Collins

England's Landscape

The East Midlands

DAVID STOCKER

SERIES EDITOR NEIL COSSONS

ENGLISH HERITAGE

First published in 2006 by Collins, an imprint of
HarperCollins*Publishers*
77–85 Fulham Palace Road, London W6 8JB

www.collins.co.uk

10 9 8 7 6 5 4 3 2
10 09 08 07

ISBN 10 – 0 00 715574 3
ISBN 13 – 9 78 0 00 715574 3

British Library Cataloguing in Publication Data
A CIP catalogue record for this book is available from the
British Library.

DEDICATION
To the memory of the Andrews sisters of St Neots (Bertha, Nora
and, especially, Kit) who first made me feel at home in the East
Midlands.

ACKNOWLEDGEMENTS

SERIES EDITOR
Sir Neil Cossons OBE
Chairman, English Heritage
President, Royal Geographical Society
The series editor would like to acknowledge the contribution of
the following people:

EDITORIAL BOARD:
Professor David Cannadine
Queen Elizabeth the Queen Mother Professor of British History,
University of London

Professor Barry Cunliffe
Professor of European Archaeology, University of Oxford

Professor Richard Lawton
Professor Emeritus, Department of Geography, University of
Liverpool

Professor Brian K Roberts
Professor Emeritus, Department of Geography, University of Durham

ENGLISH HERITAGE EXECUTIVE EDITORS:
Dr Paul Barnwell, *Head of Medieval and Later Rural Research*
Dr Martin Cherry, *Former Chief Buildings Historian*
Humphrey Welfare, *Northern Territory Director*
Graham Fairclough, *Head of Characterisation*

ENGLISH HERITAGE PROJECT MANAGERS:
Val Horsler, *former Head of Publishing*
Adele Campbell, *Commercial Publishing Manager*

All new ground and air photography was taken specifically for
this series. Thanks to: Damian Grady, Senior Investigator of
English Heritage Aerial Survey and Investigation Team, and to
the photographic and dark-room teams in Swindon; Steve Cole,
Head of Photography, and the staff of the English Heritage
Photography team. Archive material from the National
Monuments Record was researched by the Enquiry and
Research Services teams led by Alyson Rogers (Buildings) and
Lindsay Jones (Archaeology/Air Photos). Graphics lists were
managed by John Vallender and Bernard Thomason. Graphics
were produced under the management of Rob Read of 3's
Company (Consultancy) Ltd by Steve Cheshire and John
Hodgson. All other images were researched by Jo Walton and
Julia Harris-Voss.

Publisher & Commissioning Editor Myles Archibald
Production Director Graham Cook
Edited by Rowan Whimster
Designed by D & N Publishing, Hungerford, Berkshire
Indexed by Sheila Seacroft

Printed in Italy by LEGO SpA, Vicenza

Contents

Acknowledgements

When the work is done, it is a pleasure to remember the friends and colleagues who have helped bring the project to completion. Martin Cherry urged me to write the book in the first place and Graham Fairclough generously made it possible for me to do so. I am enormously grateful for Hum Welfare's care and dedication in directing my wayward ideas. Adele Campbell, who inherited the project when half-way through, has been unfailingly helpful and constructive. The script would not have become a book without the sheer hard work of Jo Walton, who grappled valiantly with archives and museums on my behalf, or without the two English Heritage photographic teams headed respectively by Steve Cole and Damian Grady. Rob Read's office worked wonders with the graphics and Alyson Rogers and her team at NMRC managed flows of paperwork with great skill and patience. The text editing was begun effectively by Catherine Bradley and completed with great aplomb by Katy Carter. I would also like to thank several colleagues and friends who have provided me with help on individual points, sometimes without realising it. These include: Nat Alcock, John Bailey, Julia Briggs, Philip Burditt, Philip Dixon, Anna Eavis, Naomi Field, Mick Jones, Edward Martin, Richard Morris, Francis Pryor, Brian Roberts, David Robinson, Dave Start, Alan Vince and Stuart Wrathmell.

In such a book it is not possible to acknowledge intellectual debts satisfactorily, but I am aware that my thinking has been deeply affected by Brian Roberts and Stuart Wrathmell, whose work over the last decade has been inspirational. I have also been impressed with the more specific landscape projects undertaken by Chris Dyer and his various collaborators in the same period, and I have been much influenced by his *Central England Settlement Project* and the *Whittlewood Project* that followed it, and together showed that forest areas are central to understanding the East Midlands. I would not think the way I do about the landscape, however, without the enlightened guidance (over many years) of Graham Fairclough. Finally, everyone needs a sounding board and, during this project, Paul Everson has played that role for me. I would not have found the confidence to proceed with a book of this type without his measured encouragement and solicitous advice.

David Stocker
Oxford

Foreword

The landscape of England evokes intense passion and profound emotion. This most loved of places, the inspiration for generations of writers, poets and artists, it is at once both the source of the nation's infatuation and the setting for grievous misunderstanding. For people who visit, the view of England offers some of their most lasting images. For exiles abroad the memory of the English landscape sustains their beliefs and desire for a homecoming.

But for those who live in England the obsession is double edged. On the one hand we cherish the unchanging atmosphere of a familiar place, and on the other make impossible demands of it, believing that it will always accommodate, always forgive. Only in the last half century or so have we started to recognise the extreme fragility of all that we value in the English landscape, to appreciate that it is not only the metaphor for who we are as a people but that it represents one of our most vivid contributions to a wider culture. At last we are beginning to realise that a deeper understanding of its subtle appeal and elusive character is the key to a thoughtful approach to its future.

The unique character of England's landscape derives from many things. But nowhere is the impact of human intervention absent. If geology and topography set the scene, it is the implacable persistence of generations who since the end of the Ice Age have sought to live in and off this place that has created the singular qualities of the landscape we have today. Not, of course, that the landscape before people was in any sense a static thing; on the contrary, the environment untouched by mankind was and is a dynamic and constantly changing synthesis. Every layer of that complex progression can still be found somewhere, making its own peculiar contribution to the distinctiveness of today's England. It is a compelling narrative. Through this series of regional studies our distinguished contributors – as authors and editors – have distilled something of what has created today's England, in order to decode that narrative.

Unique is an overused term. But it has a special resonance for the landscape of England, both urban and rural. What we hope readers of this series will begin to feel is the nature of the qualities that define the English landscape. Much of that landscape has of course been inherited from cultures overseas as conquest and migration brought here peoples who have progressively occupied and settled Britain. They created what might be called our shared landscapes, defined as much by what links them to the wider world as through any intrinsically native characteristics. The peoples whose common bonds stretched along the Atlantic seaboard have left a legacy in Cornwall more akin to parts of north-west France or Spain than to anywhere else in England. There are Roman roads and cities and medieval field systems that have their closest parallels in the European plains from whence they derived. Great abbeys and monasteries reflected in their art and architecture, their commerce and industry, a culture whose momentum lay outside these islands. And when disaster came it was a pan-European epidemic, the Black Death, that took away between a third and a half of the people. England's are not the only deserted medieval villages.

And yet, paradoxically, much of what today we would recognise as the quintessential England is only some two or three centuries old. Parliamentary enclosure, especially of the English lowlands, was itself a reaction to an even greater economic force – industrialisation, and the urbanisation that went with it. It has given us a rural landscape that epitomises the essence of Englishness in the minds of many. The fields and hedgerows surrounding the nucleated villages of the pre-existing medieval landscape are of course quite new when set against the timescale of human occupation. Indeed, when the first railways came through there remained, here and there, open fields where the rows of new hawthorn hedges were still feeble whips scribing lines across a thousand years of feudal landscape.

As Britain emerged to become the world's first industrial nation its astonishing transformation was at its most visible in the landscape, something new, indigenous and without precedent. It fuelled the debate on the picturesque and the sublime and was a source of wonder to those who visited from overseas. But in its urban and industrial excesses it soon came to be detested, by aesthetes, social commentators and a burgeoning class opposed to the horrors of industrial capitalism. What was perhaps the most decisive contribution of Britain to the human race provoked a powerful counteraction reflected in the writings of Ruskin, Morris, Octavia Hill and the Webbs. It was this anguish that a century ago energised the spirit of conservation in a growing band of people determined to capture what was left of the pre-industrial rural scene.

Today the landscape of England is, as ever, undergoing immense change. But, unlike the centuries just past, that change once again draws its energy and inspiration from forces overseas. A new form of global economy, North American in flavour, concept and style carries all before it. The implications for the long term future of the landscape and the people who live in it are difficult to predict. The out-of-town shopping mall, the great encampments of distribution warehouses crouching like so many armadillos across the rural shires, the growth of exurbia – that mixed-use land between city and country that owes nothing to either – are all manifestations of these new economic forces. Like the changes that have gone before they have become the subject of intense debate and the source of worrying uncertainty. But what is clear is that a deeper understanding of the landscape, in all its manifestations, offers a means of managing change in a conscious and thoughtful manner.

This was the inspiration that led to this new regional landscape series. To understand the language of landscape, to be able to interpret the way in which people make places, offers insights and enjoyment beyond the ordinary. It enables us to experience that most neglected of human emotions, a sense of place. These books set out to reveal the values that underwrite our sense of place, by offering an insight into how the landscape of England came to be the way it is. If understanding is the key to valuing and valuing is the key to caring then these books may help to ensure that we can understand and enjoy the best of what we have and that when we make our own contribution to change it will not only reinforce that essential distinctiveness but improve the quality of life of those who live there.

Neil Cossons

NORTH
WEST

NORTH EAST

WEST
MIDLANDS

EAST MIDLANDS

EAST
ANGLIA

WEST

SOUTH EAST

SOUTH
WEST

1

Introduction

THE EAST MIDLANDS: 'MIDDLE LAND' OR MERELY 'LAND-IN-THE-MIDDLE'?

OPPOSITE PAGE:
The regions: the red lines bound the general area covered by each volume in the series.

Everybody's geography is weakest when it comes to the midlands: rivers and towns are widely misplaced, the counties are hard to remember by name and even more difficult to sort out clearly from each other.

(Hoskins, 1949, v)

Where are the 'East Midlands'? Are these counties just an extended zone of London's dormitory, creeping over the lip of the great chalk saucer in which the capital sits? Or, on the other hand, are they merely pale imitations of the North, or the West Midlands: places where industrialisation eventually overtook England's rural heartland once food could finally be imported in sufficient bulk from overseas? A recent change of names at the modern communication hub, from 'East Midlands Airport' to 'Nottingham Airport', is symptomatic of our problem. This change was made, a spokesman said in January 2004, 'because we find the travelling public does not know where the East Midlands is' (Fig. 1.1), and the press followed up with a further bout in the contest between Leicester and Nottingham for the title of regional capital. This book aims to show, however, that the East Midlands forms neither a suburb of these two cities, nor an extension of the South or the North. It is a third place altogether, with its own distinctive landscape and history.

This is not the first book to make such a proposal: as so often, the great W G Hoskins has been here before. In several of his books, but particularly *Midland England* (1949), he made a poetic case for considering the East Midlands as a territory in its own right. More than that, however, he saw this region as the essence of England. It represented the ideal for which he had struggled between 1939 and 1945, and it was a lesson from the past for Clement Attlee's government in its mission to construct self-sufficient communities between 1945 and 1949. Its centred villages offered a contrasting model to the cosy imperial paternalism of Stanley Baldwin's world, which Hoskins, ever the radical non-conformist, associated with the unrestrained sprawl of bungalows along arterial roads in south-eastern counties before the war. Nor were the connections Hoskins drew between the East Midlands and 'Englishness' a superficial matter of fox-hunting scenes,

Fig. 1.1 Where, exactly, are the East Midlands? *East Midlands Airport was thought to be insufficiently securely located in the public mind before the name was linked with Nottingham. But can one really find such seascapes in the East Midlands at all?*

morris dancing and 'chocolate-box' villages. He had identified something distinctive about the nature of settlement itself in this part of the country, and he wanted to recommend his findings from past landscapes to his contemporaries. This region, he insisted, is the heartland of 'village' England. This is where the typical English village, and everything associated with that ideal place, is found. The village communities of the East Midlands, he implied, offered a model of how to build a peace-time world.

Before the 20th century, however, most country dwellers in England did not live in 'villages'. This realisation comes as something of a shock. But in their *Atlas of Rural Settlement in England*, Brian Roberts and Stuart Wrathmell have shown how varied England's settlements have been in the past (and remain today). In character, they can be placed on a scale extending, at one end, from isolated dwellings scattered evenly across the landscape ('dispersed settlement') to, at the other, dense concentrations of dwellings with empty landscapes in between ('nucleated settlement'). In their subsequent book, *Region and Place*, they show that parts of this complex pattern have been stable through long periods of time. Some elements, indeed, extend back at least as far as the Anglo-Saxon period. We might expect that the different settlement types would blend into each other imperceptibly, but in fact many boundaries between areas of 'dispersed' and 'nucleated' settlement are surprisingly abrupt. The most significant of these sharp boundaries show an England divided into three broad settlement 'zones'. The 'central province', characterised by villages, runs north-east to south-west through England and lies between two provinces dominated by dispersed settlement, to the south-east and north-west (Fig. 1.2). This central province includes most of the East Midlands, and such landscapes, with empty fields grouped around nucleated villages, have long been described as 'champion'. John Leland used the term in the 1540s, for example, to describe the landscape south of Leicester, but it was already a well-established term by then. It derives from the Latin *campus*, via the Norman French *champagne*, meaning 'a landscape of fields'.

The typical settlement of the central province is the village, and has been for many centuries. The same cannot be said, however, of many areas outside this province, such as Kent or Herefordshire. As in the East Midlands, the landscape in these counties is fully occupied, but instead of being grouped in villages, the houses are typically strung out along intricate networks of lanes. In Kent and Herefordshire even the churches stand (or stood) relatively isolated from parishioners' dwellings: in the East Midlands, houses crowd around the churches with little space to

Fig. 1.2 Distribution of 'nucleated' and 'dispersed' settlement types in England according to Brian Roberts and Stuart Wrathmell. *Note that the zone of 'nucleated' settlements (villages) runs north to south through the East Midlands (source: Roberts & Wrathwell 2002).*

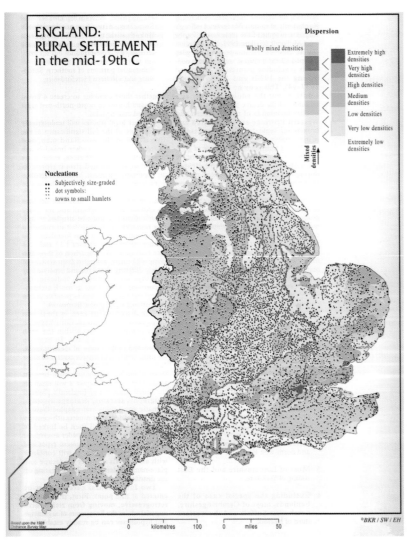

spare, contrasting with the empty landscapes between villages (Fig. 1.3). Following the expansion of local government planning powers since the war, town hall officials have pretended that the country is evenly provided with villages, putting up village name-boards around the larger clusters of houses in Kent and Herefordshire, defining 'village envelopes' and filling in the fields that have always separated individual dwellings in these parts. In these places, there has been an officially sponsored drive to create villages, where there were none before.

Such actions are not just bureaucratic perversity: they are taken because people like the idea of villages. The village represents a powerful ideal which has become deeply embedded in both the English psyche and its politics since 1945. It has become the pre-eminent symbol for all those who aspire to life in cosy houses standing side-by-side in small, friendly, self-regulating communities. Ideas like these were, however, also predominant when most of our villages were founded, in the 10th and 11th centuries; they informed not only the founding of villages, but also the layout of a landscape of common fields around them, which embodied ideas of community co-operation and stability just as effectively. Although easily mocked, the village idea continues to be politically attractive. In the 1990s it underpinned John Major's vision of communities with greens, cricket matches and pubs; of elderly spinsters walking to Holy Communion and district nurses on bicycles. But until 1945 this idea of the village only had concrete form in certain parts of England, of which the East Midlands was the most notable.

Fig. 1.3 In the East Midlands landscape buildings often huddle round their churches, with large empty spaces in between villages. These spaces were once 'common fields', which were divided up into an irregular chequerboard by 'quickset' hedges during the Agricultural Revolution. The reorganised landscape proved ideal for foxhunting and many stands of trees between villages were newly planted to provide cover. The new fields enclosed a productive mixed agriculture with pasture in the valleys and arable on the higher, more free-draining, land. The land is not occupied in this fashion everywhere in England, but it is characteristic of the East Midlands. Farthingstone stands in the foreground, Preston Capes in the middle distance and beyond that, Woodford Halse (Northamptonshire).

WHERE ARE THE EAST MIDLANDS?

When defining the limits of the East Midlands, then, we must consider the boundaries between 'village England' and the settlement provinces on either side (Fig. 1.4). The Fens to the east are another world, where villages resemble small towns yet many people live in relative isolation along remote lanes. They do not form part of our study. Further south, the line of chalk hills ('the southern wall of

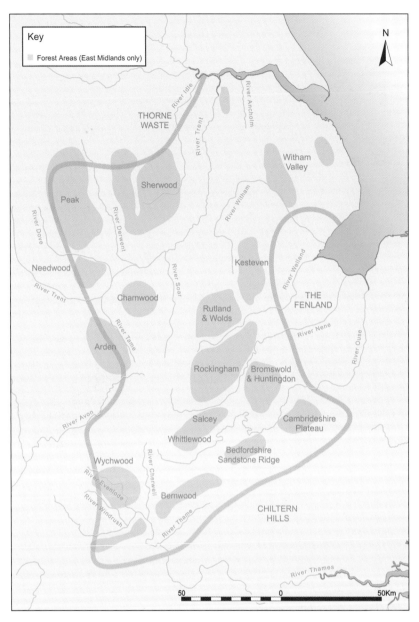

Key

▨ Forest Areas (East Midlands only)

N

THORNE
WASTE

River Idle

River Trent

River Ancholm

Peak

Sherwood

Witham
Valley

River Dove

River Derwent

River Witham

Needwood

River Trent

Charnwood

River Soar

Kesteven

River Welland

THE
FENLAND

Rutland
& Wolds

River Nene

River Ouse

Arden

River Tame

Rockingham

Bromswold
& Huntingdon

Salcey

Cambrideshire
Plateau

Whittlewood

Bedfordshire
Sandstone Ridge

Wychwood

River Cherwell

River Evenlode

Bernwood

River Avon

River Windrush

River Thame

CHILTERN
HILLS

River Thames

50   0   50Km

**Fig. 1.4 The East Midlands, showing
rivers and major areas of ancient
forest.** *The boundaries of the forest areas are
generalised from Domesday records and from
various other sources.*

the Midland park', Hoskins called it)
marches south-west from Gog Magog
beyond Cambridge towards the
Thames at Goring. Chiltern country,
concealed behind this 'wall', is still
largely without nucleated villages: it has
knots of impenetrable lanes scarcely
one car wide and, above all, woodlands.
There have also been woodlands in the
East Midlands, as we shall see, but even
today the Chiltern woods are
substantially larger. The Thames breaks
through the hills at the south-eastern
corner of our region, but the chalk wall
turns west at Goring, continuing
undiminished all the way to the western
boundary of old Berkshire (now
Oxfordshire), beyond Wantage. The
eastern and southern boundaries of the
East Midlands are clearly marked, then,
by the fen edge and the chalk wall.

Our northern and western
boundaries are a little more ragged.
The Humber estuary marks a clear
end to Lindsey (the northernmost
'Part' of Lincolnshire) and has been a
major boundary for millennia, even
though eastern Yorkshire shares a
similar geology and settlement pattern.
Further west, beyond the once
impenetrable Humberhead Levels,
Sherwood Forest to the north of
Nottingham forms an arboreal buffer
zone between the East Midlands and
southern Yorkshire.

The term 'forest' is important to this
study, yet it is not a synonym for
'wood'. The word comes from the
Latin *foris*, meaning 'out of doors', in
the sense of 'outside'. But it also
implies marginality: this is 'the beyond',
land outside normal controls and
jurisdiction. In medieval times, a forest was an area of open country, subject to
laws governing land use that were different from those in surrounding
countryside. Here the animals of the chase had priority over use of the land for
agriculture. Settlement and agriculture was permitted in such areas, but only with
the lord's explicit consent. These large forests often included woodlands.
Wychwood Forest (Oxfordshire), for example, was quite densely wooded, but
even here, less than 50 per cent of the land was covered by trees in 1086. In an
East Midlands forest, the countryside would typically have included heathland
and woodland as well as the pasture and arable used by the resident community.
Bradgate Park (Leicestershire) has preserved a small tract of such countryside
(Fig. 1.5). Typically, such forest regions would also have had a different settlement
pattern from the land around. As they were less confined by common fields,
dwellings in these regions were not so tightly grouped together; as in the Chilterns
or Fens, they could spread along the roads. One of our main themes will be the

subtle contrast between settlements established in forest areas and those in the areas dominated, until the 18th century, by common fields.

The Sherwood Forest landscape, then, is an area in which houses are dispersed across the countryside, and it contrasts with the Trent valley to the south, where villages and enclosed common fields predominate. Like the Chilterns, Sherwood is another forest along the East Midlands borders. Today it is closely identified with Nottinghamshire, although this type of landscape once extended much further west, climbing steadily higher up the Pennine slopes to join the Peak Forest of northern Derbyshire. These forest areas once formed a near-continuous boundary between the East Midlands and Yorkshire, Lancashire, Cheshire and Staffordshire beyond.

Further south, Needwood Forest (between the rivers Dove and Trent) also marks a boundary between landscapes of nucleated villages and those with more straggling settlements. Identifying it as a boundary serves to confirm Burton upon Trent (nominally in Staffordshire) as an East Midlands town, in a way that neither Luton nor Sheffield could ever be. South of Needwood, the broad, untidy basin where the River Tame joins the Trent is debatable land. Arguably, Tamworth falls on our side of the ill-defined East Midlands boundary. Even though it was the cradle of Mercia, before the rise of Birmingham the people of the Tame basin looked beyond Charnwood to Leicester as their regional capital. Further south, our boundary is more clearly marked. Yet again, the boundary of village England terminates abruptly against a forest edge – this time the Forest of Arden. This boundary bisects all aspects of Warwickshire life and runs north–south through the county, from Nuneaton through Stratford-upon-Avon to Shipston-on-Stour. East of this line is the Feldon Country which blends imperceptibly with Northamptonshire and Oxfordshire.

Fig. 1.5 Bradgate Park (Leicestershire). *Enclosed from Charnwood Forest before 1247, and abandoned by the Earls of Stamford before it could be re-landscaped, Bradgate Park by chance has retained the appearance of a medieval forest landscape. That is to say, it is a landscape managed to encourage game rather than agriculture. Yet it is not a landscape of unbroken tree-cover; many agricultural and industrial settlements co-existed with the game.*

We have returned again to Oxfordshire's western boundary, due north of Wantage but on the northern side of the Cotswolds. Even here, in what seems to be continuous Cotswold countryside, Roberts and Wrathmell found a statistical boundary that coincided approximately with yet another forest. Although not as evident as some other regional boundaries, Wychwood Forest (lying wholly within modern Oxfordshire) is also marked in the landscape by a change in the character of settlement – from village England to the more dispersed settlement pattern typical of the forests.

It is possible, then, to draw a line around a block of territory in the East Midlands using settlement forms and forest boundaries. But has this block ever been recognised as an entity before? When the various forests were first established we cannot say, but we will see that the territory defined by them approximates to the two adjoining Iron Age tribal areas of the Corieltauvi and the western Catuvellauni. These political units may have existed even earlier in prehistory, but they were certainly important to Romano-British government. Furthermore, since the 7th century much of the East Midlands as we have defined it has contained complete units of church government, subject to cathedrals located within the region. Between the 7th and 9th centuries, our region probably contained three whole dioceses, based at 'the South City' (probably Lincoln), at Leicester and at Dorchester-on-Thames. Following 10th-century reforms, the three were united in a single diocese based initially at Dorchester and, after 1073, at Lincoln. In 1109 Cambridgeshire had become a separate diocese based at Ely, but East Midlands' cathedral was at Lincoln until 1540, when the separate dioceses of Oxford and Peterborough were created – also wholly within our region. Centuries later, new cathedrals were raised at Southwell (1884), Derby and Leicester (both 1927), while in 1914 Bedfordshire became part of the new St Albans diocese. Nottinghamshire, however, has usually been considered part of the York archdiocese, and Derbyshire, Staffordshire and Warwickshire have long been associated with Lichfield.

THE FACE OF THE EAST MIDLANDS

The skeleton of the East Midlands region we have just defined is formed by lines of low hills running parallel with each other in a lazy curve from south-west to north-east (Fig. 1.6). The backbone is the broad sweep of the Jurassic limestone rocks, running in a great arc from the Rollright Stones on the Cotswolds to the Humber at Alkborough. The limestone outcrops along a steep scarp facing north-west and west which, at its highest point, stands 260m above sea level and 90m above the valley below. Sloping gently away from this scarp towards the south-east and east, a broad dry plateau is carved and moulded by rivers in steep-sided valleys. A thin veneer of boulder clay covers much of this cold plateau land, and it has accumulated to greater depths along the courses of rivers.

If rock forms East Midlands' skeleton, the rivers carry its soul. Some of these systems (the Witham, Welland and Nene) flow directly off the limestone hills and into the Wash. Others (the Trent, Avon, Ouse and Thames) exploit larger valleys between the Jurassic limestone and adjoining geological systems. North of the Trent, the older Pennine rocks raise much the highest hills in our region (up to 630m) and their greater rainfall encourages rushing rivers such as the Derwent, which even so has almost forgotten its mountain origins by Derby and become a Midlands river at its confluence with the Trent. The Trent itself winds north of Charnwood, an isolated upland north of the Jurassic hills and divided from them by the broad Soar valley. South of the Jurassic hills, the Corallian hills run in parallel; and between the two flows the youthful Thames, before it breaks through the Corallian scarp at Oxford. The Thames then winds its lazy, adolescent way towards Goring, but the Corallian hills march north-eastwards along the north side

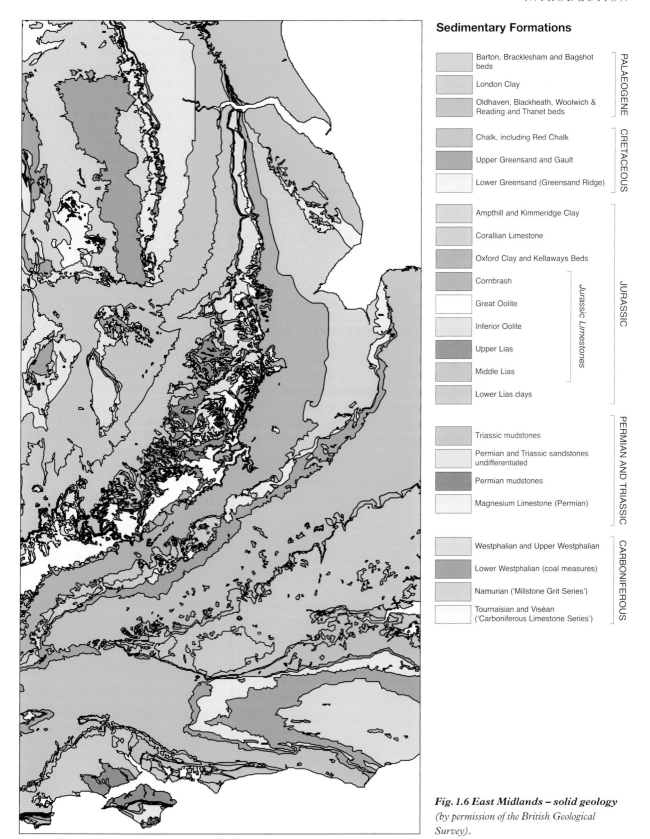

Sedimentary Formations

PALAEOGENE
- Barton, Bracklesham and Bagshot beds
- London Clay
- Oldhaven, Blackheath, Woolwich & Reading and Thanet beds

CRETACEOUS
- Chalk, including Red Chalk
- Upper Greensand and Gault
- Lower Greensand (Greensand Ridge)

JURASSIC
- Ampthill and Kimmeridge Clay
- Corallian Limestone
- Oxford Clay and Kellaways Beds
- Cornbrash
- Great Oolite
- Inferior Oolite
- Upper Lias
- Middle Lias
- Lower Lias clays

Jurassic Limestones (bracketing Cornbrash, Great Oolite, Inferior Oolite, Upper Lias, Middle Lias)

PERMIAN AND TRIASSIC
- Triassic mudstones
- Permian and Triassic sandstones undifferentiated
- Permian mudstones
- Magnesium Limestone (Permian)

CARBONIFEROUS
- Westphalian and Upper Westphalian
- Lower Westphalian (coal measures)
- Namurian ('Millstone Grit Series')
- Tournaisian and Viséan ('Carboniferous Limestone Series')

Fig. 1.6 East Midlands – solid geology
(by permission of the British Geological Survey).

of the Vale of Aylesbury to blend with the green-sandstone hills of southern Bedfordshire. Like the Thames, the Ouse rises in the Jurassic limestone, but never breaches the Greensand ridge, and is thus shepherded north-eastwards towards the Fens at St Ives. As if genetically, the local road network follows these river valleys from south-west to north-east, turning left or right into the hills when a tributary valley offers convenient access.

Such deceptively simple observations allow us to classify much of the land in the East Midlands as belonging to one of four categories: 'flood plain', 'bottom land', 'terrace' and 'top land' or plateau. This diversity of landform was a major factor in determining the locations of individual settlements in the East Midlands, because settlers have always sought to place themselves alongside contrasting terrains. The flat 'top land' is not ideal for settlement: not only are reliable water supplies rare, but rainfall is unlikely to stand on the surface. Rainfall waters crops, however, and towards the edges, the thinner drift ensures easy tillage and effective subsoil drainage. The fringes of the plateau, then, offer good land for cultivation, even if, on top, the land is intractable and well-wooded. Our flood plains in the valley floors are also not ideal for settlement, but they make excellent pasture. It is the bottom lands and the terraces, where the water runs off the tops in defined streams but which stand above the flood mark in the valley floor, which have always attracted settlement. Throughout time each community wanted, if possible, access to land of all four types. Given the choice, however, settlements themselves would cluster along the valley sides.

This pattern of land usage is perfectly illustrated by the small settlement of Wyboston, which lies west of the Ouse in north-east Bedfordshire, about 16km north-east of Bedford (Fig. 1.7). The modern village sits below the limestone plateau, covered with boulder clay, which forms the western part of Eaton Socon parish. Today the plateau is dominated by enormous fields of barley, although in 1086 it was mostly occupied by managed woodland. The soil here was both relatively poor and hard to work, and there was not much running water. But the woods could be cleared, stock could be reared and, with assiduous manuring, crops could grow. This plateau land was never occupied by settlements of any size – although people did live up here in both the Bronze Age and in the

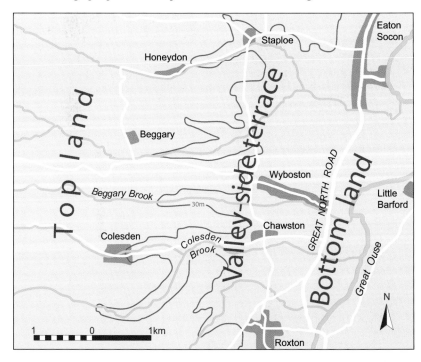

*Fig. 1.7 **The area around Wyboston (Bedfordshire).***

Romano-British period. Intrepid settlers also established themselves here in the 12th century, although the quality of living they expected was indicated by the ironic place-name they gave to the largest settlement: Beggary.

At the other end of the long rectangle of land occupied by Wyboston, the bottom lands and the flood plain were rich in hay meadows, but could be flooded in winter. As on the plateau land, settlements were founded here at times of population pressure and favourable climate – in the late Iron Age and Romano-British periods, and in the 12th, 13th and 19th centuries. Both western and eastern ends of Wyboston's land were important agricultural units, then, but they have only been used for settlement intermittently. More successful locations for settlement in Eaton Socon parish were to be found along the lower stretches of the brooks running off the plateau, at Staploe, Honeydon and Wyboston itself. The presence of permanent settlements in this zone eventually influenced the line taken through this landscape by the Great North Road. Like Eaton Socon itself, Wyboston probably began life as a settlement extending east–west, in this case along the Beggary Brook, but both places were subsequently pulled into a north–south alignment by the road itself running through them. As we explore the East Midlands, we will return again to these places to seek examples of the typical in microcosm. Why select Wyboston for this honour? For no better reason than it is where my own family comes from (Fig. 1.8).

Fig. 1.8 Wyboston (Bedfordshire), looking north. The medieval village is strung-out left to right along the village street, parallel with the Beggary Brook (in the hedge-line). The Great North Road, running northwards towards Eaton Socon, is just visible (top right), whilst the centre of this view is dominated by the grid of horticultural plots laid out over Rookery Farm (once in the common field) by the Land Settlement Association in the late 1930s. It was intended specifically for the unemployed of London's East End and each 'model' house was equipped with its standard piggery, poultry-house, glass-house and propagating shed.

Wyboston is not typical of the entire region, however. We shall find, for example, that the Lindsey Wolds are very different from the more typical East Midlands landscape. Uniquely in our region, these are chalk hills – part of the same geological formation as the Chilterns. But unlike the Chilterns, we find no scattered settlements hidden among dense woodlands here. The Wolds landscape is open and windy, with enormous views in every direction and deep valleys whose vertiginous sides are, nevertheless, ploughed. Hemmed in by their former open fields, many Wolds villages cluster around their churches in the valley floors, and have done so since at least the 10th or 11th centuries. These hills are clear proof that the manner in which settlements occupy the land is not determined solely by underlying geology. If settlement style followed geology, these hills would be an island of dispersed settlement resembling the Chilterns, anchored off the coast of 'village England'. But the Wolds villages, their medieval open fields and the rectilinear pattern of Parliamentary enclosure, declare that they belong to the East Midlands.

The identity of the Wolds has thus been moulded not so much by the chalk soils as by the ideas and habits of the neighbours to the west, and it is true that our sense of place is greatly influenced by surrounding communities. This book aims to investigate how the East Midlands landscape has been settled and used, and to explore the many connections between what may seem, at first sight, to be discrete episodes in history. Following an introduction dealing with climate, agriculture and communications (Chapter 2), the first part of the book (Chapter 3) examines the settlement history of the East Midlands. Then Chapters 4 to 7 analyse the region from different angles, seeking patterns in housing, industry, defence and belief throughout the past seven millennia, concentrating always on the landscape impact of these activities. Throughout, the book asks a simple question: does a distinctive East Midlands region really exist? Or is this part of England merely the remainder, once Yorkshire and the West Midlands, the South East and East Anglia have been delineated? The answer that emerges from the following pages may surprise some. Even if it is not always easy to keep in sharp focus, the region does have an underlying unity.

FURTHER READING

General works

General works on the history of the landscape are also referred to under many of the chapters that follow. Important introductions to English settlement and landscape as a whole include: Hoskins 1955; Roberts & Wrathmell 2000a, 2002; Thirsk 1987, (ed.) 2000.

Individual counties and areas

The *Victoria County History* has complete coverage for Berkshire, Bedfordshire, Cambridgeshire, Huntingdonshire, Rutland and Warwickshire. Oxfordshire is nearly complete whilst Northamptonshire and Leicestershire are partly covered. The *Little Guides, Shell* and *Buildings of England* series are all complete. *Royal Commission on Historical Monuments* inventories exist for Buckinghamshire (1913), Huntingdonshire (1926), Cambridgeshire (1968 and 1972),

Northamptonshire (1975, 1979, 1980, 1981, 1982, 1984 and 1985). The city of Oxford was covered by an inventory published in 1939 whilst the Cambridge equivalent appeared in 1959 and that for Stamford in 1977. These are supported by extensive unpublished data in the *National Monuments Record* in Swindon. Leicestershire Museums published a helpful series of volumes, mostly by Hartley (1983–90) reporting on all the earthworks of this county. *Historic Environment Records* exist in all East Midlands counties and in certain historic cities. In addition important regional studies for this chapter include: Bigmore 1979 (Bedfordshire and Huntingdonshire); Emery 1974 (Oxfordshire); Everson *et al.* 1991 (West Lindsey); Godber 1984 (Bedfordshire); Hill 1948, 1956, 1966, 1973 (Lincoln); Hoskins 1949 and 1957a (Leicestershire); Palliser 1976 (Staffordshire); Reed 1979,

1993 (Buckinghamshire); Steane 1974 (Northamptonshire); Taylor 1973 (Cambridgeshire).

Boundaries and woodlands

Barnatt & Smith 1997 (Peak District); Blair 1994 (Oxfordshire); Broad & Hoyle (eds) 1997 (Bernwood); Dyer 1996 (Warwickshire); Foard 2001 (Rockingham); Foss 1996 (Leicestershire); Keighley 2000 (Wychwood); Page & Jones 2001 (Whittlewood); Phythian-Adams 2000; Roberts 1976–7 (Arden); Roberts & Wrathmell 2000b; Salway 1999; Selwood 1984; Stamper 1988.

Geology

British Geological Survey (various reports and maps); Arkell 1948; Clifton-Taylor 1972; Parsons (ed.) 1990; Purcell 1967; Sutherland 2003 (Northamptonshire).

2

Passing Through: Weather and Communication Routes

PATTERNS OF CLIMATE AND AGRICULTURE

Did it rain last night? And if it did, how was that rainfall perceived? Was it seen as a familiar enemy against which defences were prepared: a sound roof, clear drains and a well-protected garden? Or was it, instead, a welcome shower, part of a predictable pattern of rainfall, expected about now and doing the garden good rather than harm? All cultures must address such questions seriously, and few places have such a diverse climate as the British Isles. Indeed, the effects of rainfall and drought, frost and sunshine, wind and calm have moulded the landscape of England just as much as terrain and settlement pattern.

English bridges, for example, are a sensitive indicator of local rainfall and landscape type. In the Pennines, where the fast-flowing rivers can rise suddenly by 5m, bridges tend to be high arches of stone, with the minimum of piers and with strong abutments set deep into the banks. Beeley Bridge (Derbyshire) takes the form of a great stone bow, because of the great rises of which the Derwent is capable. In the south and east, however, where the rain falls less intensely and where it flows off the land more slowly, bridges were usually built with many small arches. Bridge piers will not be swept away because, even in flood, the river spreads out like a slow-moving lake. Most East Midlands rivers are of this type. The difference in temper between the Great Ouse and its unpredictable Yorkshire namesake is evident in their bridges. Instead of leaping stone arches crossing the water in a single span, upstream of Wyboston on the Great Ouse, we find magnificent medieval stone bridges set in causeways across the broad valley – at Great Barford (Fig. 2.1), Bedford (the Old Bridge), Bromham, Stafford, Harrold

Fig. 2.1 Great Barford Bridge was constructed between 1427–9, with a legacy from Sir Gerald Braybroke, and masonry of this date can be seen along its upstream (western) side beneath the brick-built widening of 1874 (the last of several). With its long causeway of many small arches, it is typical of the ancient bridges on most East Midlands rivers.

OPPOSITE PAGE:

TOP: **Fig. 2.2 The broad character of East Midland's farming c.1960, before the impact of European subsidies.**

BOTTOM: **Fig. 2.3 The Bardney sugar-beet factory, symbol of national planning in British agriculture after World War I, dominates the River Witham and the modern fen-edge village.** *One chapel of the Anglo-Saxon Monastery here (founded in the late 7th century) lay within the 'Z' bend in the village centre, near the parish church. The road leading westwards across the fen towards Lincoln is the modern equivalent of ancient causeways that have crossed the peat-lands hereabouts since the Bronze Age.*

and Turvey. The many arches of such bridges have survived, though patched, for centuries because the rivers of the East Midlands in their broad valleys are slow-flowing and slow to rise.

According to the averages given in the digest *British Rainfall*, the wettest places in the East Midlands are on the hills: the Derbyshire Pennines regularly have 1.5m per year; the Cotswolds, in the south-west, have about 0.7m, as does the Charnwood massif. But the driest area, the Witham valley in Lincolnshire, has only some 0.5m. If we exclude the Pennine uplands, however, it is the evenness of the rainfall across the region that is striking – a variation of a mere 20cm per annum. Not only are the East Midlands relatively dry, but the rainfall is evenly spread throughout the year. Of Leicestershire's annual rainfall, for example, 49 per cent falls in the six months from April to September. Flash floods do occur, like the one that hit Thurcaston (Leicestershire) in July 1891, when rain fell at the astonishing rate of 159mm per hour (typical English rain falls at a rate of only 6mm per hour). Fortunately perhaps, the cloudburst at Thurcaston lasted for only five minutes, but on 29 May 1920 a cloudburst of about 51mm per hour at Louth, in the Lincolnshire Wolds, caused the swollen River Lud to sweep through the town, killing 23. Devastating though they are, such events are rare. *British Rainfall* advises that 'noteworthy', 'remarkable' and 'very rare' rainfall events occur here only about once every three years. This is the lowest rate of exceptional rainfall in England and reinforces the point that the East Midlands' rainfall is both relatively light and relatively evenly spread throughout the year.

Equability of rainfall is matched by benign temperatures. Although only two months are reliably frost-free (July and August), and although ground frost was recorded in June 10 times between 1881 and 1952, it nevertheless tends to be localised. An understanding of terrain has permitted farmers to grow a wide variety of crops throughout the long growing season between late March and early October (during which daytime temperatures stay above 6°C). In the Derbyshire Pennines, the growing season is five weeks shorter and the sun shines less, but in most of the East Midlands sunshine is plentiful, compared with many other parts of England. Between 1901 and 1961, Nottingham had about 1,300 hours of sunshine each year, evenly spread once again throughout the summer months, with the highest figures in June, July and August, when it is most needed for ripening crops. Even Skegness, famously promoted as 'bracing', has a remarkably sunny climate: over 1,500 hours per year during the same period and, on average, an hour more each day than Nottingham. These figures go some way towards explaining bank holiday exoduses from the latter to the former, like that in August 1882, when 22,000 day-trippers arrived by railway to see the newly opened pier: by 6.00 pm they had stripped the little town bare of food and drink, and then they all tried to leave at once. In the resulting chaos the last packed train left at 2.30 am, leaving hundreds of trippers to sleep on the platforms.

Exceptional temperatures do occur. When the Trent froze over during the winter of 1762–3, a sheep was roasted on the ice at Wilford (Nottinghamshire), and the temperate fell to minus 24.4°C at nearby Carlton. Who would have dared climb the hill to Lincoln Cathedral on 9 August 1911, when the temperature topped 37.1°C in the shade? Who would have flown from RAF Cranwell (Kesteven) when the wind reached 110 mph, matching a national wind-speed record held by Stornoway (Outer Hebrides)? But these events *are* exceptional and, for most of the time, the East Midlands climate is calm, warm and well, but not over, watered.

Temperature, rainfall and sunshine statistics provide the matrix for agriculture. Although this is a relatively dry part of England, rainfall is sufficient to keep the free-draining soils fertile and to turn the clay vales green. Droughts are rare and, equally important, the timing and duration of frosts encourage a wide range of agricultural crops as well as good grazing pasture. The indispensable *Reader's*

Digest Atlas for 1965 shows that within living memory most of the region was still used for arable or for mixed arable and livestock (Fig. 2.2). In the eastern part (Lincolnshire, Huntingdonshire and western Cambridgeshire), a greater percentage of the land was given over to crops than to pasture, while in Leicestershire, Northamptonshire, Oxfordshire and north Buckinghamshire proportions were reversed. Though still predominantly 'mixed', farms here were dominated by their permanent grassland. With more than 110 reliable frost-free days per year, the East Midlands has always produced grain, particularly barley (now grown primarily for beer) and wheat for bread, although peas and beans were once more important than they were in 1965. At that date potatoes were also cultivated, and the shiny green foliage of sugar-beet still dominated the valleys, much as the strategically placed sugar refineries (built as part of a national drive for self-sufficiency after 1918 at Brigg, Bardney and Spalding in Lincolnshire, and at Newark) dominated the skyline (Fig. 2.3). Sugar-beet was not the only crop generating a distinctive landscape, of course. Most agricultural regimes have required specialised buildings, and we shall look more closely at the architecture of East Midlands farming in Chapter 5.

In 1965, mixed farming was not so evident in Bedfordshire. Here, close to the London markets, farming was combined with horticulture: around Sandy and Biggleswade it was completely dominated by it. Whether seen from the East Coast Main Line or from the A1, the regimented rows of glasshouses, which seemed to fill the Ivel valley like a calm lake, were a sure sign that you had

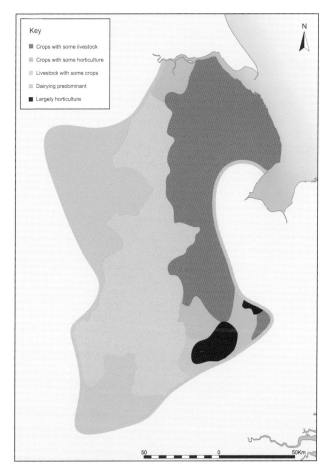

Key

■ Crops with some livestock
■ Crops with some horticulture
■ Livestock with some crops
■ Dairying predominant
■ Largely horticulture

N

50   0   50Km

reached the bottom of London's garden and were about to climb over the wall into the backyards of other cities (Fig. 2.4).

Since 1965, of course, European agricultural subsidies have led to the wholesale conversion of grassland and horticulture to arable, even in Bedfordshire, while the introduction of new arable crops such as rape now turns our springtime landscape an unhealthy yellow. So much of the countryside is now dedicated to arable that, in parts of Lincolnshire, virtually the only land unploughed is that protected by environmental or heritage legislation (Fig. 2.5). This modern landscape revolution, driven by European agricultural objectives and backed by European money, has seen the destruction of many of our archaeological sites and landscapes: by 1990 over 10 per cent of the earthworks recorded in West Lindsey a mere 20 years earlier had been destroyed through ploughing.

But was the climate always so benign? And, if it was, did farmers always respond with mixed agricultural regimes? Each passing year brings greater understanding of both agriculture and climate in remote periods, as sediments found in lake-beds and ice-cores are studied. We now know that, since the last Ice Age (which ended between 8,000 and 10,000 years ago), the East Midlands has seen many substantial climatic changes.

Although woodland clearance began around 4000 BC, it took a very long time for man to have a serious impact on the region's tree cover (pp.35–6). The

ABOVE: *Fig. 2.4 Until distortions introduced by subsidies on grain production, the light fertile soils along the River Ivel around Sandy (Bedfordshire) produced a rich crop of vegetables for the London market.* *If not travelling by rail, they were transported down the A1 (bottom left). Until the 1970s, much of the crop was grown in greenhouses, like those bottom right. Now, where vegetables are still grown, they are produced under polythene (centre). Along the river itself (top) the sandy subsoil, which gave the place its name, is eagerly quarried for the building industry.*

BELOW: *Fig. 2.5 Almost the entire parish of Wispington (Lindsey) has been turned into a 'prairie' growing subsidised grain.* *Looking eastwards to the village of Wispington (in the trees), only one large mechanised farm and a redundant Victorian church (with spire), now used as a farm store, remain.*

process can be documented precisely because the soils bound together on hill slopes by these woodlands were washed off into the rivers when the trees were cleared. The rivers carried it into the developing marsh that would eventually become the Wash, where it still lies stratified today in well-dated archaeological contexts. Yet archaeology has not yet provided much information about what happened next. Evidence for agriculture at this date is usually deduced from pollen samples, but few such samples have been taken in our region. Structures are limited to the (often accidental) discovery of a few pits, such as those which underlay the Iron Age settlement at Dragonby (Lindsey). Here fragments of sickle and quernstone were found – sure signs of cereals in the diet – and fragments of tools and animal bones also suggested the management of domesticated animals. Neolithic Dragonby, then, may have also been a mixed-farming settlement, as it remained into modern times. In both the Nene and Thames valleys 'emmer' wheat and 'naked six-row' barley were grown in the Neolithic period, and both were brought to the enclosure at Briar Hill, south of Northampton. In both valleys, however, wild fruits, berries and nuts were also being consumed in large quantities, suggesting not only that the woodland had not yet been entirely cleared, but also that it was a valuable food resource.

In the Bronze and Iron Ages, the mixed agricultural economy seems to have expanded. This was a period of great woodland clearance and in many places (along the Thames, for example) aerial photography reveals patterns of rectilinear trackways replacing the woodlands, providing arteries for a whole landscape of chequerboard fields, defined by ditches. These field ditches provide us with an insight into the new agricultural regime: such ditched boundaries (with the fences and hedges that accompanied them) are only necessary when crops and animals need to be separated. It seems, then, that mixed farming was already recognised as the most effective way to exploit the East Midlands, and so it probably continued through the Romano-British period. The balance between stock and grain may have changed from year to year and century to century, but both were of great importance.

A combination of cultivation and stock-rearing continued even though mean air temperatures gradually declined from the middle of the second millennium BC. Although there seems to have been a rise between about 150 BC and 200 AD, and contemporary viticulture has been detected around Wollaston in the Nene valley, by the 5th century AD, the end of the Romano-British period, mean air temperatures had fallen to their lowest point since the ice retreated. On the other hand, the difference between summer and winter rainfall had diminished. It may have been colder throughout the year in 600 AD, but differences between summer and winter were no longer so marked. Even if crops ripened less quickly, there was less risk of drought in the growing season. Excavations at Catholme (Staffordshire) and Goltho (Lindsey) revealed the mixed agricultural economy persisting between the 5th and 9th centuries. Despite the temperature fluctuations, the East Midlands landscape continued as a chequerboard of agricultural closes, separated by open commons and woodlands – a pattern which probably developed from that left by Romano-British farmers.

Then, quite suddenly, the temperature picked up. In the 'warm period' between the 8th and the 13th centuries AD, air temperatures were higher, with less stormy conditions, and warm summers followed cold winters. Before 1106 Henry I had a vineyard as far north as Lincoln. A few generations earlier the East Midlands had seen an agricultural revolution just as profound as that introduced by Parliamentary enclosure 800 years later. Both revolutions are considered below, but we should note in passing a great change, from the pattern of small fields typical of the previous four millennia to the enormous 'common fields' introduced in the late 10th and early 11th centuries. Theoretically the new common fields permitted an increase in arable production, compared with earlier patterns of farming (Fig. 2.6). Was this a response to the improving climate? The growing

ABOVE: *Fig. 2.6 Before the drive towards grain production in the 1960s and 1970s, typical East Midlands grassland was corrugated by 'ridge and furrow' earthworks, the most visible remnant of medieval common-field ploughing.* Such earthworks are increasingly rare and are now found mostly on non-agricultural land, as here around Watford (Northamptonshire) where, before the golf-course, it was protected within the landscaped parkland of Watford Court. The sweeping curve of each ridge as it approaches the headland and the mounding of soil at its terminal are both features created through turning the long medieval plough-team. Note the recently destroyed ridge and furrow earthworks in ploughland to the south-east (top left).

RIGHT: *Fig. 2.7 The vineyard on the terrace below the Old Bishops' Palace at Lincoln* was re-planted with Rhenish vines in 1972, donated as a gesture of friendship between the City of Lincoln and its German twin town, Neustadt-am-der-Weinstrasse to celebrate the Cathedral's 900th anniversary.

season was lengthening and temperatures were rising, so it might have been possible to get two crops from the same field in a single year. We do not know whether any increase in East Midlands' arable was accompanied by a decline in stock numbers, but there is no reason to think the one necessitates the other. Under the new rotation systems, fallow fields were now available for the community herd and, anyway, common fields did not occupy all the available land. Permanent pastures and common grazing could still be found on the heaths.

After about 1300, however, another prolonged cold spell set in, with cooler, wetter summers and longer, colder winters. Conditions in this 'little ice age', when the European glaciers advanced and the Thames froze regularly, reached their harshest in the 16th century. But the cold water also drove shoals of herring from the Baltic into the North Sea, where English coastal fisheries developed to take full advantage, eventually rescuing Grimsby from economic collapse. The 14th-century climatic downturn meant a return to shorter growing seasons, lower summer temperatures and greater rainfall, and the percentage of arable relative to pasture in the East Midlands quickly reversed. From the 9th to the 13th century, the increased arable had supported a larger population in an intensively occupied landscape. Now, between about 1350 and 1750, as the population declined, many former common fields were put down to permanent grass. Stock numbers, particularly sheep, rose as the population fell and settlements became depopulated.

Since the late 17th century, however, average annual temperatures have been rising. Ice on the Thames was last thought thick enough to hold a 'frost fair' in 1814, and in1972 a vineyard was again planted in Lincoln (Fig. 2.7). As the weather started to improve the population began to increase once again, and another agricultural revolution was required to feed industrial towns and cities. Ironically, although this agricultural revolution brought in many technological and methodological innovations, its main impact on the landscape was a return to the style of land use which had prevailed between the Bronze Age and the 10th century AD. Once again the landscape was divided up into many comparatively small enclosures, separating fodder and crops from stock. 'Improved' East Midlands farms were still, however, mixed. Once again there was a rapid increase in the percentage of arable land relative to pasture, but we have seen that, in 1965, the region remained as dominated by mixed agriculture as it always had been.

Examining long-term variations in climate alongside changes in the region's agriculture in this way, we can see apparent correlations between the two, especially during the last 1,500 years, for which we have most information. As temperatures rise, we see population growth and the introduction of communal farming systems, resulting in increased arable production. Similarly when the climate grew colder and the population shrank, the arable area shrank commensurately, in favour of a rural economy more dominated by pastoralism. Joan Thirsk, the great historian of early modern agriculture, suggested long ago that the area of grain under cultivation will always be related to population size. In periods when large populations work the land itself, or when that land is farmed for the benefit of large urban populations elsewhere, the percentage of land under arable must expand. Conversely, when rural populations fall and urban populations disappear, there is no requirement for surplus grain; the land either reverts to pasture – because surplus stock is more valuable than surplus grain – or it goes out of production all together.

Sometimes, then, connections between population, climate and agriculture can seem very direct, a slight change in one having predictable and inevitable consequences for the other. Unfortunately, it is not always as simple as this. We also have to take account of the influence of human technology, and indeed ideology. Increases in arable hectarage required heavier ploughs and more, heavier, draught animals that themselves needed good pasture. Ploughs with coulters, shares and mouldboards were introduced during the late Roman period, at a time when the total arable hectarage was probably *declining* relative to pasture. More recently, mechanisation in all areas of farming and, especially, the introduction of chemical fertilisers and pesticides, have meant that crops are simply no longer as sensitive to climate as once they were. Since 1965 England's population has stabilised, while its arable production has rocketed. Decision-making on the farm today, in the East Midlands as everywhere else in Europe, has much more to do with short-term global politics and economics than with climate.

COMMUNICATING WITH THE EAST MIDLANDS

A map of English communications routes resembles true satin cloth. In satin the dominant pattern is produced by the weft strand: the warp strand, crossing the weft from side to side, adds the substance, but is subordinate to the weft's linear design. Yet without the warp there would be no cloth. Like satin, maps of English communications routes also often emphasise the 'weft', with red or blue motorways extending radially from London. The network of lesser roads – the 'warp' – transects these main routes, often in contrasting green. Railway maps display a similar pattern: the weft is formed by the inter-city lines radiating from London, while the warp threads (greatly fragmented by Dr Beeching's axe) snake cross-country, away from nodes on the main lines.

The weft is oriented differently in the various English regions. In the East Midlands, the dominant communications routes slant across the landscape from south-east to north-west, as they thunder through. The M40 and M1 run perpendicular to the geology and breast the Midland scarps at right-angles, like a sailor approaching oncoming waves in a storm. They are crossed and re-crossed, of course, by many local roads which, by contrast, run along the grain of the landscape, following the major river valleys from south-west to north-east. The East Midlands satin, then, is placed diagonally on the map of England, and this section considers its weft: the main arteries of national communication (Fig. 2.8).

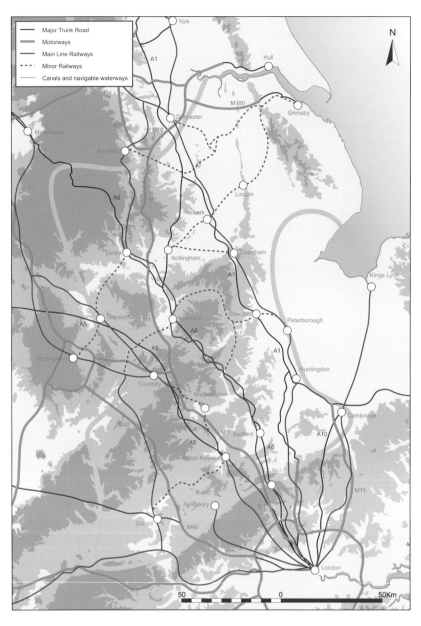

Fig. 2.8 Principle routes of communication in the East Midlands.

Some of our modern main roads are heroic; others less so. The London to Oxford motorway was an early component in the national network (although the extension from High Wycombe to Oxford was only opened in 1974), and it had priority, it was rumoured, so that ministers' chauffeurs could drive quickly and conveniently up from Westminster and arrive in time for dinner! It gives the motorist a great sense of crossing boundaries. He or she climbs steadily out of the London basin until, suddenly, the Chiltern summit (only 243.9m, though often shrouded in cloud) is boldly marked by the communications tower on Beacon Hill (Fig. 2.9). This Cold War sentinel, built in the early 1960s as part of the BACKBONE microwave communications system, guards the gateway to the East Midlands. And few gateways are more dramatic: a great concrete bow carrying a minor road (surprised, no doubt, to receive such monumental treatment) stands at the top of a majestic cutting through the chalk, sweeping in a gentle curve down the scarp towards Lewknor. By contrast, beyond the Oxford turn, the M40 extension to Birmingham (opened in 1992) now cuts across the grain of the landscape, spurning all previous routeways through this part of England, and bursts through the side of the Cherwell valley south of Banbury like a burglar crashing through a garden hedge. The railways and canals were not so brutal hereabouts. Both the Oxford Canal (completed in 1778) and the Great Western Railway (by 1850) used the Cropredy Gap in the Jurassic ridge north-east of Banbury to cross the limestone scarp, and then followed the Cherwell valley quietly southwards to the Thames. On a bright spring day it is one of the finest railway or canal journeys in lowland England (Fig. 2.10).

The M1 (opened in 1959) is a more subtle road altogether. It belongs to the golden age of motorway construction, when such roads were 'designed' rather than 'cut', and when they had more support from the communities through which they passed. Pevsner was surprised that the British did not start building motorways at all until the 1950s (a generation later than the Germans and Italians), and in 1960 he was critical of the 'backward-looking' designs used on the M1 bridges. He might have commented that the whole road was 'backward-looking'; yet in this very conservatism, perhaps, lies its success. Through the southern East Midlands the M1 is essentially a replacement for the A5 – the Roman Watling Street – from London to Chester and North Wales. Being a Roman road it follows straight lines: it was originally surveyed in the 1st century AD from hilltop to hilltop across the landscape, paying little attention to the terrain and none to the indigenous population. It speaks as eloquently of a remote bureaucracy as the M40 extension from Oxford to Birmingham. By remarkable contrast, the new M1 *used* the landscape. Unlike the cavernous chalk cutting of the A5 a mile to the west, the M1 enters the East Midlands so quietly north of Luton that concentration is required to notice its use of a natural gap in the chalk escarpment. The Greensand ridge at Woburn is clambered over rather than cut through and, having meandered across the Ouse/Nene watershed, the road follows the small valley of Whilton Brook deep into the limestone dip-slope and through the 'Watford Gap' into the Avon valley. This is as far as the M1 went until 1964 and, although it is now fashionable to deride this overcrowded road, it was a bold attempt to reconcile the needs of modern transport with the character of the countryside through which it passed. The manner in which the route of this early motorway follows the landscape makes one feel that the designers were concerned with more than simply conveying as many cars through the region as fast as possible.

Finding a path for the first railways had been just as tricky as planning the motorways. It is no coincidence, then, that Robert Stephenson's London and Birmingham Railway (now the West Coast Main Line) had explored the same route through the Jurassic ridge in 1833–8 as that taken by the M1 in the 1950s. The stretch through western Northamptonshire posed the biggest engineering problems on the whole route between Euston and Birmingham. The Wolverton embankment over the Ouse, the Weedon viaduct over the Nene and the Roade cutting near Blisworth are all major early monuments of engineering genius, but even Stephenson was almost defeated by the three-year struggle to cut the Kilsby Tunnel, which carries the line for over 2km under the Watford Gap. Underground aquifers here made the geology beneath the limestone extremely treacherous, and

BELOW: **Fig. 2.9 The communications tower at Beacon Hill on the Oxfordshire/Buckinghamshire border** *tells the motorist arriving from London on the M40 that they have reached the Chiltern scarp, and are about to race downhill through the great chalk cutting (made 1970–2) and into the East Midlands.*

LEFT: **Fig. 2.10 The Cherwell valley south-east of Banbury remains a major communications route.** *The Oxford Canal, one of the two main routes from Birmingham to London for 80 years from 1778, follows the contours along the western side of the valley, the straight line of the railway (c.1850) takes the eastern side of the valley, whilst the river itself meanders between the two. The M40 (opened 1991) ignores all these long-established lines as it sweeps insensitively across the grain of the landscape.*

a line of 13 pumping engines ran continuously for nearly a year to keep the excavations dry. For a short time, Kilsby was the longest tunnel in the world.

Even before Stephenson, the surveyors of the Grand Junction (now the Grand Union) Canal had seen the potential of this same Whilton Brook route. The Jurassic ridge was even more of a barrier to canals, and throughout the final quarter of the 18th century networks developed independently either side of it. Although the Oxford Canal eventually connected the Midlands with London in 1790, it was not until the Napoleonic Wars that funds were found to link the Severn and Trent with the Nene and Ouse systems. This was achieved by the construction, first, of the Braunston and Blisworth tunnels (opened in 1805), and then, the Crick Tunnel (opened in 1814), less than a mile east of Kilsby. 'Staircases' of locks were also needed: there were ten at Foxton, Leicestershire (completed in 1812) and seven at Watford (1814). The project was expensive and funds were short, so the canal was built to a narrow gauge. This restricted its usefulness so greatly that in 1900 a peculiar steam-powered boat lift was built at Foxton to reduce delays. Connections through the Jurassic hills linked the booming Midland textile towns with the expanding market in southern England, and branches were opened to take advantage, such as the Nottingham Canal in 1796. Suddenly such towns acquired new industrial suburbs around their canal basins: at Nottingham, a new suburb of wharfs and warehouses sprang up between the Castle cliff and Trent-side.

North of the Crick interchange, the M1 extension is a different road. Like the more southerly stretch, however, it respects the landscape and previous communication routes, shadowing the old road from Leicester to London through much of south Leicestershire. Then, north of the city, where Charnwood stood as a barrier to previous communication routes, it snakes up and down the steep valleys like an Autostrada. The Trent crossing, via a large modern causeway, is now marked only by a road sign, but the causeway itself is the lineal successor of the Harrington Causeway between Long Eaton and Castle Donington, which linked Nottingham with the Black Country and impressed Henry VIII's antiquarian, John Leland, in the 1530s. Leaving the East Midlands, the M1 penetrates the Pennine massif along the Erewash valley, and then runs cross-country to the watershed and the Doe Lea valley. This river falls into the Don system – a sure sign that we are leaving the Midlands. Our departure (or arrival) is supervised by a trio of country houses (Hardwick Hall, Bolsover Castle and Sutton Scarsdale Hall), each standing high above the valley and overlooking the huge smoking Coalite coking plant south of Staveley. Here genteel Midlands houses cough politely and confront industrial South Yorkshire (Fig. 2.11).

Fig. 2.11 Bolsover Castle turns its back on industrial South Yorkshire towards the northern end of the Doe Lea valley; the 17th-century fantasy house of the Cavendish family stands downwind of the enormous Coalite coking works (the largest in the world when opened in 1936). Standing alongside the powerful Markham coal mine, the works was a milestone on the M1 for a generation. The huge mechanised retorts (foreground) are fed by rail and, in 1939, Coalite started producing petrol from their coal-oil by-product here.

In medieval times the main road north of Leicester took a more easterly route. Leaving the town's west gate, it followed the Soar northwards as far as Barrow and then headed overland for Nottingham, where a bridge (presumably of timber) was constructed across the Trent at West Bridgeford as early as 920. This was the original road from London to York, mentioned in Domesday Book of 1086 but superseded by more easterly routes not long afterwards. North of Nottingham this road followed the eastern boundary of Sherwood Forest until it joined the Great North Road (now the A1M) that had crossed the Trent at Newark. By the 10th century the road north from Nottingham was probably already a landscape feature, as it formed a line along which parish boundaries were drawn when they were established at about that time.

The line taken by the canals, the railway and the A5 and M1 as far as Crick, must be one of Britain's most impressive long-term communication routes. Peoples moving north-west over the millennia, crossing the Ouse and the Nene, have made for the Watford Gap and breasted the Jurassic escarpment there, before heading for their different destinations further north: Birmingham, Manchester, Leicester, Nottingham or Newcastle. Although we can see landscape evidence for this route's presence since Roman times, we have to ask how many others had taken a similar route before the Romans arrived. Unfortunately we know very little about prehistoric routeways in this region. What evidence we have suggests that long-distance pre-Roman trackways ran along the Jurassic scarps from south-west to north-east. The very existence of this proposed 'Jurassic Way' has been seriously questioned recently, however, and south-west of Grantham any single line is almost impossible to establish.

Travel before the Romans would have been between local centres, strung out south-west to north-east along the sides of minor valleys and separated from each other by the major rivers. So, by cutting a new direct route (the A5, or Watling Street) south-east to north-west 'across' the countryside, the Romans were implementing a change in national transport strategy. The new road seems to have bisected the previous road network, crossing the major river valleys at right-angles, in order to link regions of the country that had not been directly linked before. It was, in effect, the first attempt to demonstrate that Britain could be a single polity.

On the A5 we still exploit this bold 1st-century initiative, which might suggest that it has been in more or less continuous use since Roman times. This cannot be the whole story, however. As you travel the A5 today, you can almost keep pace with the parallel traffic racing along the M1 a mile to the east, and this is primarily because there are few settlements to slow you down. Yet, if the road had been in constant use by the local population, surely it would have attracted settlements at some stage between the Roman period and the present? In fact, the local road network continued to ignore Watling Street, and settlements in northern Buckinghamshire, western Northamptonshire and along the Warwickshire–Leicestershire border are located elsewhere. This is a 'weft' road, while the local settlements are linked by the modern (and medieval) 'warp' road network. Between the Roman period and present, it seems, Watling Street has played little part in linking the local people of the East Midlands together. It remains what it always has been, a road for travellers passing through the region.

There *are* occasional settlements along Watling Street, however, and their character sheds light on the area's personality. Northwards from Dunstable, Fenny Stratford at the Ousel crossing was a medieval settlement near the site of the Roman station of Magiovinium. By contrast, no Roman predecessor has been found at the medieval settlement of Stony Stratford, at the Ouse crossing at the other – northern – end of modern Milton Keynes. But although apparently founded at different periods, both Stratfords were founded for the same purpose: to service traffic on Watling Street. And this was the role they played until the arrival of the M1. The most famous sights in Stony Stratford are still The Cock and The Bull, 18th-century coaching inns, where it was said that you heard tales as dubious in one as in the

Fig. 2.12 'The Cock' and 'The Bull' on Watling Street at Stony Stratford represent many fine 17th- and 18th-century inns on main roads through the East Midlands. *Like The Saracen's Head at Towcester, The George at Grantham, The Three Swans at Market Harborough and many others, these competitors developed into three-storey structures of brick. Typically they had a passage through the building, giving onto a yard behind surrounded by large kitchens, extensive stables and cheaper lodgings. Travellers such as John Byng would have stayed in the more expensive rooms on upper floors facing the street.*

other: a 'cock and bull story' (Fig. 2.12). Both Stratfords had flourishing markets in the medieval and early modern periods, but it is noticeable that, like modern motorway services, they were not self-governing settlements. Neither Fenny nor Stony Stratford was the centre of a medieval parish. They were places of work for local people, but their roots lay away from the road in the countryside through which it passed unheeding.

The Stratfords are about 16km apart, and 16km north of Stony Stratford the traveller arrives at Towcester (Roman Lactodorum). This was a more important Roman town than Magiovinium, perhaps, but just as dependent on Watling Street for its living. About 20km beyond Towcester the road reaches the abandoned town at Whilton Lodge in Norton parish, the Roman walled settlement of Bannaventa. A further 20km north still is the deserted Roman settlement of Tripontium near Churchover, where the road crosses the Swift. Another 13km further and the road reaches the site of Venonae (High Cross), a town now marked only by its elaborate antiquarian memorial of 1712.

The pattern is clear: these Watling Street settlements were founded by the Romans at regular intervals to service the road. They may have provided new local markets and services for the indigenous population, but they were there primarily to facilitate the business of government. They were bases in which troops could be lodged, staging posts where official couriers could change horses, and depositories where tax and treasure could be held safely while in transit. Usually they contained a single large building at their core to provide these services – the *mansio* (p.50). These settlements were not built to serve the local population, but to service the Empire. And once that Empire had ceased to exist, most of them dwindled and disappeared altogether. Those that were revived in the medieval period (really only the Stratfords and Towcester) did so in order, once again, to attract customers passing on Watling Street. Only Towcester seems to have been self-governing, with its own medieval castle and church. Indeed we know that Towcester was deliberately refounded as a *burh* by Edward the Elder in 917 (pp.197–9), so even here it seems it took an external stimulus; the settlement did not arise from local convenience. In medieval and later times, Watling Street passed *through* this region rather than being integrated with it, much as it had in the Roman period. The locals saw it as a source of income, but they actually lived elsewhere.

The A1(M) is a quite different type of road. Its Roman predecessor from London to Lincoln – Ermine Street – survives in the form of adopted roads today, but in the East Midlands only its central section is followed by the modern A1 – the 'Great North Road' (Fig. 2.13). South of Alconbury (Huntingdonshire) and north of Colsterworth (Kesteven), instead of following the Roman line, the modern road follows a medieval route through towns and villages. Unlike Watling Street, then, the northern and southern parts of Roman Ermine Street were evidently not such main routes subsequently, and they linked few settlements. In Lincolnshire, since the medieval period, Ermine Street (the 'Highdyke') has been mostly used as a droveway for taking animals to market in the south, and in places south of Lincoln it is still a green lane. In 1790, John Byng, the talented diarist, thought the Roman road south of Alconbury (now the A14 and A1198) was deserted because there were better inns on the Great North Road to the west, and because the latter route took the traveller into the fashionable West End of London, rather than to the City.

Like Watling Street, Roman Ermine Street cut across the prevailing settlement pattern, ignoring any existing prehistoric communications network. Even where it could have followed the prehistoric trackway along the Lincoln Edge it did not do so, running instead a mile to the east. Ermine Street, then, was another 'imperial' road, created by a remote authority to serve national and international interests rather than local ones. Like Watling Street, it also had regular stations or small towns spaced along it: Wimpole, Sawtry, Great Casterton, Ancaster (Causenna), Navenby, Owmby, Staniwells and Winteringham on the Humber. Although most of these locations (though not Owmby, Staniwells or Winteringham) were reoccupied by medieval villages, when we look in detail at the map it is clear that the medieval village centres were away from the road itself, being dictated by other factors, and in 1800 all the sites of the Roman towns themselves still lay in the fields. Within our region, Ermine Street did pass through some of the more important of Britannia's towns, such as Godmanchester (Durovigutum), Water Newton (Durobrivae) and Lincoln (Lindum Colonia). Paralleling the post-Roman history of the small Roman settlements, however, their medieval successors were also relative failures.

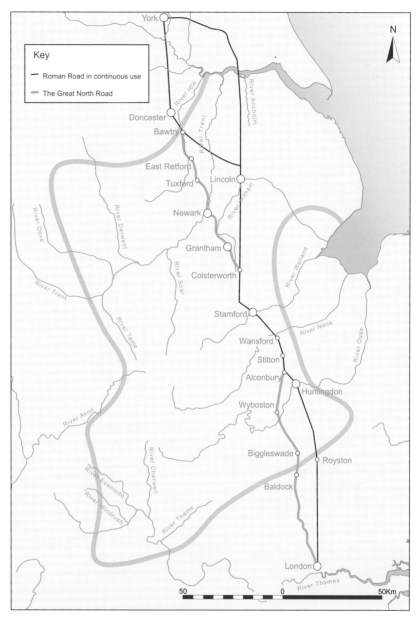

Fig. 2.13 The 'Great North Road' from London to York.

Godmanchester was only ever a small town, overshadowed by adjacent Huntingdon, and Water Newton was abandoned altogether. Only Lincoln remained a major settlement, although there were times in the 15th century when even that city was little larger than contemporary Godmanchester.

Once a bridge had been built over the Trent at Newark, the medieval Great North Road (the modern A1M) branched westwards off the Roman Ermine Street line at Colsterworth, south of Grantham. Bishop Alexander of Lincoln had obtained a licence for the bridge from Henry I between 1129 and 1133, although it was still under construction in the 1160s. In fact, Alexander's bridge may have replaced an earlier Trent crossing. The road from Colsterworth to Newark follows, in part, a trackway known as Sewstern Lane, which seems to be of prehistoric origin and was certainly a feature in the landscape by the 10th century, when it formed the county boundary between Lincolnshire and Leicestershire. Sewstern Lane has continued in use in the landscape: in the late 17th and 18th centuries it was a major drove road and was used almost exclusively for driving large herds and flocks long distances to market.

We do not know when traffic started to use the Great North Road route through Biggleswade and Buckden (now the A1M). It was a road linking settlements of medieval origin and, even at places like Alconbury, Wansford or Stamford, which lie near the line of Roman Ermine Street, the Roman site has been deserted and settlement shifted to its modern location during the medieval period. In its medieval form, the Great North Road was not so much an expression of national government as of local requirements.

As early as 1622 there had been an attempt to make the stretch of Great North Road between Biggleswade and Baldock into a turnpike (a road maintained to a good standard through toll payments), but most of the turnpikes along its southern parts were later in date and were implemented piecemeal. The long stretches of former Roman road that now form the A14 and A1198, however, were ideal for turnpiking, and the section between Wansford and Royston was among the earliest turnpikes in England (1663). Turnpiking both of the main roads north from London had the same effect as toll roads today. In 1753 complaints were made that the toll gates on the Great North Road and the Ermine Street routes forced drovers and other cost-conscious travellers to use a more westerly route through Oundle.

The motorway sections of today's A1 have few of the design values of the M1 or the M40. They are essentially bypasses around the medieval settlements, linked together to create a continuous dual carriageway. Where it does follow the Roman road – for example over the fenland escarpment north of Alconbury – the A1 resembles more closely 'imperial' roads like the A5; but to the south, where it winds through Huntingdonshire and Bedfordshire, the motorway accommodates the surrounding community, rather than being imposing itself upon it. Certainly a journey along the Great North Road in a mail coach, or in a motor car before the dual carriageway was built, would have been noticeably different from that along the old A5. It would be punctuated by frequent delays for local and market traffic. Biggleswade, Sandy, Eaton Socon, Buckden, Alconbury, Stilton, Wansford, Stamford, Colsterworth, Grantham, Newark, Tuxford and East Retford could all provide serious hold-ups. All of these towns have, or had, a wide selection of coaching inns to cater for those who decided to have lunch or to stay overnight while the traffic cleared. In 1792, John Byng gave us his preferences: The Sun at Biggleswade was good except for the beds, The Wheatsheaf at Alconbury was good except for the stabling, and The Haycock at Wansford Bridge was good except for the wine.

The coaching inns were themselves supported by a whole variety of industries. Coach-builders, emergency seamstresses, farriers, hairdressers, laundresses, tapsters, tobacconists, wheelwrights and many other trades were all in demand by the travelling public, and most would have been required since Roman times. At Stilton (Huntingdonshire), passing stagecoaches, and subsequently motor cars, provided an ideal market for the tasty cheese made in Leicestershire to the north-west. It was a great delicacy by the early 18th century, when it was sampled by Daniel Defoe. A day's journey further south, at Wyboston, conveniently close to The Bell and The Crown, Rawling Stocker (1717–58) owned a yard and stables in which he let lofts to grooms and coach drivers, and where he repaired cart and carriage wheels broken on the road. He also owned an apple orchard, whose fruit he could sell at the roadside in the autumn. Rawling ran the early 18th-century equivalent of a motorway service station, and today this part of Wyboston is dominated by his modern successors: a Little Chef, a garage and several large motels (Fig. 2.14).

Through careful planning, the designers of the East Coast Main Line railway between London and Newcastle (which did not open until 1852) coped with the East Midlands' geology much more comfortably than their equivalents on the west coast route. It has no tunnels, except where it cuts through the Chiltern chalk and the limestone of the Jurassic ridge at the short Stoke and Peascliffe tunnels (either side of Grantham). Like the navigations before them, the railways in the eastern part of the region made good use of the river systems and, compared with Stephenson's London and Birmingham Railway, the 'weft' threads were relatively minor feats of railway engineering. On the other hand the secondary 'warp' railways, linking local communities along the limestone ridges, frequently deployed engineering resources out of all proportion to their importance today. The most spectacular of these over-engineered branch lines must be that opened in 1879 to take traffic from Kettering and Corby to Oakham and Melton Mowbray. It served the infant ironstone mining industry (pp.176–7) and was provided with one of the most impressive viaducts in Britain: the 82-arch Welland viaduct, near the village of Harringworth. Similarly the Grantham Canal, which linked the town with Nottingham in 1798, had 18 locks and climbed 50m into the limestone hills, and is another prodigious feat of transport engineering, yet it was a local facility and never extended southwards across the watershed.

We have travelled the A5 and the A1, but between the two lie the A6 and the Midland Main Line railway from St Pancras to Leicester and Nottingham, which shadows it through much of the East Midlands. Leaving Watling Street for Bedford, Northampton, Leicester and Derby at Dunstable, the line of the A6 had become, by the 18th century, a principal coaching route from London to Manchester, promoting fine inns along the way, such as the Three Swans at Market Harborough. But this can hardly be described as a historic communication route to compare with Watling Street or Ermine Street. The A6 has no Roman predecessor and the lengths of medieval road, of which it is mostly formed, are merely the short-distance links between settlements. This is a connecting together of 'warp' roads rather than part of the 'weft'. Similarly, although Nottingham is said to have had the earliest railway in Britain (built in 1603–4 to carry coal from

Fig. 2.14 'Little End' Wyboston is dominated today by hotels and leisure complexes laid out on what was once meadow land between the Great North Road and the Ouse (top right).
Like the Thames, Trent and Nene valleys, large gravel pits now full of water make the whole Ouse valley appear poorly drained from the air. Archaeological excavations at such pits have revealed much of the East Midlands' prehistory. Hereabouts the pits, first dug in the 1940s and 1950s, have themselves given way to golf-courses and angling-lakes. Wyboston has made a living from the road since medieval times. The (now defunct) 1950s garage (west of the A1, centre left) was itself the successor of several more ancient inns, of which The Crown and The Bell survive (top centre), the latter, straight-jacketed by slip-roads, still offering accommodation.

pits in Strelley to Wollaton), in the 19th century the town was a latecomer to the railway revolution. The direct railway line from London to Nottingham was not opened until 1857 and, unlike the East and West Coast Main Lines, it snakes its way through the landscape in tunnels and cuttings. But the St Pancras to Nottingham line is at least still with us, the Great Central Railway (founded 1899), which was intended, eventually, to link towns like Nottingham with the continent, is now reduced to England's most comfortable commuter line (from Aylesbury and Banbury into St Marylebone) and the proposed 'Little Swindon' loco works at Woodford Halse (near Brackley) has returned to pasture.

Fig. 2.15 The hub of England; a landscape of national distribution centres. *Two kilometres north-west of the Watford Gap, lies the embryonic DIRFT (Daventry International Rail-Freight Terminal). The Northampton railway line curves westwards to join the West Coast Main Line, and DIRFT, alongside it, is linked to the M1 by its own junction. Roman Watling Street (the A5), an earlier artery of the international economy, drives straight northwards. Today, it conveys lorry-drivers quietly from DIRFT, past the thicket of radio-masts on Dunsmore, to the enormous truck-motel east of the road. In the middle distance, left, lie the gleaming sheds of distribution centres north of Rugby whilst, nearer the horizon, lie further distribution centres around Lutterworth.*

So the East Midlands really has only three main communication routes: that which follows the upper Thames and Cherwell across the limestone into Warwickshire; that pioneered by Watling Street through the Watford Gap; and that which takes the more gentle route of the Great North Road across the broad river valleys of the lower Ouse and Trent. If we really want to understand communications in the East Midlands, we need look no further today than the area round the Northamptonshire village of Watford. Here the unassuming valley of the Whilton Brook has been a major communications corridor for 2,000 years, if not longer. According to people in south-eastern England, once you are 'north of Watford' (the gap, and not the Hertfordshire town), you are in *terra incognita*. This is where 'elsewhere' starts, and it is no coincidence that so many large freight distribution depots have established themselves around here in the last decade (Fig. 2.15). Long-distance travel from the South East to the North in England always has to cross the Jurassic ridge, and the Watford Gap is the place to do it. Today the M1 boasts Watford Gap Services and, although we may think the service station a very modern concept, it is in fact the direct successor of the Roman stations alongside the A5, of the cheese-sellers of Stilton and of Rawling Stocker on the Great North Road. There can be few more traditional ways of life in the East Midlands than servicing people travelling long-distance through the country.

FURTHER READING

Bridges
Jervoise 1932; Simco & McKeague 1997 (Bedfordshire).

Meteorology and climate
Edwards (ed.) 1966 (Nottinghamshire); Jones 1954; Kinvig *et al.* (eds) 1950 (Warwickshire); Linton (ed.) 1956 (Derbyshire, Nottinghamshire, Lindsey); Martin & Steel (eds) 1954 (Oxfordshire); Pye (ed.) 1972 (Leicestershire); Steers (ed.) 1965 (Cambridgeshire).

Environmental history and archaeology
Dark 2000; French *et al.* 1992 (Nene and Welland valleys); Limbury & Evans 1978; Rackham, J (ed.) 1994; Rackham, O 1986; Robinson 1992 (Thames Valley); Scaife 2000 (Ouse Valley); Simmons 2001; Thirsk 1987.

Specific sites
Bamford 1985 (Briar Hill); Beresford 1975, 1987 (Goltho); Losco-Bradley and Kinsley 2002 (Catholme); May 1996 (Dragonby).

Communications
Aldcroft & Freeman 1983; Greenwood 1987; Hadfield 1970 (canals); Lelux 1984 (railways); Margary 1967 (Roman roads); Mills (ed.) 1989 (Lincolnshire); Palmer and Neaverson 1992; Taylor 1979 (roads); Wright 1982 (Lincolnshire).

Early travellers
Andrews (ed.) 1934 (John Byng); de Beer (ed.) 1959 (John Evelyn); Defoe 1724–6; Freeman (ed.) 1952 (Thomas Fuller); Jackson (ed.) 1870 (De la Pryme); Morris (ed.) 1949 (Celia Fiennes); Toulmin Smith (ed.) 1964 (John Leland).

3

Settling the Land

A Landscape of Individualism?
Settlement from Prehistory to the
10th Century

PREHISTORIC SETTLEMENT

In 1951 the *Ordnance Survey Map of Prehistoric Britain* depicted a mere 29 locations in the East Midlands, representing the entire period from about 450,000 BC to the Romans. Furthermore, 10 of those were in the Derbyshire Peak and a further seven were on the Lincolnshire Wolds. Of course, this apparent lack of easily visible remains does not indicate an absence of people in the East Midlands before the Roman period; it is, rather, an index of the region's agricultural success during subsequent millennia. We have seen that this is one of England's principal arable areas and, while ancient earthworks and stones rarely presented an obstacle to grazing, they were inconvenient and inefficient in arable land, so they were systematically eradicated. Thanks to later 20th-century archaeology (aerial photography, field walking and systematic excavation prior to development), we now know that prehistoric settlement in this region was just as intensive as elsewhere in Britain. As in later periods, however, it is not found uniformly across the countryside. Interesting concentrations and gaps are visible, some of which were even evident to the archaeologists who worked on those early Ordnance Survey maps.

A modern distribution map of Neolithic, Bronze or Iron Age finds in the East Midlands shows concentrations in the river valleys. But dots on maps can be deceptive, and the distribution of finds may not give an accurate picture of prehistoric settlement. Typically, the dots represent sites visible in aerial photography, yet such sites are only visible in certain geological conditions. Large gaps in the patterns of dots, for example on the plateau west of Cambridge, or on the uplands of Kesteven or Leicestershire, do not necessarily represent an absence of prehistoric settlement in those places. It may just be that the clay blanket overlying the more permeable geology in such areas produces fewer crop marks.

Occasionally the clay blanket is lifted by intensive survey or excavation, and then prehistoric archaeology is revealed – and it is plentiful. A study of Ropsley and Humby parishes in central Kesteven, for example, revealed a fully occupied landscape from the Neolithic period onwards, with a multitude of different site types scattered across the countryside. Areas of thick woodland did exist hereabouts, but they were used, not avoided, by the human population. Although knots of settlement may have clustered at favoured points in the landscape (alongside river crossings, or at springs, for example), it seems that, following some preliminary clearances of forest here in the 4th millennium BC, the 'plateau land' may have been deliberately 'maintained' as heathland for hunting. It was not ploughed for agriculture, but it was regularly burnt, a process presumably managed by the local population. A similar savannah landscape was indicated by the contemporary soil profile found beneath the long barrow at Ascott-under-Wychwood, Oxfordshire.

It was once thought that this preliminary 'clearance' of the landscape by humans could be dated by the 'elm decline' at around 6000 BC, a phenomenon observed in studies of pollen samples from across northern Europe. But we now think that the sudden disappearance of large numbers of elm from our landscape had more to do with the first appearance of *Ceratocystis ulmi*, the same 'Dutch elm disease' fungus that denuded the English countryside in the 1970s. Neolithic peoples, then, did not completely clear the woodlands and replace them with fields for agriculture, as was once thought. Rather they actively managed their woodlands, which is why Neolithic coppiced timber is occasionally found in waterlogged excavations (at Etton north of Peterborough, for example). Although in the 21st century we think of woods producing only standard timber, throughout history they have been just as important as sources of sticks for firewood, coppice poles for a whole variety of important tasks such as fencing, leaves for feed and bedding, mast for pigs and other animals, bracken for dyes and herbs for medicines. Such resources were too valuable to dispense with, at least not all at once in a general 'clear-felling'. The blanket of trees must have been removed cumulatively over many generations, and the eventual clearance of large areas may thus have been largely accidental.

Little was found at Ropsley to indicate where Neolithic peoples actually settled, but detailed research elsewhere is starting to reveal even these fugitive sites. Two sites at Milton Keynes overlooking the Ousel (Stacey Bushes and Heelands) have produced pits and gullies belonging to what are probably settlement sites. Excavations at Swarkestone and Aston (Derbyshire) revealed similar types of site, overlooking the valley of the Trent, and further north at Lismore, near Buxton, a community from about 2000 BC is thought to have been home to pastoralists (keeping cattle, sheep and pigs), who also grew small quantities of cereals and legumes on their more easily worked soils. At Corporation Farm, Abingdon, overlooking the confluence of the Ock and the Thames, another site of this sort (enclosed in this instance) has been explored, and domestic rubbish pits have been found overlooking the Thames at Yarnton, north-west of Oxford.

Many writers have envisaged a pattern of 'slash-and-burn' agriculture around such early settlements. Taking their models from ethnography, they say that clearings in the woodland around such settlements were designed specifically for agriculture, but that the land was only cultivated for, perhaps, a single generation. Without fertiliser the soil soon becomes exhausted, and farmers simply move on to create a new clearing. At Ropsley and elsewhere, such 'slash-and-burn' settlements would have occupied only small areas in the valley floors, near the water supply. The remainder of the territory would be hunting country: part managed woodland, part heathland made manageable by periodic burning. When there were local resources to exploit, some settlements might be occupied only seasonally: at Abingdon, for example, the settlement might have been used mostly by fishing expeditions.

Although fire may have been useful in maintaining the heath, it is not certain that trees of the temperate English woodlands could have been cleared for agriculture by burning, and tools must have been preferred for felling. At Ropsley, there were indications of a more systematic and permanent clearance phase during the central part of the 3rd millennium BC, followed by an extended phase of arable and pastoral occupation. A similar sequence has been found elsewhere on these uplands (at Sproxton, Leicestershire, for example). This major landscape clearance is confirmed and dated by silts from the Fens, which were deposited in a short but intense period of freshwater sedimentation, lasting only a century or two between about 2500 and 2100 BC. During this period, the Ouse, Nene and Welland rivers were choked with clay washed off the hillsides of what would become Northamptonshire, Bedfordshire, Leicestershire and Kesteven.

The rivers could not carry such large quantities of mud and, as soon as they reached the Fenland flats, it was deposited as layered sediments, which can now be identified and dated. The dramatic environmental changes revealed by such work bring to mind contemporary television pictures of torrents of mud flowing off the hills after storms in Central America and South-east Asia, once the tree cover retaining the soils on the hillsides has been removed by new settlers.

Was such clearance of the woodland made possible by the arrival of the sophisticated metal implements of the Bronze Age? This episode late in the 3rd millennium BC, though dramatic, was just one of several similar events. A little later (between about 2000 and 1500 BC) soil was being washed off the hills of Gloucestershire, Oxfordshire and southern Northamptonshire in the same way, to be deposited as thick silt in winter flooding along the Thames valley. By 1700 BC, the lower Cotswold slopes near Hanborough in the Windrush valley and at Stanton Harcourt (Oxfordshire) had been cleared and were used for grazing domesticates. Woodland on the Corallian hills was being cleared at Sidlings Copse (east of Oxford) at about the same time. The new pastures being created on these hills were probably used seasonally, with herds and flocks being driven long distances, from settlements and meadows in the valley bottoms up onto the hills for the summer.

Perhaps the most revealing studies of agricultural settlement in the Bronze Age East Midlands are those undertaken by Francis Pryor near the fen edge around Fengate, to the north and east of Peterborough. Around 1500 BC a fully occupied, intensively used agricultural landscape was revealed here. Herds of cattle were turned out to graze on rich fenland pastures in the spring and summer, and brought back to the settlements on the higher land along the fen edge in autumn. Some, at least, of the cattle were over-wintered, perhaps feeding on hay cut in the Fens, but possibly also on grain grown on the higher ground inland, beyond the settlements. A large proportion of these animals lived to maturity, suggesting that their milk (probably stored as cheese) was important. Along this fen edge, extended families lived in large single houses, dotted about within a patchwork of enclosures extending for miles north and south along the topographical zone between the fenland to the east and the higher ground to the west. This was a landscape of 'mixed farms', then, with the settlements themselves dispersed within it, rather than nucleated in 'villages'.

The enclosures themselves probably represent ditched paddocks, surrounded by 'quick' hedges, rather than cultivated fields, which each family unit would have used for managing its element of the cattle herd, and some had wells in their corners to water the stock. Although they lived a little distance from their neighbours, isolated from them by their paddocks, each family was inextricably bound up with the community, and the valuable fen grassland on which the entire community depended would have been managed in common. We know less about the cultivated fields probably located further inland, but these may have been managed communally also. Each Fengate family's house – just as was the case later, at thousands of other places across the East Midlands – was located in the most favourable spot, near the boundary between different agricultural resources, the fen and the arable. Perhaps each family worked its own long narrow strip from the 'top land' through the fen edge into the 'fenland', but a 'democratic' and 'co-operative' spirit must have prevailed among Bronze Age farmers hereabouts. Although each group of enclosures might have been managed by a single family group, the community as a whole must have overseen the much larger common resources of fen (and perhaps arable). The initial division of the fen-edge zone into enclosures might have been the work of a dominant authority with the power to divide up the land, but that conclusion need not follow automatically.

Similar Bronze Age field systems are known right along the fen edge – further north at West Deeping and Billingborough (Kesteven), for example. Crop marks are thought to represent similar patterns of droves, closes and dispersed roundhouses at Croxton Kerrial, Garthorpe and Wymondham in the Leicestershire uplands, and around St Ives (Huntingdonshire) and Fenstanton (Cambridgeshire). In Oxfordshire, along the upper Thames around Wallingford, the farming landscape was also organised in similar fashion, although it might have come into existence a little earlier, around 2000 BC. On the thin soils of the Derbyshire uplands, similarities with such lowland settlement regimes are evident. On Big Moor (on the Yorkshire boundary), timber houses were built on platforms in the angles of surrounding field systems. Some such sites are said to have been occupied for an enormous period of time, from about 3000 BC until early in the 1st millennium BC. The climate was warmer and drier through much of the Bronze Age (p.23) and it is entirely possible that lowland farming styles expanded onto these marginal uplands at this time. On the Derbyshire moors it seems that enclosures were used for arable, and not for stock management as was probably the case in the lowlands.

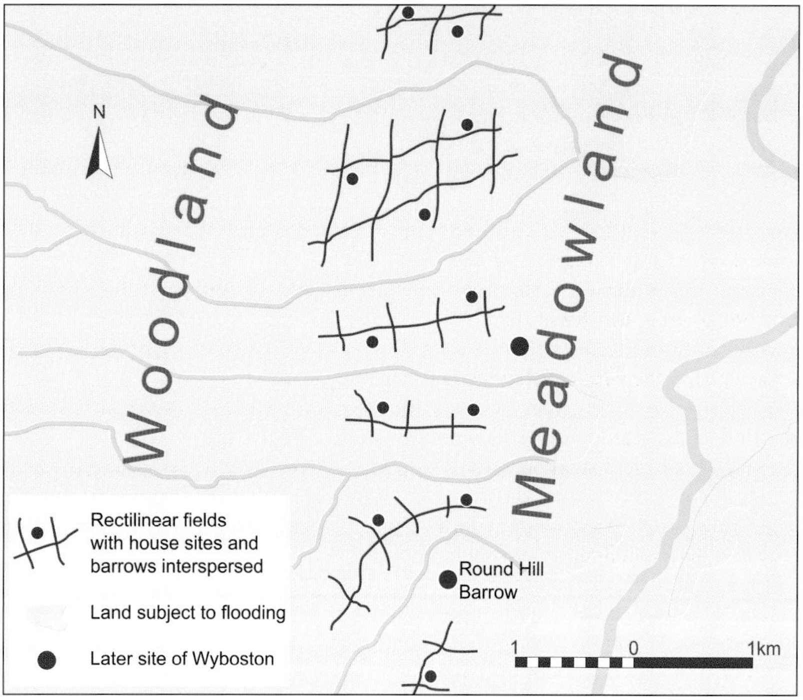

Fig. 3.1 Speculative reconstruction of Wyboston landscape in the late Bronze and early Iron Ages (compare Fig. 1.7).

From *c.* 1500 BC onwards the landscape around a place like Wyboston would also have been used more intensively. The pattern of landscape exploitation used on the fen edge and in the Thames valley would probably have been found here also (Fig. 3.1). Being a typical strip of Midlands countryside, containing 'bottom land', 'terrace land' and 'top land', we can suggest that it was the 'terrace land' around the later village of Wyboston that would become the centre of the Bronze Age agricultural regime. In this zone, as at Fengate, we might find roundhouses distributed amongst the earliest components of an extensive rectilinear field system that is still visible in air photographs (even though many of those we see are thought to be Iron Age or Romano-British in date – Fig. 3.2). Such a landscape has been slowly revealed in excavations within a similar topographical location 5km to the north at Little Paxton. The managed woodlands of the 'top land' and the meadows of the 'bottom land' are likely to have seen only temporary settlements until, just before the Romans arrived, a small settlement was established in the meadow land near the river (below).

In the deteriorating climate of the late Bronze Age, after about 1000 BC, the grazed upland pastures at Hanborough reverted back to scrub. Peat started to form on Big Moor. Settlement generally was contracting, pulling back towards the valley floors. In the Thames valley and along the fen edge around Fengate, the established agricultural regime, which had lasted for about a millennium, started to break down. Fenland water levels were rising, and the water was getting more brackish each year. Soon the old tracks became impassable on foot, even in summer, and an economy based on managing great herds of grazing animals here was no longer viable. After about 600 BC the fen-edge community consequently became less reliant on their animals, depending more on what they could grow for themselves on the higher grounds inland from their homes. Pollen samples show a dramatic increase in weeds of cultivation at this time. They were brought in with the grain grown on the higher ground and imply a larger area put down to crops. Perhaps this is also why more sediment was now being washed off the hills around the upper Thames.

It may be that the population was falling at this time, and some archaeologists have also seen evidence for the growth of an unwelcome aristocracy and their

***Fig. 3.2 Crop marks of late Bronze-
Age, Iron Age and Romano-British
roundhouses,*** *enclosed fields and trackways
on the terrace land just south of modern
Wyboston. The building in the bottom right-
hand corner fronts onto the Great North Road.*

imposition of a new social hierarchy during this period of crisis and change. At
this period, it is argued, agricultural production was less under the control of the
individual family and more under aristocratic control. In return for agricultural
produce the new aristocracy may have offered the community defence; either
actual, from surrounding groups, or metaphysical, from the wrath of their gods
and ancestors.

Certainly, it is only in the Iron Age (after about 600 BC) that the introduction of
new technology is accompanied by a new pattern of more 'nucleated' settlements.
Now certain groups of houses (not in themselves much different from those
found in the corners of the Bronze Age fields) were established within boundaries
so substantial that they are seen as security measures: either military or symbolic.
Such settlements are ubiquitous in the East Midlands, as they are elsewhere in
Britain. In upland areas they are sometimes called 'hillforts' – a hilltop site,
surrounded by a rampart, within which houses huddle, apparently for safety. A
great concentration of such sites is found in the north-west corner of our region,
in northern Derbyshire (at Ball Cross and Burr Tor, for example). These
complexes are comparable with the long line of hillforts stretching along the
southern and eastern borders of the East Midlands, along the scarps of the
Berkshire Downs and the Chilterns, but only a handful are known actually within
the East Midlands. A few good examples still stand as earthworks, but to view
these sites merely as defended settlements is to ignore much of their richness.
Later, we will ask more profound questions about their purpose (pp.214–5).

By no means all settlements of roundhouses that are bounded by a rampart
and ditch have been claimed as hillforts: many are in indefensible sites (by the
Cam at Great Shelford, Grantchester and Trumpington, Cambridgeshire; near
the Ouse at Little Paxton, Huntingdonshire; near the Witham at Short Ferry,
Lindsey; near the Windrush at Mingies Ditch (*see* Fig. 4.10) and in dozens of
other places). A study of crop marks in Leicestershire showed that about 100
sites of this type could be identified with some confidence, while in Lincolnshire
an even greater concentration of such settlements has been revealed through air
photography, sometimes along with the field systems which went with them.

Such grouping together of houses within enclosures in the landscape might
indeed speak of a more hierarchical society. Hierarchies might even be detectable
in the layout of buildings within certain settlements. At Colsterworth (Kesteven),
for example, the enclosure contained a centrally placed large roundhouse
(presumably for the premier family) surrounded by four or five smaller ones,

with similar interior fittings, but placed more peripherally within the enclosure: service buildings were placed even further away from the central dwelling. Such enclosed clusters of Iron Age houses might, then, represent a fundamentally different style of settlement from the 'dispersed' pattern prevalent at Fengate and elsewhere a few centuries earlier. But is this more 'nucleated' settlement pattern related to the rise of a new regional social and political hierarchy? In such a society, one might argue, those in authority would have the power to bring family units together, away from their individual land holdings.

Yet such profound changes in the way settlements use the landscape should probably not be allocated to a single cause. The hierarchical structuring of the settlement seen at Colsterworth was not detected at Gravelly Guy (Oxfordshire) and the rise of this Iron Age aristocracy remains hypothetical. Unlike the settlement revolution of the 10th century AD, when formerly dispersed communities were also pulled together into nucleations, any putative Iron Age aristocracy did not impose a radical change in landscape management. The chequerboard of late Bronze Age fields was developed through the Iron Age, but it was not overthrown. That only finally occurred in the 10th century.

It is also the case that most Iron Age communities of the East Midlands, along the fen edge (at Catswater, for example), along the Ouse (at Salford) and on the gravel terraces of the Thames (like that excavated at Gravelly Guy), are mostly 'unenclosed' settlements whose layout does not suggest the need to consider military defence (Fig. 3.3). Typically these are clusters of houses at regular intervals (we might call them 'villages') within the long strings of ditched enclosures, that occupy similar zones in the landscape to their Bronze Age predecessors. They flourished in the period between about 400 and 100 BC, and it is an open question whether such enclosures represented a new start or whether they simply developed the Bronze Age field pattern. The wetter weather in the earlier part of the Iron Age would have produced excellent grazing along the river. These meadows would have been enhanced by controlling the seasonal flooding (which may be why the enclosures were so prominently ditched), and the settlements had to manage drainage, too, using gullies dug both around the individual houses and around whole settlements. Pollen samples (at Farmoor, west of Oxford, for example) confirm that for most of the period between about

Fig. 3.3 A reconstruction by the Oxford Archaeology graphics office of the unenclosed Iron-Age community along the edge of the common grazing at Gravelley Guy, near Stanton Harcourt (Oxfordshire). Note that, as in later periods, concentrations of houses are located at the boundary between enclosed fields and open grazing.

400 and 100 BC this was a rich grassland environment, while the remains of many dung beetles in macrofossil samples show that the grasslands were intensively grazed.

Then the weather cleared up somewhat. The most recent studies suggest that, within a pattern of longer-term deterioration, there was an improvement in climate between about 150 BC and the 3rd century AD, with warmer temperatures and less rainfall. Thames valley settlements like those at Gravelly Guy, Cassington and Tomlins Gate, and several around Milton Keynes, like that at Pennylands, have all produced good evidence that cereals, beans and peas were grown and stored at this time. Because so many Thames valley sites have been investigated, meaningful conclusions can be drawn about the development of crops and advances have been demonstrated in both the quantity and quality of the plants grown throughout the Iron Age. Emmer wheat was replaced by spelt wheat, for example, implying an increase in productivity per hectare, while the presence of spiked rush seeds within grain stored near Abingdon shows that arable cultivation had extended into low-lying boggy areas and hints at its intensification.

On the light limestone soils to the north, Iron Age communities were also growing grain as well as raising stock. Excavations at Enderby (Leicestershire) demonstrated that Iron Age peoples were growing a large hectarage of cereals. This conclusion is reinforced by the large number of iron ploughshares, sickles, quernstones and grain storage pits found across the region.

Pollen records the impact of these communities on the landscape and shows not only an increase in arable crops but also a sharp rise in quantities of grass alongside a rapid decline in plants of scrub and waste, so the grazing was improving also. Late Iron Age farmers also knew about manuring (the collection of dung and other waste for spreading on the fields to enhance fertility): we know this because we find a 'background' scatter of domestic pottery in their fields that is unlikely to have arrived through any other mechanism. Although the area down to grain seems to have increased, then, these late Iron Age farms were still the centres of 'mixed' agricultural regimes: the rearing of stock and the growing of crops remained interdependent, as they were locally until the 1970s.

With the development of a fully occupied landscape, we should not be surprised, perhaps, that long-distance linear ditch systems, which occur throughout the East Midlands, have been interpreted as evidence for competition between different groups of farmers. Such ditch systems have been investigated by aerial photography in Lincolnshire, but they are also known in other parts of the region, sometimes surviving as earthworks, as at King Lud's Entrenchments (Sproxton, Leicestershire) and between Stow-Nine-Churches and Farthingstone (Northamptonshire), for example. If the landscape was fully occupied with competitive farming communities, the argument runs, the communities would want to demarcate their territories. This is especially true, it is said, if cattle were being run loose on large 'ranges'. According to this interpretation, the whole of the plateau north and south of Lincoln would have been divided into rectangular territories by large multi-ditched systems both crossing the hills from east to west, and running north–south along their eastern (dip-slope) side. Were these huge structures really just to keep cattle in? If so, why are they not continuous and why do they only seem to include parts of the landscape?

Areas of open 'range', woodlands and meadows, all of which will have been integrated with the Iron Age farming regime, will not usually show up as crop marks. So, if the 'top land' was grazed by free-range animals, presumably the community's grain must have been grown in the ditched enclosures around the settlements. Yet in the Bronze Age around Fengate, such enclosures were for stock management (keeping the stock out of the surrounding crops), rather than for growing grain; and in the Thames valley the closes were paddocks, not arable fields. Was this situation really reversed in Lincolnshire, with the stock being given free range on the hills while the crops were grown in secure enclosures?

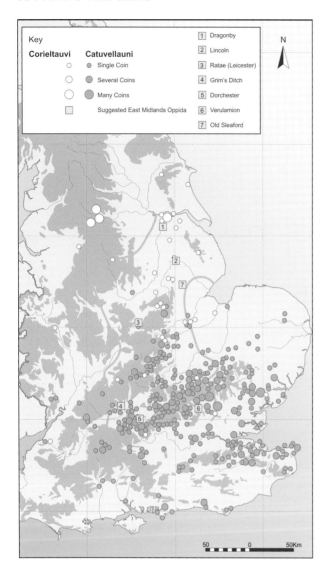

Key

Corieltauvi   **Catuvellauni**
○   ● Single Coin
○   ● Several Coins
○   ● Many Coins
□   Suggested East Midlands Oppida

1 Dragonby
2 Lincoln
3 Ratae (Leicester)
4 Grim's Ditch
5 Dorchester
6 Verulamion
7 Old Sleaford

N

50   0   50Km

Fig. 3.4 Distribution of coins minted by the Corieltauvi compared with those of the Catuvellauni (sources: Jones & Mattingly 2002, Figs 3/7–3/9 & 3/11).

Such diversity is quite plausible. In the upland areas of Britain, including Derbyshire, the open hills were clearly used for grazing and, therefore, the small quantities of grain (grown here for domestic consumption rather than surplus) had to be protected within enclosures. But does that necessarily also apply to the rich arable soils on the (relatively) low hills of Leicestershire and Lindsey? Is it possible that it was the animals here who were confined within enclosures (at least seasonally) before being led through open land, planted with grain, on droveways (many of which are represented as crop marks) to their meadows in the river valleys? The picture is far from clear, but we should beware of importing assumptions about lowland agricultural practice from the agriculturally more marginal uplands.

Many late Iron Age excavations have revealed the arrival of new cultural traditions, apparently from Europe, in artefacts (mostly pottery and metalwork) of so-called 'Belgic' style. A more glamorous marker, however, that this region was part of a larger European culture is the use of coins. Coinage indicates both a level of political sophistication beyond the simple ties of family (it has been suggested that coins were issued in the names of paramount chiefs and their sub-kings) but, even more usefully, coin distribution patterns show where particular political groupings were to be found. Coins issued by the rulers of a late Iron Age tribe called the Corieltauvi dominated the northern part of the region, although only isolated finds have been made north of the Trent valley (Fig. 3.4). In Derbyshire the only Corieltauvian coin found was well to the east of the Peak hillforts – reinforcing the suggestion that these structures relate to political groupings based further north: indeed, the north-western Corieltauvian boundary may have been the Trent valley itself, between the Tame and the Derwent rivers.

Leicester became the regional Romano-British centre for Corieltauvian gatherings and its Latin name, Ratae Corieltauvorum, seems to mean 'rampart of the Corieltauvi', perhaps indicating that, in the late Iron Age, it had been enclosed within banks and ditches. But if Ratae was an important place in the late Iron Age, was it in any sense a capital? In fact, the Corieltauvi may have been not so much a tribe as an alliance between perhaps four otherwise unconnected political groups. Such an alliance, it is argued, could have been founded on opposition to the Catuvellauni. We will encounter them as the powerful and expansionist tribe which, by the time of the Roman invasion of AD 43, apparently occupied most of the southern part of the East Midlands.

Significant though Iron Age Ratae may have been, the settlement at Old Sleaford (Kesteven) may have been even more important. Not only was this a large and wealthy settlement, but the gold blanks, from which coins were struck, were made here. Such activity, it is thought, would only have taken place at the principal seats of political power. Consequently Old Sleaford may have been an *oppidum* – a political centre and gathering place. No traces of dykes like those characteristic of the southern British *oppida* have yet been found around Old Sleaford, however, although in Corieltauvian territory they may have existed at Lindum (Lincoln) as well as Ratae. The hillfort on Burrough Hill, near Melton Mowbray, represents a fourth potential gathering place for this late Iron Age political grouping. Alone among the East Midlands hillforts it has produced late Iron Age material, suggesting a continuing political role in the 1st century BC.

Corieltauvian settlements of less exalted status are regularly identified and occasionally explored through excavation. The enclosed settlement at Colsterworth is largely of this date, as are similar sites at South Ferriby, Kirmington and Owmby (Lindsey) and Harston, Loughborough and Oadby (Leicestershire). A thoroughgoing investigation of a community of this period was undertaken at Dragonby, on the limestone ridge north of Scunthorpe. Here a rectilinear 'village' plan was laid out with individual enclosures – many if not all containing large roundhouses – probably in the 3rd century BC. The Dragonby excavations are of interest because they reveal the slow development of a community through an extended period of late Iron Age contact with the Roman Empire, and subsequently through the conquest itself and far into the Romano-British period. They show a community continually adapting to change, where new cultural influences arrived incrementally. But although the indigenous community had contact with occasional new artefact types over an extended period of time, they were probably not newcomers themselves.

Pollen samples from the higher ground above the Dragonby settlement show that the development of the large, unenclosed 'nucleated' community in the 3rd century BC here coincided with a decrease in tree pollen and an increase in the growth of cereals and weeds of cultivation. These are signs of arable cultivation on the 'top land', not of cattle ranges. Dragonby, however, is also located on an easily worked outcrop of ironstone, and in a culture where this material was highly prized, control of this resource would be both economically important and prestigious. Iron production may therefore have played a significant part in the settlement's economy. Furthermore, it is said that it takes 630kg of charcoal to produce 1kg of iron and, as only certain thicknesses of wood make good charcoal (pp.180–1), this staggering conversion rate must suggest that Iron Age peoples were skilful woodland managers. We should presume, therefore, that Dragonby may have had access to large areas of managed woodland, perhaps on the sandy heaths to the south-west.

Accounts by Roman writers ensure that we have more information about the intrusions of the Catuvellauni into the East Midlands in the generations before the Roman invasion than we have for earlier periods. This 'tribe' certainly possessed *oppida*, of which the most famous lie in Hertfordshire, outside the East Midlands. Within their new western lands (ie the southern East Midlands), the Raw Dykes at Dorchester, enclosing the extensive late Iron Age settlement here, might have become a gathering point for political groupings within the Upper Thames valley (Fig. 3.5), although a similar establishment has recently been

Fig. 3.5 The 'Raw Dykes' cut off a promontory of land between the Rivers Thames (foreground and top right) and Thame (top left) immediately south of the modern village of Dorchester-on-Thames (Oxfordshire). *Despite some levelling, these earthworks remain massive, are presumed to be late Iron-Age in date and to relate to an* oppidum *of the western Catuvellauni. Crop marks of an extensive settlement have been recorded in the fields to the south (right), which would have occupied a man-made island in the river (see also Fig. 7.11).*

Fig. 3.6 The late Iron-Age settlement by the Ouse near Wyboston, seen in an aerial photograph from the west taken before excavation in 1954–6.

proposed at Abingdon. The mysterious Grimm's Ditches, on the high plateau between the Cherwell and the Evenlode valleys north-west of Woodstock, may also be a site of this type, although it is possible that this centre might have lain on the eastern edge of the territory of the Dobunni, a tribe based in the Severn valley (p.134). From their political heartland beyond the southern and eastern borders of the East Midlands, a Catuvellaunian advance into the East Midlands is also visible in the distribution of their coinage (*see* Fig. 3.4). It is more common than the Corieltauvian coinage, and is plentiful in the valleys of the Ouse, Nene and Thames. Consequently, excavations in these areas have hunted for signs that the Catuvellauni drove out earlier peoples and destroyed or reoccupied their settlements.

Some evidence for such a late Iron Age conquest has been proposed in Bedfordshire where, in marked contrast to the continuity evident at Dragonby, there are some signs of abrupt changes in the settlement pattern. A number of small Bedfordshire agricultural settlements do date from this phase of hypothetical Catuvellaunian expansion. Down by the river at Wyboston, in the prime meadowland, a small settlement of two roundhouses within an enclosure was established at precisely this time (Fig. 3.6). It is likely that this was established at some distance from older Iron Age settlements further up the slope in the vicinity of the modern village. Although on rich grazing land, the new settlement would have been prone to flooding and stayed wet for much of the year. Its inhabitants were using new styles of pottery and metalwork, yet this new settlement in the Wyboston landscape looked very much like its predecessors elsewhere. It was surrounded by a small group of rectilinear enclosures, which in such a low-lying location must have been paddocks for stock control rather than fields for crops. The settlement's agricultural economy, as represented by artefacts, was based on cattle-rearing, although sheep and pigs were also important.

At Odell (Bedfordshire), Blackthorn Farm (north of Northampton), Dorchester (Oxfordshire), Woughton (Milton Keynes), Willington (Derbyshire), Cambridge Castle and many others, excavations have revealed similar evidence for the planting of new settlements on what had been farmed land in the late Iron Age. Typically these settlements contain a cluster of roundhouses, either grouped within an enclosure ditch or set individually within groups of paddocks. But, apart from the fact that these new settlements represent more families living on the land, what evidence we have suggests that the landscape itself continued to be managed as it had been in the previous few centuries. Wherever appropriate sampling has been undertaken, we find grain-growing still taking place on the 'top land' and stock-rearing on the meadows in the valleys. Both activities took place within the same community: the East Midlands 'mixed farm' was already well established when the Romans arrived.

THE ROMANO-BRITISH SETTLEMENT: CONTINUITY

At Dragonby the impact of the Roman conquest on a large and flourishing late Iron Age community can be read in the excavations. Here at least, the central years of the 1st century AD saw a recession, when quantities of Iron Age pottery used on the site declined, but they were not immediately replaced by wares of Romano-British design. It was not long before the settlement recovered, however, and by about AD 100 it was flourishing again and generating more pottery than ever, although now mostly Romano-British wares. The impact of the invasion of AD 43 was thus not felt at Dragonby immediately, but rather over a generation or two.

Dragonby's field system may have continued in use through these decades without a break, and in this respect it appears typical of contemporary sites across the East Midlands. However, we have indications that the Romano-British farmer obtained greater yields from his land than his predecessors. In Langton Hundred in south-east Leicestershire, distinctive 'halos' of broken pottery have been found around each settlement site, derived from manuring. Although such manuring had also occurred in the Iron Age, the far greater quantities of Romano-British pottery suggest an intensification within the arable infields nearer the settlements, while a much thinner pottery scatter further out also indicates that, now, the arable was encroaching on the 'top land'. By the end of the 2nd century, it is thought, the hectarage of land hereabouts under arable was similar to that under the 13th-century 'common field' regime.

Not only did Romano-British farmers manure their arable intensively, they were also practising sophisticated crop rotations. At Gravelly Guy and Barton Court Farm (both in Oxfordshire), weedy legume seeds were found amongst the stored cereal grains. Such plants often thrive on arable land when lying fallow, and are beneficial as they nitrogenate the soil. Further evidence for the intensification of arable between the 1st and the 3rd centuries comes from excavations at Ashville (near Abingdon), where first the decline, and then disappearance, of spiked rush pollen strongly suggests large-scale land drainage. Romano-British farmers persisted with the principal foodstuffs of the Iron Age: in the Upper Thames valley, breadwheat remained the dominant crop in the Romano-British landscape. Yet an increasingly wide range of other plants was under cultivation, and flax and beans were grown in addition to cereals at Ashville. More adventurously, evidence for vine-growing has emerged from excavations at Wollaston (Northamptonshire), both in the form of pollen and an excavated planting trench. How widespread viticulture was is hard to say, but in the warmer, drier climate prevailing between the 1st century BC and the 3rd century AD, the limestone slopes of the upper Welland, Nene and Ouse valleys would have been ideal.

Cultivating cereals would have been made easier by the introduction, usually credited to the Romans in the 2nd or 3rd centuries AD, of a heavier plough with an asymmetrical share, coulter and mould-board. This not only allowed heavier clays to be cultivated, but also suppressed weeds by turning the sod. The Romans are also thought to have introduced the scythe, an early example of which was excavated at Farmoor. While they could be used for harvesting cereals, scythes were especially useful (compared with earlier sickles) for cutting hay to provide winter feed for stock. Evidence for haymaking comes from large quantities of seeds from hay-meadow plants found on settlement sites. The greater areas under arable cultivation would have required more cattle as draught animals, of course, and such widespread haymaking hints at the feeding of many beasts through the winter. Statistical analyses of animal bones from several Romano-British sites have shown that cattle were becoming increasingly common, perhaps replacing sheep in the diet.

The great majority of people in Roman Britain, however, were not living in settlements of a distinctively Roman type ('villas' or 'towns'): they lived instead in small rural settlements very similar to those of their forebears. The survey of 12 representative square kilometres of Langton Hundred identified some 20 Romano-British settlement sites (Fig. 3.7). Of these only one was a villa, established in the late 2nd or early 3rd century, although three others had imported Roman finds. The remaining 16 settlements were farmsteads, many of which had been previously occupied in the late Iron Age. All of them produced quantities of 1st- or 2nd-century pottery, showing that they were not dependent on the villa's agricultural regime, as they were established before it arrived. Indeed, four of the smaller settlements disappeared in the late 2nd century: two of these were close to the villa and may have been replaced by it. The Roman landscape was fully occupied, with an even greater density of small settlements than had existed in the Iron Age. In the Nene valley, Iron Age settlements identified through crop marks occur (on average) once every kilometre, while Romano-British settlements occur every 500m.

Many East Midlands farmsteads of this type have been investigated (at Dunston's Clump, west of Retford; Willington, on the Trent below Burton; Goltho, east of Lincoln; Empingham, Rutland; Kempston, Bedfordshire and elsewhere). Some of these settlements grew large, such as that identified from aerial photography near Fotheringhay, Northamptonshire, and by no means all of them are enclosed within ditches. The fully excavated site at Odell (Bedfordshire) seems typical. Here, several large circular buildings of late Iron Age date continued in use after the conquest, until replaced by similar circular buildings when renewal became necessary. Contemporary ancillary domestic and agricultural buildings here were, however, usually rectangular. The settlement was partly enclosed by a substantial ditch which, although probably stock-proof, was not a serious defence. The field system around the Odell settlement also developed between the 1st century BC and the 3rd century AD, mainly by subdivision, suggesting an increasingly complex agricultural regime.

Intensification of arable farming and an expansion of the settlements themselves would probably have been the outward sign of the assimilation of a settlement like Wyboston into the Roman Empire. The excavated late Iron Age farmstead on the 'bottom land' (see Fig. 3.6) was evidently joined by others (identified from aerial photographs) scattered more evenly across the landscape, and at this time it grew in size, acquiring more buildings, some rectangular rather than circular. The Iron Age field systems hereabouts remained in use and became more complex (see Fig. 3.2). In the 2nd century a grain-drying oven was constructed in a field corner near the settlement near the river, another sign of increasing grain cultivation. The national distribution of such ovens is concentrated in the East Midlands and demonstrates that the region was producing substantial grain surpluses, requiring storage (for which we also

Fig. 3.7 The hundred of Langton (Leicestershire) showing the occupation periods of the known Romano-British settlement sites, as deduced by P Bowman (source: Bowman 1996, Fig. 2).

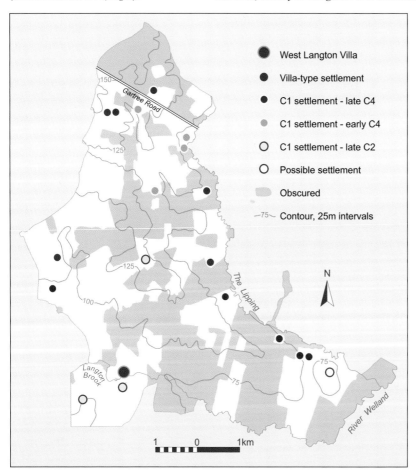

have evidence in the form of barns), and therefore drying. The Wyboston oven would have been wood-fired with fuel from coppice or pollards on the 'top land', although the primary function of this woodland may already have been wood pasture for cattle and pigs. The 'bottom land' by the Ouse would have provided hay meadow, but by the 2nd century much of the land between the meadows and the woods was probably given over to arable, producing a substantial grain surplus. We need to ask why, during the 2nd and 3rd centuries, such investment was put into producing surplus grain. And to approach this question we need to ask whether the increase in arable hereabouts was related, in any way, to the arrival of a villa on the gravel terrace near the river in Eaton Socon.

THE ROMANO-BRITISH SETTLEMENT: CHANGE

In the 21st century two entirely different interpretations of the Roman Empire are put forward by historians, both based on our more recent national experience. The account given by contemporary Roman writers themselves, and repeated in different forms by generations of historians and archaeologists, describes a beneficent empire bringing civilisation's fruits to benighted peoples. This model parellels British imperial experience in Africa and other territories where – to Victorian eyes – the natives appeared backward. The archaeological remains of Roman Britain have been explained in this way for centuries, yet the dramatic change implied by this narrative is often invisible in the landscape. In some places, the moment of conquest is indeed marked by highly visible constructions, sealing Iron Age layers beneath them and permitting no debate about the impact of Rome. But it has become clear that such structures represent only a thin veneer on the country's surface and affected only a tiny proportion of the contemporary population. In the East Midlands countryside, at least, it is not the dramatic break with the past (implied by traditional narratives of conquest), but rather the continuity between the late Iron Age and the Romano-British periods, that impresses. More like the British in 18th-century India, the Romans might have tried to strike alliances with the Iron Age peoples. Perhaps they attempted to manipulate indigenous politics: bolstering the regimes of regional rulers favouring imperial policies here, mounting a military expedition against a local warlord there. Like many English sahibs, no doubt many ambitious Romans aimed to marry into the indigenous aristocracy. How else, after all, could the Romans keep control of Britannia with such a small (yet expensive) military force, and ensure that the Empire received the profits from its valuable economy?

Yet, although we have noted remarkable continuity in the countryside through the 1st and 2nd centuries, there was clearly a period following the conquest of AD 43 when changes in East Midland power structures were reflected by the intrusion of two distinctively Roman institutions in the landscape: first, the foundation of towns and, second, the construction of villas.

Representing major intrusions into the previously rural landscape, towns were very visible expressions of the new political order (Fig. 3.8). Symbolically, at least, the relocation of the principal Corieltauvian political centre (if that is what it was) from Old Sleaford to Ratae (Leicester) must have seemed revolutionary, although we have already seen that an Iron Age centre may already have existed at Leicester, associated with a dyke system (p.42). The equivalent centre for the western half of Catuvellaunian territory (the southern part of the East Midlands) lay outside our region at Verulamium (St Albans), but it is possible that the western Catuvellauni looked to a sub-capital within our region. Perhaps the political centre for the western Catuvellauni was Durobrivae (Water Newton, Cambridgeshire), because at least one milestone directs travellers to that town. Lactodorum (Towcester) and Alchester (Oxfordshire), however, being walled and linked directly with Verulamium by road, are equally realistic candidates.

Fig. 3.8 The East Midlands in the Romano-British period.

As at Ratae, recent archaeological work at Lindum (Lincoln) has shown that the pool formed by the Witham had long been a place of importance for the Corieltauvi. Not only was much valuable metalwork found around the river crossing (p.210), but a late Iron Age dyke system has also been identified. There may even have been an Iron Age hilltop enclosure here as well, although no such structure has yet been identified. Following the invasion of AD 43 a legionary fortress, built on the hill overlooking the pool, might have replaced the focus of tribal gatherings, while a new causeway leading to it was constructed across the pool. This pool had previously been so important to the identity of the place that the Romans based their place-name on it (Lindum means 'the place by the pool'). Was this a calculated act of desecration? Was the construction of the causeway across the revered waters merely practical necessity – undertaken at the behest of the military engineers – or was political and religious humiliation intended? However we interpret them, both Lindum and Ratae are unequivocal statements in the landscape that the Roman government now controlled the key locations of earlier political regimes.

Lindum and Ratae both began as military establishments, although they had been demilitarised by the end of the 1st century. Both had streets laid out on a grid system (Figs 3.9 and 3.10) containing many impressive public buildings: public bathhouses, gymnasia, market halls and temples. Both individually and as an ensemble, these buildings were the settings for imperial ceremonies and public water supplies ran from sculpted fountains in the streets. The aim was to bring the flavour of Rome itself to Britannia. But once the public buildings were completed, during the 2nd century, the towns seem to change in character. During the 3rd century the small artisans' houses of timber and rubble, formerly packed in between public buildings, disappeared, and in the 4th century they were replaced by large stone-built private houses, many with hypocausts and mosaics. These *palazzos* sometimes resemble rural villas, and occasionally they may have been the centres of agricultural operations themselves. Whereas there had been considerable industrial activity in Ratae in the 2nd century, it is hard to find any in the 4th. It is not that these two towns had declined economically, although they may have done; but rather that their role in the surrounding countryside seems to have changed. Early on they were genuine foci of populations, but later they appear more like empty strongholds of the ruling imperial elite.

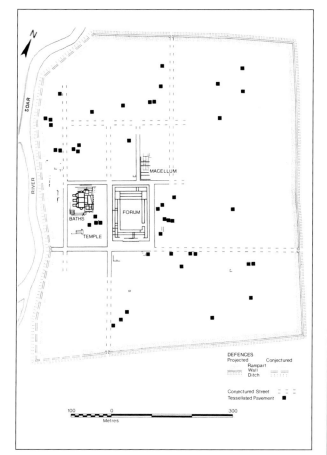

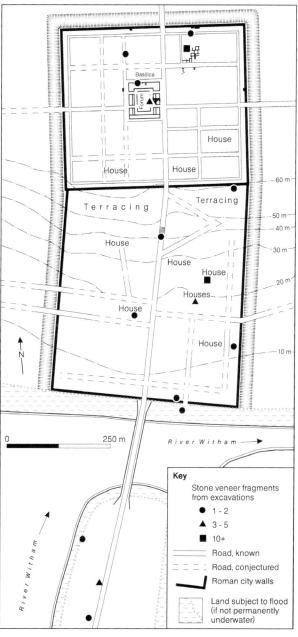

Ratae and Lindum were not the only models of urbanism. The so-called 'small towns' were not just imitations of such places in miniature – they looked quite different, and had an entirely different role in the economy. Much the largest town of this type in our region was Durobrivae between Chesterton and Water Newton, south-west of Peterborough (Fig. 3.11). As at Lindum, a new fort had been built on the hilltop, on the north side of the river. A large walled town grew up along the road to the south, as the merchants and traders, who kept the fort's garrison supplied and entertained, also established themselves. When the soldiers left, the commercial settlement consolidated its position in the local economy and kept going.

It has been calculated that it would have required 166ha of crops to supply a garrison of 500 troops for a year. Clearly there would have been a substantial surplus of grain for sale once the garrisons left. The surplus would still be required, of course, by troops in northern Britain, and East Midlands towns like Durobrivae presumably changed their roles to market their produce to an imperial, rather than a local commissariat. Such changes may explain the development of urbanism at Lindum and Ratae, too, although tribal administration and politics must have made the situation here more complicated.

Many East Midlands towns may have grown up around a fort and then outlived the military (p.197 and *see* Fig. 3.8). Though individually small, from the 1st century their impact on the landscape was large, through their stimulation of local economies. Although the initial fort would have been a dramatic

ABOVE LEFT: *Fig. 3.9 Late Romano-British city of Lindum* (source: Jones, M J 2003).

ABOVE: *Fig. 3.10 Late Romano-British city of Ratae Corieltauvorum* (source: Buckley & Lucas 1987).

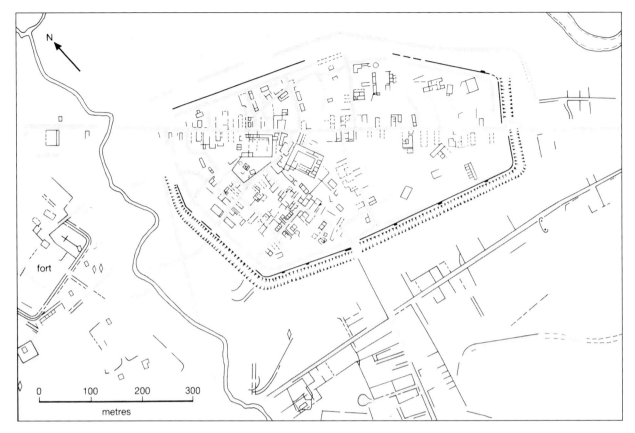

Fig. 3.11 Late Romano-British town of Durobrivae (Water Newton, Huntingdonshire), as mapped from the earthworks and aerial photography (source: Jones & Mattingly 2002).

intervention into people's lives, the revolution in the local agricultural economy represented by their successor towns was to last until the end of the 4th century.

Some forts were not established in open country for strategic reasons; instead, they were deliberately placed on top of existing Iron Age settlements (at Durolipons, Cambridge and Great Chesterford, Cambridgeshire; Kirmington, Lindsey and Dorchester, Oxfordshire). None of these forts continued after about AD 70, when the East Midlands were demilitarised, so presumably they had served their purposes. It is not clear why these native communities should have been singled out for military occupation, or indeed whether such an occupation was an honour or a punishment. It is clear, however, that small towns could also develop out of existing Iron Age communities without the apparent intervention of the military: examples include Owmby (Lindsey), Sapperton (Kesteven), Kettering, Duston and Irchester (Northamptonshire), Sandy (Bedfordshire) and Frilford (old Berkshire).

Even though they may have had differing origins, the small towns developed similar ranges of facilities. Public buildings, and even temples, are almost entirely absent until the 3rd century, for example, and in the 4th century the small towns apparently lacked the large, stone-built private town houses which are such a feature of Lindum and Ratae at this date. Several contain only a single substantial building, usually identified as a *mansio* (p.30). The typical layout was not a grid as at Lindum and Ratae, but long, narrow, house plots extending back from a main road. Very few have a subsidiary road network, even though some are quite large and the houses at Durobrivae extended along Ermine Street for nearly a kilometre.

The mere fact that buildings in such towns are laid out with their gables along the main road emphasises the fact that these are the houses of traders, whose access to the street front was crucial to their livelihood. The *mansio* was here for similar reasons: like the traders, it provided a service to travelling officials and their emissaries. These small towns were thus genuine economic centres, and as they continued in active use through the 3rd and 4th centuries we can suggest that, unlike Ratae and Lindum, they were integrated with the local economy and not simply floating on top of it.

It was the market infrastructure, of which the towns were a part, which enabled East Midlands farmers to capitalise on their surpluses. This infrastructure was provided by the Romans, and it marks the greatest distinction between the late Iron Age and the Romano-British periods, and indeed between the Roman period and the early medieval. Towns were essential to house the middle men and the administrators of imperial government. Initially major towns like Lindum and Ratae were at the centre of this commerce, but after the 2nd century it seems this role was also adopted by the 'small towns'. Political and social power was transformed, then, between the 1st and the 4th centuries. Initially the economic lead lay with the political imperialists, in the quasi-Roman 'public' towns of Lindum and Ratae. But, while the administrative and symbolic importance of these towns did not diminish until the end of the 4th century, the economic initiative passed sometime in the 3rd century to the markets of the small towns. This shift might be a reflection of profound changes in the imperial economy. The rise of the small towns might imply, for example, that agricultural surpluses were no longer being sent around the Empire, but now remained within the locality. If so, presumably the only export leaving the East Midlands after the 3rd century, bound for Londinium, or for Rome itself, would have been coin, squeezed from agricultural surpluses in the form of taxes. Such a system is, of course, very vulnerable. It can be terminated abruptly, either because the taxes cease to be paid by the population or, more typically, because the taxes are interdicted by local chiefs who no longer feel obliged to pass them further up the hierarchy.

Such economic considerations lead us directly to the disintegration of the Roman landscape. We have seen that, until the 3rd century, the East Midlands economy was based on the generation of agricultural surpluses – particularly, perhaps, of grain. By the 5th century, however, the East Midlands countryside was dominated by pasture, and it is increasingly clear that this changeover from arable to pasture occurred, not following a decision in Rome to leave Britannia to fend for itself at the start of the 5th century, but rather during the late 3rd and 4th centuries. Furthermore, there is clear evidence in both Lindum and Ratae that large numbers of cattle were processed for meat, hides and horn within the walls in the 4th century. In south-east Leicestershire, only 12 of the 20 identified settlements continued into the 4th century – a clear sign that the numbers living on the land were declining, and a development consistent with a switch from arable to pasture. The same trend is illustrated by a dramatic decline in quantity of 4th-century pottery reaching the fields – evidence that the land was no longer being manured with the same enthusiasm.

We will consider villas later (pp.135–6), but here we should note that many fell into ruins long before the end of the 4th century; although, as we shall see, the agricultural land around them remained in use as pasture. This may tell us something important about the villa economy. If we are right in thinking that most villas reflected a vibrant rural economy based on the marketing of surplus crops, we have to ask whether or not the change from arable to pasture evident in the 4th century is the key to understanding their disappearance also.

SETTLEMENT, *c*.400–850

The 5th-century theologian known as Gildas has had a huge influence on our approach to his own times. He may not have reported many historical facts but he described such an atmosphere of destruction and collapse in Britannia that subsequent landscape historians have often seen the Anglo-Saxon landscape as a new beginning. Yet we must struggle with Gildas's legacy. Writers on the Anglo-Saxon landscape often start with the simplified and incomplete chronology that arises from the literary sources and superimpose a narrative derived from place-names, many of which are presumed to date from this period. Early charters describing estate boundaries can offer a more reliable understanding, but very few exist for the East Midlands (although a group relating to old Berkshire and western Oxfordshire survives). Excavations have not produced much evidence for the East Midlands landscape between the 4th and 8th centuries either, and it is probably true to say that we know less about the region in the four centuries between about 400 and 850 than we do about any other period between about 600 BC and the present.

Our relative ignorance is due, partly, to the character of remains left by the English of the immediate post-Roman period. As engineers in wood, their structures do not survive so well in the soil as do the Romans' stone ones. Similarly, where they used pottery at all (and wooden vessels were widely used instead), it was of poor quality and is consequently less easily seen than its Romano-British equivalent as archaeologists diligently search ploughed fields. The land itself was now more thinly occupied. Most writers agree that, between the 3rd and the 7th centuries, the population fell rapidly, reaching perhaps less than 1,000,000: fewer people than in the Iron Age. It seems clear that the Anglo-Saxons suffered from colder, wetter climatic conditions prevailing between the 4th and 9th centuries. There may also have been natural catastrophes, such as the so-called 'narrow ring event' of about AD 536 in which the health and growth of trees (as seen in their annual growth rings) was greatly limited for about a decade across much of the northern hemisphere. Whether this represents a volcanic eruption, an asteroid strike or some other phenomenon, remains hotly disputed, but environmental damage was clearly considerable, and this must have put further strain on subsistence farmers.

In this darkness it is perhaps not surprising that writers have, like Gildas, imagined no more than the Roman landscape run to seed; but the Anglo-Saxon landscape of the East Midlands was more complex than this. Much of the extensive landscape of rectilinear fields established by the Iron Age and Romano-British peoples, for example, clearly continued in use between AD 400 and 800. This relatively large-scale survival of Romano-British field systems seems to represent a genuine difference between the East Midlands and the north-western and south-eastern provinces, where the woodlands seem to have regenerated considerably.

At Shotover (Oxfordshire), Romano-British arable fields were not merely abandoned to the wild in the Anglo-Saxon period. Instead they were converted to pasture. Here agricultural land was not taken out of use on a large scale and replaced by woodland until the 11th or 12th century. At Catholme, on the Trent south of Burton, some (if not all) the existing field boundaries continued to be maintained (Fig. 3.12). At Willington (Derbyshire), the Romano-British field system also seems to have continued in use through the 5th and 6th centuries. Romano-British field boundaries were also probably maintained through the 5th, 6th and 7th centuries at Caldecote (Milton Keynes), and a study of boundary clauses in the charters of an Anglo-Saxon estate at Uffington (old Berkshire) also reports Romano-British field boundaries continuing in use. Something similar may have occurred along the Bourn Brook west of Cambridge, while at Royston Grange (Derbyshire) it seems clear that, although the Romano-British arable enclosures were no longer ploughed, they may have become pasture rather than being completely abandoned.

At Goltho (Lindsey), on the other hand, excavations seemed to show that the settlement there was abandoned between the 4th century and its 're-foundation' in the 9th century. In the absence of environmental studies we cannot judge whether the clay vale in which it sits was deserted, or whether, as at Catholme, the centre of local agricultural operations merely shifted to another site. Elsewhere there was probably some withdrawal of land from use, particularly at the margins. Some writers have suggested that the widespread use of the word 'thorn' in place-names of this period indicates that land had simply been abandoned (as at Chawston – 'Cealf's thorn bush' – just across the brook from Wyboston). Others point out, however, that thorns might have been deliberately planted as boundary markers. In fact isolated thorns are often the only standard trees to survive in an intensively grazed landscape, and their use in Anglo-Saxon place-names may be evidence, not of abandonment of land, but of the spread of pasture. In the Thames valley, the rate at which soil was being washed off the hills north and west of Oxford slowed up dramatically in the 4th century, even though there is plenty of evidence from other sources that rainfall had increased markedly. This can only be accounted for by presuming that the Romano-British arable fields had been converted to grass or other permanent vegetation cover.

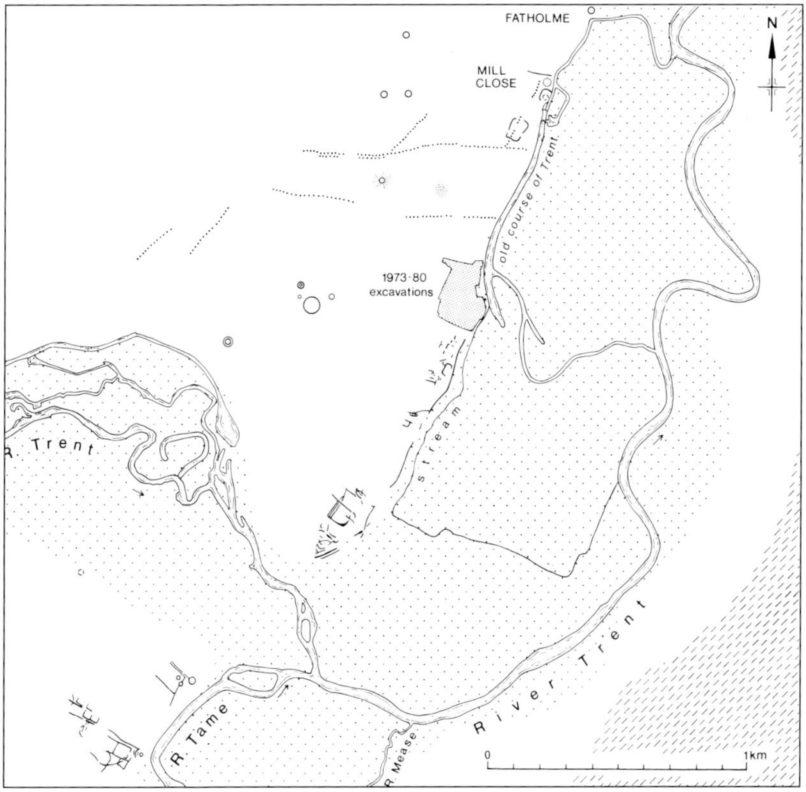

Fig. 3.12 Plan of the clusters of settlement crop marks around the excavated Anglo-Saxon settlement at Catholme (Staffordshire) (source: *Losco-Bradley & Kinsley 2002*).

In the Leicestershire Wolds most of the land away from the river valleys was being used for grazing by about AD 500, and a large-scale study of land use around Brigstock (Northamptonshire) seemed to show something similar. At Uffington, although the Romano-British field boundaries survived, relatively little of the available land was laid down to arable. Soil conditions at Catholme were not conducive to the survival of pollen, but it seems that many of the closes used by Romano-British farmers for growing grain were in permanent pasture by the 5th century. Some confirmation that the Anglo-Saxon economy relied on extensive pasture has been provided by studies of excavated animal bones: at Quarrington (Kesteven), for example, cattle seem to have played a major role in the diet, and were more important than sheep.

Accentuating the positive, then, what evidence we have suggests that the Romano-British landscape of small rectilinear fields in this region continued in use through the period between 400 and 800, at least on the less marginal lands, even though many were converted from arable to pasture. If field boundaries were maintained, they must have remained useful and consequently they may not have been intended to keep animals out of the arable but to separate one herd or flock from another.

Although it may be tempting to relate the replacement of the grain-growing economy by one based on stock-rearing to 'waves' of invaders, and to the warfare that dominates our (highly suspect) documentary sources for the 5th, 6th and 7th centuries, we have already seen that it may have had more to do with both the deterioration in the climate and changes in the Europe-wide economy during the 4th century. Many East Midlands villas, like that at Totternhoe (Bedfordshire), went out of use in the 4th, rather than the 5th, century, and although the agricultural regimes focused on them were 'mixed', their main business had been the production of a grain surplus that made large cash profits for their owners. This Empire-wide economy was designed to provide a grain surplus to feed the large urban populations, and to generate coin to pay taxes, on which the Empire depended. But the Empire's political collapse in the West in the 5th century meant that there would be no coin or taxes and, without such mechanisms, urban populations disappeared, at least in Britain. In such a world, grain was largely grown for domestic consumption rather than for paying taxes. Within a society based on small family and kinship groupings, wealth, status and physical well-being were better served by raising stock. For local leaders, large feasts given to neighbours would have replaced submissions of tax. In the East Midlands, the economic situation around 400 is symbolised perfectly by the late 4th-century cupellation furnace in the former *macellum* in Leicester, being used for reducing silver coinage to bullion (a process which the imperial government had already decreed was illegal and punishable by execution). The furnace was housed in a rough timber shelter within the ruins of a largely abandoned city.

Occupation in Lincoln also came to an end at the end of the 4th century. As in Leicester, small quantities of early and middle Anglo-Saxon pottery have been found; although these cannot represent 'urban' occupation, exactly what they do imply is still open to debate. Excavations at St Paul-in-the-Bail raised the possibility that the former Roman enclosure was appropriated by the church between the 5th and 9th centuries (p.226), but ecclesiastical sites would have generated much greater quantities of pottery, and of different types. Urban ruins were valuable quarries of *spolia*, so they are very likely to have had 'owners' and been managed as a resource in the landscape, like the woodland, but we have yet to discover whether they had any other use.

Woodland remained just as important to the rural economy of the Anglo-Saxons as it had been earlier. It is thought that England's 'central settlement province' had a more open landscape in the Anglo-Saxon period, with relatively less woodland than the provinces to the north-west and south-east. There were major managed woodlands in the East Midlands, however, and as a rare resource they would have been of great importance. To a greater extent than the Romano-British, the culture of the Anglo-Saxons laid stress on woodland skills. Not only was their architecture and engineering entirely dependent on understanding the structural qualities of timber, but much of their mythology was located in, and on the fringes of, woodlands. Anglo-Saxon woodlands were certainly not abandoned thickets: they were carefully husbanded resources, managed with just as much attention and skill as open pastures and the field boundaries, and fully populated by grazing animals: cattle and horses, but especially pigs. In King Ine's laws (early 8th century), the sizes of trees are measured by the number of swine they can shelter, and in Bedfordshire and Buckinghamshire in 1086 the size of woodlands was measured by the number of pigs they could support. Little such wood pasture survives in England today, but it can still be seen in the East Midlands at Bradgate Park, Leicestershire (*see* Fig. 1.5). Bradgate contains only certain types of tree: there is no elm, hazel or hawthorn, because the deer eat the shoots, but there is plenty of oak, beech, aspen and hornbeam which they find less palatable. Even these species are browsed below a certain level, and poles have to be grown above the browse-line as a pollard. Place-names may indicate that some Anglo-Saxon wood pastures contained more specialised trees. Apley (Lindsey) was 'the woodland clearing with the apple trees'; plum trees were grown at Plumtree south-east of Nottingham and at Plumtreeley west of Oxford; and woad was grown at Woadley (Oxfordshire). Within 8km of Wyboston, in the woodlands on the plateau, the lost settlements of Peartree and Perry grew pears.

The community's specialised resources, like woodland, were often held directly by the king or his aristocracy – a phenomenon which is often explained by the royal desire to maintain hunting grounds. However, given the high value of woodland, the nobility's direct responsibility could have come about through the need to police scarce resources shared amongst local communities. In certain areas, parish boundaries (although much later impositions on the landscape) converge on woodlands, great pastures, lakes and similar landscape features in order to ensure that each parish obtains its share of the valuable common resource. The entire Forest of Charnwood, for example, is divided into sectors like a cake, with slices allocated to individual lowland parishes around the periphery, as was the great pasture in the Lindsey clay vale known as the 'Lissingley'. The same pattern can be seen fossilised within the layout of parish boundaries on the wolds of Leicestershire north of Ratcliffe (Fig. 3.13). At Flittermere the subdivision of a lake (presumably used for fowling, reeds and clay, as well as fish) between the communities of Lutton (Northamptonshire) and Great Gidding (Huntingdonshire) was so controversial that it gave rise to its placename (Old English 'flitt' means strife, or a dispute). Such controversial divisions of scarce resources would need oversight, which is most likely to have been provided by the Anglo-Saxon aristocracy. The Fens, marking the eastern border of our region, also represent a 'rare' resource, for example, and during the Anglo-Saxon period they were controlled by royal monasteries. Such sharing of rare resources in the landscape, under the supervision of the aristocracy, probably goes back at least to the Iron Age. After all, we have seen that the population had been larger, and agriculture more intensive, during the late Iron Age and Romano-British periods. Rare resources would have come under even greater pressure at these earlier dates than during the Anglo-Saxon period.

The need to share resources might explain why so many of the royal forests of Anglo-Saxon England lie along political boundaries. Wychwood in western Oxfordshire occupies the eastern boundary of the Anglo-Saxon grouping called the Hwicce ('Wychwood' is literally 'the wood of the Hwicce'). We have already noticed that many of the East Midlands' other borders are also marked by woodlands, many of which are first documented as royal forests in the late Anglo-Saxon period. Sherwood is 'the shire wood', for example – that is, it belonged to an arm of royal government; the Peak is 'the forest of the Pecsaetan', who were a sub-kingdom like the Hwicce.

Certain internal political boundaries might also be visible as woodland zones. Most obviously, the southern border of Lindsey, along the north bank of the Witham, was, and still is, occupied by a belt of woodland (sometimes known as Linwood), which was already present by 1086. More speculatively, we might also ask whether the woodlands between the Ouse and the Welland (the forests of Salcey, Rockingham, Bromswold and Whittlewood) also represent another political boundary within the East Midlands. Whether once more continuous than

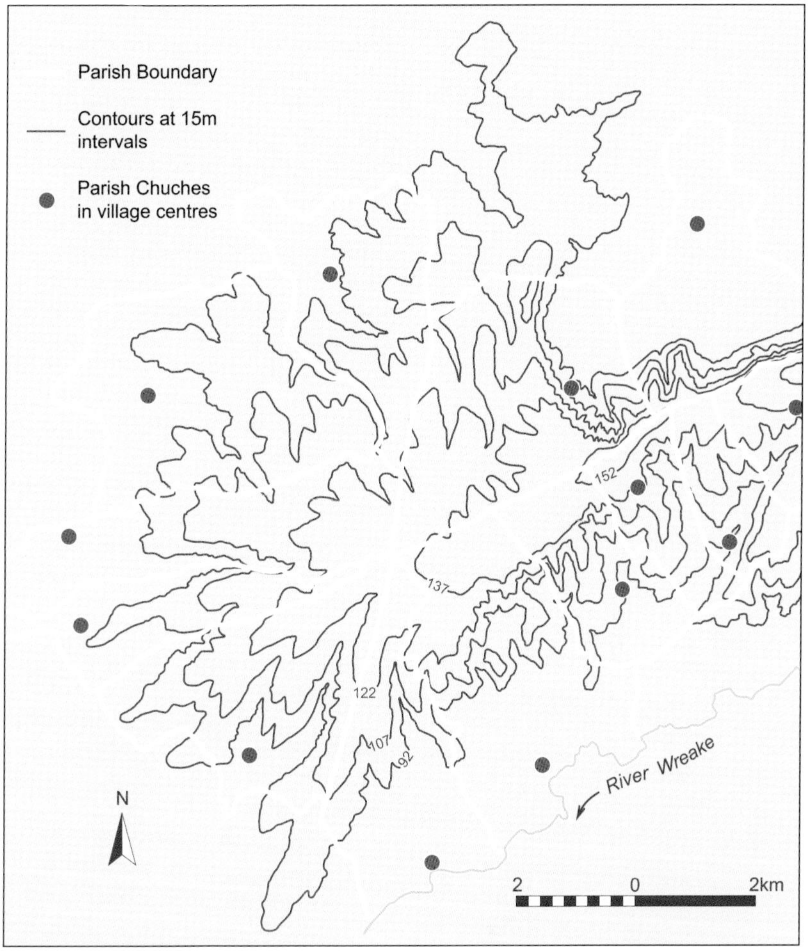

Fig. 3.13 Layout of parishes on the topography of the Leicestershire Wolds, north of Melton Mowbray.
Note the way in which the valuable upland grazing resources are equitably divided amongst the settlements on the lower ground.

Within the figure:

Parish Boundary

Contours at 15m intervals

Parish Chuches in village centres

152

137

122

107

92

River Wreake

N

2   0   2km

when first recorded in the late Anglo-Saxon period or not, they evidently lie approximately along the Iron Age boundary between the Corieltauvi and the Catuvellauni (*see* Fig. 3.4). Neither Iron Age boundaries, nor their Anglo-Saxon equivalents, had to be drawn along a narrow line, especially if they followed important resources exploited by dwellers on both sides. Indeed we might also ask not only whether the Northamptonshire forests were once more continuous, but whether they extended further northwards into Rutland (the medieval forest of Leighfield) and on into Kesteven (whose name means 'the wooded district'). Perhaps Northamptonshire should be thought of as border country, a zone of woodland resources since at least the Iron Age, shared by peoples from both north and south. When it came to measuring the land in 1086 it was found that most of Northamptonshire was measured in hides (the southern English unit of measure), whereas in the north of the county, carucates (the northern equivalent) were used. Is this another reflection of the same ancient boundary? Northamptonshire was certainly an area with a marked concentration of royal demesne land in 1086, which would also be appropriate in a 'border' zone under royal control.

To the east, the East Midlands region is bounded by famous Anglo-Saxon boundary earthworks, the Cambridgeshire Dykes. Significantly, perhaps, they 'fill' a gap in the circuit of natural boundaries around the region, lying between the Chiltern woodlands and the Fens. These enigmatic landscape monuments consist of four colossal bank and ditch systems, the longest 12km in length, and they clearly mark boundaries between distinct territories (Fig. 3.14). They are not well dated, but the limited evidence implies construction in the 5th or 6th centuries. Their appearance suggests, however, that this was a period when communities on either side were unable to agree over the distribution of common resources along a political boundary – in this case, perhaps, grazing rights on the extensive heaths now used for training Newmarket racehorses.

Within these potentially ancient political boundaries, long-term stability may also be indicated by the many East Midlands settlements of the 5th and 6th centuries that remained in the vicinity of pre-existing Romano-British settlements. This was the case, for example, in Toddington parish (Bedfordshire) where four out of eight Romano-British settlement sites have also produced material of post-Roman date. In Leicestershire, the large Anglo-Saxon settlement site in East Langton was within 200m of its Romano-British predecessor. At Empingham, Rutland, one of the three excavated Romano-British settlements continued in use, apparently without a break through the period from the 4th to the 7th centuries. Similarly at Higham Ferrers, Wollaston, Marston Trussel and Brackley (all in

Fig. 3.14 Devil's Dyke, one of several major landscape divisions on Newmarket heath, *perhaps constructed during the Anglo-Saxon period, still survives as a large earthwork bank and ditch cutting north-westwards past the modern racecourse (left) and into the fens. To the right (north-east), today's heath land is still carefully parcelled-out, amongst competing gallops.*

Northamptonshire), Wavendon Gate and Caldecotte (Milton Keynes) and Maxey (north of Peterborough), the Iron Age, Romano-British and Anglo-Saxon settlement sites all lie within a few hundred metres of each other. Distinctive Anglo-Saxon buildings (*grubenhauser* – *see* pp.115–16) were constructed within the standing ruins of the villas at Shakenoak (Oxfordshire), Orton Hall Farm (Peterborough), Stanwick and Brixworth (both Northamptonshire), suggesting perhaps that the architectural ambitions of the owners had changed, but that the focus of the settlement had not. An even clearer example of settlement continuity emerged from the important excavations at Barton Court Farm near Abingdon, where a scattering of Anglo-Saxon structures lay around the ruins and within the courtyard of the villa. The relationship between the former Roman buildings and the Anglo-Saxon ones here suggests that the occupation sequence was more or less continuous.

At Catholme, the excavated Anglo-Saxon settlement was laid out on a new site early in the 7th century. But it sits within a long string of crop marks along the river and midway between two further settlement sites, which we would presume – from their plan-forms – were late Iron Age or Romano-British in date (*see* Fig. 3.12). Given that the field system which interconnects these rich valley-bottom settlements seems to have continued in use from the later Iron Age right through to the 7th century, we have to presume that one or both of the settlements adjacent to Catholme continued in use long after the end of the Roman period and that, for reasons not yet understood, the farmers of this land did not relocate their accommodation for 200 years.

The plan of the 7th to 9th century settlement at Catholme, with its nine or ten small stockaded enclosures separated by well-defined trackways, each with a similar range of structures, strongly suggests a group of pastoralists, living in family units, within a single 'village' (Fig. 3.15). But it remains uncertain how many of the enclosures were occupied at any moment. Given the difficulties of dating such deposits closely, it is possible that the settlement here only ever consisted of a single hall, presumably belonging to the head of the extended family, and a number of smaller structures round about. When these buildings came to the end of their useful life (perhaps after a generation or so) the entire group of buildings might have been recreated within a new enclosure a few metres away. Such a narrative would certainly provide the mechanism to explain the so-called 'settlement drift', which has

Fig. 3.15 Layout of the Anglo-Saxon settlement site at Catholme (Staffordshire). Not all the buildings shown can have been occupied contemporaneously.

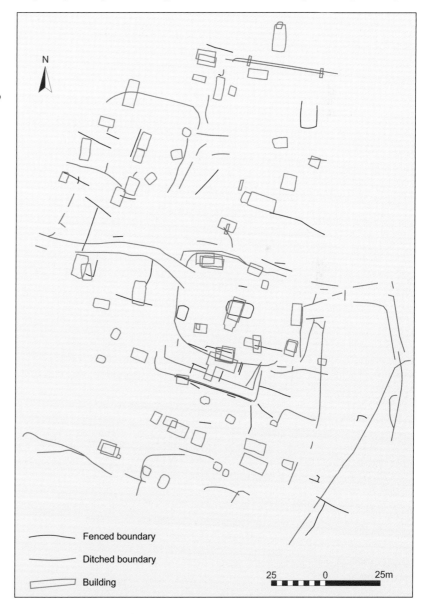

N

Fenced boundary

Ditched boundary

Building

25   0   25m

been proposed at a number of contemporary settlements (like Yarnton, Oxfordshire) to explain the slow progress of buildings across the landscape with the passing generations.

The most significant differences between the Anglo-Saxon landscape at places like Barton Court Farm and its late Iron Age and Romano-British predecessor, then, was the change from large-scale arable to large-scale pasture. On the whole the settlements themselves remained in approximately the same locations and remained scattered across the landscape. Their structures changed character, in line with the changing material culture of their inhabitants, and these changes were marked most dramatically by the ruination of the villas. However, whether we are dealing here with the perpetuation, intact, of early estates is a question of a different type, and a harder one to answer. Peter Bigmore suggested that the fact that Eaton Socon had its own 'soke' (ie independent jurisdiction; including Wyboston of course) from an early date might indicate the survival of a Roman agricultural estate, based on the former villa north of the church, long into the Anglo-Saxon period. Unfortunately the idea remains no more than an interesting suggestion, and Peter Addyman's excavations east of the church found no evidence for such an early settlement.

At Catholme, Yarnton and several sites beyond our region, writers have suggested that a significant change came about in the 7th century. Such a change might be indicated by settlements 'drifting' away from the Iron Age and Romano-British locations and it might reflect various political changes which are suddenly revealed to us though early surviving documents. The sophisticated and complex political hierarchy reflected in these early sources, it is argued, had its most obvious physical manifestation in a group of 'palace' sites, of a type which had not existed in the 5th and 6th centuries. East Midlands palaces of this type have been identified at Drayton, near Dorchester-on-Thames, and at Northampton (*see* Fig. 4.25). The 8th-century Northampton palace, if such it was, might have been the successor to a Romano-British power centre at Duston, 1km west, where earlier material has been found. There is also some evidence that Northamptonshire hillforts at Irthlingborough and Rainsborough were also reoccupied in the 6th and 7th centuries, suggesting a multiplicity of high-status sites in the Northamptonshire landscape. The excavated buildings at Northampton are so exceptional, however, that scholars have speculated that they may have represented a superior centre of power for a much larger area than just the upper Nene valley. Certainly it is hard to believe that similar structures would have existed at all the other known or presumed 8th-century estate centres such as Kings Sutton, Fawsley, Rothwell and Finedon.

FURTHER READING

General
Barrett and Bradley 1980; Brannigan, 1985; Brown 1974; Cunliffe 1991; Dark 1994; Fowler 1983a; Fox 2000; French *et al.* 1992 (Nene and Welland valleys); Frere 1987; Gelling 1984; Hamerow 2002; Hill 1981; Hooke 1998; Jones & Mattingly 2002; Millett 1990; Phythian-Adams 2000; Pryor 1998a, 2002; Rackham 1986; Roberts & Wrathmell 2002; Robinson 1992; Salway 1981; Stafford 1985; Taylor 1975; Todd 1991; Van der Veen & O'Connor 1998.

Areas
Barclay *et al.* 1996 (Thames valley); Barnatt 1987 (Derbyshire); Benson and Miles 1974 (Thames valley); Bewley (ed.) 1998 (Lincolnshire); Blair 1994 (Oxfordshire); Boutwood 1998 (Lincolnshire); Bowman 1996 (Leicestershire); Briggs *et al.* 1986 (Oxfordshire); Dark 2000 (Oxfordshire); Dawson 2000 (Ouse valley); French and Wait 1988 (Cambridgeshire); Garton 1987 (Nottinghamshire); Hingley & Miles 1984; Hooke 1985, 1998 (Oxfordshire/Berkshire/Warwickshire); May 1976, 1996 (Lincolnshire); Miles 1997 (Thames valley); Pickering & Hartley 1985 (Leicestershire); Pryor 2001 (Peterborough area); Simco 1984 (Bedfordshire); Wild 1974 (Nene valley).

Early towns
Burnham & Wacher 1990; Jones 2003a, b (Lincoln); Jones & Mattingley 2002 (*Durobrivae*); Sawyer 1981, 1988; Vince 2003a (Lincoln); Wacher 1995; Williams *et al.* 1985 (Northampton).

Specific areas and sites
Allen & Robinson 1993 (Mingies Ditch); Cook & Rowley (eds) 1985 (Dorchester); Dix 1981 (Odell); Grimes 1961 (Colsterworth); Lambrick & Allen 2004 (Gravelly Guy); Lane 1995 (Ropsley & Humby); Losco-Bradley & Kinsley 2002 (Catholme); Mackreth 1996 (Orton Hall Farm); Miles 1986 (Barton Court Farm); Tebbutt 1957 (Wyboston).

A Landscape for Communities: Settlement from the 9th to the 18th Century

THE COMMON FIELDS

One Tuesday in 1790 the diarist John Byng, out and about on holiday, rode across the common fields of Sandy, Bedfordshire, on his favourite horse Poney. 'Here', he wrote, 'culture is brought to great perfection and cucumbers cover the ground'. The cucumbers were growing in Sandy's unenclosed common fields and, although they obviously belonged to someone, Byng felt no guilt in selecting a few for his tea; many more were probably squashed under Poney's hoofs. This was not merely the autocratic behaviour of an irredeemable aristocrat towards the peasantry. Byng's behaviour expressed the universally held belief that communal agriculture was just that: 'worked in common'. The community farmed the land co-operatively, and the produce was, to some extent, shared. Feeling that his family connections made him a part of this Bedfordshire community, Byng expected that (in return for his intangible service to the community as a civil servant) he was entitled to a share of the communal produce. But his ability to behave in this way was seriously threatened by the movement to enclose the common fields: indeed, a little later that day he encountered some newly enclosed land and 'broke down some rails most courageously'.

The enclosures of the late 18th century were particularly controversial in the East Midlands because, in this region, farming in common fields had been brought – as Byng said – 'to perfection'. The truth of the claim is most clearly demonstrated by the system's survival here, with adaptations, for nearly a millennium (Fig. 3.16). It was not a technique favoured in every part of England, and studies of the distribution of common fields all emphasise how, in its fully developed form, it was found mostly in the East Midlands and in adjacent regions to the north and south-west. In other parts of the country, East Anglia for example, communities frequently farmed certain fields 'in common', but such fields occupied only a small percentage of any given township.

The fully developed common fields of the East Midlands represented a revolution in agriculture. For some two thousand years – probably since the late Bronze Age – the region's agriculture developed within a landscape of ditched closes, surrounded by hedges or fences. These had been used for both arable and pasture at different times but they remained relatively small and were probably individually owned and farmed. In such a landscape, homes and farms did not have to be concentrated together in clusters; in principle they could be located anywhere that proved convenient for the individual farmer, even though, in practice, some

Fig. 3.16 The spacious landscape of East Midlands' common fields, *captured here in R Relhan's early 19th-century painting of Barton (Cambridgeshire).*

59

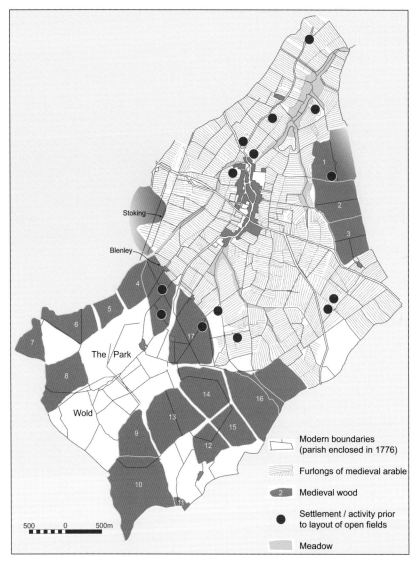

locations were considered much more convenient for settlement than others. So far as we can tell, however, the locations of such settlements were not governed by the layout of the fields around them. This seems to be the single greatest change in the landscape brought about by the wholesale conversion to farming in common fields: the location of the settlement became subordinate to the layout of the fields, rather than vice versa (Fig. 3.17).

The single most important characteristic of this agricultural revolution was that, afterwards, agriculture could no longer be undertaken by an individual in isolation, whether he or she was the lowliest peasant or the lord of the manor. Instead, all members of the social hierarchy now had to pool their activities – to co-ordinate what they did on their own lands and when they did it – with the community within which they lived. The individual family did not lose the right to farm its land, but could no longer do so in isolation from its neighbours. In East Midlands' common-field systems the individual's land was held as long, thin, unenclosed strips within each of the community's large common fields. The great bulk of the community's land now lay in two or three such great fields. The community as a whole became responsible for co-ordinating what individuals grew, and when. The entire field (or subdivisions of the field,

Fig. 3.17 David Hall's map of the common fields and other resources of the parish of Yardley Hastings on the north-eastern edge of Salcey Forest (Northamptonshire). *Note the scatter of earlier settlement sites lying beneath the medieval arable. Although there were five fields of common arable, they were organised (in the 16th century) into a three-field rotation. The south-western woodlands were worked in 15 named blocks, with one block being coppiced, in rotation, each year.*

known as furlongs, which was the more usual unit of crop) had to be ploughed and cropped as a single unit, and it needed to lie fallow at the same time (or alternatively, to grow peas and beans) so that the soil could recover.

The individual farmer could no longer run his few cattle and sheep in his own private close; instead, the community's stock was combined into a single herd or flock to graze the common fallow, or the stubble, when appropriate. As always, the stock spent most of the time on commons and heaths, where grazing rights were inherited with membership of the community itself. Such commons and heaths did not disappear when the common fields were laid out, but they often became smaller and more intensively used than previously, and they were increasingly found only on the margins of the community away from the common arable. Something similar happened with the community's woodlands. Like commons and heaths, these were valuable resources, housing a variety of industries as well as providing specialised pasture – particularly for pigs. But even the woodlands were marginalised within the new landscape, often separated from the dwellings by the new common fields.

Common-field landscapes were carefully designed, then, with all the elements closely integrated. They required firm management and a strong resident authority if they were to work effectively. This authority usually resided in the 'great meeting' or 'court'. Such meetings (and their various sub-meetings) were sometimes, though not always, held under the auspices of manors, but the critical thing was not so much the legal framework within which they operated, but the support they commanded within the community. The common-field system was in the hands of the villagers themselves, both through their own individual agricultural activities and through their appointment of officers and functionaries from among their number. The village herdsmen and women held responsibility for grazing the community's herds in the correct place at the right season, and ensuring that they did not stray into the arable. Community 'woodwards' ensured that the woodland was effectively managed. Bailiffs, reeves and other petty officials ensured that ploughing was done in the right field at the right time and in an equitable way. Some of these figures were appointed directly by the village meeting, but all were responsible to it. This was a society where the individual was required to play a clearly defined role in the community. Similar concepts of community commitment were also woven into the fabric of the criminal law, not just in the stipulated penalties for infringing the agricultural regime, but in the king's courts, where more individual infringements could be punished by fines on an entire community. In the common-field world, everyone was, literally, his brother or sister's keeper.

Inevitably, the introduction of a common-field system also had profound effects on the distribution of settlements within the community. Houses could no longer be scattered among the fields – the space was needed to ensure maximum output of the agricultural land. This was not just a matter of convenience: it was also a matter of equity. There was now less distinction between the farmer living on good land, with his fields around him, and his poorer neighbour living in a hovel on the marginal land. Great stress was laid on the equitable division of community resources. Everyone needed to have similar quantities of good, mediocre and poor land distributed through the fields. Thus, for the system to work well, the settlements which had formerly been scattered around the landscape had to be brought together ('nucleated') in a single place, into what we now call a village. Now all holders of lands in the great fields would share the same advantages and disadvantages. They would all live at similar distances from their land in the fields, be it good, bad or indifferent. Once dwellings were grouped together near the centre of the common fields they would also be able to share a number of other communal facilities, such as the manure heap. A common green, on which stock might be gathered for counting, slaughtering, shearing, or just for the night, could also be located conveniently in the centre of the community, and perhaps serve as a market place for goods produced within the village to be exchanged for goods manufactured elsewhere. There could be a church for communal worship, and a communal alehouse.

Consequently, the common-field revolution brought with it a revolution in settlement pattern. A map of the locations of genuine 'villages' in England will coincide with one showing the locations of two- or three-field agricultural systems – and both maps focus on the East Midlands. The decision to create common fields necessitated densely packed villages with large spaces in between. There had been groupings of houses into quite large settlements in the Iron Age but, by comparison, this was 'nucleation' on a much smaller scale, which still left many small settlements scattered across the landscape, each set within its own individually farmed fields, sometimes on good land but often not. Under the common field regime in many East Midland parishes, such 'nucleation' was so thoroughgoing that hardly anyone lived outside the new villages. These village settlements, and the field systems around them, gave the East Midlands its distinctive character for a millennium and, despite the 18th-century enclosure movement, these villages are still the foundation of the East Midlands landscape today. The region remains quintessentially what the Edwardian historian FW Maitland called England's 'village country', to be contrasted with the South East, the South West, the West and the North West, which he called the 'hamlet country', and which landscape historians, more prosaically, call 'zones of dispersed settlement'.

This landscape revolution was therefore just as significant as the enclosure movement of the late 18th century. Indeed because that movement represented a return to the more individualistic style of farming and landscape management, more typical also of the period prior to the establishment of common fields, one might even see the common fields themselves as an aberration, albeit one that lasted a millennium. Although we can see the landscape impact of common fields well enough, as with all revolutions, understanding their causes requires much harder work. As the topic was once a debate between documentary historians, for a long time it was dominated by the surviving documents, which are mostly court records concerned with infringements of the community's agricultural rules. Such documents are also late medieval or later in date, and give little idea of the circumstances in which common fields might have originated. More recent work has sought to amalgamate archaeological evidence with the surviving documentation and has produced new insights into how common-field systems came into being.

It was once thought that common fields came about slowly through the operation, over many generations, of 'partible' inheritance – the system whereby land was shared out between the heirs, rather than descending through the eldest son. After several generations of such subdivisions, it was argued, maintaining the boundaries between strips became pointless and, consequently, common fields were created almost by default. According to this view, common fields developed only slowly and were an inevitable consequence of rising populations. It was believed that the earliest examples might have been as early in date as the 7th century and the latest were still in the process of formation in the 12th or even the 13th century. Many objections have been raised to this proposal since it was first put forward, but perhaps the most telling is a rhetorical question. If the common fields are an inevitable consequence of steadily rising population, why did they not develop in East Anglia, where the population growth in the period between the 9th and 13th centuries was even greater than in the East Midlands? There is certainly no direct correlation between population size in 1086 in England and the presence of common fields.

Increasingly, archaeological results also argue against this thesis. Huge quantities of pottery have now been systematically obtained, both from the former common fields and from the villages at their cores, and the distribution pattern is remarkably consistent. In both Northamptonshire and Leicestershire dense concentrations of pottery, indicating the existence of former settlements in the common fields, always date from between the 5th and the 9th centuries. Furthermore, a very high percentage of such sites have no pottery of later periods. The common-field systems were therefore not in existence between the 5th and the 9th centuries. Pottery of later dates (from the late 9th century onwards) is found, instead, in a uniform scatter, indicating that it has been spread across agricultural land with manure. This indicates that, up until the 9th century, relatively small settlements were scattered across each community's land area, but subsequently, those settlements had gone under the plough as the common fields were laid out over them as, for example, at Yardley Hastings (*see* Fig. 3.17). Conversely, although some of today's villages clearly had earlier origins, the pottery sequence in most parts of them begins in the late 9th century onwards. In Leicestershire, 90 per cent of pottery of 9th–11th-century date comes from sites in, or adjacent to, modern villages, while in Northamptonshire the equivalent figure is 80 per cent.

Studies in Northamptonshire show that most, if not all, the county's common-field systems were in existence by the year 1000, and they seem to have been created quickly, over a period of less than a couple of generations in the 10th century. Similar conclusions have been reached in West Lindsey, while in Oxfordshire, north of the Chilterns, the common-field systems are thought to have taken somewhat longer to develop. Even so, the astonishing reality must be that, in any single village, the common-field system must have been laid out following one harvest and been in operation quickly enough to safeguard the next.

The 10th and 11th centuries have recently been christened as the East Midlands' 'village moment'. We must ask what unique new pressures on the East Midlands rural community resulted in the formation of common fields and their villages. One variation of the 'population pressure' argument has newly arrived Danish landlords of various settlements imposing common-field systems, and its villages, on the community, either to ensure that the peasantry's numbers were maintained, or simply to ensure the maximum income from their holdings. This argument fits comfortably into the traditional historical narrative, as it allows this landscape revolution to be associated with documented political events. Even so, the proposal that reorganisation of the landscape was imposed following the conquest of the Danelaw in the second half of the 9th century seems implausible, as the pattern of common fields does not correspond with the areas known to have been under Danish control. The whole of Oxfordshire and Warwickshire, most of Buckinghamshire and parts of Northamptonshire were all outside the Danelaw, as were other areas dominated by common-field agriculture further to the south-west. The 'reconquest' of the Danelaw by the Wessex kings in the first half of the 10th century might also provide a political framework within which to place a wholesale reorganisation of the landscape. But this too fails to satisfy, on similar grounds.

A more recent 'political' explanation proposes that replanning of the landscape came about as lords set their 'slaves' free. Slavery in later Anglo-Saxon society is little understood, but it is widely agreed that, as a practice, it was passing out of use by 1086. It is argued that, if any lord decided, or was required, to set up a community of former slaves as free men, he or she would have had to establish a village and its fields to accommodate them. Unfortunately this explanation also falls foul of regional differences in settlement and field types. Both large-scale common fields and the nucleated villages at their cores are confined to the 'central province', yet the lords emancipating slaves here also had land and slaves in other parts of the country where villages do not arise.

There are thus serious objections to the proposal that the East Midlands style of common fields, with their concomitant villages, was established at the *diktat* of lords. In addition to those objections raised already, we should also note a great similarity in the layouts of streets from village to village in the East Midlands, with only a handful of different types of plan being identified. Yet there is a great variety of combinations of different types of lordship in villages across the region. Even more tellingly, it is increasingly clear that only holdings within 'village England' are planned like this. In the holdings of the same lords in other parts of the country, both the field systems and the settlements which support them use the land quite differently. In the East Midlands the lords may therefore have been responding to something distinctive in this part of England, which is not present elsewhere. As one contemporary manual on estate management put it:

> *… the customs of estates are various … nor do we apply these regulations to all districts … If we learn better, we will eagerly delight in what we learn and maintain it according to the custom of the district in which we then live. Wherefore one must delight among the people to learn laws if one does not oneself wish to lose honour on the estate …*
> (*The Rectitudines* – Douglas (ed.) 1981, 878)

So, if the landscape revolution was not imposed from above, what persuaded 10th-century communities to abandon their traditional agricultural regimes and start working the land in a new way, and living in newly laid-out houses in a new village? Perhaps we should ask what the benefits of the new system were, and in whose interests they operated.

From an agricultural point of view, the main benefit of common fields was the efficient use of communal plough teams and other resources needed for arable agriculture. In a common field, the plough team could work the strips of many farmers. The loss of the close boundaries also maximised the area which could be laid down to crops, and this area could be enhanced further by organising the ploughing in such a way that it formed 'ridges' of soil – providing a greater surface area for the seed bed. The furrows, or gullies, between each strip provided for more effective water run-off than was possible in flat ground, while the turning area (or headland) for the plough team at either end of each ridge could be positioned over the fallow or over communal tracks, again permitting the maximum area of the strip holding to be ploughed. The so-called 'ridge and furrow' earthworks which were once so typical of the East Midlands countryside were formed in this way (*see* Fig 2.6). It might even be the case that the common-field revolution was only made possible through the introduction, apparently in the 9th century, of the wheeled plough, which allowed large teams of draught animals to plough even the toughest claylands efficiently. In the common field, manuring was made easier by the establishment of a communal dung heap; but even more important, bringing the community's individually owned animals together to graze in a communal herd meant that they could be grazed effectively on the fallow or the stubble and their dung would contribute to bringing the land back into productive use year after year. Furthermore, a herd belonging to several dozen peasants could be looked after by only one or two individuals, releasing more hands to manage the arable.

These advantages all seem to point in one direction: those with the most to gain from the common-field system of agriculture were the peasants themselves. In particular, they were now able to manage the arable more effectively, and produce more grain, without compromising the size of their herds. Indeed such documentary information as we have suggests that arable production did rise in the East Midlands between the 10th and the 13th centuries, once the common fields had been established. But there is no reason to think that the increase in arable production made possible by the common-field system was forced on East Midlands peasants purely because populations were rising. There were evidently more mouths to feed, but it may have been more important that surplus arable produce could be sold for a good profit. It can be no coincidence, surely, that the 10th century also sees, for the first time since the Romans, the introduction of a truly mass coinage. Although sustaining an increased population, much of the additional produce of East Midlands' common fields was probably marketed for cash. Although profit might go to the individual peasant initially, it quickly found its way up the social hierarchy in rents and in commutation of peasant services. Increasing arable output was therefore good for all sections of society. The common-field revolution, then, might represent a *collaboration* between lords and peasants, brought about because it was in the interests of the entire community.

As we might expect, Domesday Book confirms that there were many prosperous peasants by 1086, the wealthiest of whom must have been indistinguishable from the lesser gentry. The 'sokeman' class, for example, seems to have been composed of largely autonomous farmers, quite capable of organising the agricultural regime on their relatively small holdings to maximum advantage. Although the legal implications of the term 'sokeman' may have been archaic by 1086, these were, nevertheless, substantial and prosperous figures. Numerically speaking they were rare in Oxfordshire, Bedfordshire and Buckinghamshire, but here their economic role was probably taken by 'freemen'. In Lincolnshire, however, sokemen accounted for nearly half the population. In a considerable number of nucleated villages surrounded by common fields, Domesday Book records no lords as resident at all. In Lincolnshire communities like Blyton or Great Hale, or Tilbrook in Bedfordshire, where only sokemen are reported, it is likely that the common fields owe their origins to decisions made by these sokemen's ancestors to replan their agriculture. They would not have done so without the consent of their feudal lords, who would hope to benefit from the changes also, but the evidence seems to suggest that the initiative for this revolution must have come from below. No doubt there would be losers, particularly among the poorest and the un-free, but compared with many developments in medieval England, the planning of the common fields and their concomitant villages appears to have been a genuine community effort.

THE TOWN RETURNS

Important though it is, the arrival of common-field agriculture is only the first of two great landscape changes in the East Midlands between the 9th and 11th centuries. At this time also urbanism was re-established here and it is hard to believe that such dramatic contemporaneous changes in lifestyle were not related. It was once thought that, for consideration as a town, a village had to achieve a particular legal status. However, such definitions might rule out such obviously urban places as Market Harborough (Leicestershire), which throughout the Middle Ages was, legally speaking, a secondary settlement in Great Bowden parish. We now usually deem a town to be any settlement where a substantial proportion of the population was not involved directly in working the land. Towns were, therefore, 'service centres' for the country round about: they had a 'hinterland' from which the people would come to sell agricultural produce and to purchase goods not made in individual villages: pottery, more sophisticated metalwork, horn-work, textiles, leatherwork and luxury goods.

The first such service centres may have been associated with monasteries. Early monastic settlements, such as Peterborough, Oundle, Bardney or Breedon-on-the-Hill, might have had some urban characteristics before the 10th century, and Bede sometimes called such places *civitates*, a word later routinely used to describe towns. None of them has yet been explored on a sufficiently large scale archaeologically to reveal much about middle Saxon urbanism, although many specialised crafts were undertaken in such locations. Such churches might have sponsored early markets at convenient locations on the road or river network, such as on the Roman road at Stow Green near Bourne (Kesteven), perhaps at Flixborough (on the Trent north of Scunthorpe) or at Torksey (about 32km further upstream, on a sandy island on the Lincolnshire side). It is highly likely that markets of the 7th and 8th centuries occurred on the Nene under the supervision of Peterborough, on the Ouse under the supervision of Ely and perhaps on the Thames under the supervision of monasteries at Dorchester and Abingdon.

But it is far from clear how many people actually lived at such markets. Towns where traders lived and worked probably disappeared with the Romans. Many East Midlands towns were eventually re-established on the sites of Roman predecessors, but not one has produced evidence for continuity of urban occupation. In the East Midlands, and probably in most other parts of the country as well, towns (as places where goods were both manufactured in large numbers and traded widely) were 'reinvented' in the late 9th and 10th centuries. But was the re-foundation of such places an inevitable result of the re-organisation of the landscape between about 900 and 1100?

As in the landscape around, the fundamental change in the late 9th or 10th century may have been one of marketing strategy. Indeed it may be represented by the arrival of middle men. Whereas formerly foreign traders had appeared at market sites, done their trading and then gone away, in the 10th century, such traders seem to have set up home in or near the markets and traded continuously. Settlements of this type were set up at earlier dates in other parts of England, at 'Hamwic' (near Southampton) and Ipswich, and it is possible that there were such places in our region (at Torksey, perhaps). But the earliest places with evidence for resident traders – the earliest 'towns' yet confirmed in the East Midlands – are late 9th-century in date. Such traders may have either begun

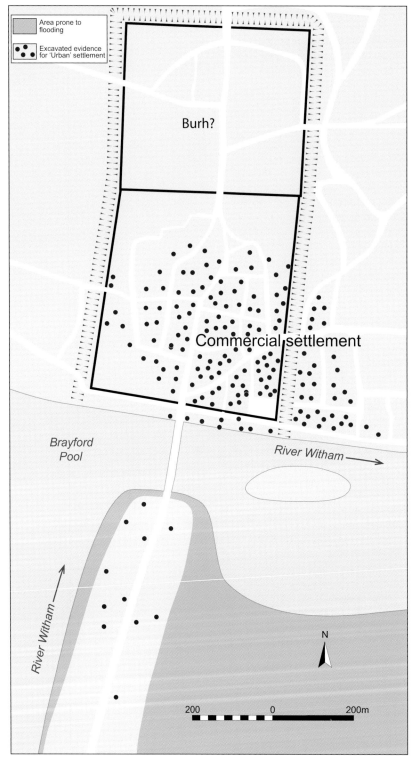

Fig. 3.18 The distribution of settlement in 10th-century Lincoln, based on archaeological finds (source: Vince 2003b).

manufacturing near their new homes, or trained locals to manufacture for them. No doubt the reasons behind this major economic change are complex. It may represent an eclipse of ecclesiastical power, or of the power of the aristocracy, during the Viking incursions of the 9th century. After all, following their military defeat by the Danes in the 870s, it would have been hard for Anglo-Saxon landlords (secular or ecclesiastical) to resist the incoming Scandinavian traders who wanted to establish themselves more permanently on their market sites.

Throughout the 10th and 11th centuries, such manufacturing and trading settlements were established at political centres across the East Midlands. Around the river crossing at Lincoln a resident community of pottery manufacturers, metalworkers and textile workers sprang into existence. Similarly, Stamford, Northampton, Nottingham and Leicester all seem to start with an industrial settlement: in all four cases pottery kilns, and evidence for metalworking and textile production dominates the earliest levels. At 10th-century Derby, Bedford, Buckingham, Towcester and Oxford, housing sprang up for new classes of urban artisan, whose lifestyle revolved around manufacturing goods that were then traded in great market places close to their workshops.

The isolated scraps of documentation we have for towns of this age, however, are concerned not with industrial production but with the establishment of *burhs*. All of the political centres listed above, and also Tempsford (Bedfordshire) and Wallingford (Oxfordshire), were described in this way. Clearly such places had some defensive capacity, but whether *burhs* had much to do with the development of true urbanism may be doubted. At Lincoln, for example, the *burh* was probably the former Roman upper enclosure, which is several hundred metres (and up a steep hill) from the 10th-century 'urban' settlement along the riverside, both inside and outside the Roman walls of the lower city (Fig. 3.18). This matter is considered further in Chapter 6 (p.198).

The profound changes in the way goods were exchanged, implied by the new urban markets, cannot have been independent of the development of the more market-based economy implied by the expansion of the coinage at precisely this time (nor of the licensing of new urban mints). If we are correct in suggesting that the main aim behind the introduction of the common-field system in the countryside was the production of an arable surplus, then that surplus must have also played an important role in the development of the new urban markets. The manufactured goods of the new towns would have been purchased by the new 'villagers' with their surplus grain, while the grain would have been required by the manufacturers, who no longer had time to grow their own. Although most East Midlands towns had their own common-field system, just like the settlements around them, and although there must have been a period early on when these systems supported the entire urban population, in towns like Lincoln and Stamford the common fields rapidly became less important as a source of food than their markets. Clearly inhabitants in the developing settlement south of the river at Lincoln could manage well enough on food purchased in the city markets, because they were never given any rights to land in the town fields.

MAXIMUM OUTPUT

Whatever its origins, by the 12th century the 'village moment' seems to have passed. After this date few, if any, common-field systems or their villages were established in the East Midlands. But that is not to say that no new settlements were established. The population expanded throughout the 13th century and more land and settlement space were required. England's most rapidly expanding counties between 1086 and the Hundred Rolls of 1274–5 were Bedfordshire and Northamptonshire, which may have seen an increase in population of between 300 and 400 per cent. The population of north Buckinghamshire also grew considerably, while in much of Lincolnshire, parts of Nottinghamshire and in south-eastern Leicestershire and Rutland, the population probably increased by more than 100 per cent. This population was growing most rapidly, however, in precisely those areas that were already relatively densely populated in 1086. Meanwhile the less densely occupied areas, such as Charnwood and the Northamptonshire plateaux, retained relatively low populations. Both areas, of course, were occupied by forests and, although the population of such areas may not have been expanding at quite the rate of surrounding areas, they were absorbing people nevertheless.

East Midlands settlements responded to the growing population between the 11th and 13th centuries in several ways, often detectable in village plans today. They were most easily accommodated through an expansion of the original village onto the common arable fields, with new plots (tofts) in a block running back from one or more of the access roads. Such added settlement blocks could be of any size, from a few tofts to a whole new suburb. At Grantchester (Cambridgeshire), the village expanded southwards from the original Anglo-Saxon settlement around the crossroads, and today's picturesque village street zigzags its way along what were originally headlands within the common field (Fig. 3.19). Many similar settlement extensions, of similar date, have also been identified in Lindsey: at Blyton, West Firsby, South Carlton and at least a dozen others.

The modern village at Wyboston was probably laid out at this period (in the 9th or 10th century) with individual properties strung out along the Beggary Brook, to the west of the Great North Road (Fig. 3.20). In the 18th century the village was still surrounded by its common fields, Norton, Bellam and West (or Bills Minks) fields. Taken in isolation, Wyboston was probably a typical 'three-field' community with the various furlongs planted, harvested and grazed according to an intricate rotation controlled through the village meeting. In modern Wyboston the

ABOVE: *Fig. 3.19 The village of Grantchester (Cambridgeshire) is thought to have originated around the junction towards its northern end (top centre).* *The road southwards towards the church zigzagged its way along the boundaries of groups of closes and furlongs in the common fields, before they were built over as the village expanded. The earliest fabric in the church (with its clock set at 2.45 p.m.) dates from around AD 1000, suggesting that the settlement had extended this far southwards by that date. By the 19th century it had reached the River Cam bridge at the bottom of the picture.*

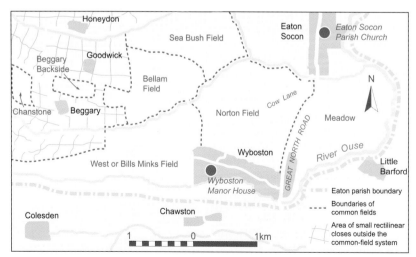

Fig. 3.20 The medieval landscape of Wyboston and Beggary, showing the extent of medieval common fields and enclosed closes.

properties all front onto the east–west road which runs parallel to the brook, but earlier properties may have faced onto the stream, the common source of water. The plots on the north side of the modern road are of roughly uniform sizes in the earliest mapping we have (of the late 18th century) and imply that they were laid out in several episodes. The earliest group to have been established may be that at the west end of the village, around Manor Farm and the road junction; further to the east, a sequence of extensions may be marked by regular parcels of tofts, accommodating an expanding population. The final development may have been the filling in of the narrow strip of land between the modern road and the stream itself, presumably at a time when the population was reduced and community access to the water was no longer so vital (perhaps in the 14th century or later). Wyboston, however, was a relatively unusual village in the East Midlands because, even though it had a relatively large population, a self-sufficient common-field agricultural system and numerous manors, it still contained no church. It remained within the enormous parish of Eaton Socon and, until a chapel of ease was provided in the 15th century (p.223), parishioners walked to services, and carried their dead, down Cow Lane to St Mary's, Eaton Socon. We shall also see, in a moment, that it also contained a second, entirely different, agricultural system on the higher ground to the west.

Wyboston village grew by extending towards the River Ouse, but some East Midlands settlements grew towards their neighbours and eventually amalgamated with them. Lincolnshire contains many examples of discrete settlements which, between the 11th and 13th centuries, grew together to form single villages (Great and Little Corringham, Lindsey; Silkby and

Willoughby Kesteven). Here the component settlements remain visible in the 'polyfocal' layout of such villages today, having, for example, two greens. If amalgamation did not occur until after about 1100, such villages might have two parochial churches, which belonged to their original component settlements, such as Spridlington or South Kelsey (both Lindsey). The field systems might even remain distinct in such settlements. Although after amalgamation Spridlington's fields were run as a single agricultural unit, they retained their original names.

Throughout the period between the 11th and the 13th centuries, the edge of the cultivated land was pushed outwards, away from the new villages. In particular the common woodlands, now mostly confined to the edges of the community, beyond the common fields, came under pressure for conversion to arable – a process known as 'assarting'. Surviving documents sometimes record such encroachments. Large-scale assarting had taken place at Holywell, Careby and Aunby (Kesteven) in the late 12th and early 13th centuries and 97ha of assart were incorporated into the common fields of Barwell (Leicestershire). At South Scarle (Nottinghamshire) in 1225–31, 25 landholders in the common field agreed to clear a new assart into the woodland on the fields' edge and take one bovate of the new land each. We can identify many similar assarts on the edges of existing villages through surviving field names: 'Sart Field' in Islip (Oxfordshire), for example. As at South Scarle, presumably the new strips created in such operations were allocated largely to those who had cleared the land.

BREAKING NEW GROUND

There were, however, other ways of accommodating extra people in the landscape, apart from simply expanding existing settlements and field systems. Population pressures in the 12th and 13th centuries drove some settlements onto common heaths and wastes, where animals from many villages might be grazed seasonally, but where there was evidently still enough room for new cottages. Such settlements were found on Oxfordshire heaths by the late 12th century (at Newton Purcell, Newton Morrell and Caulcott) and on the edges of marshlands in the same county (like Standlake), and they were still springing up at Desford, Earl Shilton and Normanton on the heaths of western Leicestershire in the late 13th century. The most famous settlement of this type, however, is the impoverished community of Juniper Hill on Cottisford Heath on the Oxfordshire/Northamptonshire border, later immortalised as Flora Thompson's *Lark Rise*.

Another strategy was to create entirely new settlements in woodland areas, with their own dedicated field systems. Such new settlements are found most frequently (or at least they are best documented) in the royal forests which, although not uniformly or densely covered with trees, still occupied a large part of the East Midlands in 1086. Such settlements are frequently mentioned in documents, usually because, in creating the new settlements, the colonists had fallen foul of 'forest law'. In Whittlewood, Rockingham and Salcey forests, there were about 60 13th-century offences against forest law (such as 'damaging the *vert*' – the vegetation cover – and making it unsuitable for game animals). There were about 20 offences in Leighfield Forest (Rutland) during the same period, and the picture was similar in Bernwood, Wychwood, Huntingdon, Sherwood and other royal forests. Between 1200 and 1350 more than 2,400ha of woodland were cleared to form new settlements in Rockingham, Salcey and Whittlewood alone. But the total forest area cleared during this period here was even greater, because the documents only record the infringements of forest law, making no mention of those assarts agreed with the Crown. In a different type of document, for example, we hear by chance that 200ha of Rockingham Forest in Rushton parish (Northamptonshire) had been assarted by agreement with the Crown in the 13th century, and this accounts for more than a quarter of the entire parish.

Village names give some idea how many settlements originated in woodland. In Northamptonshire, a county where much of the land was governed by forest law by the 13th century, the names of 37 settlements include the word *-ley* (a woodland clearing), 12 include the word *-worth* (an enclosure within woodland), and nine the word *-feld* (a grazed clearing within forest). Some of these settlements, at least, must indicate woodland clearance between the 10th and 13th centuries. There are also records of woodland clearance outside royal forests, for example in Charnwood and central Bedfordshire (on the Greensand) where the dynamic Cistercian abbey at Old Warden was an important agent. The abbey was known as St Mary-of-the-Asserts, and was granted many small holdings of woodland in expectation that the monks would clear the wood and cultivate the land. Many other monastic houses were also enthusiastic promoters of assarts: both Ramsey Abbey (Huntingdonshire) and Eynsham Abbey (Oxfordshire) increased the value of their holdings considerably through this means. Pipewell Abbey (Northamptonshire) is said to have been responsible for a staggering total of over 5,200ha of assart, and it became an important source of income for several monastic houses in the Witham valley.

The new settlements in forest areas, with their own independent agricultural systems, enabled the landscape to absorb considerable increases in population. At Brigstock, a royal manor in Rockingham Forest, we can calculate from the surviving court rolls that the resident population in 1310 might have represented a full 600 per cent increase since 1086. In this manor, at least, we know that this swollen population was only sustainable because new minor settlements were carved out of the surrounding forest, mostly out of woodlands. We also know (from the same sources) that the assarts generated more extra space than was needed simply to accommodate Brigstockers and their descendants: many occupants of the new minor settlements were incomers. In the Bishop of Winchester's great manor of Witney on the edge of Wychwood Forest, 32 out of 36 freehold farms in the vill of Hailey in 1279 were described as assarts, and new tenants from outside the manor paid a uniform rent of 6 pence an acre, a somewhat higher price than many of the bishop's older tenants.

The forest areas, however, also often contained significant industries, and some of these were already served by a resident population, which was not displaced by such assarting. Whereas the economy of the common-field villages was largely geared to producing agricultural surplus, inhabitants in the forest areas, including many colonists of assarts, would have balanced agricultural labour with work in one of the woodland industries (explored in more detail in Chapter 5 – p.179), at least until all the woodlands were felled. In the forest of Rockingham, for example, many communities engaged in ironworking and pottery manufacture as well as working the land. In Bernwood Forest in 1622, lawyers representing four Oxford colleges provided an excellent description of the economy of the straggling settlement of Brill (Buckinghamshire) in an attempt to prevent it being disafforested, which provides us with a glimpse of how diverse the economy of such forest places could be. It was, they said:

> *A town … delicately situated upon a fertile, fruitful hill in the midst of the Forest, and blessed with all kinds of commodities, as corn, hay, grass, wood, herbs and roots, wells and springs, that the earth can bring forth in the upper parts of the earth. And the earth within serving for the best brick and all earthen vessels, and the stones for lime, of any one place.*

(Lipscomb 1847)

For the aristocracy, on the other hand, such forests were primarily for hunting and the woodland areas within them were most important as covers for game. Industrial and agricultural activities were certainly not precluded, but infringements of the *vert* were prosecuted enthusiastically. The Domesday Book entry for Fotheringhay (Northamptonshire) makes this dual use quite explicit, explaining that the woodland in the vill was worth 10 shillings, but 'only when it beareth mast [leaf-litter] and the King hunts not'. All East Midlands forests were occasionally used for hunting by the king and his aristocracy, and the requirement that forests were kept in suitable condition must have placed even more pressure on the increasingly over-used landscape. Such pressures were sometimes increased by the aristocracy themselves and occasional pollen records show tracts of agricultural land (at Shotover, Oxfordshire, for example) incorporated into adjacent forest areas, presumably for hunting purposes, in the 11th and 12th centuries. Pollen records for the forest of Harthay (Huntingdonshire) accord with surviving documents to show that forest trees were deliberately established over former agricultural enclosures. In the case of Leicester Forest, called *Hereswode* ('the wood of the people' or 'the wood of the army') in Domesday Book, forest resources which may have once belonged to the community became a private hunting ground belonging exclusively to Leicestershire's sheriff.

Fig. 3.21 Laxton (Northamptonshire) is characteristic of villages in former forest areas. Not only do surviving woodlands crowd around the settlement, but the modern field pattern shows little sign of the great common fields more typical of 'champion' villages. Even so, they have produced evidence for extensive Roman and medieval charcoal-burning and iron-smelting. The medieval village house-plots line up in a row along the north side of the street, with the church isolated to the south. They are now mostly occupied by 19th-century houses, rebuilt by the Evans family. Note also the more dispersed pattern of outlying farms, away from the village centre. In 'champion' areas these would be enclosure farms, but here they are mostly on more ancient sites; indeed Laxton's original manor site (at Fineshade) lay so far east it became a separate parish.

Before the establishment of assarts in the forest areas, settlements here were still, on the whole, much smaller in size than was usual in 'village England', often being a few properties laid out in a simple row: an example is Laxton in Rockingham Forest (Fig. 3.21). The population in such places was actually quite sizeable, but it was scattered through the forest, more like the earlier dispersed East Midlands settlement patterns before the 'village moment'. Twelfth- and 13th-century assarts, then, were not creating a novel settlement form; they simply exploited these forest areas in ways that had been traditional. By contrast with the new common-field landscape beyond the forest, the landscape here continued to be populated by smaller settlements with their fields and closes grouped around them.

Eighteenth-century reports show that some of these settlements had no common fields at all, but in others certain 'closes' were farmed in this way. The language is the same, but the fields so described were quite different from the large open expanses of the common fields around more typical villages beyond the forest. In the forest such 'common fields' were often indistinguishable from the privately managed closes around them. These fields were certainly not at the heart of a large integrated agricultural regime and they may have been farmed 'in common' only in the sense that stock was grazed here by more than one owner. This explains why, instead of having two or three common fields like the true common-field villages, some forest communities often had large numbers of them: up to 40 in certain cases.

The two common fields at Beggary in Wyboston vill, called Beggary Backside and Chanston fields, were of precisely this type (*see* Fig. 3.20). They did not resemble the common fields of Wyboston itself, but looked like larger versions of the privately owned and individually farmed closes round them. Beggary Backside and Chanston fields therefore hint at assarting around Beggary. Wyboston is typical of this part of Bedfordshire, on the southern edge of Huntingdonshire

OPPOSITE PAGE:

TOP: *Fig. 3.22 Principal features of medieval Nottingham* (various sources).

BOTTOM: *Fig. 3.23 Principal features of medieval Leicester* (source: Buckley & Lucas 1987).

Forest, in having a group of remote settlements, typically called 'ends' (although in Eaton Socon parish they were called 'hamlets'). These remote settlements (Beggary, Staploe, Honeydon, Goodwick etc) are all on the higher, poorer boulder clay soils of the parish, once occupied by large areas of wood pasture. In 1086 Eaton was notable for containing woodland for 500 pigs, but between 1086 and the late 13th century much of that woodland had been felled to make way for the hamlets, with their patchwork field systems. Some of these new settlements are recorded as having been speculative ventures by prospective landlords, such as Bushmead Priory, whose assarting in the northern part of Eaton parish was extensive. These new settlements were not all easy places to colonise, as is revealed by the name given to the community cut out of the woodland west of Wyboston's West Field: it was probably called Beggary because the land was so poor.

At the time they were created such settlements might have been described as 'Stocks' or 'Stockings' (from the Old English word *Stocc*, meaning a 'tree stump'), a place- and field-name which occurs repeatedly hereabouts (for example at Little Staughton, otherwise 'Little Stocking'). New inhabitants of such settlements might take this term as their surname, when that became more usual for the lower orders of society during the 13th century. By 1227 the handful of families living on the assart at Beggary included one that had done just this: the head of the family was known as Hugh le Stocker. By 1297, this little community had grown to about 15 families and Hugh's descendant, Juliana le Stocker, owned not pigs (because the woodland had virtually all gone) but a heifer, a cow and a bullock, which were numbered among Beggary's herd of 50 beasts (including three oxen for ploughing). Juliana probably rented one of the small closes into which the land around the settlement's central moat had been divided, in which to run her few beasts. She probably had common rights in the limited Beggary arable and in a meadow from which she gathered hay. More significantly for the future of her family, however, Juliana also owned five sheep in Beggary's flock of 24.

THE TOWNS BOOM

In 1086 the populations of Nottingham, Leicester, Stamford and Northampton were greater than 2,000, while Oxford might have had 4,000 or 5,000 residents. Much the largest town in the East Midlands, until its catastrophic crash around 1300, however, was Lincoln, where up to 10,000 people may have squeezed into the city by 1100. Although the pace of expansion probably slowed during the 12th century, people were still migrating to the towns throughout the 13th century. Their migration is recorded in their newly minted surnames. Of surnames in Leicester's tax records between 1269 and 1318, 78 per cent indicate individuals from villages within 32km of the city, while in a Stratford-upon-Avon rental for 1251–2, perhaps 90 per cent of those with topographically distinctive surnames came from within 25km of the town.

From the 13th century, Oxford attracted scholars and students from across Europe, and the city developed a distinctive economy to service them. Other East Midlands towns also attracted migrants from further afield – often merchants motivated by commercial prospects in the town. A study of Leicester merchants' surnames between 1300 and 1320 reveals that they, or their recent predecessors, had come from Derbyshire, Staffordshire, Lincolnshire, Suffolk and Kent, while one of the most important Lincoln merchant families was named 'de Paris'. This picture of more wide-ranging contacts emphasises the point that, from the 10th century onwards, the East Midlands' growing marketing economy could not be sustained without external contacts. In the 10th and 11th centuries, towns like Lincoln and Nottingham conducted a vigorous international trade with Scandinavia and the Low Countries. The great fair held annually at Northampton, first mentioned in the 1140s, had an international clientele, and was visited, particularly, by continental cloth buyers, who imported luxury goods to pay for their cloth. From the 12th century, however, London became the single most important market for imported goods from the continent. Increasingly, a percentage of the East Midlands' surplus grain went to London for sale also, rather than to local market centres. In the 14th century, for example, villeins on Ramsey Abbey's estates were required to carry grain to London after harvest; and by the 14th century, East Midlands merchants looked to London for supplies of fine cloth, dyestuffs, wine, spices and virtually all other luxury items, rather than to travelling continental merchants, and even for some foodstuffs, such as dried fish. It would have been unusual for such imports to be marketed directly in the villages, however – they would have been sold through urban markets first.

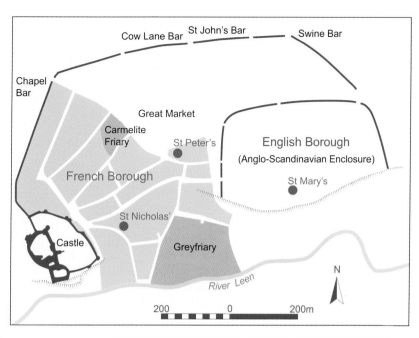

Specialists were required to deal with the increasing range of commodities being brought to urban markets and the lists of tradesmen to be found in larger towns continued to grow through the 13th century. Leicester's guild merchant was joined by members of 60–65 different occupations between 1298 and 1380, including cutlers, bell-makers, jewellers, a sculptor and a 'samiter' (a dealer in fine silks), while representatives from 70 different occupations contributed to the town's lay subsidy of 1524. Inevitably, some new trades dealt with the newly created paperwork: scriveners and lawyers had arrived in most large towns by the 14th century.

Increasing population usually meant physical expansion. Extensions to individual towns have been readily identified through analysing their street patterns. At Lincoln, as many as nine distinct market places have been identified, most of which represented additions to the urban area when they were first laid out. In Nottingham the huge market place was also an addition to the 10th-century *burh*, being established on open ground west and north of the so-called 'English borough' on the hill around St Mary's church (Fig. 3.22). By the early 12th century it had become the principal mart for a large area: in Henry I's charter, the men of both Nottinghamshire and Derbyshire were required to come here to buy and sell. At Leicester also, although there had been three market places within the walls (including a new one – the Saturday Market – laid out in the late 13th century), the two largest lay outside the north and east gates. Outside the east gate, the Beremart ('Barley market') dealt with much of the grain surplus from Leicestershire's common fields (Fig. 3.23). Northampton also had two large market places outside the north and east gates (Fig. 3.25). The latter was probably the 'Newland' mentioned

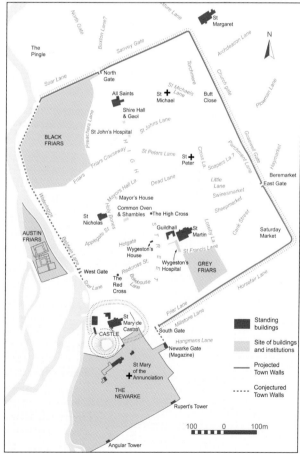

in 1086 and may have been founded in the early 11th century, while at Stamford the main markets also seem to have been west of the original *burh*, becoming enclosed

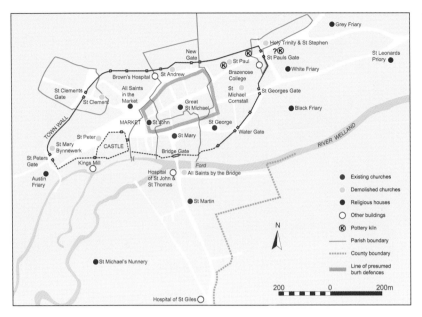

Existing churches
Demolished churches
Religious houses
Other buildings
Pottery kiln
Parish boundary
County boundary
Line of presumed
burh defences

200   0   200m

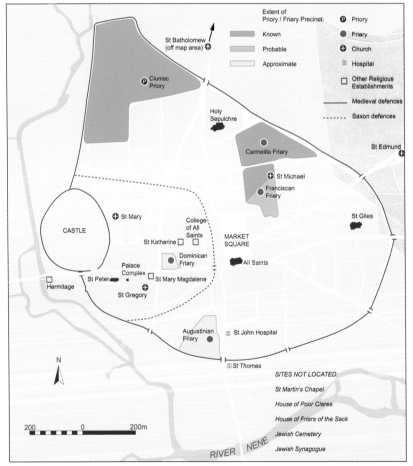

Extent of
Priory / Friary Precinct:
Known
Probable
Approximate

Priory
Friary
Church
Hospital
Other Religious
Establishments
Medieval defences
Saxon defences

SITES NOT LOCATED:
St Martin's Chapel
House of Poor Clares
House of Friars of the Sack
Jewish Cemetery
Jewish Synagogue

200   0   200m

TOP: *Fig. 3.24 Principal features of medieval Stamford* (various sources).

ABOVE: *Fig. 3.25 Principal features of medieval Northampton* (various sources).

within the medieval walls only later (Fig. 3.24). Many, if not all, of these new 10th- and 11th-century markets were lined with newly erected properties, presumably intended to attract new traders. In Lincoln, the earliest documents suggest that most markets had specialised functions: the meat market, cloth market, hay market etc. At Northampton there were street markets for cloth, wool and straw. Even small towns like Daventry had separate markets for cloth, meat and pigs, and where the market was held in a single space, as at Brackley (Northamptonshire), different zones would be colonised by traders in different commodities.

Brackley is a good example of a medieval planted town (Fig. 3.26). The original settlement lay within Halse parish, and is still easily distinguishable in the town plan by the knot of lanes around the river-crossing near St Peter's church (itself originally a chapel of Halse). A broad market street was laid out, probably before 1173, alongside the main road from Oxford to Northampton, with regular 'burgage plots' lining at least one side. Landlords could make money by establishing such towns throughout the 12th and 13th centuries. Stratford-upon-Avon was founded in 1196 by the Bishop of Worcester beside the bridge carrying the salt road from Droitwich over the Avon. Market Harborough originated a little earlier at the Welland bridge on the main Leicester–Northampton road. St Neots is also a completely re-planned 'new-town' at the Ouse crossing although, in this case, superimposed on an earlier settlement. Some new towns, such as Thame (Oxfordshire), developed to become modern boroughs but others, like Stratton Audley (Oxfordshire) or Langworth (Lindsey), struggled to retain their population when their markets failed to attract traders. A striking number of these new foundations were either within, or adjacent to, forest areas and may have been developed specifically to bring products of woodland industries to market, as such industries developed in the 12th and 13th centuries.

LATE MEDIEVAL READJUSTMENT

Then the economic bubble burst. The early 14th century was a period of crisis in the English countryside, one that probably had a greater impact in the East Midlands than any other part of England. The changes which overtook the landscape were not quite as large, perhaps, as those that followed the layout of the common fields in the 10th century, or those that finally removed them altogether in the 18th and early 19th centuries, but between those two revolutions this was much the largest upheaval.

The outcomes of these 14th-century landscape changes are easier to describe than their causes. By the end of the 13th century, in all but the forest areas of the East Midlands, the agricultural regime in each community was an integrated and efficient machine, dedicated to maximising arable output. The East Midlands climate and soils made this part of the country well suited to intensive production and, in the booming cities here, and elsewhere in England, there was a demand for all the arable produce local farmers could get to market. By the late 14th century, however, this drive for arable output had dissipated. The common fields still produced some arable crops, but they were no longer being enlarged, and the creation of new fields and settlements in forest areas had all but ceased. There was still a market for surplus grain, but after 1300 the populations of most towns ceased to grow, and in some cases it fell quite dramatically, further reducing the market for surpluses.

Even so, the market remained just as receptive to animal products, especially wool. Whereas in 1300 the village herds, including sheep flocks, had been subordinated to the needs of arable (grazing the fallow and the stubble and providing manure for the next season's crops), by 1400 sheep were less valuable for maximising arable yields than they were for the quality of their fleeces. The 14th century saw great changes in the English wool and cloth industry. In 1300, most English wool was still being produced by large landowners, especially monasteries, before being transported to towns such as Lincoln to be processed into cloth by an army of dyers, fullers, spinners and weavers. The whole production process was co-ordinated by great merchants who then took cloth to the international markets, like those at St Ives and Northampton, for sale. By 1400, however, there were virtually no professional cloth workers left in Lincoln at all: cloth production there had become a cottage industry, undertaken within the household by people whose main income came from elsewhere. Sometime in the early 14th century the Lincoln merchants, who formerly controlled the whole cloth production process, had realised that it was more profitable to concentrate on procuring, shipping and selling the raw wool to continental cloth producers, rather than maintain the whole process in England. They became early 'multinationals'. Fortunately, they still wanted good quality wool in ever increasing quantities, and this opened up opportunities for smaller rural producers whose market for surplus grain had begun to fail.

If one key feature of the dramatic 14th-century changes in the landscape was the development of the wool market, another was a fall in population. Together, in the

Fig. 3.26 The planted town of Brackley (Northamptonshire). The town is characterised by the long plots extending back from the broad market street, laid along the main road north of the castle in the 12th century. The pre-existing village, with its parochial church, lay away to the right, nearer the river crossing. The former St James' Hospital (top right) was founded about the same time as the market town, to cater for travellers, although a now vanished parochial chapel represented the parish church at the market. The town remained discretely prosperous (see the fine market hall of 1706, with its prominent cupola), but did not expand greatly until the later 20th century.

East Midlands, these two factors ensured that land was taken out of arable production and given over to 'sheep-walk'. It took fewer people to manage a sheep farm than the intricate agricultural regime of the common field, but it is unclear which development came first – the change in agricultural regime or the decline in population. Arable land could not have been turned over to sheep-walk unless there were fewer mouths to feed, which rather suggests that the decline in population came first. For many years it was presumed that the arrival of plague in England in 1348 (and its return on subsequent occasions) reduced the population to such an extent that the survivors had to capitalise on growing wool. In Brigstock manor the population was at an all-time peak in the decade between 1310 and 1320 but it then declined dramatically (by 25 per cent) before 1348. The population continued to fall sharply here after 1348, even though there is no record of plague having broken out. Clearly the years between 1310 and 1347 must have been very difficult. In 1341–2 a government inquiry into suspiciously low levels of taxation showed that dozens of communities in Lindsey were producing less than half the value of corn, wool and lambs that they had in 1291. Some villages (like Woodthorpe-on-the-Wold) had already been abandoned. Lindsey was the most badly affected area in the East Midlands, but 49 settlements of 111 investigated in Bedfordshire had also abandoned some arable land: in Segenho (on the Greensand) this amounted to 97ha. In Cambridgeshire the same commissioners were told that some 2,025ha of arable had gone out of production in the county, while at Radclive, near Buckingham, the greater part of the arable lay uncultivated. Such reports suggest that the population was reduced as much by famine in the period between 1310 and 1340 as by plague after 1348. Famine was indeed widespread in every year between 1315 and 1322 due, contemporaries said, to unusually heavy rainfall.

Although such statistics demonstrate that the rural economy was in crisis before the Black Death struck in 1348–9, we cannot deny that the disease's arrival had a profound impact on population numbers and, perhaps even more important, on community morale. The Louth Park Abbey chronicler said that many places in Lincolnshire lost four-fifths of their population in this year. This sounds like an exaggeration, but records of institutions by Bishop Gynewell of Lincoln for the year following March 1349 show that, in the archdeaconry of Stow, 45 per cent of benefices fell vacant (implying the death of the priest in charge); in the archdeaconry of Lincoln the figure was 57 per cent. In both Northamptonshire and Leicestershire, mortality among the clergy was somewhat lower, with some 37 per cent of benefices falling vacant, but this still represents an extraordinarily high death-rate. Occasionally documents show us the scale of mortality in particular settlements. On Crowland Abbey's Cambridgeshire manors of Oakington, Dry Drayton and Cottenham, the deaths of 35 out of 50 tenants are recorded at the first, 20 out of 42 at the second and 33 out of 58 at the third.

The plague's longer-term impact would have been different in each settlement. Even with mortality at about 40 per cent it is unlikely that many viable rural communities would have been completely wiped out in 1348–9. Historians have searched hard for examples of annihilation, but found only a few. Contenders are frequently in Lindsey, reinforcing the impression given by Bishop Gynewell's registers that this area was particularly hard hit. North Cadeby was one of a small number of communities here granted 100 per cent tax exemption in the early 1350s, implying that there were no inhabitants at all, while in 1398 Middle Carlton had had no taxable inhabitants for 40 years. Occasionally similar records suggest such annihilation elsewhere: in 1349 all the tenants of the north Buckinghamshire village of Kimble, for example, were said to have died of disease. But, although they reeled from the blow, most communities recovered; even Kimble, which survives today. In 1352 the manor house at Caldecote (Huntingdonshire) was collapsing, many houses were ruinous, as was the mill, and disease was said to be still rife; yet, although it is largely deserted today, Caldecote continued as a viable community into the 16th century.

Although few settlements were abandoned as a direct result of the plague, many more were to be deserted within a few generations of 1348–9, and the steady retreat away from the more marginal settlements did not stop until the population started to rise dramatically again in the 18th century. The Black Death was merely the most dramatic of a series of reversals suffered through the 14th century; in some places the biggest falls in population came later in the century. Elkington (Northamptonshire) had 39 taxpayers in 1377, for example, but was reduced to a handful of farm servants by 1412. Little Newton, in the same county, had 18 families in 1377, but only four in 1449. Opinions and statistics vary, but it is abundantly clear both that there was a dramatic decline in the population during the 14th century and that this was not due solely to disease. Taken as a whole, however, these figures all depict a much smaller rural population and a completely different agricultural regime by 1400.

Throughout the period between 1400 and 1700 the main reason for abandoning settlements was not disease but the change-over from arable to sheep farming. Kingsthorpe in Polebrook parish (Northamptonshire), for example, was reported to have been near to desertion because it had been turned over entirely to sheep-walk as early as 1386. The most prosperous farm in the community became the base of operations for the new sheep-farm, and the other house sites and the common arable were simply fenced off and grassed over to create one large pasture. Law-suits demonstrate that the agents behind such transformations were often monasteries, secular lords and members of the moneyed professional classes. Bicester Priory was accused of having enclosed the common fields and driven away the community at Wretchwick (Oxfordshire) in 1489, while London lawyer Thomas Pigott enclosed the manor of Doddershall (Buckinghamshire) in 1495 'with fences and ditches', so that 24 houses were left to fall into ruin and 120 people 'departed tearfully'.

But it was not only the rich and powerful who introduced sheep farming. In 15th-century Clipston (Northamptonshire), certain peasants were keeping up to 400 sheep in their personal holding, in defiance of the traditional limit (set by the manor court) on numbers of sheep that individuals could own. This was how the 'woolmen' of late medieval England grew and prospered. Typically they started with just a few sheep and, season by season, they enlarged their flock, began to sell their own wool and to buy their neighbours'. Eventually they bought the sheep as well, and organised the preparation and transport of the wool for export. Some East Midlands woolmen have left us lasting monuments to their prosperity, like John Curteys of Wymington (Bedfordshire), whose magnificent brass records his death in 1391, or John Lyndewood of Linwood (Lindsey) who, on his death in 1419, left bequests for a fine brass in his own parish church (showing him standing on a woolsack), and to 30 other local churches in whose parishes he had owned or marketed the clip.

In Wyboston too, a family of woolmen was also putting together a commercial empire. Juliana Stocker (p.72) was a mixed farmer and stood 16th in order of wealth in her community, but she did run five sheep with the Beggary flock in 1297. Her 14th-century descendants, however, moved up the income scale – from 16th to second place in the community by 1334. Although we cannot be certain how this was achieved, three 14th-century generations of Stockers expanded Juliana's small flock to become the largest in the vill. By the early 15th century Thomas Stocker (*c.* 1368–1440) was called 'merchant of Wyboston' and was dealing with the sale and export of wool and cloth in London: his son John was to become one of the wealthiest wool merchants in England. Later still Thomas' nephew, Sir William Stocker (*c.* 1420–85), was to become both mayor of the Calais wool staple and (briefly) Lord Mayor of London in 1485.

We do not know how the generations between Juliana and Thomas achieved this impressive rise from the peasantry to the commercial elite, and then to the gentry, but we can make some assumptions. We have seen that Juliana lived in

Beggary, a marginal settlement on the fringes of Wyboston vill, representative of many settlements of the 12th and 13th centuries driven into the former woodland by population pressure. By the mid-14th century, however, the family had moved from marginal Beggary to the vill's centre at Wyboston. If it was like many other 'ends' in this part of Bedfordshire, it is likely that the settlement at Beggary was reduced during the 14th and 15th centuries from an independent community with its own field system to a single farm surrounded by sheep-closes. No doubt increasing numbers of the sheep running here bore the Stocker brand, and we have some documentation from the 15th century recording the family buying, selling and organising local wool production. It was presumably a slow process of purchase and amalgamation, lasting at least three generations. The end result, however, was not just the conversion of the Beggary landscape into sheep-walks, but the conversion of the peasant family of 1297 into international traders in wool and cloth by the reign of Henry VI.

Like that at Beggary, many marginal cultivation systems in the East Midlands were abandoned altogether. These abandoned field and settlement systems now account for most of the 2,500-odd entries on the list of 'deserted medieval villages', around which the infant subject of medieval archaeology coalesced in the 1950s. A map of deserted 'villages' (as opposed to deserted settlements of all types) shows that they are almost exclusively located in the central province of England, where the villages themselves are located. Deserted medieval villages are concentrated in the East Midlands, because that is where the greatest concentrations of villages themselves were to be found.

Desertion was most frequent where settlements themselves had been thickest on the ground before the 14th century: in the wolds of Leicestershire for example. The most recently founded settlements – those established on the more marginal land at the time of maximum pressure on population and resources – were, it seems, the first to vanish. In Lindsey, where perhaps as many as 150 settlements were deserted, they went mostly from the Wolds and clay vales. West Wykeham, for instance, received tax relief in the 1350s and by 1377 had disappeared, with no taxpayers at all. Similarly West Ravendale and Raventhorpe were deserted by the late 14th century. None of these places had been long established in the landscape (Fig. 3.27). They were at the top of dry Wolds' valleys, occupying the most unpromising outlying parts of parishes centred on villages further down the slopes. Such places disappeared completely, but in most other parts of the East Midlands, it was more common for the marginal settlement to dwindle in size to a single farmstead, as at Beggary. Such more marginal settlements were affected to a much greater extent than the older, well-established parochial centres, which shrank in size, but continued as viable communities and complete desertion of villages with parochial churches was actually infrequent.

In north Buckinghamshire, settlements throughout Aylesbury vale were deserted, but almost all were peripheral vills, a sure sign that they had been established relatively recently. Here settlement was only withdrawing from the margins. The same seems to be true of many deserted settlements in

Fig. 3.27 The earthworks of the stone-built deserted medieval village of Gainsthorpe (Lindsey) *reveal the layout of lanes, yards and house-plots in this photograph taken from the east in the late afternoon of 2 November 1999. The settlement was always marginal, established high up on the limestone edge in Hibaldstow parish and by 1616 it was said 'there is nowe neyther tofte tenemente or cottage standinge … it keepes neer 1500 sheepe'.*

Oxfordshire, although the most famous images of desertion in the county come from Hampton Gay and Shifford, which both retain parish churches set among the silent earthworks of their former communities. More typical of the Oxfordshire pattern of desertion were the marginal assart settlements of Tangley and Tilgarsley in Wychwood Forest, which were probably created in the 12th century, prospered until the 14th century and then disappeared completely. In Bedfordshire, in addition to marginal settlements like Beggary in the upland north-east of the county, shrunken and abandoned settlements are most frequent in the clay vale and on the Greensand hills. In Northamptonshire, deserted settlements are spread more evenly across the county, but here too most sites deserted in the late medieval period were peripheral settlements, for example the cluster with -*cote* place-names around Towcester (Foscote, Wood Burcote, Caldecote, Duncote and Heathencote).

TOWNS IN DECLINE

Perhaps the clearest signs that town and countryside were interdependent are the simultaneous economic crises they both suffered in the late Middle Ages. Although people sought relief by moving to the towns during the years of famine in the early 14th century, the towns gained no long-term benefit. In general urban populations declined at similar rates to the countryside around. The causes of the long period of contraction experienced by late medieval English provincial towns have been debated as fully as agrarian decline, and a similar range of contributory factors has been identified. Even so, the experience of different towns was evidently not identical.

Perhaps it was because the East Midlands had been so dominated by common fields and nucleated villages (in a way that the West Midlands, for example, was not), that difficulties in the countryside had such a marked impact in its towns. After all, if the common fields really were aimed at producing arable surpluses to be sold to feed town-dwellers without fields of their own, the 14th-century change from intensive cultivation of crops to the production of wool must have had a serious effect on the urban economy. Lincoln's economy, for example, was completely dominated by cloth. There were, perhaps, 2,000 cloth workers in the early 13th-century city, importing dyes from the Mediterranean and exporting cloth all over Europe. Cloths were produced in sheds grouped in the south-west corner of the lower city, around streets given names like Walkergate ('the street of the dyers'). But when its long, expensively produced, single-colour 'russets' and 'scarlets' suddenly fell out of fashion at the end of the 13th century, Lincoln was extremely vulnerable. It had built its prosperity on a single product range and it proved incapable of developing new ones during hard times. Between 1321 and 1331 there were no weavers left in the city at all (and probably no other cloth workers either), and by 1345 only a handful of people remained who described themselves as textile workers. By this time the small amount of Lincoln cloth still being made was for domestic purposes only.

Lincoln was not the only East Midlands town dependent on the cloth industry's prosperity. Northampton, which had seen the most dramatic urban growth in the region during the 12th century (when its tax value briefly overtook even Lincoln's), was heavily dependent on this industry also. When its new town wall was built in the 12th century, the town's footprint was exceeded in England only by Norwich and London itself (*see* Fig. 3.24). Three hundred weavers were recorded at work in the early 13th century, but by 1275 it was reported that 'fullers … weavers … and other craftsmen of this sort have left Northampton because they are too heavily tallaged [taxed]'. While Northampton's population may have reached 6,000 in about 1200, by 1377 it had fallen to fewer than 2,500, and by 1484 it was granted tax relief because the town 'hath fallen into so great desolation and ruin … so that almost half of the same town remains desolate and destroyed'. Throughout this dark period, however, the great cloth market was held annually and was starting to flourish again by the 16th century, even though textiles from Northampton itself were rarely on sale.

Similarly Stamford's population virtually halved between 1300 and 1500, although here the decline of cloth manufacturing was partly compensated for by increasing traffic on the Great North Road. Leicester and Nottingham also lost population during this period, but neither experienced economic collapse on Lincoln's scale. Both continued to produce cloth and sell it at regional markets, though that at Nottingham was reduced in length from 15 to 5 days in 1378 through lack of business. Nottingham weavers had been granted the monopoly of weaving all dyed cloth within 10 leagues of the town in the 12th century, but by 1348 the weaver's guild was complaining that its membership had dwindled and by 1433–4 the town was officially listed as 'impovershed' and incapable of fulfilling its taxation obligations.

Oxford was another centre of cloth production. The earliest references to the town's trade in wool and leather occur before 1107 and there was a strong guild of weavers working Cotswold wool in the town by 1130. As in other places, its textile-based economy went into reverse in the final quarter of the 13th century. There had been over 60 weavers in the town in about 1220, but only 15 in 1275 and none at all by 1323. Here, as in Lincolnshire, cloth production did not cease (although there were changes in the types of cloths produced) but it moved from the town into the countryside: in particular to large villages like Bampton, Witney and Standlake. By the 14th century, the handful of merchants remaining in Oxford, like William of Bicester, transferred their activity from production to shipping raw wool – in William's case via London. In a petition of 1334, William himself was actually blamed for Oxford's decline during his time as mayor (for nine years between 1311 and 1332), but there is plenty of other evidence – falling rentals and waste burgage plots – which absolves him of personal responsibility. By 1388 three times as many workers were involved in Oxford's building trade as in textile manufacture which, by now, was aimed only at a very local market. Only Chesterfield among East Midlands towns increased cloth production through the 15th century, apparently facilitated by bipartite trade with Southampton, whereby wagons taking lead for export returned with imported dyestuffs.

As in the countryside, plague was also a factor in urban depopulation. Among burgage-holders in Lincoln, mortality in 1349 was 30 times greater than the average for the period between 1315 and 1376. In Leicester, Henry of Knighton wrote that over 1,400 people had perished in three city parishes in 1349 'and so in all the parishes in great multitude'. Perhaps 2,000 out of a total population of 6,000 died here. Yet, as in the countryside, plague struck an urban economy which was already faltering. Lincoln and Northampton had already plummeted down the ranking of English towns in terms of size and wealth, and Leicester, Nottingham, Bedford and Stamford quickly followed them. Smaller East Midlands towns suffered a similar marked decline. In a Royal charter of 1363 it was reported:

> The town of Huntingdon, as well as by mortal pestilences thereunto coming, is so impoverished and injured that the forth part of the town is not inhabited, and the remaining few have scarcely the wherewith to live.

Huntingdon's 13th-century prosperity had been largely due to the success of the international Easter fair at St Ives, from which it claimed a toll from goods bought and sold. Like Northampton, the fair at St Ives was primarily for cloth and, although it also traded in wool, it too was badly affected by the 14th-century restructuring of the cloth industry. The fair continued to be held, but by 1536 it was thought to be worth only £50 to the owners of the charter (Ramsey Abbey). In a world of such commercial contraction it is not surprising, perhaps, that 60 per cent of village markets in Lincolnshire disappeared during the 14th century. If the marts of the large towns could not survive, what chance did these gatherings stand?

By the 15th century, therefore, most East Midland towns presented a dramatic contrast with their 13th-century predecessors. Not only were there far fewer residents, but whole districts had simply been abandoned. They must have looked very much like the recently shrunken and deserted settlements in the countryside around. In Lincoln, settlement withdrew completely from all the suburbs except Wigford and Eastgate (near the cathedral), where the church had created its own micro-economy (Fig. 3.28). Regular attempts were made to stimulate economic activity in such deserted areas: new market rights were granted at Newport in Lincoln (1327), for example. But none stimulated regeneration. In Nottingham the subsidy roll of 1523–4 seems to show that parts of French Borough away from the great market place, as well as the eastern parts of English Borough, were very thinly populated. The population here had deserted outlying districts within the walls to cluster around the market place. In Leicester, Northampton and Derby the picture is broadly similar.

Lincoln's southern Wigford suburb would probably have been abandoned also, if it had not been for the concentration here of the city's economic elite. Wealthy merchants such as the de Sutton family had survived, as purchasers and exporters of raw wool. The de Suttons built a large new stone house in Wigford in the late 14th century. Though they lived in suburban palaces, the only significant urban employment such merchants offered was to warehousemen. Most cloth-manufacturing merchants of the 13th century had evolved into wool merchants by the 15th. William Wigston was such a figure in Leicester, and William Browne ('a merchant of a very wonderfulle bigness', according to Leland) was important in Stamford. Both founded hospitals in their communities. In Nottingham, the 1473 list of freeholders shows the town's wealth concentrated in the hands of a small number of merchants, although not all were in the wool trade. Here the Mellour family made themselves wealthy, using locally mined coal in their bell foundry. Their fortune eventually endowed the new Free School in 1513.

Fig. 3.28 Lincoln, seen from the south-west in the Buck Brothers' engraving of 1743. Lincoln was a sylvan city, dominated by trees rather than buildings.

EARLY MODERN STASIS

The pattern set for agriculture in the East Midlands during the later 14th century was followed for another four centuries. Although arable production did not cease, it lost the dominant role it had played in the 13th-century agricultural economy. On the wetter land (in the clay vales of Lindsey, for example) cattle became important in the 14th and 15th centuries, but on higher, drier land, corn and sheep, or sheep alone, became the mainstay of the rural economy. Wool remained the region's principal cash crop until the mid-16th century, when war in the Low Countries affected the stability of the trade, and the final loss of Calais in 1558 made shipping English wool to Flanders a more complicated business. But rather than revert to arable (for which the workforce had now dissipated) East Midlands livestock farmers turned to meat production, especially for the London market. Some graziers such as the Lee and Spencer families purchased manors with the specific intention of enclosing them and running sheep, cattle, or both, to be fattened for sale in London. Sir John Spencer's flock numbered between 13,000 and 14,000 between 1510 and 1520, and was scattered over many Northamptonshire manors, but he eventually centralised his enterprise at Althorpe. At about the same time, Robert Lee had enclosed all the common arable in Burston (Buckinghamshire), specifically to run sheep, and by 1620 his descendant Sir Henry Lee fattened 1,200 head on this land for the London mutton market, from which he expected an income of £522 per annum.

Whether the sheep were raised primarily for wool or meat, the impact on the resident population was similar. What happened to the villagers of Burston is not reported, but their houses were reduced to earthworks and only the manor house now remains. Extra pasture, needed for increasing sheep numbers, was always most conveniently obtained through enclosing parts, or all, of former common fields and laying them down to grass. But the manoeuvre was difficult if the common-field system was still working and numbers of villagers owning land there had been maintained. Such villagers knew that sheep-farming profits would go to the sheep owners and that many fewer workers would be needed. The Spencers employed only five shepherds to look after 10,000 sheep at Wormleighton, Northamptonshire, in 1577. Furthermore, sheep farming was a much less communal activity. Under the common-field system, the lowliest peasant had an equitable share in the best land along with the worst, whereas once the village land was divided up into private closes, it was likely that any land he was able to retain would be of poorer quality.

The landlord aiming at running sheep in a common-field parish would mount a campaign to acquire field strips, through purchase or exchange – a process called 'engrossment'. Such campaigns would eventually lead to the survival of only a single farm, surrounded by open grassland in which sheep could be run. The descendants of the original villagers, meanwhile, whose land in the common fields had been purchased, would be living in reduced circumstances in rented cottages on the marginal land. It was a well-recognised transformation, feared by the peasantry and viewed with suspicion by many establishment figures such as Sir Thomas More (1477/8–1535), who said:

> Your sheep, that were wont to be so meek and tame and so small eaters, now, as I hear say, be become so great devourers and so wild, that they eat up and swallow down the very men themselves. They consume, destroy and devour whole fields, houses and cities.

It is therefore not surprising that the slow process of enclosure was a constant source of friction in the countryside throughout the early modern period. Proposals to reorganise a community's common fields were sometimes met with resistance, which occasionally developed into more widespread insurrection (for example in 1548–9 and 1607). Such insurrections were sometimes followed by government inquiries into rural grievances, in which East Midlands cases usually figured prominently. Following the 1607 enquiry, for example, 31 per cent of the prosecutions of landowners for illegal enclosure came from the counties of Oxfordshire and Northamptonshire alone.

Many individuals prosecuted in 1607 were not members of great families. The majority were 'new men' whose families had been quietly prospering, often at the expense of their neighbours, for several generations. The Dissolution of the Monasteries in the late 1530s had ensured that much common-field land came onto the market, stimulating the land market for the following generation. Of 129 landed families paying tax to support the Lincolnshire militia in Armada year (1588), only 44 had appeared in similar lists in the 1550s. Such statistics imply that the number of families owning more than a few strips in the common field was increasing considerably, although because they were disproportionately influential, and because they tend to be recorded in documents, it is possible to exaggerate their overall numbers. In Lincolnshire, such landowners represented only between 1 per cent and 1.5 per cent of the population in 1603, although equivalent percentages in Northamptonshire and Leicestershire may have been somewhat higher.

In Wyboston, the engrossing Stocker family of the 14th and 15th century had effectively divided into two. The London branch, with all its power, wealth and social contacts, was killed off in the 'sweating sickness' of 1485, leaving the farming branch of the family at Wyboston running a large sheep flock in enclosed parts of the vill. It seems clear, however, that they were never able to acquire a sufficient holding in Wyboston's common fields to enclose them. This is probably because they never managed to acquire any manors with land in Wyboston, which passed instead through the hands of a bewildering variety of absentee landlords. Nevertheless, the Stockers were able to acquire some Wyboston land which had formerly belonged to St Neots Priory (which they were probably already renting before the Dissolution), and they were probably also renting a Wyboston manor house. For a century past they had called themselves 'gentlemen' but, to become enclosing landlords, they would have had to look outside the village of Wyboston. By the 1620s the head of the family, John Stocker (c. 1577–1659), was living in the depopulated village of Little Barford, 5km away across the Ouse, and in the 1650s his younger brother Richard (1579–1656) was the first of several who returned to live in the manor house at Beggary. Whether John or Richard was responsible for the larger areas of permanent pasture that were created at both places is not known.

From the landlord's perspective, the easiest communities to enclose were the assarts made originally in the 12th or 13th centuries where, as we have seen, the populations had often already dwindled during the agricultural crises of the 14th century. Like Beggary, they frequently had no integrated common-field system anyway and in such places the entire settlement, including its fields, could easily be converted into single sheep-walks by the engrossing farmer. Aunby (Kesteven), for example, was an assart community with its own field system, created in 1219, and here, by the 16th century, the Hatcher family had created a single farm surrounded by sheep-walk.

Enclosing well-established settlements like Lamport (Northamptonshire) was a tougher proposition. Although there had been some enclosure by the Cecil family, the village and common fields were still vigorous in 1560, when the manor was bought by John Isham, a typical woolman. His accounts show how, over a 20-year period, he set about systematically enclosing his own holdings, amalgamating them and adding to them by purchase. By 1583 he had enclosed enough land round the manor house to run a flock of over 1,500 sheep, which brought him an

Fig. 3.29 Lamport (Northamptonshire).
The Isham family, successful graziers and typical enclosing landlords of the 16th and 17th centuries, eventually gained control of Lamport. Ridge and furrow of the former common fields can be seen beyond the avenue south-east of the house. The earthworks of the former village street, and of properties facing onto it, extend westwards from the church. The fine rectory beyond the church dates from 1727–30, but most of Lamport's houses were rebuilt in the 1850s for estate workers. Although late 16th century in origin, Lamport Hall itself has been rebuilt twice; by John Webb (1650s) and by Francis and William Smith (in 1732–42). Its open parkland was laid out after 1761 and replaced geometrical garden layouts against the south and west fronts, both of which survive as earthworks.

income from butchery, wool and live sheep of some £300–£350 per annum (Fig. 3.29). The villagers were pushed to the margins of the enclosed land, although there were still common fields here in 1795.

In both Northamptonshire and Leicestershire, enclosure gathered pace through the 17th century: Hoskins thought that fully half the agricultural landscape of Leicestershire was redesigned at this time. At Great Stretton, for example, there were still 15 families in the time of Elizabeth I, but by 1800 there were only two houses alongside the church. Here, although enclosure had begun around 1500, the common-field agricultural system was not threatened until the mid-17th century, when the more prosperous peasants started amalgamating strips in the common fields and enclosing them to create discrete land holdings, enclosed with new dykes and hedges. By 1670 there were only five houses left, representing five successful peasant families during this period of intense competition. Similar self-promotion schemes among the peasantry are common. For example a 'Mr Peeps' (father of diarist Samuel) was only one of many such small independent landowners who fell foul of Brampton's manorial court (Huntingdonshire) in 1635 and again in 1644–5 for creating closes for his own stock on the common pasture.

Fig. 3.30 The extent of Parliamentary enclosure of the late 18th and 19th centuries *as compared with private enclosure in England and (inset) in Lincolnshire. The private enclosure is usually earlier in date.*

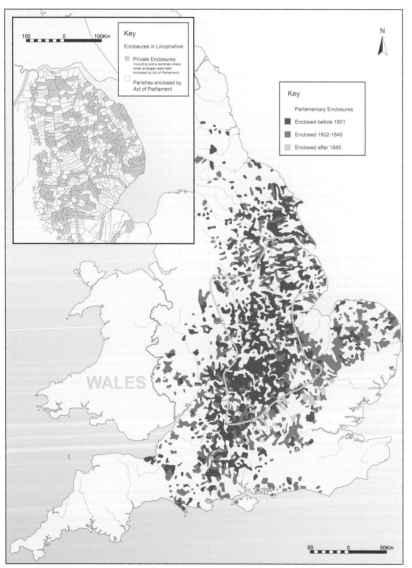

The government inquiry of 1607 found that 12 villages in Kesteven and 17 in Lindsey had been depopulated through enclosure for sheep pasture. Here much enclosure was undertaken by the Earl of Lincoln, who was reported to have enclosed 4,000 acres (1,600ha) between 1585 and 1616. In Lincolnshire a total of more than 5,300ha had been converted to sheep pasture. The Northamptonshire figure was less (4,350ha), but it represented a much larger proportion of the (far smaller) county. Equally large proportions of Leicestershire and Huntingdonshire had been enclosed by 1607. Lincolnshire was also top of the 1607 commissioners' list of numbers of farmhouses decayed, deserted or converted into cottages (1,292) but, again, there were more farmhouses in Lincolnshire initially. Although documents such as these show the landscapes of Northamptonshire, Leicestershire and north Buckinghamshire altered out of all recognition between the 14th and the 18th centuries, in Lincolnshire such total transformations were confined to certain parts of the county, such as the southern Wolds. In spite of the enclosures, Lincolnshire remained predominantly a county of arable production in common fields (Fig. 3.30).

In the southern Wolds, however, enclosure continued apace through the 17th century. Drayner Massingberd enclosed the village of South Ormsby after 1647 and Calceby in 1672, converting the former common fields of both into sheep-walks. In South Ormsby there had formerly been six farms and 11 cottages; by about 1800 there were only three farms but 24 cottages. As in so many places, the enclosures had reduced the number of independent farmers here (though no doubt improving their incomes), while greatly increasing the number of poor wage-labourers, whose land in the common fields had been sold or exchanged away. Like the Lees and the Spencers, the Massingberds aimed to produce meat rather than wool and in the 1650s and 1660s they began to fatten their sheep on Lindsey marshland, purchased for the purpose, at Huttoft and Ingoldmells, 15km further east. By the 1670s Massingberd was selling carcasses in London and in the 1680s flocks of live sheep were being driven down the long road from South Ormsby to Smithfield.

Beasts had always been driven to London, and into the regions' towns, for slaughter, but while the populations of most East Midlands towns had fallen, London continued to expand exponentially. Despite the fame of specialist regional markets like Nottingham's Goose Fair (probably first instituted in the late medieval period), more and more of the meat produced in the East Midlands was going direct to London and by the 17th century, herds and flocks from much further away than South Ormsby were passing along East Midlands roads. These huge migrant flocks and herds themselves posed a threat to common-field agriculture, as they would eat or trample crops as they passed through. At Hockcliffe, on Watling Street in southern Bedfordshire, the drovers' herds actually precipitated enclosure before 1620 because the common fields were 'spoiled and trodden with cattle, sheep, pack horses and hackneys, because of the nearness thereof to a high road … and because of the driving of cattle to and from Leyton …' (Bigmore 1979, 161–2). Some farmers, however, were able to take advantage of the drove roads, by providing overnight pasture for the animals and accommodation for the drovers: such pastures themselves would have been enclosed from the common fields or heaths. In Huntingdonshire in 1613 most of the parishes crossed by the drove road known as Bullock Lane (which continued Sewstern Lane southwards) still had common fields, but groups of closes along the road in Glatton parish are thought to represent such overnight pasture. Farms in such locations are sometimes named Coldharbour, and there are several with this name along Bullock Lane.

Once falling populations had relieved the pressure for settlement expansion, the rate of clearance of East Midlands' woodlands slowed. Even before 1300 the aristocracy had sought to seal off particular hunting grounds from the vast areas controlled by forest law – where they had to share their hunting grounds with the inhabitants' day-to-day activities – by creating exclusive hunting reserves or parks, where the environment could be managed for the maximum benefit of chase animals. The earliest such parks in the region were created in the 12th century (such as Beaumont Lees, cut out of Charnwood Forest by the Earls of Leicester), and dozens of such parks were cut out of the former forests from then until hunting changed its character in the 18th century. In Leicestershire, the two tracts subject to forest law (Charnwood/Leicester Forest and the fringes of Rutland Forest) gave way to at least 25 such enclosures, each surrounded by a park pale to keep the deer inside, and often equipped with specialised accommodation for the hunting parties. Much the most famous of these Leicestershire parks is at Bradgate, looking southwards from the slopes of Charnwood (see Fig. 1.5). It is, in effect, another type of enclosure, this time cut out of woodland rather than common fields, and more than 6.5km in circumference. It probably also dates from the 12th century, but its unusual post-medieval history lends the place magic today. Because the Earls of Stamford abandoned the house at its centre in 1720, the parkland was never converted into the setting for a great house. So, although formal gardens were laid out, the park itself retains its medieval hunting-park appearance, with standard trees in groups and singly and a varied undergrowth including clearings or 'lawns'. Similar 'enclosure' of land subject to forest law to create private parks went on across the region in the final medieval centuries. In Bedfordshire new parks were concentrated along the Greensand ridge, while in Huntingdonshire they lie mostly across the centre of the county where Bromswold Forest once was.

Hunting parks are particularly frequently met with in Northamptonshire, because such large areas of the county were designated as forest; John Speed showed 27 such parks on his map of 1610. Elizabeth and James I sold off Northamptonshire forest to the aristocracy to make money and much of this former crown land was used to create hunting parks. In 1604, however, Sir Robert Cecil devoted 900ha of the former royal forest of Rockingham around Brigstock to new assart, destroying the greenwood and creating 24 closes for agricultural purposes. Cecil's actions were revealed when Charles I revived forest law in the 1630s, and the Crown claimed that such land had only been sold on the assumption that it would continue to be used for hunting. But Sir Robert was simply treating the former royal forest in the same way as former common fields, or indeed common fenlands to the east. They were no longer community resources to be managed by the community, but private resources belonging to owners who had the right, indeed the duty, to make the most they could of them.

More typically, a large chunk of Whittlewood Forest around Wakefield Lodge was first emparked by the crown in the 17th century and subsequently sold to the Dukes of Grafton, who turned the hunting park into an ornamental landscape around their new house. Major new houses had always required an appropriate landscape setting, but the scale of landscape manipulation for such purposes had been increasing since the 13th century. Wakefield Lodge was one of many great houses in the forest areas created within newly enclosed parkland settings. Neville Holt (Leicestershire) and Goltho Hall (Lindsey) are early examples, and Houghton House (Bedfordshire) may be a later example: building there is said to have begun in 1615. Splendid settings for new houses were often created only by removing the villagers' houses among which the hall had developed. The Ishams did just this at Lamport (see Fig. 3.29), and the village of Quenby (Leicestershire) was probably removed to create a setting for the Ashby family's grand hall, reconstructed between 1620 and 1630. The desertion of Stapleford (Leicestershire) was connected with the rebuilding of the house around 1633, as was that at Wistow (Leicestershire) before 1641. Something similar happened at Canons Ashby (Northamptonshire), although the village here had been enclosed before by monastic landlords (Fig. 3.31), whilst at Woburn (Bedfordshire) the village was moved to a new location outside the newly enclosed hunting park by the Russell family before 1661. Although begun in the late 17th century, a similar process at Wimpole (Cambridgeshire) was not completed until the 1840s.

Between 1400 and 1700, then, the East Midlands landscape of open common fields and more open tracts of forest was gradually divided up, both physically into sheep-walks, agricultural closes and parks, and socially, between landowners and the landless. However, we must not exaggerate the impact of pre-Parliamentary enclosure. In 1697 Celia Fiennes observed a diverse landscape. Leicestershire was, she said, full of:

Fig. 3.31 A rich archaeological palimpsest is preserved in the beautiful park of the Dryden's late 16th-century mansion at Canons Ashby (Northamptonshire). *Behind the house (to the north-east) lie the earthworks of the deserted village of Ashby, with (to the south) the nave and tower of the Augustinian Priory church (founded c.1150). The monastic buildings lay to the south again and were converted into a mansion by Sir John Cope in the 1540s before his son-in-law shifted it to the present site.*

*… good corne of all sorts and grass, both fields and inclosures. You see a great
way upon their hills ye bottoms full of Enclosures, woods and different sort of
manureing and herbage, amongst which are placed many little towns …*

(Morris ed. 1949, 161)

Although enclosures were common by the 18th century, in many parts of the region
common fields were still the dominant feature of the landscape, and horsemen like
John Byng could ride for many miles without encountering a single hedge. In
Oxfordshire, Frank Emery estimated that no more than three in ten settlements had
been enclosed in the 16th and 17th centuries. In the whole of Bloxham hundred, for
example, only the villages of Drayton, Adderbury and Broughton had seen much
enclosure before the late 18th century. Peter Bigmore's view was that:

*The landscape of Bedfordshire and Huntingdonshire on the eve of …
parliamentary enclosure … must have been as devoid of trees and hedges as at
any time in the long history of its evolution, although the recent rapid removal
of hedgerows has come perilously close to reproducing that same landscape.*

(1979, 168)

EARLY MODERN TOWNS

Through the 15th and 16th centuries, many lesser towns quietly reverted to
villages. Derbyshire had 28 medieval market charters granted, but by the end of the
17th century only nine or ten were still in operation. Leicestershire had had 30, but
by 1693 there were just 12, and some of those were clearly ramshackle affairs – that
at Waltham-on-the-Wolds was described in 1670 as being 'very inconsiderable and
in a manner disused'. Many East Midlands towns fell back on their roles as market
centres for their local agriculture. Good examples are Banbury, Loughborough,
Market Harborough and Olney, where large 17th-century sheep markets attracted
buyers from a wide area for animals raised locally on upland enclosures and sheep-
walks. On the back of its market, at the focus of several major drove roads, Banbury
developed a new local textile industry. Woollen cloths called 'shag' or 'plush' were
woven here and finished cloths from the north and west were brought to the town
for dyeing – presumably with dyes traded at the market. Sheep were also the
principal commodity for sale at large markets in Horncastle and Sleaford, which
also stood in areas that had seen a maximum of private enclosure. Market
Harborough had a horse market, which specialised in plough animals, bred in the
district. Lutterworth and Uppingham were also flourishing agricultural markets
and, at the latter, Celia Fiennes saw dealing in corn, cattle and leather in 1697, all
produced locally. At Melton Mowbray the market attracted pigs from a wide area
around. These places were all towns of the second rank in 1600, however, and their
success, especially when compared with first-rank towns, demonstrates how
fundamentally the 14th-century economic crisis had realigned the regional
economy. The production and supply of complex manufactures over long
distances was simply no longer profitable – the successful towns were those that
concentrated on servicing their local communities. This replacement of an
international urban economy with a local one is reminiscent of the replacement of
the imperial cities of Roman Britain with late Roman small towns (p.51).

Between 1400 and 1700, the first-rank towns also tried to fill similar service roles
to their lesser counterparts. Derby, in particular, became an important regional
agricultural centre. But it had never been much larger than many of the second-
rank towns anyway, with only 1,300 inhabitants in 1524. Its relative success was
probably due to its concentrating not on manufactures but on its flourishing corn
market, with which it supplied most of Derbyshire (Fig. 3.32). Traffic in grain led to
a large brewing industry and by 1693 Derby had 76 malthouses, 120 alehouses and

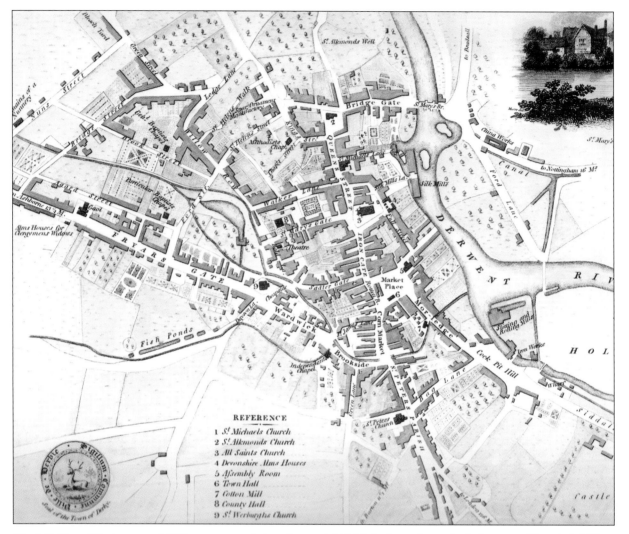

REFERENCE

1 St Michaels Church
2 St Alkmonds Church
3 All Saints Church
4 Devonshire Alms Houses
5 Assembly Room
6 Town Hall
7 Cotton Mill
8 County Hall
9 St Werburghs Church

Fig. 3.32 Map of Derby around 1800.
The market zone extended from Market Place along Irongate and Cornmarket Street to Brookside. Lombe's great mill stands in the Derwent and is marked 'silk mill'.

a population of around 6,000. It had no other major industry until Lombe's Mill was built on the Derwent in 1717–18 (p.162). Burton-upon-Trent's dominant 19th-century brewing industry also began in this way, with a large regional market concentrating on the buying and selling of barley grown in the Trent valley.

Leicester, with a population of 3,000 in the 1520s, was twice the size of Derby and Burton, however, and having lost its major indigenous industry there were many idle residents. As in Lincoln, the council attempted to provide make-work schemes, often involving woollen weaving and knitting, simply because the raw materials were still to hand even if their markets were now largely local. More than half those admitted to the freedom in the 16th century were involved in services – making clothing, food and drink. John Evelyn captured the atmosphere of the stagnant town in 1654: 'The Olde and Ragged Citty of Leicester, large and pleasantly seated but despicably built, the chimney flues like so many smiths' forges' (de Beer ed. 1959, 346–7). There was no longer a growing industry to drive expansion and to put the population to work. The static population figures reflect this – under 4,000 people in 1600 and fewer than 5,000 a century later. By 1700, however, the population was swelled by the first workers in Leicester's new frame-knitting industry. The first framework knitting machines were set up in the town in the 1670s and by 1714 it had between 500 and 600 frames, employing 7,600 people (although these figures must have included many knitters in the surrounding villages). With this new impetus the city expanded again for the first time since the 13th century, and by 1801 there were 18,000 inhabitants.

Lincoln was not so successful in its efforts to revive its former economic position. At its lowest point, probably towards the end of the 15th century, the city was no larger than a large village (with a population of 1,700 in 1445–6), with economic contacts and range to match. Now, only the cathedral's contacts with a wider world brought news and goods from outside the region. Its economic collapse since *c*. 1300 been more complete than many of its fellows, and by the 16th century there was insufficient money to undertake the most basic repairs. The council exaggerated only slightly in 1528 when they said that 'eight- or nine-tenths' of the town was 'in ruins'. John Evelyn called it 'ragged', like Leicester, and Defoe thought it 'ancient, ragged, decayed and still decaying' in 1726. Agricultural markets were held to attract peasants from the surrounding area, but they too were declining in value, despite the council's brigading of the disparate markets in a single street. What had been the East Midlands' regional capital in the 13th century had long been overtaken in size by the other shire towns, and by 1600 Lincoln was not even the largest town in Lincolnshire, having been overtaken by Boston, Stamford, perhaps Grantham (said to be 'rich and populous' in 1700), and also by Newark (a town of about 2,700 people in 1600). From the late 16th century onwards these towns had diversified from wool and cloth to general agricultural markets servicing surrounding farming communities. By 1650, if not earlier, Stamford, Grantham and Newark had all also made money from increasing coach traffic on the Great North Road. In the 18th century all three towns boasted competitively of the finest inns on the route to Scotland.

Northampton and Nottingham both managed the decline of the international wool market during the 16th century more successfully than Lincoln. Nottingham seems to have taken to the role of servicing its local agricultural region readily (a rental list of 1459 shows it full of chandlers, saddlers, lorrimers, smiths and similar trades, whose business was to keep agriculture working) and its population doubled between 1500 and 1660 (from 3,000 to 6,000). It is not clear why Nottingham should have succeeded, relatively speaking, where similarly placed Leicester failed. It did attract the patronage of several great aristocrats – the Earl of Kingston's heir and Lord Mansfield both built fine townhouses here in the 1650s and 1660s – and such figures do not seem to have been present in Leicester. Their houses clustered around Castlegate (where some can still be seen today), leading up to the ducal palace in the castle (Fig. 3.33). It is hard to believe, however, that these aristocrats made the critical difference between economic success and failure. Even so, most visitors thought the city a fine place to live. Leland, writing in the late 1530s, said: 'Nottingham is both a large town and well built for timber and plaster, and standeth stately on a clyminge hill'. To Celia Fiennes 150 years later, it was still 'the neatest town I have seen', whereas in the 1720s Defoe said it was 'one of the most pleasant and beautiful towns in England'. By the time the last two travellers visited, it had (like Leicester) re-entered the market for manufactures, and there were 1,200 knitting frames at work between 1732 and 1750. By 1768, Richard Arkwright had erected his first spinning mill operated by horses, in the English Borough, and several other industries had been established. Glassmaking had developed on the

Fig. 3.33 An impression of Nottingham's fine 17th- and 18th-century townscape, praised by so many contemporary visitors, can still be gathered in Castlegate. *The fine residence on the right is Newdigate House (of c.1675–80), opposite a terrace built about a century later.*

eastern side of the built-up area, alongside new pot-kiln banks, and brewing and industrial tanning were also important by the mid-18th century. New industries were attracting workers into the town in increasing numbers. The population was well over 10,000 by 1739, by which time the city contained some 2,000 dwellings.

By 1700, Northampton was also turning its manpower to manufacturing once again. The shoe industry, using local leather from cattle reared in those same enclosures noted by Celia Fiennes in valley floors, had become important by the mid-17th century. Thomas Fuller could write in 1662 that,

… the town of Northampton may be said to stand chiefly on other men's legs; where (if not the best) the most and the cheapest boots and stockings are bought in England.

(Freeman ed. 1952)

Boots and shoes now filled stalls, loaded three centuries earlier with cloths, in the great market place north of All Saints' church. Even the potential catastrophe of a great fire, which swept through most of the town in 1675, was quickly turned to advantage. There was enough money to rebuild much of the centre of the town in brick (and in the process stimulate a resilient brick trade) so that when Defoe visited in the 1720s he thought it 'the handsomest and best town in all this part of England' (Fig. 3.34).

Fig. 3.34 This steel engraving by Wilkinson (c.1820) shows the famous market square at Northampton, looking south towards All Saints Church. *Most of the buildings lining the square were rebuilt piecemeal following the fire of 1675.*

FURTHER READING

General

Astill & Grant (eds) 1988; Beckett 1988; Blair 1994 (Oxfordshire); Bourne (ed.) 1996 (Leicestershire); Briggs *et al.* 1986 (Oxfordshire); Campbell & Overton 1991; Court 1938; Darby (ed.) 1973, 1977; Dyer 1989a, 1994, 1996 (Warwickshire); Glasscock 1973; Godber 1984 (Bedfordshire); Gray 1915; Hallam (ed.) 1988; Harvey 1989; Hodgett 1975 (Lincolnshire); Holmes 1980 (Lincolnshire); Lloyd 1977; Miller (ed.) 1991; Phythian-Adams 1977 (Rutland); Platts 1985 (Lincolnshire); Sawyer 1998 (Lincolnshire); Short 2000; Thirsk 1957 (Lincolnshire), 1987, (ed.) 2000; Williamson 2003.

Villages and settlements

Allison *et al.* 1965 (Oxfordshire), 1966 (Northamptonshire); Aston *et al.* (eds) 1989; Beresford 1983; Beresford & Hurst (eds) 1971; Bond 1985 (Oxfordshire); Brown &

Foard 1998; Brown & Taylor 1989, 1991 (Bedfordshire); Dodgshon 1981; Dyer 1989b; Everson *et al.* 1991(Lindsey); Foard 1978 (Northamptonshire); Fox 1989 (Leicestershire), 1992, 2000; Hadley 2000; Hall 1989, 1995, 2001; Hatcher 1977 (Black Death); Hooke (ed.) 1985, (ed.) 1988; Hoskins 1946 (Leicestershire); Leadham 1897 (Nottinghamshire); Lewis *et al.* 1997; Roberts 1977, 1987; Roberts & Wrathmell 2002; Rowley 1981; Seebohm 1915; Taylor 1975, 1977, 1983, 1995; Thirsk 1973, 1987; Unwin 1983 (Nottinghamshire); Williamson 2003.

Forests and parks

Cantor 1970–1, 1976–7 (Leicestershire), 1980 (Rutland), 1982, 1983; Foard 2001 (Rockingham Forest); Pettit 1968; Squires & Humphrey 1987(Charnwood); Stamper 1988; Taylor 1998; Watkins 1993 (Arden); Woodward 1982 (Oxfordshire); Young 1979.

Towns

Aston & Bond 1976; Baker *et al.* 1979 (Bedford); Barley 1949 (Newark), 1969 (Nottingham); Beresford 1967; Brown 1970 (Leicester); Clark 1984; Clarke & Ambrosiani 1995; Courtney 1998 (Leicester); Dodd (ed.) 2003 (Oxford); Dunn 1977 (Huntingdon); Fasnacht 1954 (Oxford); Foard 1995 (Northampton); Green 1977 (Godmanchester); Hall 2001; Harvey 1969 (Banbury); Hodges 1982; Holt & Rosser (eds) 1990; Laughton & Dyer 1999; Lobel 1975 (Cambridge); Rodwell (ed.) 1975 (Oxfordshire); Rogers 1965 (Stamford); Schofield & Vince 1994; Vince 2003b, 2003c (Lincoln); Williams 1984.

Individual sites and areas

Addyman 1965 (Eaton Socon); Beresford 1975, 1987 (Goltho); Croft & Mynard 1993 (Milton Keynes); Foster 1994 (Brigstock); Holderness 1972 (South Ormsby); Jackson & Foard 1993–4 (Yardley Hastings); Orwin 1967 (Laxton); Parry 1994 (Raunds); Steane & Bryant 1975 (Lyveden).

The Individual Returns?
Industrial and Modern
Settlement, *c.*1750–2000

INNOVATION AND THE INDIVIDUAL

Between about 1750 and 1850, with the impact of parliamentary enclosure, the East Midlands landscape experienced greater changes than at any time since the 10th century. With the survival now of copious documentation, we can see that these changes were aspects of even greater movements in society. They were, it seems, an inevitable concomitant of industrialisation and the growth of a property-owning democracy. The reorganisation of the countryside represented another agricultural revolution.

Since the 14th century, enclosing landlords had been demonised for destroying communal farming systems, and replacing them with ones allegedly aimed at benefiting landowners at the peasantry's expense. The peasantry had frequently appealed to government to preserve them from such rapaciousness, and government had occasionally fined landowners. Parliamentary enclosure seemed, however, to give wickedness official sanction. Some viewed this new and systematic wave of enclosure as the legalised theft of the peasantry's common rights; the donation of their economic livelihoods by officialdom to a much smaller, newly created, class of fortunate tenant farmers and landlords. No one put it better than John Clare, writing in the 1820s in Helpston, north of Peterborough:

> *Inclosure came and trampled on the grave*
> *Of Labours Rights and left the poor a slave …*
>
> (The Mores)

Unlike many earlier enclosures, which were frequently undertaken by single owners in the more marginal common-field systems (often creating 'closed' villages), enclosure by act of Parliament was certain to be controversial as it affected precisely those relatively large rural communities (usually 'open' villages) where common-field agriculture had worked well (*see* Fig. 3.30). It appeared to be unilateral action, taken by the most substantial figures in a community, sometimes including the clergy, against their poorer neighbours. The holders of more extensive lands in the common fields had to be persuaded that exchanging their strips for a compact farm, over which they would have individual control, would be to their advantage:

> *Each little tyrant with his little signs*
> *Shows where man claims earth …*
>
> (The Mores)

But for the majority, who had little or no land in common fields, the small measure of economic control they had held over their lives was removed.

Nor was it just members of the educated working class, like John Clare, who expressed their anger. John Byng, a blue-blooded aristocrat wrote: 'As a sportsman I hate enclosures, and as a citizen, I look on them as greedy tyrannies of the wealthy few, to oppress the indigent many' (Andrews ed. 1934, 7). Byng's anger was at least partly because the new enclosure walls and hedges made the traditional style of hunting obsolete. He was accustomed to pursuing game on horse-back across open heaths and former forest areas which, after enclosure, was no longer straightforward:

But paths to freedom and to childhood dear
A board sticks up to notice, 'no road here'.
… the very birds should learn to know
When they go there, they must no further go.

(The Mores)

Not only did the new field boundaries place difficult obstacles in the horseman's way, but the game animals themselves had lost much of their cover during the landscape's re-organisation. Shortly after enclosure, therefore, landowners and hunters urgently promoted new plantations to provide new cover for game animals, often given contemporary sounding names like 'Botany Bay', planted *c.*1790 near Tilton (Leicestershire). The land chosen for such 'coverts' was often marginal (disturbed land above a tunnel on the Melton Mowbray to Nottingham railway, at Grimston Gorse, for example) and tolerant, rapidly growing, tree species were selected to provide thick underbrush. A further problem for the post-enclosure huntsman was that the former heath was now demonstrably owned by a particular individual. It had been 'privatised'; individual farmers had become autonomous business units, be they tenant or landlord. No longer able to call on fellow strip-holders for informal help, or blame them if things went wrong, the farmer was now on his or her own, to prosper or to go bust according to his or her own energies and talents. To maintain their welcome the huntsmen had to present themselves to such farmers, less as sportsmen, more as a vermin-control service.

If holders of the new enclosure farms had become their own masters, however, so had their labourers. Now they were free of traditional bonds and informal patronage within the village, they too could take command of their earning power and sell their labour where it would achieve the highest price. Unfortunately John Clare was not unique in being defeated by this challenge. There is no more poignant image of the destructive impact of late 18th-century capitalism on the landscape and its inhabitants than the lonely poet tending the limekiln among the earthworks of the deserted village of Pickworth (Rutland) in 1817. Pickworth had been enclosed in the 17th century, leaving only the church standing (Fig. 3.35), and the

Fig. 3.35 'There's not a foot of ground we daily tread … but holds some fragment of the human dead.' *The houses of modern Pickworth (Rutland) represent a recent re-occupation; the medieval village (whose earthworks survive around the centrally placed manor house) was deserted by the 18th century, the church was ruined and landowners' incomes came from lime-kilns along the busy drove-road. John Clare found employment here in 1817 after leaving his native Helpston following enclosure, and wrote the lines above. Though the quarry scarp is still visible, the remains of the kilns themselves have mostly been swept away by the modern houses and gardens.*

new owners had seen the potential for converting the rubble of the former common-field community's cottages into lime to improve the new fields of isolated enclosure farms around. They had also taken advantage of displaced and destitute former common-field villagers, like Clare, to work the kilns. Lime burning was once a communal activity, undertaken by the whole community on the village common; now it was an opportunity for the new breed of farmer to make a profit at the expense of both neighbouring farmers and of the itinerant poor.

As a more complex, market-oriented society developed, large numbers followed John Clare off the land to sell their labour in manufacturing and service industry in the towns – where they might make a more profitable living than in their home villages. By 1901, two in every three people in Leicestershire lived in a town, whereas only one in six had done so in 1700. But unlike some northern industrial towns expanding at this time, into which labourers flooded from far-flung parts of Britain, immigrants to Leicester, Nottingham and Lincoln during the 18th and 19th centuries came predominantly from surrounding villages.

This flow of people from the land combined with national and international economic trends to undermine the dominant social position of local aristocrats in the towns. Hitherto towns had been centres servicing the countryside immediately around and, consequently, local landowners had a dominant voice in their development. But between 1750 and 1850 the new industrial-scale manufacturers, now established in the towns, applied themselves to other markets, both national and international. As a direct result, the towns' new masters became shareholders in London, and customers were scattered around the world. In the East Midlands the greatest change was one of urban industrial scale. There had been ironworking in Lincoln, for example, before 1800, but during the 19th century it expanded from an industry of a few dozen self-employed artisans serving the local market to one employing an industrial proletariat of tens of thousands, serving an international market. In a few towns (like Stamford, for example) the rural aristocracy managed to retain their dominant position and manage limited industrial expansion for their own benefit. But in many East Midlands towns, industrial development was simply too rapid, diverse and hungry for cash, and rural landlords were replaced as councillors by new generations of self-made men.

It was not the presence of industry *per se* that made towns expand, then. After all, there had been ironworking in Lincoln since the Romans, frame-knitting machines in Leicester and Nottingham since the late 17th century, and leatherworking in Northampton for many centuries. Rather it was the construction of great factories, mostly in the 19th century, that caused new towns to be founded and old ones to expand. Much of the machinery powering the industries was invented long before the first signs of major expansion amongst East Midlands' towns. It was the scale and quantity of machines that was novel. Such scale and quantity were only made possible by harnessing new power sources. The distinguishing feature of new East Midlands factories was their bringing together of larger numbers of larger machines powered by water or steam. It was the search for power that brought the first factories to our region. To the Derwent valley, for example, where communities of the first industrial generation were powered by water. The finest surviving group of mill-workers' houses is at Milford, founded in 1781 by the Strutt family, but the earliest had been established in central Derby by Thomas Lombe around his new water-powered silk mill on an island in the Derwent in 1718–22. It is claimed that this was 'the earliest factory in England'.

But this early use of water power on the Derwent associates it with the North, not the East Midlands. Similarly, early use of water power for woollens manufacture around Witney, at the other end of our region, associates the town with the early Gloucestershire textile industry (*see* Fig. 5.10). These new water-powered industrial communities depended on fast-flowing streams, but the gentle slopes and slow-flowing rivers of the Midland counties seem to have been less easily adapted to power factories. It would take the harnessing of steam power to drive the machinery halls, before Nottingham, Leicester and Lincoln could join Derby and Witney in the list of major regional industrial centres. Although steam engines were available for such purposes from the end of the 18th century, the coal to power them had to be brought into such towns. Both Leicester and Nottingham had access to nearby coal delivered by cart and canal, but it was not until the railways made coal transport cheap and quick that these towns could really join in the industrial prosperity seen in the new cities of Lancashire, Yorkshire and the North East. More so than Leeds, Manchester and Newcastle, Leicester, Nottingham, Northampton and Lincoln are industrial cities of the second generation – the age of the railways.

COUNTY TOWN OR INDUSTRIAL WEN?

Until the railway arrived in 1846, Lincoln was a small city with little manufacturing. Economy and politics had been dominated by a small group of families with local business interests, typically the wholesale or retail marketing of the county's agricultural products. These activities placed them in subordinate (though not powerless) relationships with local landowners. The Ellisons, who during the late 18th century dealt in agricultural produce, had identified new markets among the expanding populations of West Riding manufacturing towns. They invested heavily in water transport and soon had enough capital to set up a banking empire. The Ellisons were not manufacturers, however, and they employed only a small urban workforce, quite unlike the industrialists who arrived with the railways. Railways brought with them the capacity to manufacture agricultural machinery in Lincoln, remote from sources of water power, iron and coal. Several investors arrived intent on converting existing small-scale workshops into a mechanised engineering industry. These new men, including the Claytons, Shuttleworths, Fosters and Joseph Ruston, were neither from distinguished families, nor (mostly) from Lincolnshire; they came to Lincoln because they saw an investment opportunity for their capital. Joseph Ruston, for example, was of Cambridgeshire farming stock, but in 1856 he found himself working in a cutlery firm in Sheffield and (so the legend goes) he heard at his local barber's that a small metal-bashing company employing 25 men in Lincoln was looking for an injection of capital. Ruston hurried to purchase the company, and within 20 years he had built a multinational engineering combine worth £500,000 in 1889 and employing a workforce of nearly 3,000. Ruston's story, though perhaps more colourful, was not markedly different from those of dozens of men (they were typically men) who turned the same trick in East Midlands towns in the period between 1750 and 1950.

Lincoln's common fields, north of the town, had been enclosed in 1803, while to the south of the city much of the land was also in private hands. Consequently large land reserves were available for expansion to house the new industrial workforce, as the city's population rose from about 17,000 in 1851 to about 60,000 in 1911. In this respect Lincoln was similar to Leicester and presented a marked contrast with Nottingham. Industrial Leicester and Nottingham were like rival siblings, similar to each other in many respects, yet always emphasising their differences. Both towns were production centres for hosiery and other knitted products before the end of the 17th century (pp.88–9), yet their physical development through the 18th and 19th centuries was markedly different. The differences between them were rooted in their internal politics. Leicester's ruling oligarchy promoted the enclosure of the town's common fields. They commanded enough support among holders of common-field rights to enclose West Field in the late 17th century and East Field in 1764. These large tracts were therefore already in the hands of individual owners, who could then be persuaded to sell land to house an expanding population of industrial workers. The population increased from 6,000 in 1750 to 17,000 in 1801, and spacious housing was laid out on the newly enclosed, well-drained, gently sloping land west, east and north of the walls. Attempts to enclose the South Field in the 1750s failed, but the final extinction of common rights here in 1804 stimulated a new period of speculative house-building which lasted for 30 years. By 1841, there were more houses in Leicester than there had been in the entire county in the 16th century.

Nottingham, on the other hand, was not able to develop in the same relaxed and ambitious way. Like Leicester, Nottingham had not expanded much beyond its medieval walls by 1750, but here enclosure of the town fields by larger landlords was fiercely resisted by the commoners, and opposition was supported by the ruling oligarchy. Consequently the population drawn into Nottingham during the city's expansion between 1750 and 1850 was housed in increasingly overcrowded conditions in the ancient centre, where the earliest recorded back-to-back housing was present by 1785. Unlike Leicester, the town failed to develop contiguous suburbs. Nottingham's politics therefore forced new industries, such as brick-making, pottery and glass production, into outlying townships and villages away from the centre, both in the Trent valley at Carrington, Lenton and Sneinton, and at Arnold, Basford, Bulwell and Radford. Even as late as 1840 Nottingham's town centre remained encircled by its common fields and, although the population had increased from 11,000 in 1750 to over 60,000 in 1850, the town's footprint had increased by less than one-third. It is not surprising that living conditions in the centre became a national scandal and in 1845 the Health of Towns Commissioners' *Report* stated that:

> … *nowhere else shall we find so large a mass of inhabitants crowded into courts, alleys and lanes as in Nottingham, and those too of the worst possible construction. Here they are so clustered upon each other; court within court, yard within yard, and lane within lane, in a manner to defy description … some parts of Nottingham [are] so very bad as hardly surpassed in misery by anything to be found within the entire range of our manufacturing cities.*

Leicester, on the other hand, was 'spread over an unusual extent of ground in proportion to its population'.

In Nottingham, the common-field right-holders were finally overcome in 1845, an Enclosure Act was passed, and substantial areas of common field north of the medieval town were rapidly developed for housing. By 1900 only the areas designated as public open space by the Corporation in 1845 (the Arboretum, Corporation Oaks and Robin Hood's Chase) had not been built over. In Leicester the population had gradually spread outwards from the historic centre and eventually the factories moved out to be with them. But in Nottingham the reverse occurred. Densely occupied slums within the old town rapidly decanted into the new suburbs after 1845, leaving large spaces in the town centre which were recolonised by factories and commercial establishments. Around the ancient parish church of St Mary, in particular, a new commercial and manufacturing district was constructed between about 1850 and 1914.

Ironically perhaps, in the light of what was to happen later, the well-to-do of 17th- and 18th-century Nottingham had lived in spacious townhouses, whose quality had been noticed by many travellers (*see* Fig. 3.33). But many such houses were overwhelmed during the housing shortage within the medieval walls before 1845, and most of the well-to-do moved a mile to the west, putting the Castle Rock between themselves and the seething city. Here they occupied an early private estate, The Park, laid out at the foot of the Rock, where the earliest terraces were built in 1827. The estate was comprehensively replanned in 1851 with large, rather old-fashioned houses imitating the crescents and squares of Regency London, designed by T C Hine, the Duke of Newcastle's surveyor (Fig. 3.36). The duke himself also evacuated the castle following its destruction by a mob of *sans-culottes*,

enraged by the defeat of the 1831 Reform Bill in the House of Lords. But personal disaster did not dissuade the duke from investing in the city. Above all, he seized the opportunity created by enclosure in 1845 to parcel up his estate at Mapperley, 2km north-east of the centre, and sell lots for development by the new middle classes, who now flocked to the town to capitalise on its booming new industries. Before the First World War this was where the cigarette magnate J D Player lived. Player's architect was Arthur Marshall, and his lavish neo-Elizabethan villas in Mapperley quietly compete for attention with Hine's gloomy-looking Gothic houses.

In more tranquil Leicester, founders of industrial dynasties, like the Coltmans and the Parrs, built fine brick townhouses closer to the town centre, in The Newarke and Friar Lane, for example. In the 1820s, the *Leicester Journal* offered 'plots suitable for building genteel residences' in the exclusive suburban development to the south, now known as New Walk. As the century progressed, the well-to-do sought the higher ground, south-east of the medieval town between the London and Humberstone roads and overlooking the city centre: the area is still dominated by leafy streets and prosperous brick villas (Fig. 3.37). In Lincoln also, but on a smaller scale, Ruston, Clayton and several other industrial barons staked out an exclusive suburb in the bosky quarter between Wragby Road and the cliff edge, overlooking the forest of smoking chimneys in the plain below. The lead given by such figures was followed throughout the next century by many members of Lincoln's growing middle class, who huddled together, as if for reassurance, around the industrialists' villas. The most famous, and still the most intact, of these well-to-do suburbs in the region grew up on agricultural land belonging to St John's College north of the extra-mural market place in St Giles parish, Oxford. Begun in the 1850s as a speculative venture, north Oxford's combination of architect-designed villas (many by local architect

TOP: ***Fig. 3.36 The Park, Nottingham, was a middle-class enclave laid out by the Duke of Newcastle on the Castle's former hunting park in the 1820s.*** *The earliest houses were neo-classical terraces ranged along the hill side (in the trees) but, from the 1850s, large architect-designed villas were laid out in symmetrical patterns around the central amenities seen here. Urban developments of this type became the inspiration for much larger working-class suburban developments in the 20th century, like Leicester's Braunstone estate.*

ABOVE: ***Fig. 3.37 The New Walk, lined with distinctive trees,*** *was laid out as a promenade in 1785 for Leicester's bourgeoisie along the boundary of the city's South Field and, to that extent, was a middle-class encroachment onto the working agricultural landscape. After common rights in South Field were extinguished in 1804, fine villas sprang up in new side-streets, 'enclosing' the promenade itself. By 1847 it was 'the only solely respectable street in Leicester' heading uphill away from the walled city, where Victoria Park would be established in 1883.*

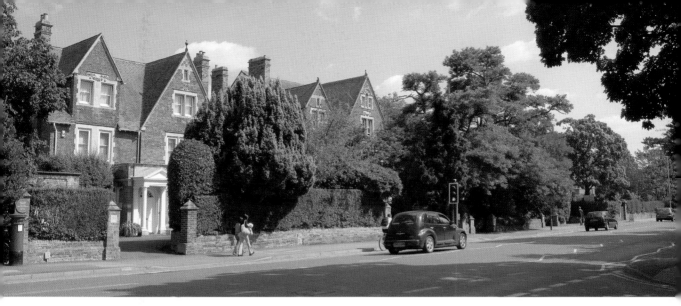

William Wilkinson), sweeping vistas and mature trees, is the epitome of the well-to-do Victorian suburb, and residents still fight fiercely to keep it that way (Fig. 3.38).

The new populations of working people attracted to Lincoln in the second half of the 19th century were rapidly accommodated in large areas of new terraced housing built with locally made fiery red bricks, and wood and Welsh slate imported by railway. They were laid out in rectilinear blocks, with generous streets, often built by, or in conjunction with, the works' owners. Indeed their aspirations for their workforces outstripped the council's ability to provide public services. The new housing estates on Monk's Road, Burton Road and Bargate Close were all provided with both water and sewage infrastructure, but the council was quite unable to make it work effectively. In 1870 a Home Office inspector reported that 'there is not a town in England that offers a more flagrant instance of the dereliction of … duty than the city of Lincoln' and, even though there were improvements in the following decade, the city also endured a major cholera outbreak in 1904–5, traced to the water supply. Having been inaugurated as early as 1876, the city's sewage network was not finally completed by the council until 1912.

A map of Leicester made in 1828 shows many streets of workers' housing under construction around the old centre, gobbling up the former common fields to the north and east. They were urgently needed, as the population grew by 20,000 in the 1850s and 1860s, reaching 210,000 by 1901. During Victoria's reign houses were constructed in huge new estates in St Margaret's parish and towards New Humberstone. Leicester's new houses, on all four sides of the city now, were mostly of good quality. Bricks were made from the local Liassic clays exposed in the valley sides (initially in South Field), while after 1840 Welsh slates were brought in via the town's new connection to the railway network. In 1883 South Wigston was founded as a new industrial suburb, complete with factories, houses and churches. The ambition of the new settlement was considerable. W G Hoskins remarked that, on a foggy November afternoon in the 1950s, the sight of South Wigston was 'an experience one is glad to have had'. The long, uniform frontages of bright red brick houses lining the street grid, with breaks in the façades provided only by the more showy factory entrances, seemed to him to represent the very essence of English provincial life. There was, he said, something 'profoundly moving' about it.

In Nottingham, houses built in the late 19th century on the land released by the 1845 Enclosure Act were also of a good standard and, almost as if to make amends for the city's earlier shocking state, the corporation now enforced detailed building regulations and installed forward-looking water supply and sewerage schemes. Its new attitude was symbolised by the appointment of a borough surveyor as early as 1859, the wonderfully named Marriott Ogle Tarbotton (who is also remembered for having been the first such officer in England) and, with its new team of engineers,

Fig. 3.38 Comfortable villas of the late 19th century in north Oxford provided respectable accommodation for the city's burgeoning bourgeoisie and their servants. Although many such properties are now subdivided, a strong local community remains and struggles to ensure that redevelopment here is 'in keeping'.

the corporation began a campaign of civic projects. It extended its boundaries (1877), replaced the old Trent Bridge (1871), converted the shell of the ducal palace into a city art gallery and museum (1875), bought out the gas supply company (1874) and constructed an integrated water supply and sewage system (from 1872). In 1875–7 Nottingham Corporation was one of the first to experiment with genuine 'council housing' through the construction of Victoria Dwellings on Bath Street – a forbidding block of 82 tenements, which represented the most advanced social housing in the Empire (Fig. 3.39). By 1888, a quarter-century of civic improvement was symbolised, in the manner of northern industrial oligarchies, by the planning of a new guildhall. Although a latecomer to effective local government, in 1897 Nottingham was awarded the enhanced status of 'county borough' as part of the Diamond Jubilee celebrations. It was thought at the time, probably with some justification, that the borough's improved condition had also been responsible for the sudden diversification of its industrial base. In 1850 Nottingham had been largely dependent on the textile trade, but by 1900 bicycle and cigarette manufacture, chemicals and pharmaceuticals all employed many more people. These new industries were located alongside their workforces, not in the centre of the town, but in suburbs similar to South Wigston, at Radford and Lenton (John Player Cigarettes), Radford (Raleigh Cycles) and Beeston (Boots Pharmaceuticals).

Leicester's water supply of wells and conduits had been comprehensively replaced a whole generation earlier, in 1853–5, by a piped water supply leading from a new reservoir at Thornton. A general sewage system, with a pumping and drying station near Leicester Abbey, was inaugurated two years later and, by 1874, the corporation was rewarded by the lowest death rate per thousand (23.3) of any large city in the country. Derby Corporation also provided water and sewage early and efficiently. In 1849 the workers in the new 'railway town' on Litchurch marshes lived in overcrowded enclosed courts, 352 of which had no drainage, sanitation or water supply of any sort. But by 1851 the Corporation had opened a new waterworks: a sewage works was constructed in the following decade and, as in Nottingham, the corporation enforced strict new building regulations regarding water supply and sanitation. By 1885 Derby had achieved the lowest death rate per thousand (18.1) in the region. Derby is also reputed to have opened the earliest public park in England at Osmaston Road in 1839, designed by J C Loudon and donated to the town by the industrialist Joseph Strutt.

Compared with Leicester and Nottingham, Northampton grew slowly before the railways came. Even so, the population doubled (from 7,020 to 15,351) between 1801 and 1831, a growth fuelled partly by military orders for boots and shoes during the Napoleonic wars. By 1831 fully one-third of men living in the town were shoemakers. Boots and shoes, made in a thousand backyard workshops in the town, were exported to Weedon and other barracks by canal, although they had to be carted to wharves at Gayton (8km south-west) before the Grand Union spur arrived in the town in 1815. Population figures jumped with the canal's arrival – rising in the 1820s by 42 per cent – and other industries were attracted. There were three iron foundries by the 1830s, for example, and many brickyards capitalised on the Nene valley clays. But footwear's economic dominance was increased when the railway finally arrived in 1845 and by 1871, 43 per cent of the male population worked in the industry. Like Leicester, Nottingham and Lincoln, Northampton expanded across the former suburban orchards and common fields, especially to the west and north, where an enclosure Act of 1779 had extinguished common rights (Fig. 3.40). To the east, the land was developed by a single speculator, Thomas Grundy, who had established both a brickyard and Northampton's first building society and was therefore

Fig. 3.39 Victoria Dwellings, Bath Street, Nottingham. *Recently refurbished, this large apartment block stands today as a reminder that, after an uncertain start, Nottingham became one of the most dynamic of Victorian City Corporations. It was erected to house council workers and their families in modern conditions in 1876–7 and designed by the architectural firm Bakewell & Bromley.*

well placed to take a profit at each stage of house purchases. He promoted six streets of villas and middle-class housing along the Wellingborough Road. Grundy was supported by the council in his single-handed attempt to plan the development of Northampton: throughout the 1840s, 1850s and 1860s they stipulated that only 'high-class' housing could be built south of the Billing Road. As in all the other towns we have looked at, then, the layout of Northampton reflected precisely the rigid social stratification of Victorian England.

Until the 1850s, shoemakers had some autonomy over production in their backyard workshops, collecting their raw materials along with their wages from overseers once a week, and returning the following week with finished boots and shoes to collect more leather. From the 1850s, however, some of the various shoemaking processes became mechanised, and the new machines were housed in factories driven by steam engines burning coal brought by railway. In 1875 the *Northampton Mercury* exaggerated in saying that backyard shoemakers' workshops had become a thing of the past and henceforth 'the homes of their workers would be for resting and not for work'. Production in domestic workshops was becoming rarer, however, and factories were thicker on the ground, but they could still be found as late as 1939. Even so, by 1901 Northampton had become a typical East Midlands town, of red-brick workers' terraces intermingled with factories, and with a middle-class ghetto to the east. Although the population had reached 87,021, this was small compared to Leicester and Nottingham. Here too, the council had been active in promoting water and sanitation schemes (a secure water supply had been established by 1847), and also in enforcing building regulations. Northampton's terraces were usually built with party walls extending upwards through the roof, for example, to reduce the impact of fire.

In many ways 19th-century Oxford stood apart from other East Midlands towns. Its economy had always been based on an uncomfortable mixture of the local market place and the international exchange of learning. In the 17th century the university had stated:

> ... the towne of Oxford lyes out of the road; and is in no way usefull to the publique by any trade or manufacture. It serves only for the intertainment of Schollers, and the Townesmen have no other possible meanes of subsistence but by the Universitie.
>
> (quoted by Snow 1991, 14).

Throughout most of the 19th century, the university struggled to keep it that way, fiercely opposing, for example, the construction of Great Western Railway repair workshops on meadows west of the city. They had cast themselves as Canute, but the attitude explains why it was suppliers of the town's own market who responded most positively to industrialisation. As in many market towns, Oxford's local service industries, brick-making and metal-founding, expanded

Fig. 3.40 The common fields north-east of Northampton, where the racecourse survived well into the 20th century (now the recreation ground top left), were overwhelmed c. 1870–90 by the small factories and terraced housing of the boot-and-shoe industry. The factories are often on corner plots. With their many subtle distinctions of plan and decoration, houses were frequently rented from factories, and skilled workers made boots in enlarged back rooms or in characteristic – and increasingly rare – back-to-back workshops at the ends of gardens.

exponentially with the arrival of the railway in 1844 and ironworks such as Lucy and Co of Jericho became quite large, employing over 600 workers in the 1950s. However, none of these 19th-century industries approached the pre-eminent position of the university as an employer within the town, and indeed some of the industrial development was stimulated by the university itself, through enterprises like the large printing works, whose new steam-driven plant (of 1826–30) was also established in Jericho, like Lucy's, in order to secure coal supplies brought by canal. Compared with Leicester, or even Lincoln, only small areas of working-class housing were laid out in Oxford, in areas like St Clement's, Jericho and St Ebbe's, to accommodate the new industrial workers.

It was only later that one of Oxford's many small backyard metalworkers – William Morris – graduated from repairing students' bicycles to their new automobiles. In 1912 Morris purchased a former military college at Temple Cowley (then a small community 4km from the city centre) and began assembling motorcars. The first buildings were nothing more than a lightweight roof suspended over the former parade ground, but they were well placed to take advantage of the railway, through which Morris imported components (none of which were made in Oxford initially) and exported the finished cars. By the 1970s the site occupied 75ha and employed 30,000 (Fig. 3.41). The effect on the physical shape of Oxford was as profound as the impact on its social mix. The town's entire centre of gravity was shifted to the south-west, with large estates of workers' housing being laid out in Cowley between the wars, occupied by a substantial industrial working class drawn from other parts of England, something Oxford had had little experience of hitherto. Over 3,000 council houses were built between the wars, although double that number were provided by private developers, including the Morris company itself.

After 1945 the Morris workforce was swelled by Commonwealth immigrants, and by 2001 12.9 per cent of the city's population was from an identifiable ethnic minority. Although Pakistanis and Bangladeshis, who came to work here in the 1960s and 1970s, constitute the largest single group (at nearly 3 per cent), there are also large Chinese and Indian communities. These diverse peoples have brought their cuisines with them, and they make Oxford among the most exciting places to eat in England. The south Asian communities, in particular, lend an exoticism to the modern Cowley Road, while west Oxford has welcomed the Chinese. Motor manufacturing, however, is no longer the dominant employer (Cowley works now employs fewer than 5,000), and the university is determined not to exclude itself from the new technological revolution in the way it did in the 19th century. High-technology firms have been established in the city in astonishing numbers. In the late 1980s dozens of new businesses were being started up in Oxford every week, and the number of such businesses in the city was growing at the rate of 26 per cent per year – faster than anywhere else in England. The workers in this latest industrial revolution have snapped up the small terraced houses put up for workers of the first, in

Fig. 3.41 Cowley works, south-east of Oxford, on 12 June 1969. In 1925, *dependence on the railway line (crossing the site from south-west – top – to north-east) pulled the core of Morris' automobile assembly works, with its long parallel 'north-light' roofs, away from the former Military College, 500m north-west. This enormous works attracted much of Oxford's 20th-century house-building into this quarter of the city. West of the railway lie the curving avenues of the newly-built Blackbird Leys estate.*

Jericho, Osney Island and the Cowley Road, and have pushed house prices in the city as high as anywhere in England.

Leicester, always a town interested in novel ways of doing things, was quick to explore new types of housing provision in the 20th century. In 1893 a co-operative society was formed around the workforce at Anchor Boot and Shoe, aimed at raising enough share capital to build houses for its members, and between 1907 and 1915 about 100 houses were built on the outskirts of New Humberstone. A similar scheme was floated at Swanpool in Lincoln slightly later, but was markedly less successful (Fig. 3.42). This type of housing development was soon superseded by local government schemes, ushered in the by the 1909 Town Planning Act, which laid responsibility on local authorities for ensuring good housing standards and (after 1919) for grant-aiding construction. In the early 1920s much of Leicester's effort was directed at ambitious and exemplary council housing schemes to the south-west of the city, in what became the Braunstone estate. Here houses were fully equipped with services and laid out in a carefully landscaped setting around a huge park. The city had built itself, or had sponsored the construction of, more than 12,000 houses before 1939. Lincoln had a similar estate at St Giles, also built at the far end of the transport system, but the city's engineering industry wobbled after the First World War and then went into a long decline, so funds for rehousing were harder to find. Lincoln still had slums in the lower city after 1945 but Leicester's, between Humberstone Gate and Belgrave Gate, were even more extensive. Leicester Corporation had drawn up extensive slum-clearance schemes in the 1930s, under the Housing Acts, but many were not fully implemented until the 1950s and 1960s. By then, these schemes were decanting the population from cleared areas of the inner cities into new tower blocks such as those on Rowlatt's Hill (built 1967–8). Even in Lincoln, tower blocks were used to rehouse families from areas of sub-standard housing, at Stamp End (Fig. 3.43), and on the last undeveloped part of the former common fields north of the city (the Ermine estate). By 1970 about 40 per cent of the city's population occupied council-built properties, although by this time over 60 per cent of the population worked, not in manufacturing, but in service industries.

Between the wars Nottingham also developed its housing stock, showing more determination, perhaps, than its fellow county towns. Twenty estates were built by the council on the northern and western fringes of the city: between 1919 and 1965, 33,178 council houses had been provided out of an overall total of 48,296 new homes. No other East Midlands town could match that effort. Symbolic of new civic priorities in housing, perhaps, was the purchase of 800 acres (320ha) of the Wollaton estate, around the famous stately home (p.146), in 1924 and the immediate earmarking of all but 20ha for new housing estates. By 1961 Nottingham was the eighth largest city in Britain (with a population of 300,630), although by 1981 it had lost about 25,000, and had been overtaken by Leicester as the region's largest city (328,835).

Leicester's continued rapid expansion, at a time when Nottingham was losing people, is mostly accounted for by immigration. This comfortable town, with its diverse range of industries (predominantly engineering by 1990) was an attractive destination, first for immigrants from the West Indies and, subsequently, for ethnic Asians from Kenya and Uganda. These new communities have concentrated in the Highfields and Belgrave districts and by 1983 they formed about 25 per cent of

Fig. 3.42 Houses 'fit for heroes' at Swanpool, Lincoln. These carefully designed homes represent the short period of industrial philanthropy in housing provision before legislation made Local Authorities responsible for the housing stock. The new estate, located well away from the city centre and following 'Garden City' principles, was erected by a local Co-operative Society following its establishment in 1919. The Society was bankrolled by Colonel Ruston, the managing director of one of Lincoln's major employers, who claimed he was inspired by model workers' villages at Port Sunlight and Bourneville.

ABOVE LEFT: *Fig. 3.43 Some of Lincoln's working class housing was laid-out in a grid of red-brick streets (typical of so many East Midlands towns) east of the centre, on the slopes above the engineering works in the valley.* *The terraced Edwardian houses in the foreground, with their superior architectural details, were tenanted by the more senior workers, whilst most lived in more simple terraces running down the hill behind. Shuttleworth House was one of two tower blocks erected by Lincoln Corporation in the 1960s to replace the worst of these down by the river. Behind is the Titanic Building, a huge assembly shed built in 1912 by Clayton and Shuttleworth. It remains uncertain whether it was named because its great length recalled the famous liner (launched in that year), or because it 'sunk' the company, which finally ceased trading in 1930.*

ABOVE RIGHT: *Fig. 3.44 The Asian community has successfully established itself in parts of northern Leicester.* *The dour red-brick terraces remain, but their modern occupants bring a splash of colour and exoticism, especially in Belgrave Road during Diwali, the festival of lights.*

LEFT: *Fig. 3.45 Warwicks & Richardson's, Newark, proclaims the dominant position held by breweries in so many East Midlands towns.* *The tower brewery here (behind the street range) was the largest of six in Newark in the 1870s, but before 1900 it had assimilated four of its rivals. In 1890, the firm celebrated its position in Queen Anne style by constructing this enormous gatehouse block along the street (architect William Bliss Sanders). It contained offices and storage, but has been at risk for many years.*

Leicester's population. Their contribution has made the city one of the most exciting and diverse in England (Fig. 3.44).

Compared with Nottingham and Leicester, Derby was decidedly reluctant to accept responsibility for house-building. In the 1920s, however, the Ministry of Housing persuaded the corporation to seek advice from more dynamic councils on coping with its housing crisis. The corporation chose to go to Sheffield, where new houses were being built using locally made cast-iron frames, and so it was that Derby had acquired 500 of these unusual structures by 1927. It was nowhere near enough and only 6,852 new houses were built in the city between 1919 and 1939. After 1945, however, the pace of construction quickened and the Mackworth estate, north of the historic centre, and the Chaddesden estate, to the north-east, are among the largest in the East Midlands. Latterly, since Derby's industrial base has diversified away from railway equipment into aero engines and artificial textiles, there has been much new building by the private sector.

Bedford, more typical in some ways of the smaller towns than of the centres of county government, remained a market town with a population of less than 10,000, offering professional services (legal and banking) and shopping, but little else, until the railway arrived in 1846. But immediately the railway came, as in Oxford, the town's traditional firms of maltsters and brewers started to increase the scale of their operations. By 1910, Charles Wells was importing malt by rail and exporting its famous beers all round the East Midlands by the same means. Similarly in 1859, some 10 years after the first trains arrived, the Britannia Ironworks was founded, amalgamating a number of local foundries. By 1874 these works covered 6ha producing much the same range of agricultural machinery that was also flooding out of Lincoln's factories. As at Lincoln, the Bedford enterprise was entirely dependent on the railway, and the 1859 works were laid out alongside it. The town grew rapidly in size, but with a population of only 28,023 by 1891, it was still not a large place.

Unlike many East Midlands towns further north, however, Bedford was close enough to London to become, in the 20th century, the base of manufacturing industries seeking to exploit the capital's huge market. In 1894, W H Allen established an engineering works at Bedford rather than at Derby, specifically to be near the London market. The Igranic Electric Company declared that they established themselves here in 1913 for the same reason. Bedford's greatest period of growth, then, came later than Lincoln's and by 1961 it had a population of 63,334. Like all the other towns we have looked at, its development before 1939 was also strictly zoned, with working-class districts laid out to west and south, and a leafy suburb laid out around a park to the north (incorporating Bedford School) for the well-to-do.

TRADITIONAL MARKET CENTRES AND INDUSTRIAL NEWCOMERS

East Midland towns of the second rank, the market centres of the pre-industrial age, also acquired their own industries and accommodated miniature industrial revolutions. Without exception, such towns needed a railway link, although industrial development in some, like Grantham and Louth, was stimulated earlier by canals. Others developed more slowly, even if beside navigable rivers. Loughborough was on the Soar, but it was not until the railway arrived here that the Brush electrical engineering works and Herbert Morris's crane works were established. Despite the canal, Grantham only grew large once the arrival of the railway made heavy engineering possible, then Hornsby's could grow from a local blacksmith into a major manufacturer of agricultural machines. Though always a prosperous market centre, the railways permitted Newark's traditional malting and brewing industries to expand greatly, and Warwick's magnificent 'tower-brewery' still stands in its Queen Anne disguise (Fig. 3.45). The arrival of

railways at Gainsborough turned the sleepy little port into a stereotypical red-brick manufacturing town, huddled around the impressive Marshall's factory – yet another producer of agricultural machinery (Fig. 3.46). Yet more machinery was made at Banbury. The great livestock market here continued to dominate the town, but Banbury's medieval suburb of Newland (closest to the Cherwell and the Oxford Canal – which arrived in 1778 – and to the railway when it arrived in 1850) was redeveloped in the 19th century as a manufacturing community, producing a similar range of agricultural machinery to Grantham, Lincoln and Gainsborough. Here too, Samuelson's Works was accompanied by rectilinear streets of new terraced housing in which the workers lived.

The story is similar in many other smaller East Midlands towns. Places like Abingdon, Bicester, Bletchley, Cambridge (Fig. 3.47), Daventry and Huntingdon all saw a gradually increasing population from the end of the 18th century, followed by a period of overcrowding and popular discontent from the defeat of Napoleon until Victoria's coronation. Then the railways arrived and the coal they brought enabled the mechanisation of local industries and

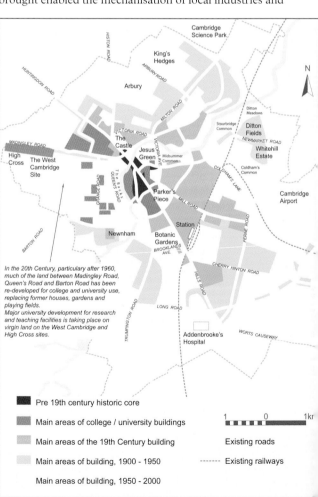

ABOVE: *Fig. 3.46 Gainsborough joins the consumer revolution.* On 22 July 1948 (top) this archetypical, red-brick, East Midlands manufacturing town was emerging from World War II. Marshall's engineering works (first established here 1850) occupies several blocks on the eastern side of the medieval centre, ranged along the Trent. In 2004 (bottom picture) Marshall's has gone. The southern part of this rip in the townscape is already colonised by the anonymous shed and car-park of a retail outlet. Further north, only the factory façades will be retained, amongst further new shopping malls.

RIGHT: *Fig. 3.47 The growth of Cambridge in the 19th and 20th centuries* (source: Kirby and Oosthuigen 2000).

the development of a national market for the town's product, which rapidly replaced sales in its own market place. Industrialisation in these towns always involved the layout of areas of terraced housing and, always at a slight distance, an enclave for the well-to-do. Albert Park estate in Abingdon is an excellent example of the latter, laid out in 1864–5, where the new villas all turn their backs on the rest of the town and gaze serenely across the fine new park.

Some towns were, of course, dependent on the railways for more than transport. We have already noted Derby's role as a centre of railway engineering, but major works at Rugby, Wolverton, Bletchley (Fig. 3.48) and Peterborough were all developed by railway companies, often on sites where relatively small settlements had existed before. In all these places the pattern was the same. Large working sheds were established alongside main railway lines, and new streets of houses for the workers were developed on adjacent green-field land. Although

Fig. 3.48 Bletchley is typical of several East Midlands small towns that owe their 19th-century prosperity to the railways. *The medieval village lay 1km to the west (right), whilst today's town centre (upper left) was largely built by the L&NWR after 1838. In 1850 the main line (top left to middle right) was crossed by the Oxford to Cambridge route and Bletchley became an important junction with extensive goods-yards. Important brickworks (now a wildlife sanctuary – top) and London overspill increased the town's population to some 20,000 before inclusion within the new Milton Keynes in 1967. In the foreground, however, between the A5 and the railway, Denbigh West industrial estate (1960s) is typical in relying on road, rather than rail.*

Peterborough was an ancient urban centre, it was in much reduced circumstances by the early 1840s (with a population in 1801 of only 3,500) when five railway companies established a junction and boosted the population fourfold (to 17,429 by 1851). The new rail works and their associated housing schemes were laid out along the railway, north and south of the new station, which was on the western edge of the existing settlement, completely re-orienting the town. For 1,500 years Peterborough had been drawn out east–west along a main route into the fens; now, it was suddenly extended north and south, along a more dominant communication route. The last railway company to arrive, the Great Northern, could only find room for its new works and associated housing a mile to the north of the medieval centre, at the optimistically named New England.

Rugby had been a respectable market town long before first the canals and then the railways arrived (in 1840), whereas Wolverton (at the eastern end of the medieval parish) was developed slightly earlier on a site without earlier settlement. Wolverton was halfway between London and Birmingham and so was the ideal place on the new railway line to change engines. A repair yard was begun by the London and Birmingham Railway in 1837, and by 1839 the company had begun to erect streets of model houses, a gasworks, a public house (the Radcliffe Arms) and (by 1844) St George's church. By 1844 the turnpike had been re-routed to go through the new town, rather than through Old Wolverton village. The town remained dominated by its single industry, with nearly half the population (7,384 in 1911) being directly employed by the railway. Didcot was in a similar position to Wolverton on the Great Western, and saw a similar development, but although it lies just north of the Berkshire Downs, its history properly belongs to the South and West.

Industrialisation in the East Midlands was not a purely urban phenomenon. Many industries were already present in parts of the pre-industrial countryside, mostly within former woodland areas and those which had once been governed by forest law. The more dispersed patterns of settlement in such areas may have been

ABOVE: *Fig. 3.49 Westhorpe Colliery, near Worksop,* was sunk
in the open countryside by local landowners J and G Wells Ltd in
1923. A new pit-head baths complex including a medical centre was
constructed following Nationalisation in 1949, and a powerful electric
ventilation fan was installed in 1955. The colliery closed in 1984 and
the site awaits redevelopment.

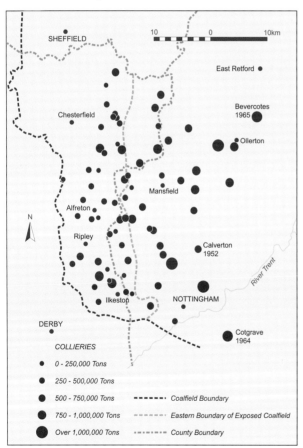

*Fig. 3.50 The expansion of the Derbyshire/Nottinghamshire
coalfield.* Although the symbols for each mine are graded by output
tonnage, the more recently sunk collieries, along the eastern side of the
coalfield, also have the largest output (source: Edwards (ed.) 1966).

even more suitable for industrial development than areas
where ancient villages dominated the landscape. In the
Nottinghamshire coalfield the great intensification of mining
and processing between 1891 and 1931 took place against a
largely rural background (Fig. 3.49). Improvements in
equipment meant that deep seams, which earlier had been
chased along the Derbyshire border, could now be reached
from new, larger, deeper mines located further east. But the
result was not a new town or towns, as was to occur, for
example, after 1945 at Asfordby near Melton Mowbray.
Instead the dozens of small, dispersed communities of central
Nottinghamshire suddenly expanded as landowners cashed
in on the bonanza made possible by new technology (Fig.
3.50). What had been small market towns at Mansfield,
Sutton-in-Ashfield and Kirkby-in-Ashfield expanded, but
most of the mines were actually set up in small hamlets round
about, with telling place-names like Coxmoor, Three Thorn
Hollow, Forest Town and Whinny Hill. Eventually, of course,
these settlements agglomerated and spread to form a loose
semi-urban landscape, with Mansfield at its centre, extending
more or less from Alfreton in the west to Ollerton, deep
within Sherwood Forest, to the east.

Nor was Nottinghamshire the only part of the East
Midlands where industry developed in this 'dispersed'
manner. In other former forest areas, such as the coalfield
north-west of Leicester (and extending over the county
border into Derbyshire), the intensification of industry
resulted in an enlargement of the existing hamlets and small
settlements, which eventually grew together, forming long
strings of houses and works along the country lanes. But no
new civic centre emerged (despite the grandiloquent new
clock tower at Coalville – Fig. 3.51) as it had done, for
example, in Scunthorpe. Although the last mines hereabouts
closed in the 1980s, the landscape around Coleorton and
Hugglescote remains difficult for outsiders to navigate. The
roads originated as service tracks for mines and scattered
houses and frequently, it seems, there are a dozen ways of
reaching the next settlement. A similar pattern of 'dispersed'
settlements underlies the continuous industrial landscape of
the Erewash valley, although here, greater diversity (in the
shape of textile manufacture and ironworking) and greater

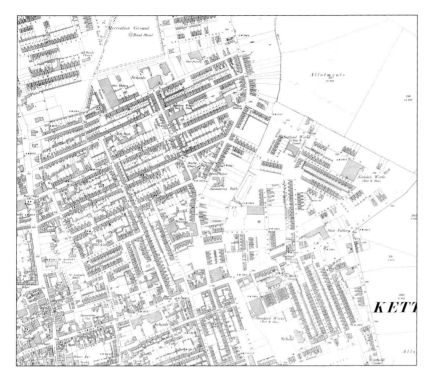

intensification of industry has resulted in larger settlements with more credibility as modern towns. Long Eaton, which had a population of only 1,000 in 1851, had 13,000 in 1901, and places like Eastwood, Heanor, Ilkeston, Ripley and Stapleford are all now substantial communities even though none were more than hamlets in 1800.

These industrial landscapes in the north-west of our region have a quite different look to the contemporary landscape of the boot-and-shoe industry further south. Kettering was typical of the smaller market towns and villages of Northamptonshire and Leicestershire that benefited from industrial investment, following the opening of the St Pancras–Leicester railway in 1857. Large government orders and the mechanisation of the industry, made possible by the cheap coal brought by rail, meant that by 1870 Kettering had 20 substantial boot manufacturers. By 1901 its population had swelled to nearly 30,000. The biggest manufacturers, such as Meadows and Bryan and J T S Stockburn, built large estates of good quality terraced housing north and east of the old town centre. As in Northampton, the characteristic 'boot-and-shoe' townscape of terraces, with workshops at the bottom of the garden – often built and owned by the footwear companies and rented out to the workers – still survives. The terraces are interspersed with small factories where the more mechanised operations were undertaken (for example in and around King Street and Wellington Street – Fig. 3.52). The prosperous and stylish 18th-century market town of Wellingborough nearby underwent a very similar transition between about 1850 and 1914. Here the population trebled but, although much of the increase was accounted for by the new boot-and-shoe industry, at least some of the town's new workers earned their living at new blast furnaces constructed to exploit the ore revealed by the new railway cuttings (p.184).

The arrival of railways meant that boot-and-shoe manufacture could be undertaken anywhere with good rail connections to the market places in London and the North. Once they arrived in a village, there was nothing to prevent the local boot-maker with capital from setting up a factory alongside the railway line. The railway brought coal to fire the machinery and carried the finished boots and shoes to market. Consequently many medieval villages alongside the new railway lines developed into towns: Burton Latimer, Desborough, Earls Barton, Finedon, Irchester, Irthingborough, Raunds, Rothwell and Rushden. These

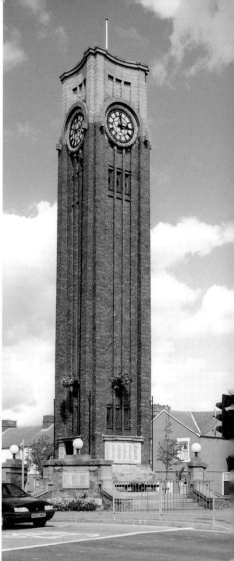

ABOVE: *Fig. 3.51 The clock tower, Coalville (Leicestershire). Being a new industrial community in the Charnwood area, where settlement was traditionally dispersed across the landscape, Coalville struggled to develop any sense of urban identity. In an effort to stimulate a sense of place the Council sponsored this huge clock tower (vaguely reminiscent of winding gear at the more modern local coal mines) in 1926 as a war memorial, marking a major cross-roads. The architect was Henry Collings.*

ABOVE LEFT: *Fig. 3.52 Map of north-eastern Kettering in 1900. The map shows a rapidly developing 'boot-and-shoe' townscape of terraced houses, with workshops in their back gardens, interspersed with factories where the more mechanised operations in boot-making were housed.*

settlements had all been substantial communities before the railways arrived and, thanks to the common fields which had separated them from their neighbours for a millennium, the new industry simply developed as a thick carapace around the villages' existing cores. The new building took the form both of factories, and of rows of comfortable red-brick terraced houses for the new workforce, often with workshops at the bottom of the garden. Here no new settlements were built around former farmsteads, as was the norm in the Leicestershire and Nottinghamshire coalfields, and the agricultural landscape retained its simple road network inherited from enclosure.

As they changed from dependence on their local markets to national and international ones, engineering towns such as Lincoln depended more heavily on railways leading to ports. Rustons had agents in 28 countries around the world in 1889 and the two 'new' Humber ports of Grimsby and Immingham could not have existed without the export trade in manufactured goods such as theirs. Grimsby, of course, was an ancient port, but its late medieval decline had been exacerbated by the silting up of the harbour. In 1346, 11 ships and 171 mariners had sailed from here to join the siege of Calais but, by 1629, only 'one poore coale ship' visited the port all year. By the mid-17th century Grimsby borough may have been smaller than the nearby village of Old Clee, and between 1789 and 1792 not a single cargo was landed; John Byng, writing in 1791, thought it 'a wretched borough, existing only by venality; and with such an alehouse as could not have been slept in' (Andrews ed. 1934, 389).

Grimsby was a rather unusual case of an important town that almost disappeared completely. The arrival of steam power and railway connections, however, rapidly breathed new life into it. The East Midlands and Yorkshire Railway arrived in 1848 and a huge new dock was constructed in 1849. The town then experienced a boom as large as any in the East Midlands: by 1901 it had 63,000 inhabitants (more than Lincoln), and by 1905 it was the fifth port of Britain. In 1865, £4 million worth of manufactured goods, most made in the East Midlands, were exported from here. The famous fish docks were also a by-product of the railways. The Grimsby Deep Sea Fishing Company was established by a consortium of railway companies in 1854 and by 1865, 10,000 tons of fish were being landed annually and a second, specialist, dock had been provided.

Throughout the 19th century the port of Grimsby was developed jointly by the borough and the railway companies, but as Grimsby's share of the import–export market rose, space for new docks ran out. In 1904 the Grand Central Railway took the bold step of creating a new deep-water port at Immingham 8km north. In 1889 Immingham was 'a small scattered village one and a half miles from the Humber' but by 1912 some £2.6 million had been spent creating docks covering 18ha set in an industrial estate of over 400ha. Unfortunately for Immingham, the imperial optimism of the Edwardian era was fading, even while the huge facility was being opened by George V and Queen Mary in 1912, and by 1952 one writer recommended the electric tram ride through the barley fields to see Lincolnshire's 'Folly' (Barley 1952, 22). This was Immingham's lowest ebb. In the 1960s oil terminals were established in the area, and in 1970–1 British Steel opened a huge facility for the import of coal and iron ore to feed Scunthorpe's greedy maw (Fig. 3.53).

Like Grimsby and Immingham, Scunthorpe is also an interloper in rural Lincolnshire. It takes it name from the village where Rowland Winn realised the potential of the ironstone on his land and the Dawes brothers began mining it in 1860, and smelting it five years later. In the 1860s the town had something of the 'gold-rush' about it, and in 1866 the local newspaper reported that a sale of building plots 'presented an animated appearance' as prices were bid up by competing developers. The new town spread rapidly across agricultural land to the west and south, but its growth was restricted by the location of the ironstone mines themselves to the north-east and east. Existing villages in the area (Ashby, Brumby,

Crosby, Frodingham and Scunthorpe) were, like all those along the Lincoln Edge, oriented east–west, clustered along the spring line at the foot of the slope. Almost perversely, these different settlements clung to individual identities even as they were overwhelmed by the rising tide of new building. By 1900 there was a series of small town centres within the conurbation, of which Scunthorpe was just one. But, as at Stoke-on-Trent, the name of this individual constituent settlement became applied to the whole new urban area. Scunthorpe itself, and Ashby further south, were laid out almost exclusively with working-class terraced housing, whereas neighbouring Frodingham was occupied by the detached houses of the managers. We have seen this sort of territorialism in all our Victorian towns, but in 1894 not one, but several, rival urban district councils (UDCs) were formed in Scunthorpe. Leaders of Scunthorpe UDC made the obvious case that a single authority would have much more effective control of the new town's water supply, drainage, lighting and roads, but the move was fiercely resisted by Frodingham and Brumby councillors: one of them proclaimed in 1903 that 'one might as well try and unite Sweden and Norway'. By 1901 there were two separate gasworks, and by 1908 separate waterworks and fire brigades. Although Crosby and Ashby joined Scunthorpe UDC in 1913, it was not until the town had industrial collaboration imposed upon it during the First World War that Frodingham and Brumby were finally assimilated. By then the new town's population was the third largest in the county and by 1971 it was nearly 71,000.

The other purpose-built East Midlands iron town, at Corby, avoided some of Scunthorpe's parochialism. Although the extent of the underlying ironstone deposits had been identified in 1851, the necessity of a rail link meant that early ironstone quarries developed along the Kettering line further west; early furnaces were established in Wellingborough, Heyford and Finedon rather than Corby. The railway did not pass near here until the opening of the Midland line between Kettering and Melton Mowbray in 1879, but when it did, ironstone quarries opened here too.

Fig. 3.53 Secreted away amongst the Humberside 'fitties', Immingham's deep-water docks remain an installation rather than a small town. *The workforce itself is surprisingly small and most travel from outside the immediate area to work. Though long considered a 'white elephant', the railway investment of 1904–12 now pays a handsome dividend, through imports of fuel oil, iron ore and containers.*

Corby owed its pre-eminence among the many ironstone-quarrying villages of Northamptonshire, however, to the introduction of mechanised mining machines – 'steam navvies' – at Stewart and Lloyd's works here in 1897. The new machines were themselves local products. Many of the earliest were built by Rustons in Lincoln and were brought from factory to workplace by rail. Corby began to smelt its own ironstone in 1907 and, although it never rivalled Scunthorpe's size, the town's population had reached 49,000 in 1970. It expanded particularly rapidly after 1934, when Stewart and Lloyd reconstructed the steelworks and brought in workers from a depressed Clydeside (Fig. 3.54). This was the zenith of the Northamptonshire iron industry, however: most viable local deposits had been worked out by the 1970s and the furnaces were finally extinguished in 1980. The land formerly occupied by the smelters has now been reclaimed for modern industrial units and less than 10 per cent of the town's people now depend on the remaining steelworks for employment.

*ABOVE: **Fig. 3.54 Stewart and Lloyd's new steelworks (reconstructed 1934) at Corby (Northamptonshire)**, seen from the north along Rockingham Road on 29 September 1948. In the foreground, the newly built housing estate, created to accommodate workers brought from Clydeside in the late 1930s, is laid out around a school complex and a crescent of shops. The medieval village, clustered around the church, lies beyond.*

Spectacular though they were, Scunthorpe and Corby were not the only examples in the East Midlands of small villages becoming large towns. If the combination of a natural resource, far-sighted investors and railways was in place, even the most unpromising locations could be transformed. In 1801 there were a mere 23 houses at Skegness, housing 134 people. The Vine Inn, which John Byng visited in 1791, had 'no garden, no walk, no billiard room; nor anything for comfort or temptation', and was run by 'Mother Notable, in all filth, shelling beans and making tarts'. Although he obviously hated the place, the shrewd Byng noted that 'if a good house were built here, with a clever landlord, it would draw much company and answer well' (Andrews ed. 1934, 372). Just such a landlord arrived to open the New Hotel in 1811 and started to attract aristocratic sea-bathing parties. This hotel became Hildred's Hotel, much the most interesting building in Skegness, which was demolished in the early 1980s, despite a national outcry. The facilities were far from extensive, but the sea-bathing public were attracted and the small town grew steadily. Skegness' equivalent of Rowland Winn or Joseph Ruston was Vivian Tippet, the local land agent for the 9th Earl of Scarborough. In 1873 the railway finally arrived from Nottingham and almost immediately the town started to receive day-trippers. Tippet's genius was not to respond to them piecemeal, but instead to plan a 'new town' on the earl's marginal seaside lands. From the start, the town was strongly associated with Nottingham – it is still sometimes called Nottingham-on-Sea, and branches of the Nottingham Co-op Society in Skegness still sell copies of the *Nottingham Evening Post* (Fig. 3.55).

*BELOW: **Fig. 3.55 The Lindsey coast looking south from Chapel St Leonards towards Gibraltar Point; Skegness lies between the two.** The enormous Ingoldmells caravan-parks create a silver-plated landscape, separated from Skegness itself by Billy Butlin's first holiday camp (established 1936).*

The natural resource which drove Buxton to expand was spa water, rather than sea water, but the effect was much the same. In this case it was the Dukes of Devonshire who made more profit from marginal land on their estates. In the 1780s the 5th Duke conceived the idea that Buxton could become a northern Bath, and crescents and terraces were planned around the ancient St Anne's Well (*see* Fig. 4.2), below the medieval town. Unlike Skegness, however, Buxton was already a recognisably urban place. Indeed it had been a minor spa town since at least the 16th century, although, according to John Byng, before the duke's investment it was 'a most uncomfortable and dreary place'.

MODERN NEWCOMERS

Today the East Midlands is also home to Milton Keynes. Established with the highest of ideals in 1967, it was initially conceived, like the new town of Peterborough (launched in the same year), as an expansion, and growing-together of existing settlement centres. At Peterborough the old city was to be dominant in the newly created topography, and no alternative centres were to be built to rival the huge new shopping and service centres around the old market place. Attractive though they may have been, neither the Stratfords, nor Wolverton nor Bletchley, were thought appropriate to become the focus of the new city. Among the 10 ancient settlements in this corner of Buckinghamshire, the partially deserted village of Milton Keynes was selected to provide the new city's physical centre, although some attempt has been made to ensure that the other original settlements survived as 'islands' within the sea of new housing. In 1967 the total population of the area was about 40,000: by 2001 the new city approached 200,000. But this city is experimental, turning its back on a millennium of nucleation in this part of the country, and on earlier new towns: Milton Keynes is conceived as a low-density (or dispersed) settlement, with a mere 30 houses per hectare, extended over an enormous area (8,900ha).

Milton Keynes will bear no resemblance to the nucleated cities of the Midlands, which we have watched develop since the 10th century. In Nottingham, for example, population densities of 240 dwellings per hectare are not unknown today and they have been much higher at earlier periods. Instead Milton Keynes's population will sit in this landscape more as the 19th-century population of the Leicestershire coalfield sat in theirs. The main difference between the two areas will be that, whereas the coalfield population was dependent on canals and railways, the citizens of Milton Keynes will be dependent on motor transport. Yet paradoxically, where Coalville has merely a clock tower, Milton Keynes has an enormous civic centre. The great glass and concrete palaces of the 2km^2 between Portway and Childs Way rear up suddenly out of the trees, which dominate the low-density housing estates all around (Fig. 3.56). Milton Keynes has not quite made up its mind. Perhaps it wants to be a nucleated city, like the other great 'monofocal' East Midlands centres, after all. Yet before it has established its urban identity Milton Keynes is being challenged to think again. In 2002 the New Labour government identified this region as a new growth area, making it likely that low-density

Fig. 3.56 As a settlement, the character of Milton Keynes is still but partly formed. Like other 'nucleated' cities of the East Midlands, it has an impressive centre with a concentration of dominant public buildings. But immediately adjacent, amongst the trees, is low-density housing. Further out, however, we find other foci, sometimes established around once-distinct villages, but sometimes newly created, whilst on the outskirts we find, not suburbs, but the city's industrial centres.

settlement will spread much further towards the north and east.

Milton Keynes is only the most recent of several East Midlands towns where efforts were made in the 20th century to solve problems of economic overheating and social congestion in the South East. The earliest 'Garden City' was at Letchworth, just beyond the region's southern border, in 1903. However, by 1950, the buffer of Hertfordshire's new towns was failing to cope with expansion and in 1952 the Town Development Act gave Westminster, in consultation with local authorities, the powers to expand designated towns drastically. Ironically the first choice for such a town, long before the birth of Milton Keynes, was Bletchley: where the huge Lakes estate at Water Eaton (population 17,095 in 1961) was built in the early 1960s by the Greater London Council. Peterborough was identified in 1967 for redevelopment as a conventional new town with a population of 150,000–200,000, and Abingdon, Corby, Daventry, Huntingdon, Northampton, St Ives and St Neots were all subsequently accorded similar treatment. In St Neots, the cosy little market town, with little industry aside from a small wood yard, maltings and breweries, and with a population of only 5,000, found itself at the western edge of a large London 'overspill' project in the 1960s, which took its population to 20,000 in less than a decade, and to 25,000 by 1997. Many of St Neots' new inhabitants found themselves commuting back into London each day, but several thousand jobs were created in new light industrial estates. Equally dramatic, however, was the expansion of Aylesbury, a small market town with a population of 13,000 as recently as 1931. A large new estate, intended for displaced East Londoners, was built during the 1930s at Southcourt, and Aylesbury was also targeted for expansion under the 1952 Act. Today the population has risen to over 50,000 and it has joined the lengthening list of small East Midlands towns paying a high aesthetic and social price for its proximity to London (Fig. 3.57).

The 20th-century coalfield expansion eastwards into Nottinghamshire meant that a large incoming population had to be housed, but the existing dispersed settlements of the area were too small to accommodate the new workers. One solution was to build a number of 'model villages'. The finest example of such a new settlement is at Creswell (on the Derbyshire border), built between 1896 and 1900, where the miners' cottages occupy both sides of a back lane laid out around an octagon (Fig. 3.57). The houses around the outside faced outwards, while those on the inside faced into the centre of the octagon, which was a landscaped green. The houses had only small yards, but allotments and social facilities were provided in a separate plot adjoining the development. After 1918, the spirit of enlightened paternalism that had found expression in Lloyd George's pre-war government was given a physical form in Bedfordshire, at Forder's enormous new brickworks south-west of Bedford (see Fig. 5.41). At Stewartby (named after a member of Lloyd George's own government) the workers were provided with excellent new houses from the 1920s. These are set in a spacious model village with a neoclassical village hall, old people's home and a school all lurking bucolically among the carefully placed specimen trees. From the top of the small hill to the south you can see the entire community laid out around its green in its brick-built splendour, with the giant chimneys rising like a theatrical backdrop behind. The chimneys carry the words 'London Brick

Fig. 3.57 As recently as 1930 Aylesbury was an attractive small market town, but its late 20th-century expansion has given the place a quite different character. The town centre is now isolated from its citizens' homes by a crazy ring-road, whilst the baleful shadow of the County Offices (of 1963–6, designed by the County Architect's department headed by Mr F B Pooley) is cast for many miles around.

OPPOSITE PAGE:

Fig. 3.58 The perfect geometry of the model mining village at Cresswell (Derbyshire) is very evident in the vertical view (top) taken on 17 September 1954. By 2004 (bottom), however, not only is the pit-head south of the village reduced to a forlorn yard, with the spoil-tips landscaped away, but the allotments, which were such an important part of the original concept behind the geometrical layout, have also gone.

Company' and 'Stewartby' in huge white letters: the whole landscape has been recruited to make one of England's finest advertising hoardings.

Nor has the paternalistic idealism that informed Creswell and Stewartby been entirely lost subsequently. In eastern Bedfordshire, where the natural resource takes the form of vegetables grown for the London market, there have been a succession of schemes designed to settle smallholders on the land. In 1911 the Duke of Bedford sold off his estate at Maulden in smallholdings of 8.5ha, each with its own house and outbuildings. Although he also expected a profit, the duke was aiming to alleviate agricultural poverty. In 1915, Bedfordshire County Council let out 962ha in similar smallholdings in the Sandy area. After the Land Settlement Act of 1919, intended to establish returning soldiers on smallholdings of this type, the council established another 660 such holdings on land purchased for the purpose. During the slump of the early 1930s, Forder's (the brick-makers) bought 216ha near Potton, to be worked as smallholdings exclusively by unemployed labourers who would be trained in horticulture by a resident Warden. In 1935 this settlement evolved into a member of the newly established Land Settlement Association (LSA), who invited unemployed Durham miners to migrate and work at Potton and some ten other sites in the East Midlands (at Chawston, near Wyboston, and at Fen Drayton – Cambridgeshire – for example).

With Potton well established, the LSA expanded into a purpose-built settlement at Wyboston itself. Here, on the former Norton Field, a group of about 45 plots was laid out (*see* Fig. 1.8). Each plot was approximately 1 acre (0.4ha) and each house, standing at the centre of the plot, alongside the access road, was originally designed to the same up-to-date specification (often by architects Packington & Enthoven) and came with a standard group of outbuildings. The LSA struggled within the European subsidy regime in the late 1970s and collapsed amidst controversy

Fig. 3.59 The perimeter track of former RAF Oakington clearly restrains the housing at the 'overspill' village of Bar Hill (Cambridgeshire). *Different planning philosophies (the earliest dating from 1965) are on show. The largest, most recent, most informal housing (marked by regularly distributed swimming-pools) has escaped the original boundary altogether. It intrudes into a new man-made golf-course landscape of lawns, bunkers and fast-growing shelter-belts; an increasingly dominant element in many East Midlands views.*

when government support was withdrawn in 1983. Plots have subsequently been sold separately from the houses, while others have been amalgamated, and most of the houses have been extended beyond recognition, but their regular spacing, at intervals of about 66m, and staggered across the road, ensures that the place remains quite unlike any other English housing scheme.

The idealistic tradition represented by such developments did not end with the smoke-stack industries. Planners still believe such new 'village' communities have a role to play in a part of England, which we have seen has contained settlements of this type for over a millennium. In Oxford there have already been major extensions to the city itself (including huge soulless estates at Blackbird Leys and Barton), but in the new millennium it is proposed to alleviate the housing shortages of Oxfordshire by creating a new 'village' on the former US air force base at Upper Heyford. The Cambridge planners had responded in the same way in the 1960s to

the need for substantially more houses adjacent to the city. Extensions to the urban area were built in the 'necklace' villages of Milton and Hardwick, and an entirely new 'village' was also inaugurated at Bar Hill, 16km north-west. In 1967 this was 'probably the most ambitious private housing development in the country' and it was intended that a population of 4,000 would be housed in a planned settlement within the perimeter track of the former RAF Oakington. In addition, there would be a church, 40 shops, two schools and office accommodation. In fact progress has been slower, and the *dirigiste* approach taken in the early planning documents has been relaxed somewhat (Fig. 3.59). Bar Hill is now, effectively, a dormitory; but it is full up, and Cambridgeshire planners of the 21st century are placing their faith in another 'new village' at 'Cambourne'.

FURTHER READING

General
Beckett 1988; Bennett & Bennett 1993 (Lincolnshire); Chadwick 1966; Chambers 1966 (Nottinghamshire); Chambers & Mingay 1966; Everitt 1974; Mills (ed.) 1989 (Lincolnshire); Seeley 1974; Wright 1982 (Lincolnshire).

Enclosure and agricultural revolution
Beastall 1978 (Lincolnshire); Chambers 1957 (Nottinghamshire, Derbyshire, Leicestershire); Hall 1997 (Northamptonshire); Olney 1979 (Lincolnshire); Russell & Russell 1982, 1983, 1985, 1987 (Lindsey); Thirsk 1957 (Kesteven); Williamson 2002.

Older towns
Beckwith 1988 (Gainsborough); Birch 1994 (Aylesbury); Brazier *et al.* 1985 (Nottingham); Church 1966 (Nottingham); Cooper 1971 (Newark); Gillett 1986 (Grimsby); Greenall 1975 (Kettering); Hatley 1966 (Northampton); Heath & Christian 1985 (Derby); Hill 1966, 1973 (Lincoln); Hinchcliffe 1992 (Oxford); Honeybone 1980 (Grantham); Kellett 1969; Owen 1978 (Burton-on-Trent); Pawley 1996 (Sleaford); Potts 1958 (Banbury); Rogers 2001 (Stamford); Scopes 1965 (Corby); Simmons 1974 (Leicester); Tebbs 1979 (Peterborough); Tebbutt 1978 (St Neots); Wedlock 1954 (Loughborough).

New towns and other settlements
Armstrong 1981 (Scunthorpe); Baker 1983 (Coalville); Dearlove 2000 (Wyboston); Markham 1973–5 (Milton Keynes); Seeley 1974; Walton 1983.

Landscape of early industry (*see also* Chapter 5)
Beaver 1982–3 (iron mining); Church 1986 (coal mining); Cooper 1983 (textiles); Flinn 1984 (coal mining); Morrison with Bond 2004 (shoemaking); Mounfield 1964–5, 1966, 1967 (shoemaking); Palmer & Neaverson 1992.

4

Patterns of Accommodation

Housing the People

Having explored the way that the East Midlands landscape has developed, from the earliest settlements to the present, we can now consider how different types of building fitted into their contemporary landscapes. Some adapted to the landscape and its uses; others adapted the landscape around them. This chapter begins by looking at people's housing, before reviewing the dwellings of society's elite.

TEMPORARY STRUCTURES

Before the First World War, archaeologists followed the last genuine charcoal-burners and bark-peelers around working woodlands, photographing their distinctive, simple shelters in the belief that such structures were replicas or lineal descendants of prehistoric houses. These woodland craftspeople, however, were building *temporary* structures, 'wigwams' of coppice poles covered with turf, which were perfectly adapted to fulfil their seasonal role as shelters whilst they worked. Although some of these woodland workers lived in brightly painted caravans, many actually lived in small brick-built houses, like everyone else. The simplicity of their temporary structures was illusory; to understand the woodland workers' housing, one needed to understand the social and economic context within which the buildings were constructed.

Houses of past ages were rarely all-purpose structures; rather, they were usually specific to particular social and economic contexts. We do the cultures that erected them a disservice unless we try to understand their buildings in the appropriate context. For example, a presumed 'house' of Neolithic date excavated at Ecton (Northamptonshire) amounted to little more than a scrape in the ground with a number of posts to support a simple lean-to roof. This structure would have closely resembled the Edwardian charcoal-burners' wigwams, but we should not draw the conclusion that the charcoal-burners' wigwams were of prehistoric design; rather, we should consider the possibility that the Ecton 'house' was a temporary structure. Where the economic and social context of such primitive structures has been investigated, in fact, their temporary character has been clear. The late Iron Age structure of this simple type excavated at Farmoor (Oxfordshire), for example, was associated with the summer grazing of cattle on rich alluvial meadowland. It too was a temporary structure, rather than a typical Iron Age one, and it produced many loom-weights, which show that stock-keepers kept themselves occupied with textile manufacture – which, incidentally, may therefore have been just as seasonal an activity as summer grazing.

Temporary structures of this kind look remarkably similar to the distinctive buildings known as *grubenhauser* which English archaeologists have presumed are typical of the earlier phases of Anglo-Saxon settlement in the 5th and 6th

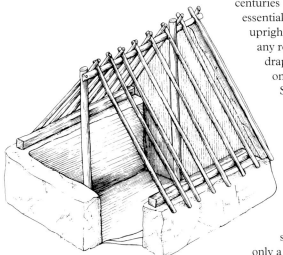

Fig. 4.1 Philip Dixon's reconstruction of a grubenhaus from remains at Catholme (Staffordshire).

centuries (Fig. 4.1). Like the bark-peelers' lodges, these structures are essentially shallow pits with a simple roof structure, supported on two upright poles bearing a ridge pole between them, over which a roof (of any readily available material: turf, thatch or leather) was simply draped. Early Anglo-Saxon structures of this type have been found on many East Midlands sites (Willington, Derbyshire; Catholme, Staffordshire; Riby Cross, Lindsey and many others). They often occur, however, on sites which are also occupied by larger and more permanent buildings. Why do we not think of them as temporary structures also, like those of similar character of both earlier and later dates?

If *grubenhauser* did represent temporary Anglo-Saxon structures, at least two different scenarios for their construction on sites also containing more permanent structures might be envisaged. One might be that that these *grubenhauser* represent the initial phases of permanent settlement by incomers – a temporary shelter lasting perhaps only a matter of months, possibly required during negotiations with indigenous occupants. In this scenario, these buildings might have been constructed on marginal land or in woodlands (where similar structures have been found at other periods), and they need not necessarily imply any particular ethnicity. Another possibility is that such structures were erected for temporary, probably seasonal, purposes within a more permanent settlement. Discrepancies in numbers, often found between the settlement's many *grubenhauser* and the few more substantial buildings, suggest that this second scenario was more likely, and that the activity undertaken in such buildings would also have been undertaken repeatedly by inhabitants of the permanent buildings nearby.

Five hundred years later, *grubenhaus*-like temporary structures were probably called 'cotes', as in the place-name 'Cotswold' ('the hills with many cotes') where they were shelters for stock-keepers. Sometimes the place-names suggest that they were occupied by young men or boys, as they tended the stock: as at Chilcote (Northamptonshire) and Childerley (Cambridgeshire). The seasonal nature of such 'cotes' is also recorded in certain place-names, for example at the two 'Somercotes' on the Lincolnshire marshes: these were temporary buildings occupied, like Farmoor, by stock-keepers in summer.

POSTS, FRAMES AND CRUCKS

Permanent domestic architecture also had its origins in the Neolithic period. At Fengate, one of the few, well-dated Neolithic 'houses' in the East Midlands (built between 3310 and 2990 BC) is nothing like the charcoal-burner's wigwam. Square in plan, it was also quite large (7m by 8.5m) and had upright corner posts, indicating vertical walls, apparently made of woven wattle covered with clay daub. It was built around a regularly laid-out wooden frame, which would have supported a pitched roof carried on a ridge pole running at right-angles to the frame. Other excavations around Peterborough have produced evidence for serviceable Bronze Age carpentry joints, and this building's frame might have been held together using similar techniques, perhaps in addition to bindings. The roof was thatched. Although it is not a complex structure, and is thought to have been a 'house for the dead' rather than for the living, this building is little different from many East Midlands houses of medieval and later dates. The timber-framing tradition, called 'post-and-truss', is thought to belong particularly to these later periods, but we must beware of thinking it too complex for earlier societies. Although such buildings take much longer to erect than any temporary structure, they are strong and durable, capable of being maintained and repaired almost indefinitely. Unlike wigwams, post-and-truss buildings indicate permanent (or at least long-term) occupation. It is not surprising, then, that we can now trace their origins back to the late Neolithic period – to the first settlements of the East Midlands. This type of structure is typical of the landscape's farmers; it will survive until next season, and the season after that if repaired. It is even robust enough to cope with climatic extremes; examples have also been found in marginal upland locations, at Lismore (near Buxton). Here two rectangular houses, also of framed construction, were excavated in the 1980s. The smaller (10m by 8m) was subdivided into two 'rooms', while the larger (20m by 8m), which seems to have been extended, contained a complex sequence of spaces within.

As large-scale agricultural landscapes developed in the East Midlands in the Bronze Age, styles of domestic architecture were altered. Whereas most known permanent Neolithic houses were rectangular in plan, from about 1500 BC circular or oval structures seem to have been almost universally adopted. Hundreds of such houses have been identified from aerial photography and scores have been excavated. Excavations at Blue Bridge (Milton Keynes), for example, revealed buildings about 20m across with flimsy upright walls less than 2m high. Most of the structure was roof, carried on long sloping timbers or rafters, which were sometimes supported halfway along their length by further upright posts, so forming, with their connecting purlins, something like a circular arcade within. Although the earliest of the Blue Bridge houses dates from the early Iron Age, they are almost indistinguishable from houses of the late Bronze Age found at Fengate. Well preserved examples of the late Iron Age have been excavated at Mingies Ditch (Oxfordshire) and Brigstock Park (Northamptonshire), whilst the basic design may have survived right through the Romano-British period (at Quarrington, Lindsey, for example). All these buildings presuppose both considerable skill in carpentry, but also extensive woodland management capable of producing long straight poles as well as a variety of smaller posts and withies.

Famously, however, the Romans favoured rectangular building and their arrival probably precipitated a marked shift away from houses of circular plan after the 1st century AD. Whether this implies a decline in the areas of managed woodland or just a change in the way timber was used within buildings is a moot point. Early rectangular buildings have frequently been excavated; at Dragonby, for example, where the remains of at least 10 such buildings were identified. Similarities in construction and use between these rectangular structures and the Iron Age roundhouses that preceded them suggest that they were rectangular replacements for the same family groups that had previously occupied the roundhouses.

At Dragonby internal posts in some rectangular buildings have been interpreted as evidence for the aisles of single-storey buildings rather than as posts supporting an upper floor. Even so, it is very likely that two-storeyed Romano-British buildings, of timber-frame construction, existed outside the towns. As currently interpreted, several Dragonby buildings belonged to a class of aisled 'hall' that we more readily associate with the Anglo-Saxons, although similar timber-built aisled halls of Romano-British date have been identified elsewhere in the East Midlands. At Dunston's Clump (Nottinghamshire), for example, a group of such buildings was constructed in the 1st or 2nd century AD within a ditched enclosure. Similar groups of rectilinear timber-framed buildings were found north of the small villa at Stanwick (Northamptonshire).

The fate of such timber-framed Romano-British buildings has become part of the debate over the end of Roman Britain itself. Some writers stress the similarities between the Romans' timber buildings and those of the Anglo-Saxons in order to bolster claims for a gradual and peaceful transition between the two cultures. Others have searched for differences in style or construction technique, and used their findings to illustrate discontinuity between them. Some have seen an ethnic distinction between methods of building using 'earthfast' posts (posts set deep into individual post holes, which are not part of pre-constructed 'frames') and those employing a trench, within which an entire wall was constructed, using a horizontal sill beam to support uprights and including partly pre-constructed frames. This second technique might have been used at some of the buildings at Dragonby; by contrast, the Dunston's Clump buildings employed earthfast posts.

The earthfast post tradition is best suited to buildings where the carpentry skills for making strong timber joints are less well developed. This conclusion is important because it directs our attention towards the distribution of timber-working skills (and perhaps, therefore, to the availability of timber) for vernacular building. It also suggests we should be studying the development of such buildings regionally. The earthfast post tradition was vigorous between the 6th and 8th centuries at Catholme, and the miscellaneous post holes excavated there can be reconstructed as satisfactory buildings in all cases, provided that the reconstructions aim for regularity of plan at wall-plate level, rather than foundation level (*see* Figs 3.15 and 4.2). If one constructs the building 'downwards' from the wall-plate, rather than 'upwards' from the post holes, the locations of the post settings become much less critical and there is less need for precisely worked timber joints.

Many buildings were constructed in this way until recent times: latterly, their posts were not sunk into the ground at all, but merely lodged on large stones (padstones) or even left simply to stand on the ground surface. Buildings employing posts dug deep into the ground seem to have become less common by the 11th century, being replaced by buildings supported on stone pads, and by the 13th century most of the peasant buildings excavated at Goltho (Lindsey) were supported in this way. It used to be thought that the earthfast post tradition was quite distinct from the traditions of both cruck and post-truss framing (which we will explore later), but recent writers have downplayed the extent to which superstructure can be read into excavation plans. Several cases have now come to light where buildings with jointed frames supported on both cruck and post-and-truss systems were dug into the ground, and would have left evidence which, if excavated, would seem to belong to the earthfast post tradition.

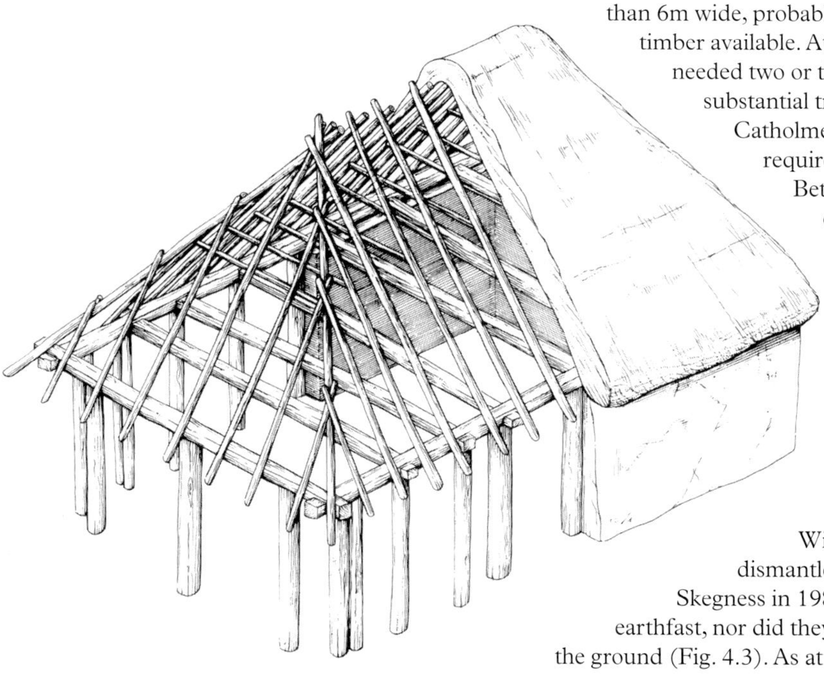

Fig. 4.2 Philip Dixon's reconstruction of a post-built 'hall' from remains excavated at Catholme (Staffordshire).

The Goltho dwellings were up to 15m long, while earlier buildings at Catholme ranged in length from 4m to 12m. But at neither site were any more than 6m wide, probably indicating the maximum length of timber available. At both places each house would have needed two or three beams of this length, implying substantial trees. Apart from these beams, the Catholme and Goltho buildings would have required only (relatively) small pieces of timber. Between the upright posts (whether earthfast or not), walls at both places were of clay, probably daubed onto spindly uprights of timber – a technique known as mud-and-stud construction that lasted in the region into the 19th century. Indeed, when reconstructed some of the Catholme and Goltho buildings look remarkably similar to those erected centuries later.

A direct descendant of this type of building constructed in about 1790 at Withern, on the Lincolnshire marshes, was dismantled and moved to Church Farm Museum, Skegness in 1980. Unexpectedly, its posts were not earthfast, nor did they sit on padstones: they simply rested on the ground (Fig. 4.3). As at Catholme and Goltho its timbers were

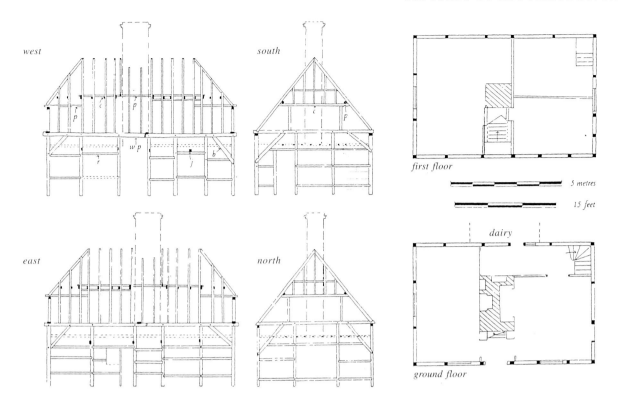

west

south

east

north

first floor

5 metres

15 feet

dairy

ground floor

b=brace, c=collar, p=purlin, r=rail, wp=wall plate

Drawn and reproduced with kind permission of Naomi Field

Fig. 4.3 Naomi Field's record of the 'mud-and-stud' cottage at Withern (Lindsey), *dismantled in 1980 and now re-erected at Church Farm Museum, Skegness.*

not regularly sized, nor were they regularly spaced. More than 200 similar buildings are known from Lincolnshire, the great majority from the north-eastern parts of the county, the clay vale, the Wolds and the marshes.

These building traditions were therefore remarkably long lived. Beneath the castle at Eaton Socon, for example, they clearly pre-date the 12th century, but at Stratton (Bedfordshire) and at Burystead, Raunds and West Cotton (Northamptonshire) they are of the later medieval period. Requiring a couple of major beams and only basic carpentry skills, they could probably be constructed within each community, without the need to call in outside specialists. Trees for major beams would have been 'standards' in managed woodlands (ie they would have been allowed to grow on through several cycles of coppicing). The few necessary standards could be obtained from the limited communal woodlands which existed in most parishes. Such major timbers might be re-used in building after building (*see* Fig. 4.13). Throughout much of the region, the roof was of wheat or barley straw, plentiful in an area with much arable land. Although thatching skills are quite specialised, they were held by many in each village community, learnt not just for thatching cottages but used more frequently for thatching haystacks. Floors also used local materials. Typically they were made from beaten clay dug from designated places in the common fields, but they could also be of a plaster made from lime, made by burning the local limestone, or – particularly in the Trent Valley – from gypsum derived from deposits in Derbyshire and Nottinghamshire (p.170).

Further up the social scale more specialised carpentry skills might be required, and buildings deploying such skills have survived better than those with more simple construction methods. Among extant East Midlands buildings we find examples of both widely used methods for building rigid, free-standing frames:

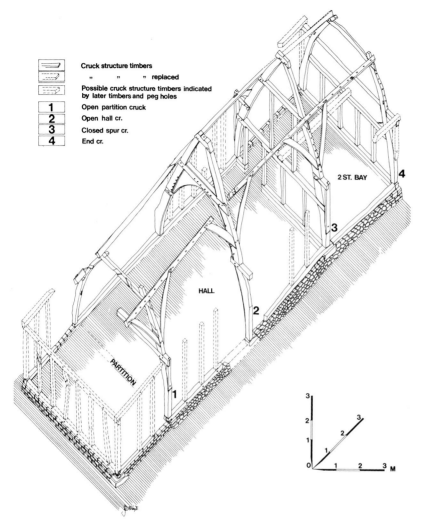

Cruck structure timbers
" " " replaced
Possible cruck structure timbers indicated by later timbers and peg holes

1 Open partition cruck
2 Open hall cr.
3 Closed spur cr.
4 End cr.

Fig. 4.4 Nat Alcock and Peter Woodward's three-dimensional record of the cruck-framed cottage at Husborne Crawley (Bedfordshire).

cruck framing and post-truss framing. In cruck framing, the building's weight is carried by pairs of large, usually curved, braces, extending from the floor to the roof's ridge beam (Fig. 4.4). There are usually at least two such pairs in each building, with the remainder of the frame supported on these principal structural elements. As with earthfast post buildings, cruck frames usually require other major timbers for tie beams spanning the width of the building. The enormous, often naturally curved, braces, which form the cruck 'blades', were carefully grown to provide an appropriate shape. Cruck building, then, implies access to extensive and carefully managed woodlands, with a choice of standard trees. But common-field village communities typically had relatively limited woodlands and very few of the hedges (where we know standard trees were sometimes grown in East Anglia). Even though such standard trees may have been beyond the resources of many common-field parishes, no parish in the region was further than 30km from a forest where such specialised timbers might have grown. Erecting cruck blades and cutting complex joints may also imply specialist carpentry skills, and these may also have been held by workers from the forest areas, who might have travelled to common-field villages to undertake building work.

Many writers have drawn attention to the asymmetrical distribution of cruck-framed buildings within England (Fig. 4.5). They never seem to be found east of a line running northwards through central Bedfordshire, and along the line of the Great North Road to Newark. In Nottinghamshire the only crucks north of the Trent are found in the western parts of the county. This distribution is also puzzling to those with interests in the wider landscape because, as we have seen, most distribution patterns in this part of England follow the south-west to north-east boundaries established by the pattern of settlement nucleation. The distribution of cruck-framed buildings seems to ignore these deep-seated landscape boundaries and, instead, is concentrated in western England and the Welsh borders. If cruck-framed buildings were made possible by a combination of the supply of specialist timber and skills based in major woodlands, this distribution map suggests that the woodlands in question were mostly within the north-western settlement province. It is also noticeable, however, that there are concentrations of crucks near some of the East Midlands' forests. They occur in Derbyshire, south-east of Charnwood, in Northamptonshire (a county with many forest areas) and in north Buckinghamshire and southern Oxfordshire, adjacent to the forests of Bernwood and Wychwood.

In southern and eastern England (including the East Midlands east of the Great North Road), a different style of timber framing was dominant: the post-and-truss system. Here the building was supported on a series of upright posts, each of which carried a frame constructed to support the roof, known as a truss; the whole was held together with sophisticated carpentry joints. Such post-and-truss assemblies were often made in prefabricated units and sometimes hauled upright on the building site (Fig. 4.6). These buildings also required standard trees from extensive and closely managed woodlands and, even though the major components were differently shaped, the trees would be grown just as carefully as those for cruck blades.

Stuart Wrathmell's recent study of these intriguing distributions suggests, however, that there was a distinctive approach to vernacular building in the East Midlands. It may not be the way the frame of the building is made that shows that we are in 'village England', but rather the manner in which panels within that frame are filled. No matter how the frame was built, the elaborate infillings used within such panels in the South East or in the West are absent from the East Midlands. Here we find virtually no ornamental panels (close studding or herringbone framing), which would require a ready supply of substantial planks. Instead, in the central province, where timber was in relatively short supply, panels within frames are filled in as they had been in the earthfast post tradition, with mud-and-stud – a technique which requires only split pollard poles

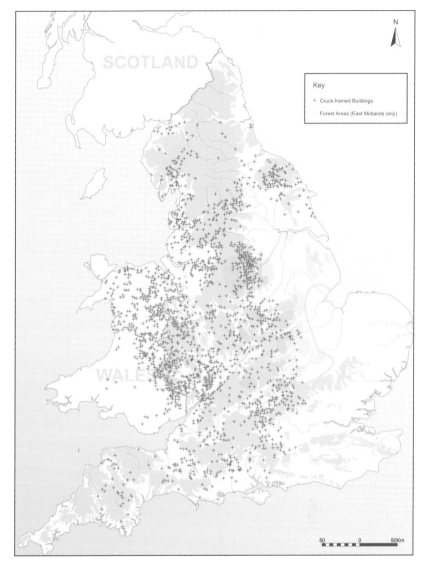

ABOVE: **Fig. 4.5 Distribution of recorded cruck-framed buildings in England and Wales** (source: Alcock 1981).

Fig. 4.6 Nat Alcock's record of the timber-framed hall and cross-wing building at Basmead Manor, 2km north of Wyboston.

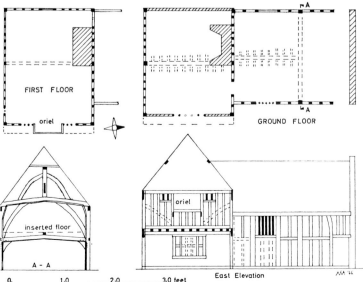

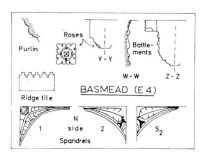

121

and other 'underwood'. This quality of wood was, we can be sure, readily available within the limited woodlands of each common-field parish. Such distinctions between village England and the South East and North West were already a talking point in 1577, when William Harrison could write:

> *In the open champaign countries they are forced, for want of stuff, to use no studs at all, but only frankposts … whereunto they fasten their splints or raddles, and then cast it over with thick clay to keep out the wind.*
>
> (Withington ed. 1876, 113)

So, in the East Midlands, vernacular buildings, constructed around simple frames supported on irregular posts, first appeared in the Neolithic period and continued in use until recent times. Such buildings used a couple of major beams (sometimes re-used from earlier buildings) and required minimal carpentry skills. From the 13th century onwards, however, more sophisticated structures, belonging either to the cruck or the post-and-truss tradition, were the products of specially grown timber and more specialised carpentry skills. Such timbers and skills may have been indigenous more to the larger areas of woodlands, either to the south-east or the west, or perhaps within the more limited East Midlands forest areas, but in much of village England, the frame itself may have been imported into the village. Local resources and skills were used only to fill in the frame once erected, and the region's individuality was expressed in this secondary process. Planks were not common in most East Midlands communities, though split coppice poles were plentiful, and so was clay and straw from the extensive arable. Consequently mud-and-stud panelling was widely used in the East Midlands for the walls of houses, no matter how the frame itself was made.

In such buildings, the frame would be quite robust, but the wall fabric would need continual repair and replacement. In 1799 the agriculturalist Arthur Young said that a mud-and-stud cottage could be built for as little as £30, whereas its equivalent cost in brick might be double that. No doubt such discrepancies would influence many landlords in their choice of materials, but it was often tenants who were responsible for maintenance. Consequently, once brick became cheap and readily available, mud-and-stud infilling was quickly replaced with brick. The replacement occurred, however, at different times in different parts of the region. It was once thought to be a 17th-century phenomenon, but we now know that it extended over a much longer period, spreading only slowly through the economic classes. Virtually all vicarages and rectories (relatively high-status buildings) in Bedfordshire and Buckinghamshire had the infilling of frames replaced in brick between 1700 and 1800. In parts of Lincolnshire and Nottinghamshire, however, entire villages were rebuilt in brick between 1770 and 1870, leaving few signs that there had been any earlier dwellings at all.

STONE AND BRICK BUILDING

It is only a short step from filling-in the frame with brick or stone to making these materials carry the weight of the roof itself, and doing away with the frame altogether. This building technique, called mass-walling, also has a long history. It occurs, after a fashion, in some Iron-Age buildings, and certain Romano-British stone buildings at Dragonby had neither timber frames nor earthfast posts. These buildings used mass-walling in local limestone, sometimes with rounded corners, and they may have carried sill beams for timber framing higher up the walls. None of them is thought to have been of more than one storey, but taller buildings of stone mass-walling were widespread in the Roman world, and East Midlands communities would have known such structures. They were certainly present in the region's towns.

We have already noted continuities between Romano-British and Anglo-Saxon timber building, but the archaeological record seems to show a clear break in the use of mass-walling, at least in larger houses. Although great churches and palaces with mass-walling in stone are known from Anglo-Saxon England, it seems the technique was not generally used for vernacular dwellings between the 5th and the 9th centuries, although stone rubble was used for infilling timber frames where it was readily available. Even following the common-field revolution in the 10th century, buildings in areas of limestone tended to use stone only for non-structural purposes. The stone walls of the simple buildings of 10th- to 12th-century date at sites such as Gainsthorpe (Lindsey – *see* Fig. 3.27), rarely took the weight of the roofs. Where such villages have been excavated (for example at West Cotton and Raunds, Northamptonshire) the only buildings with mass-walling in stone are churches and high status houses. Until the 12th century, most other buildings were supported on timber frames.

Why should this be? Were stone-working skills only available in limited circumstances? We shall see (p.166) that each community along the East Midlands limestone belt had its own quarry, and used its stone for a wide variety of purposes. Winning such stone, however, involved little more than prising it out of the cliff, while for many purposes working it involved hitting it with a hammer. Such quarries and methods would have yielded only rubble, useful for paving and boundary wall construction. To make walls strong enough to take structural weight, however, requires the skill to extract substantial blocks intact and to cut them. It also requires the ability to make mortar, which implies a lime kiln and an entire industrial technology, which, although not rare, might not have been available within each community until later in the medieval period.

By the late medieval period, however, stone walls in the East Midlands limestone belt *were* providing a ground storey, upon which timber frames were placed to support the second storey. Initially such buildings were still restricted to the upper orders of society, as at the Old Vicarage, Sleaford (Kesteven) (Fig. 4.7). At Kings Sutton (Northamptonshire) and Bloxham (Oxfordshire), however, such stone walls were also used in vernacular two-storey buildings that belonged to more prosperous 16th-century peasant farmers.

Being apparently restricted to the more prosperous members of the community, it is not surprising, perhaps, that few 16th- and early 17th-century examples survive, even in villages where stone was used extensively in subsequent years. By the mid-17th century, however, stone-built versions of the 'three-in-a-row' plan (which, as we shall see, had become the dominant house-plan form in many Lincolnshire and Nottinghamshire villages) are more common. Moor Farm Humby (Kesteven), for example, is dated 1631, whilst nearby, The Pryory, Heydour, takes this type of stone house one critical stage further, having not only a symmetrical façade, but also three chambers over the three ground-floor rooms (*see*, for example, Fig. 4.8). This layout remained remarkably popular amongst small farmers throughout the late 17th and early 18th centuries and depended on a local stone-building industry. Such buildings are often tricky to date, although sometimes they have distinctive fashionable details (the early 18th-century two-storeyed bay windows found in Rutland, at

Fig. 4.7 The Old Vicarage, Sleaford (Kesteven) is a late-medieval building with a timber-framed upper storey sitting above a stone-built lower storey. *Originally built within the churchyard, it may have been occupied by the cantarist of St Mary's Guild by 1440.*

ABOVE: *Fig. 4.8 Simple two-storeyed houses with five or six rooms, built and roofed in local materials, provided accommodation for many prosperous East Midlands families after c. 1650. This late 17th-century example is at Cranford St John (Northamptonshire).*

BELOW: *Fig. 4.9 The mid 17th-century east wing of Aslackby Manor (Kesteven) is decorated with the elaborate brickwork that defines the local 'Artisan Mannerist' style.*

Bidwell Farm, Clipsham, for example). Such architectural features were probably produced to order at the quarries from standard templates.

By the 18th century, village buildings of this status were also appearing in brick. Although used in prestigious late medieval projects like Tattershall Castle, in the 16th and 17th centuries brick had only been used extensively for vernacular building along the banks of the Trent and the Humber. At this time bricks were usually made immediately adjacent to the building site. Between 1593 and 1600, the bricks for Doddington Hall (Kesteven) were made in clamps two fields away from the house itself, while in 1649 William Occarbie of Crowle (Isle of Axeholme) was arraigned for 'making bricks on the common of the parish and selling them out of the manor'. At South Ormesby, Drayner Massingberd (pp.84–5) was making about 80,000 bricks per year in the later 1670s and used them, particularly, for building chimneys of estate cottages which were otherwise of mud-and-stud construction.

In the 17th century bricks were novel and fashionable, and were flaunted further down the social scale. In Nottinghamshire, Lincolnshire and Cambridgeshire particularly, decorative brickwork was used to ape classical architectural details and to give buildings pretensions beyond their station. There are splendid (but undated) examples at Coningsby (Lindsey) and Aslackby (Kesteven) (Fig. 4.9), whilst at North Wheatley (Nottinghamshire) the manor is dated 1673. By the 18th century, however, bricks were becoming an unexceptional sight in East Midlands villages, and good supplies of local clay meant that they did not have to be transported far. Many towns with suitable clays (Lincoln, Newark, Derby, Bedford, Northampton and Oxford) developed a ring of 18th-century brickworks around their fringes, and exported bricks along the river network. In April 1710 eight barge-loads of bricks, made east of Bedford, passed down the Ouse through Hemingford Lock (Huntingdonshire) on their way to fenland building projects. The bricks of each area were distinctive in colour and texture, from the deep reds of the Trent valley to the creamy whites of the Gault clay, which runs parallel with the chalk escarpment south-westwards from Royston. But they were still not cheap. Costs only fell dramatically with the industry's expansion in the 19th century (pp.191–3), largely because the railways reduced the cost of transport. The impact of this 19th-century traffic on East Midlands architecture was dramatic. The railways spelled the end of the regional diversity in building styles and materials to which England had become accustomed, and in its place local builders purchased their materials from remote centres by catalogue.

THE FAMILY WITHIN

Most later Bronze Age and Iron Age roundhouses had internal hearths, and the distribution of finds within them tells us that different activities (sleeping, cooking, recreation, craftwork etc) were allocated distinct areas within the great open circular space.

At Mingies Ditch (Oxfordshire) the houses had mysterious clay-lined pits adjacent to their doors, and although their purpose is not yet known, they are evidence for conformity in the planning of internal space. Even more striking is the observation that virtually all the doorways in prehistoric houses face east or south-east. Both functional and symbolic explanations for this have been put forward, but we shall see later that, in pre-modern societies, practical requirements were usually overlain with ritualised meanings; consequently, both explanations are probably applicable.

The Gravelly Guy excavations (Oxfordshire) revealed about 30 roundhouses from a single settlement (*see* Fig. 3.3). At any given time the excavated part of the settlement may have included a dozen families: a similar population density to that presumed in 14th-century Wyboston. But why should individual houses, and individual families, be brought together in a single place, whether they were built in the Iron Age or in the 10th century? We have already explored a number of factors which might provide an answer (pp.62–5) and, although lordly *diktat* has lost its popularity as an explanation for the phenomenon in the 10th century, it is still often proposed for the Iron Age. Perhaps the architecture of the houses themselves can help our thinking about this problem? No matter how rigidly divided into activity zones, a circular house plan is, after all, a fundamentally non-hierarchical architectural form. The single hearth, placed somewhere near the centre, is visibly 'shared', as are many other domestic facilities. In a rectangular house, however, it is inevitable that parts of the house will be further from the fire than others. Distinctions in status are intrinsic in the very plan itself.

Few distinctions in plan, or patterns of use, were visible between most of the houses at Gravelly Guy. All were buildings of approximately the same size, laid out within the settlement in similar groupings in an apparently uniform way, with no one house being given particular prominence. To a visitor approaching the settlement, there would have been few indications where the more powerful members of the group dwelt. This more 'democratic' view of Gravelly Guy seems to parallel the most recent views on medieval nucleations in the East Midlands. Both see the grouping together of houses in nucleated settlements, and the more communal styles of agriculture that implies, as a community enterprise, undertaken by the whole community for communal benefit.

Although the relative sizes and spacing of buildings at certain Iron Age settlements, such as Colsterworth, might indicate some level of social hierarchy, there are other ways to interpret features such as the 'defensive' ditches surrounding some sites, which are also said to be evidence for social competition between settlements. In the river valley below Gravelly Guy stood the enclosed settlement at Mingies Ditch (Fig. 4.10). Gravelly Guy was established several centuries before Mingies Ditch, and occupies the more favourable location for settlement in this area. Mingies Ditch appears to be an outpost of the community at Gravelly Guy, established at a relatively late date in the development of the community, on the more marginal land. In fact Mingies Ditch may have been originally cut out of woodland, and was perhaps associated with specialised grazing. Indeed, Mingies Ditch appears to be the Iron Age equivalent of a medieval assart. Seen in this way, its surrounding ditch appears less a military feature than the equivalent of enclosures around medieval 'stockings', a feature aimed at securing domesticated stock in the woodland environment. Thinking of enclosed Iron Age settlements as specific, not to a location in a social or military hierarchy, but to a marginal location in the landscape, may help resolve diametrically opposed views about the character of Iron Age society.

Fig. 4.10 Iron-Age 'assart'? *The small enclosed settlement, occupied between about 250 BC and 100 BC, at Mingies Ditch (Oxfordshire), as envisaged in a watercolour reconstruction from the south by the Oxford Archaeology Graphics Office.*

If the Iron Age was more communally minded than was once thought, was it the Romans who introduced hierarchical concepts into the village? At Dragonby, the continuity between Iron Age roundhouses and the rectangular Romano-British ones was impressive, but we should beware of thinking that the changes introduced by the Romans were merely of decorative style. It may be difficult to transfer patterns of social inter-relationships from roundhouses to rectangular buildings; consequently, the change in house-plan form, seen at so many Iron Age sites that continue into the Romano-British period, may represent a more profound change in society. The inward-looking Iron Age building, where all activities faced the fire and were to some extent communal, was replaced with one where it was possible, for occupants of different status, both to retire to different ends of the house and, at least in theory, to look outwards through windows into the landscape. Such views had been potentially available for centuries, but we might ask why it seems they were only appreciated now. Is that also something to do with new ideas of ownership and status? Was keeping an eye on your land, and on your neighbours, now felt to be especially important?

Buildings at sites such as Catholme can offer glimpses into hierarchies within Anglo-Saxon society. There was no return to circular houses, at least not in the East Midlands, whilst the presence of halls of differing sizes might suggest continued observance of the social hierarchies observed in Romano-British settlements. Several major halls with annexes and satellite buildings occupy the community's core. They may be sequential in date, rather than contemporary, however, and it would certainly be easier to explain a single hall for the community's leading family than it would be to explain two or more rival establishments. Scattered around the larger halls in a loose arc are as many as 10 smaller rectangular dwellings (more in some phases than others), often accompanied by even smaller utility buildings (*see* Fig. 3.15). Presumably these structures represent accommodation for the village rank-and-file, although the floor area of some of them is not much smaller than the centrally placed hall(s). Virtually all these lesser buildings have doorways in their long sides, sometimes opposed by a door in the other wall (Fig. 4.11a). The interiors of such buildings were often divided into two, to one side of the 'through-passage' (although little evidence was recovered for physical barriers at Catholme).

Similar layouts continued to be standard for the majority of the population until the early modern period. Houses of this type are depicted on the Bayeux Tapestry; the last of them were built in brick on the Lincolnshire fen edge in the 19th century, and the author Flora Thompson knew them as a girl in Juniper Hill (Oxfordshire). Between the 11th and 13th centuries the type is well represented at the excavated villages of Goltho (Lindsey) (Fig. 4.11b) and Barton Blount (Derbyshire), but at neither village is it possible to match individual buildings to peasants of known status. Indeed, such buildings were occupied by a broad spectrum of social classes. This is the type of house Chaucer had in mind for the milkmaid in the 14th-century *Nun's Priest's Tale*, 'Ful sooty was hir boure and eek hire hall'. In Long Crendon (Buckinghamshire) some 20 cruck-built cottages of 15th- and 16th-century date survive, many with this layout. These were occupied by yeomen and tradesmen as well as smallholders, so this house plan was evidently common to quite a wide range of income groups (Fig. 4.12).

This building type was also the most frequently encountered in East Midlands inventories of the later 16th

Fig. 4.11 Comparative plans of houses at (a) Catholme (Staffordshire) – 7th century, (b) Goltho (Lindsey) – probably 13th century, and (c) Wyboston – perhaps 16th century (sources: Loscoe-Bradley & Kinsley 2002; Beresford 1975; Alcock 1969).

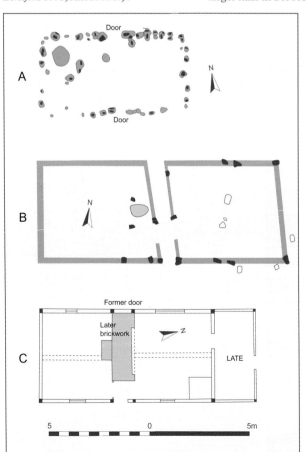

and 17th centuries, but it had ceased to be universal amongst the common people during the late medieval period, as more prosperous peasants invested in their properties by enlarging them. A greater standard of privacy and comfort was expected if it could be afforded, but the investment also reflects rising confidence in security of tenure: heads of families were increasingly likely to take their children's prospects into account when considering investments in property. Such enlarged buildings were often swept away in late 18th- and 19th-century rebuilding, but Thimbleby (Lindsey) has a number of single-storeyed, three-roomed houses with hall, parlour and an extra 'buttery' (a room for agricultural work and also sleeping) all in a line (Fig. 4.13). In contemporary inventories, this three-roomed arrangement occurs more frequently from about 1600: a Duchy of Lancaster survey of 1608 showed that in Toynton (Lindsey), 11 out of 23 houses were of this type. Here such buildings were called 'houses', whereas most of the remainder were 'cottages' of the earlier two-roomed type (although two 'cottages' still had only a single room).

In the Duchy survey as a whole, 25 per cent of houses were larger, with a hall, parlour, service room and two chambers (usually at first floor). Between 1600 and 1650, three-quarters of the Lincolnshire population lived in houses with two rooms over two, even though few examples survive today. In Bedfordshire in the same period, most people describing themselves as yeomen and husbandmen lived in houses with three, four or five rooms on the lower floor and two or three chambers over. Half of

ABOVE: *Fig. 4.12 No. 134 Great North Road, Eaton Socon. This typical example of the 'two-roomed' type of cottage found across the East Midlands in the 16th, 17th and 18th centuries was one of seven surviving examples still standing within the village in the 1960s.*

BELOW: *Fig. 4.13 A typical 'three-roomed' cottage, probably of the early 17th century. This example, built in the mud-and-stud tradition, is at Thimbleby (Lindsey). Note the reused timber post supporting one corner of the additional third chamber.*

those describing themselves as labourers lived in single-room cottages, although during the late 17th century numbers of such cottages declined sharply. Whereas during the Anglo-Saxon and medieval periods it was not easy to define an individual's social status by looking at his or her accommodation, from the late medieval period onwards, it seems that housing in the East Midlands became an increasingly accurate indicator of the occupier's position in society.

A new landlord, particularly one like Piggott, the London lawyer who purchased Doddershall in 1495 (p.77), might have built houses on his estate for the remaining workers which emphasised his newly acquired social position. In 'closed' villages of the 16th and 17th centuries across the East Midlands, many buildings with carefully judged differences of detail or plan were put up by landlords keen to realise their vision of local society. At Langar (Nottinghamshire), Lord Howe rebuilt the rectory, the inn and several farmhouses in the first three decades of the 18th century, while the grammarian, lawyer and wrestler Sir Thomas Parkyns (1662–1741) provided the nearby closed village of Bunny with a hall, a school, almshouses, an inn, a range of farms, houses and cottages, many of which he designed himself. The size and ornamentation of new buildings at both places was carefully judged and suited to the proposed social status of the occupants. Earl Harcourt was equally socially conscious at Nuneham Courtney (Oxfordshire) where, during the 1760s, the village was relocated to make way for parkland, and new buildings were established along the Oxford–Reading road. Here the inn, the curate's and the blacksmith's houses were clearly distinguished by their size and details, whilst other tenants were subdivided into a more favoured group occupying houses with a tiny upper floor and those with only two rooms. The impression created by the buildings of estate villages of this sort became an important symbol for the paternal landlord, particularly in 'closed' villages in the 19th century. The East Midlands boasts many fine examples (Fig. 4.14): the over-perfect thatched cottages of Great Tew (Oxfordshire) are said to have been designed by J C Loudon between 1809 and 1812; those at Wimpole (Cambridgeshire) belong to the 1840s, whilst the delightful houses of Warden (Bedfordshire) re-created the village as an extension of Lord Ongley's 'Swiss style' garden in the 1820s. Ongley had his tenants dress in red cloaks to harmonise with the buildings!

Between 1750 and 1850, Parliamentary enclosure left more of a mark on the East Midlands' building stock than the piecemeal private enclosures that had preceded it. The former common fields were suddenly dotted with new two-storeyed farmhouses – often with distinctive names like Waterloo (Fringford, Oxfordshire) or Victory Farm (Moulton) – now sitting at the centre of their new lands. Such late 18th- or early 19th-century buildings are so ubiquitous in our landscape that we hardly notice them. They are frequently functional structures, often with paired rooms downstairs and upstairs either side of a hall and with a two-storeyed range projecting at the back, for kitchen and servants. They are always of brick and could be bought 'off-the-peg' from local builders. In fact they were often similar in size and design to the new parsonages, built by rectors who had used the mechanism of the enclosure award to extinguish tithes in return for income from a new enclosure farm.

The reorganisation of land and labour implied by enclosure also resulted in at least one new building type in some villages. This was the row of small cottages aimed at attracting the landless labourer or the lower class of servants, like that at Achurch (Northamptonshire). An example, containing numerous cottages, in Bletchingdon (Oxfordshire) dates from 1794 and is typical in that each cottage has one room downstairs and another over (Fig. 4.15). Such rows represent new thinking by landlords, who now believed that society's lower orders needed to be mobile to service the new market economy. They had to be able to rent accommodation cheaply and to move when economic circumstances dictated.

Although newly built and with little requirement for maintenance, such rows represented only a small step upwards for the rural poor. Concern for the living

conditions of the established peasantry, who had lost out during the upheavals of Parliamentary enclosure, drove a number of other housing schemes. Much the most famous of these was the Chartist Land Company, whose houses at Charterville (Oxfordshire) were an embodiment of what was thought necessary and appropriate for the agricultural labourer in the 1850s. They were single-storey structures with two rooms, one on either side of the front door (Fig. 4.16) – not much different in plan form and size from the lesser buildings at Catholme erected 1,500 years earlier. As at Catholme, a few utility buildings were grouped outside the back door, for storage and other tasks associated with cultivating the land. Charterville did not meet with the success anticipated by its idealistic founders, but such schemes continued to be inaugurated, and both that established in 1901 at Carterton (Oxfordshire) and the Land Settlement Association estate in Wyboston (p.113) of the late 1930s still adhered to the simple two-room plan with centrally placed front and back door. By the 1930s, however, even lifestyles for the rural poor had developed to a point where they could no longer be contained in two rooms: these houses also had space upstairs.

TOP: **Fig. 4.14 Estate cottages and almshouses at Revesby (Lindsey).** *The entire village was rebuilt c. 1850–70 by the Banks family of Revesby Abbey, to whom it belonged, and included a school and home farm.*

ABOVE: **Fig. 4.15 Terrace of workers' cottages at Bletchingdon (Oxfordshire),** *newly built of local Jurassic limestone in 1794. Such rented accommodation aimed to attract, as well as to exploit, the new, more mobile, workforce in the re-invigorated post-enclosure landscape.*

BUILDING THE TOWNS

We know surprisingly little about minor urban structures in the Romano-British East Midlands. Modern excavations have been aimed at the more distinctive and prestigious buildings, and few lesser buildings are known of either stone or timber-frame construction. Several examples are from southern Lindum (Lincoln), a mile from the forum, where a group of at least nine traders' houses have been excavated (Fig. 4.17a). All were timber-framed structures, serving three roles:

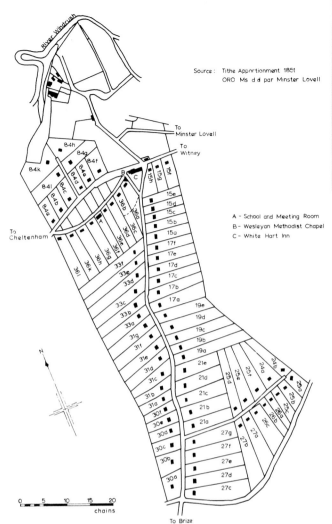

Source: Tithe Apportionment 1851
ORO Ms d d par Minster Lovell

To Minster Lovell

To Witney

A – School and Meeting Room
B – Wesleyan Methodist Chapel
C – White Hart Inn

To Cheltenham

To Brize Norton

0 5 10 15 20
chains

accommodation, workshop and shop. As is usual in towns of all dates (where street-front space is valuable) they were laid out with their gable ends onto Ermine Street. The earliest dated from the early 3rd century AD and was constructed with regularly spaced aisle posts at ground level. Although this might have represented an aisled hall structure, like the Dragonby buildings, it is more likely that it was of two storeys, with the posts supporting the upper floor. Such buildings bear comparison, in structure and plan, with the 'strip buildings' discovered in many small Romano-British towns, such as those excavated at Staniwells, further north on Ermine Street.

Little evidence has come from most East Midlands towns for domestic occupation before the 9th century (p.65). Only within Northampton have three early Anglo-Saxon *grubenhauser* been recovered, although the remains of two such structures have also been found outside Roman Leicester's south gate. Such ephemeral structures are not always easily spotted in excavations, however, and other towns may eventually yield similar examples. If such buildings really are

ABOVE: **Fig. 4.16 Layout of the Chartist settlement at Charterville (Oxfordshire) in 1851** *(source: Tiller 1985), and (above right) a cottage of 1847–50 from Charterville, with relatively few more-recent additions.*

RIGHT: **Fig. 4.17 Plans of urban house types from Lincoln, from the Romano-British period to the 14th century:** *(A) Romano-British 'strip building' in Wigford; (B) 10th- or early 11th-century house on Flaxengate; (C) late 12th- or 13th-century house at Flaxengate; (D) Row of commercial properties on Steep Hill (sources: Jones, M J, 2003; Jones, R H, 1980; Perring 1981; Jones, S, et al. 1996).*

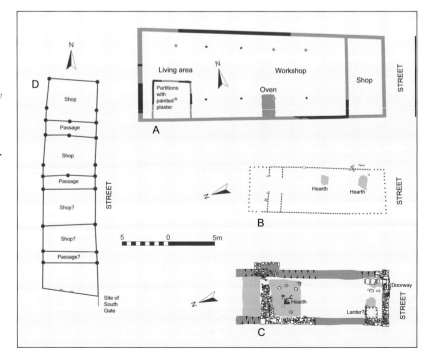

temporary structures (p.115), however, one would expect to find them in places that were *not* used for permanent settlement. In a former Roman town, like Lincoln or Leicester, *grubenhauser* might have been occupied, perhaps seasonally, by those involved in recycling stone; but in Northampton it is unclear why temporary occupation might occur. Occupation in mid-Saxon Nottingham might also have been of temporary nature: in the first, 9th-century, reference to the place it is called *Tigguocobauc*, 'the place of the cave dwellers'. Genuine urban occupation suddenly developed at all of the region's shire towns shortly afterwards however, and those urban buildings of the 10th century so far discovered have been almost exclusively timber-framed; even in Lincoln, which not only lay on a zone of exposed limestone, but was also dominated by the ruins of Roman stone structures. As in the countryside, in the 10th and 11th centuries stone was only used in the towns for stacking around timber frames, not for taking structural weight. Mass-walling in stone was a technique still reserved for churches. Urban timber-framed buildings were similar in form to many structures in the contemporary countryside. Although their construction techniques vary, 10th- and 11th-century buildings from Flaxengate, Lincoln are remarkably similar in size (about 5m by 10m) to the earliest structures at Goltho or Eaton Socon (Fig. 4.17b). Some Lincoln examples had gable ends onto the street, and therefore probably had doors in their end walls, like their Romano-British predecessors; but we are unsure whether this was the norm, and at least one Flaxengate structure had its doorway in the long wall, like the Goltho examples, being accessed from the street by a passage between buildings. Such buildings, with side passages, fitted neatly onto even the smallest burgage plots at Oxford (which were laid out at the same time and were as little as 6m wide). Remains of such buildings have been discovered in St Aldates, Cornmarket Street, High Street and beneath the Norman castle. Fragments of buildings of this date and type have also been excavated in Bedford, Northampton and Nottingham.

Later medieval Leicester may have had many stone-built houses, but the only medieval domestic buildings known with certainty are all timber framed, lining the four main streets of the town within the walls. We know little about the domestic architecture of medieval Nottingham, Derby or Northampton, but, having been spared serious industrialisation, Stamford, Oxford and uphill Lincoln are among the finest places in the country to study the development of urban domestic architecture from the 12th to the 18th centuries.

In the second half of the 12th century, Lincoln (and probably the other towns as well) acquired fine stone-built residences: several still stand, and the footings of many more have been excavated. It appears, indeed, that central Lincoln was extensively rebuilt in stone, between about 1150 and 1250. The surviving buildings of this date, like the famous Jew's House, are presumed to have belonged to the wealthiest figures of the 12th- and 13th-century town and thus might qualify for consideration as elite buildings. However, stone buildings like those excavated behind the main street front in Flaxengate, for example, can hardly be placed in this category (Fig. 4.17c). All these buildings, with mass-walling in stone, represent a new building tradition, not just in terms of construction but also in their layout. Several of the standing examples, and several more of those whose plan is known through excavation, stood along the street, rather than gable end onto it, with their doorway near the centre of the long side. They adopted, therefore, a very ancient rural house plan rather than following the urban norm. Similar houses with mass-walling in stone and with doors in their long sides are known from Stamford (no. 15 and nos 16–17 St Paul's Street) and have been identified at Leicester (Guildhall Lane and St Peter's Cemetery) and Oxford.

Following Lincoln's economic collapse at the end of the 13th century, however, most domestic architecture in the town was of timber-framed construction, as was most late medieval building in other East Midlands towns. As the long, thin,

property plots were well established, in most places the components of later medieval urban houses – kitchen, hall, private chambers and shops/warehouses – often extend in a line away from the street. The Governor's House at Newark (a building dated by dendrochronology to 1474) had a range of shops along the street front, with a narrow passage leading to the rear (Fig. 4.18). To one side of the passage, and behind the street range, the hall range mimicked the halls of rural lords, with its screens-passage entry and its 'high' and 'low' ends. The kitchen lay beyond the hall and spaces above the shops in the range along the street were probably used as the owner's private chambers. Similar layouts have been found in all our major towns, and occasionally examples survive intact, like Number 34 St Peter's Street, Stamford. Takeley's Inn in Oxford, built between 1291 and 1300, was of this general type, but it had a double row of buildings along the street front, which probably housed shops at first-floor level.

Whereas there had previously been some similarities between urban and rural buildings of similar status, this becomes less true after the 16th century. In the late 16th and 17th centuries, most rural houses below gentry status were of two rooms; but in the towns, simple buildings of this type have proved less easy to find. Equivalent accommodation in towns may have been provided by rows (similar to those erected in villages in the 18th and 19th centuries), a building type which can be seen today at the top of Steep Hill in Lincoln, where nos 26–29 were built in the 14th century (*see* Fig. 4.17d). Most surviving urban houses of 15th- to 17th-century date reflect the urban rich – the retailer and merchant class who were not, for the most part, found in villages. Their servants (who must have formed the majority in the urban population) presumably lived in the recesses of their masters' houses. Consequently, shops (often the transverse range along the front of the property plot) are a distinctively urban building form. The 'Jews House' at Lincoln retains the remains of an early shop front in its ground floor and there two late medieval examples in Elstow (Bedfordshire) (Fig. 4.19), where the local abbey encouraged the growth of commerce at its gates. The abbey also ensured that six shops were included in the ground floor of the newly built moot hall. The White Horse in Cumbergate, Peterborough, is a late medieval merchant's house of similar plan to the Governor's House at Newark, but here the range behind appears to have been a two-storey warehouse used, it is said, for storing cloth and displaying it for sale.

Another frequently used urban building type, which is related to retailing and not often found in the countryside, is the stone-built undercroft (sometimes supporting a timber-framed building above). These structures were frequently used as 'wine bars', with access down steps from the street. Even though some towns had many such undercrofts (at least five still survive in Stamford – Fig. 4.20), not every house with an undercroft was occupied by a vintner. It seems more likely that merchants of all commodities liked to offer patrons a drink, and that patrons, coming in to slake their thirst, might also be tempted to buy the merchandise. Such undercrofts also survive in Lincoln, Nottingham and Oxford.

Fig. 4.18 The 'Governors' House', Newark, is a fine example of a typical late-medieval urban house-plan.

The street range contained commercial premises beneath private chambers (with large windows), which were part of a bourgeois house focused on the ground-floor hall that extended away from the street to the rear. The hall was reached through a broad passageway from the street.

OPPOSITE PAGE:

TOP: ***Fig. 4.19 John Bailey's reconstruction studies of the surviving shops at Elstow (Bedfordshire).***

BOTTOM: ***Fig. 4.20 The 13th-century undercroft at 13 St Mary's Hill, Stamford,*** *is an elaborate example of a relatively common urban building type. The staircase in the far corner is a later feature, originally access was via stairs down from the street.*

A more sophisticated level of hospitality was offered by the late medieval inn, where the whole entourage of a major aristocrat could be housed and fed. These institutions were probably also confined to towns, most of which boasted at least one such establishment by the 16th century. Famous East Midlands examples still surviving include The Angel and Royal at Grantham, which was rebuilt in the late 15th century, possibly following a visit by Richard III; The Saracen's Head at Southwell, of *c.* 1500; The White Hart at Newark (*c.* 1475); The George at Huntingdon, and The Golden Cross at Oxford.

The terrace and the square were the distinctive urban building forms in the 17th and 18th centuries, and both were erected in the more prosperous of East Midlands towns. In Northampton, the fire of 1675 stimulated rebuilding of the Market Square, redeveloped with rows of large townhouses around the edges. Most of these have now gone, but their attraction lay in the diversity of minor differences of height and elevation detail (*see* Fig. 3.34). Even though the rebuilding had been overseen by a single architect – Henry Bell of King's Lynn – these houses did not form true terraces. This was not a unified redevelopment of the type seen at Covent Garden in London some 30 years earlier, presumably because of the great number of property owners. Similarly, although it too was praised for the handsome townhouses lining it, Nottingham's market place was never redesigned to form a unified square either. In 1792 a design to replan the market space as a single architectural whole was drafted for Leicester, but it also failed to overcome opposition from individual landlords.

In the East Midlands, then, even the most admirable 17th- and 18th-century terraces are not that impressive and, in itself, that speaks of the vitality of political and social factions in major East Midlands towns. But the finest terraces of this date in England were not in diverse commercial centres but at places like

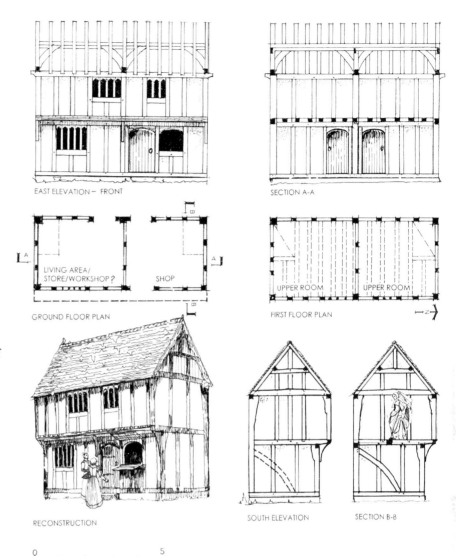

EAST ELEVATION – FRONT

SECTION A-A

LIVING AREA/ STORE/WORKSHOP ? SHOP

GROUND FLOOR PLAN

UPPER ROOM UPPER ROOM

FIRST FLOOR PLAN

RECONSTRUCTION

SOUTH ELEVATION SECTION B-B

0   5

Fig. 4.21 John Carr's magnificent crescent looks inwards towards St Anne's Well, the spa on which Buxton hoped to make its fortune. Unlike Bath's Royal Crescent, on which it was modelled, only part of the building was taken up with houses for rent. The prestigious central location was occupied by a smart hotel and assembly room.

Bath, Brighton and Tunbridge Wells, all of which were major resorts. Such terraces were built for rent by property speculators aiming to capitalise on the annual influx of wealthy visitors. There were few such resorts in the East Midlands, although where they did exist, for example at Buxton, grand terraces like The Crescent (designed by John Carr of York in about 1780) can be found (Fig. 4.21). Similarly, the Marquis of Hastings' attempt to promote a similar resort at Ashby-de-la-Zouche in the 1820s was accompanied by the construction of terraces at Bath Gardens and Rawdon Terrace.

Terraced housing in East Midlands towns is therefore much more likely to belong to the 19th century and to a lower social status. Buildings of this type have already been considered (in Chapter 3), but here we should note that, in the 19th century, with the arrival of mass communications and the long-distance transport of building materials, once again building types found in towns start to converge with those of the countryside. Terraced houses by the same builders who erected the suburbs of 19th-century Northampton can be seen in villages such as Earls Barton; as the economies of town and country became increasingly interconnected, it was once again hard to distinguish the house of a shoemaker from that of an agricultural labourer.

FURTHER READING

General
Barley 1961; Brunskill 1990 (brick building), 1992, 1994; Goodburn 1992; Grenville 1997; Hurst 1988; Innocent 1916; Johnson 1993; Quiney 1990; Smith 1965; Stenning (ed.) 1998.

Prehistoric and Roman building types
Drury (ed.) 1982; Garton 1987 (Dunston's Clump); May 1996 (Dragonby); Pryor 1998a, 2001 (Peterborough area); Salway 1981; Whitwell 1992 (Lincolnshire).

Anglo-Saxon building types
Addyman 1972; Dixon 1982, 2002 (Catholme); Hamerow 2002; Marshall & Marshall 1993; Tipper 2004.

Rural building types from *c*.1000
Addyman 1965 (Eaton Socon); Alcock 1969, 1981 (crucks generally); Alcock & Woodward 1976 (Bedfordshire); Bailey 1998 (Bedfordshire); Beresford 1975 (Goltho, Barton Blount); Cousins 2000 (Lincolnshire); Dyer 1986; Field 1984 (Withern); Roberts 1974 (Kesteven); Roberts & Wrathmell 2002; Smith 1970; Tiller 1985 (Chartists); Wrathmell 1994.

Urban building types
Bailey 2001 (Elstow); Courtney 1998 (Leicester); Faulkner 1966; Jones 2003b (Lincoln); Jones 1980 (Lincoln); Jones *et al.* 1984, 1987, 1990, 1996 (Lincoln); Ottaway 1992; Pantin 1947 (Oxford), 1962–3; Perring 1981(Lincoln); Schofield 1994; Stenning 1985; Vince 2003a, b (Lincoln).

Housing the Elite

'The greatest advantages men have by riches are, to give, to build, to plant and make pleasant scenes.' The words of Sir William Temple (1628–99) give eloquent expression to the aspirations of the wealthy and powerful throughout time. As in all parts of England, the East Midlands landscape has been shaped by many such gifts, buildings and pleasant scenes, extending back through history. This section explores the distinctive landscape contribution made by the region's upper classes.

Although many writers have been convinced that the Iron Age peoples of Britain lived within clearly defined hierarchies, with inferior and superior lords as well as peasants, only limited evidence for such hierarchies has been found in their buildings (pp.39–44 and 124–5). Perhaps we should remember that evidence for these hierarchies is partly based on written accounts by Roman historians, who did live within a clearly stratified society, and who might have interpreted society in Britain in line with their own expectations. After all, it was not until the Romans arrived that a class of buildings appeared in the landscape which expressed the social status of their owners by taking an extravagant form that was completely different from other round dwellings. These are the 'villas', and they provide clear architectural evidence of a two-tier society in the Romano-British countryside. The word 'villa' is not simply equivalent to 'farm'. Indeed, the villa excavations at Empingham (Rutland) showed that, although there was no farmstead around the villa itself, there were three contemporary Romano-British farmsteads within 1km. The villa recognised through aerial photography to the north of the church at Eaton Socon, similarly, is less that 1km from a concentration of coin and pottery finds that may indicate another farmstead on the road to Staploe. Some villas, indeed, had agricultural units attached (at Winterton, Lindsey, for example). But many did not, and villas are better defined as the rural retreats of the Romano-British elite, which is probably why many are so ostentatiously decorated: they are the setting for the display of wealth, not for its production. Many villas developed from less ostentatious farmsteads (which themselves often had origins in the Iron Age, like that at Deanshanger, Northamptonshire). Like most, Barton Court Farm villa (Oxfordshire) only became distinctively different from surrounding farmsteads (i.e. 'villa-like') in the late 3rd century.

Villas were not distributed evenly throughout Britain. Their distribution had a markedly south-eastern bias, with the great majority lying south-east of the Fosse Way. Most of the East Midlands lay in 'villa country', and more than 100 such sites are known, but within this overall distribution, intriguing concentrations and gaps occur. Very few, if any, villas are found in north Buckinghamshire and southern Bedfordshire, for example, or in south Warwickshire or southern Nottinghamshire. Some gaps may be explained by the presence of woodland but, elsewhere, areas which we might think were well-wooded seem to attract them. As villas represent only about 1 per cent of known Romano-British rural settlements, however, an absence of villas does not imply an absence of activity in the countryside.

Equally intriguing is the clumping together of villas at certain locations; some clustered around towns, especially those containing government administration. There are a number around Lindum (Lincoln) and Ratae (Leicester), at least three within a mile of Durobrivae (Water Newton, Cambridgeshire), and many close to other small towns such as Margidunum, Irchester, Godmanchester and Great Casterton. Many of these villas blossomed into large houses during the 3rd century, at the same moment that the 'small towns' (which have few really grand houses of their own) were themselves booming. Consequently it has been suggested that such villas might have belonged to the 'owners' of the agricultural market economy based in such towns. Like 19th-century factory owners, villa owners might have chosen to distance themselves from the markets on which their wealth depended.

Other intriguing groupings also occur. In western Oxfordshire up to eight villas all lie within the large ditched 'enclosure' formed by Grim's Ditch. If these ditches do represent an *oppidum* of the Dobunni (p.44), this might suggest that the descendants of individual Iron Age clan leaders, having become Romanised, established their family 'headquarters' on sites of ancestral power, within their tribal centre. This seems to have happened within the former *oppida* at Chichester, Bagendon (Gloucestershire) and Verulamion (Hertfordshire). A modern parallel might perhaps be that of King Lobengula of the Mtebele who built his detached Edwardian suburban bungalow within the royal Craal outside Bulaweyo, following his treaty with Rhodes. The cluster of villas on the upper reaches of the Witham south of Grantham (at Great Ponton, Gunby, Denton and Stoke Rochford) is less well understood. They might have been belonged to salt industry owners, as an ancient salt route from the Fens to the Midlands crosses the Witham in this area. The proximity of the small Romano-British town at Saltersford in Little Ponton parish might also be relevant.

Some villa sites may have been selected for the extensive views they afforded, though in many cases we are unsure whether the villas were the earliest buildings on these dramatic sites. Such buildings were, like 18th- or 19th-century country houses, frequently isolated from other types of settlement in the landscape. Examples of such strategic siting include some Lincolnshire villas: Claxby, Horkstow, Norton Disney, Roxby, Scampton, Walesby, Winterton and Worlaby all command big views across the adjacent valleys. Not only were the owners of such villas probably seeking views of their own land, but the villas' design may have dramatised the buildings within their landscapes. In both respects the villas established a tradition whereby the elite announced their domination of the local landscape through strategically located distinctive dwellings – a tradition which reached its epitome in the 18th century, and has still not vanished.

Even when they originated as relatively simple structures, villas frequently evolved into complexes of many rooms and buildings. The villa at Winterton (Fig. 4.22a) had a most dramatic location, with wide views to the west across the Trent valley. It had a great symmetrical range, of six architectural units, facing the western view, no doubt decorated with Vitruvian details. The rooms along this front were probably the 'state' rooms of the villa, but two other blocks of chambers (some also very fine), including a bathhouse, extended eastwards and formed a great walled courtyard, with its own gatehouse. Parts of these 'wings' were given over to stables and other agricultural activities, just as they were many generations later at the Duke of Marlborough's baroque palace at Blenheim (Figs 4.22b and 5.16). Unlike Blenheim (planned and built within a generation), Winterton grew by accretion in the 3rd and 4th centuries, but its owner may have had a status in his society not unlike that of an 18th-century peer, and the architectural expression of wealth was broadly similar in both cases. As at Blenheim, Winterton villa's large household and estate workers did not live in the nearest Romano-British settlement, but instead they populated this alternative architectural world. Not only were there buildings of more than one storey here, with mass-walling in locally quarried stone, but there were also expensive mosaics, hypocausts

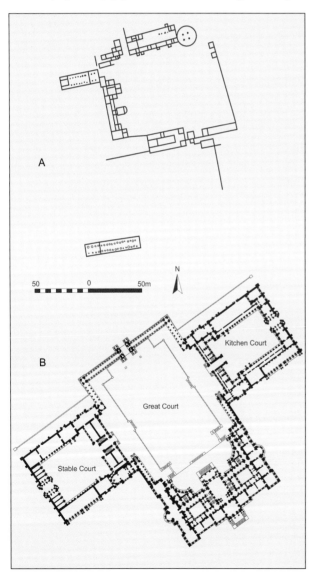

Fig. 4.22 Plan of the Romano-British villa at Winterton (Lindsey) (A), *excavated by Ian Stead, compared with the intended plan of the 18th-century palace at Blenheim (Oxfordshire) (B).*

A

50   0   50m

N

B

Kitchen Court

Great Court

Stable Court

and wall paintings: fittings that would have been as far beyond the experience of the contemporary rural population as the decorations by Grinling Gibbons and Sir James Thornhill at Blenheim were beyond theirs.

When away from home, aristocrats of the status of Winterton's owner would not be meanly housed. Indeed, the growth of such villas is matched by an increase in the scale and quality of private accommodation in major administrative centres. Although the minor towns of the East Midlands had few grand buildings in the 3rd or 4th centuries, Lindum and Ratae both acquired several large stone-built house complexes at this date, with levels of architectural finish similar to those of the finest villas. These are thought to have been the urban residences of the late-Roman aristocracy, used when governmental duties called them into town. The same late-Roman mosaic artists were employed at both the great villas and the finest townhouses, and archaeologists have grouped these artists into regional schools, which seem to cut across the old Romano-British tribal divisions. Most mosaics in the East Midlands are thought to be products of a school working out of Durobrivae, and examples of their work are found in the territory of both the Corieltauvi and Catuvellauni.

Durobrivae mosaicists found patrons, not only in villas, but also at an exceptional 'palace' complex terraced into the valley side just across the Nene at Castor (Fig. 4.23). This enormous building, apparently with wings and loggias, was 110m across – twice the width of the main range at Winterton. It was clearly related to the town at Durobrivae, which it overlooked, but no owner or administrative role has yet been demonstrated. It invites comparison with the enormous 'palace-like' structure off Greetwell Road, 1.5km east of Lindum (Fig. 4.24), which was even larger than the Castor building and arranged around an enormous arcaded courtyard, like the palace at Fishbourne (Sussex). This is clearly not a villa of conventional type, and it may be the residence of the Roman governor of Britannia Secunda, one of the four provinces into which the country had been divided by AD 312. We do not know the boundaries of this newly created administrative unit, but presumably it occupied most of the East Midlands, although the southern parts of our region would have been part of Maxima Caesariensis or Britannia Prima.

One of the principal distinctions between the Romano-Britons and the early Anglo-Saxons is the absence of aristocratic structures of the villas' scale or distinctiveness in the Anglo-Saxon period. There were, of course, relatively prestigious Anglo-Saxon buildings: at Catholme and many other places, relatively large halls stood near the settlement's centre (*see* Fig. 3.15). But such buildings were *within* the settlement, alongside other dwellings, and were similar in type. It seems that social hierarchy within the Anglo-Saxon settlement lacked the dramatic architectural expression it had been accorded during the Roman period. The Roman villa, with its many chambers and circulation routes, reflected the social

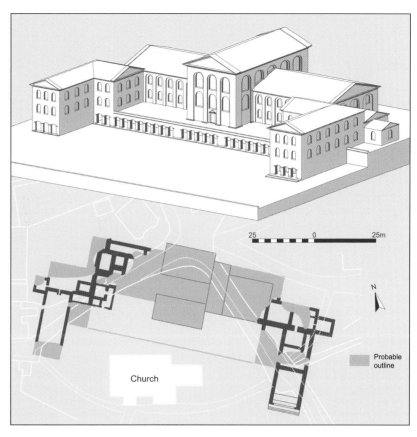

Fig. 4.23 One possible reconstruction, according to Don Mackreth, of the extraordinary Romano-British 'palace' beneath the village of Castor near Peterborough. *The plan shows how it relates to modern features and to the church site (whose origins lie in the 7th or 8th century).*

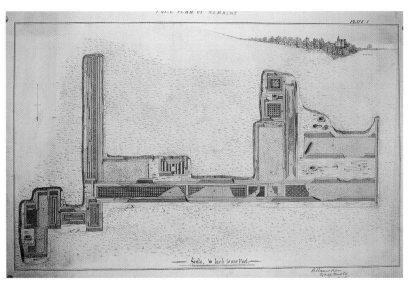

Fig. 4.24 Plan by B Ramsden of the tantalising remains of the huge 'palace' complex located just to the east of Lincoln. The complex was revealed during quarrying in the 1880s and known as the 'Greetwell Villa' (Lincoln City and County Museum. Copyright, Lincolnshire County Council).

Fig. 4.25 Reconstruction study of the earlier of the two Anglo-Saxon 'palace' halls in central Northampton. The important church of St Peter stood less than 100m to the west (source: Williams et al. 1985).

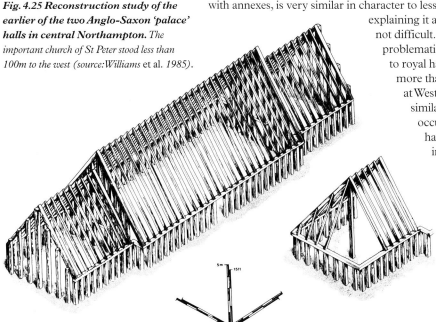

complexity of its society. Similarly, the simple architecture of the Anglo-Saxon hall was, quite consciously, a microcosm of this community's less complex hierarchy. It was an inclusive building, in which every community member had an allotted place, within sight of his or her neighbours. In some settlements there may have been only one hall, representing, as it were, the entire community. The hall's rectangular plan could be used to demonstrate social distinctions between the elite at the 'high' end, perhaps on a dais, and servants serving food at the other, but it was important that the entire community was contained under a single roof. In this respect, even though rectangular rather than round, the Anglo-Saxon hall seems more similar to the Iron Age roundhouse than to the rectangular buildings of Romano-British settlements.

A few buildings of distinctively higher status than the typical Anglo-Saxon hall are known from the 7th to 9th centuries, and one was excavated in the centre of Northampton in 1980–2. Here, to the east of the presumed early church of St Peter, the superimposed plans of two great halls lying east–west were recovered, near the top of a gentle slope leading down to the Nene. The earlier hall was timber-built, with posts set in trenches, and dated from the mid-8th century. It was very large: the hall itself was more than 25m long (compared with, for example, the 12m length of the largest hall at Catholme) and it had substantial square annexes at either end, adding another 10m to the overall length (Fig. 4.25). In the early 9th century this building was replaced by an even larger hall, more remarkable still for being made of stone. The stone hall was in the region of 35m long, with a single annex at the west end.

The first Northampton hall, with doors centrally placed in its long sides, and with annexes, is very similar in character to lesser Anglo-Saxon halls, and explaining it as the residence of a senior lord is not difficult. However, although a couple of problematic contemporary documents refer to royal halls built of stone, we have to wait more than 250 years (until William II's hall at Westminster) before a secular building similar to Northampton's stone hall next occurs in England. Such peculiarities have led to the alternative interpretation that both Northampton buildings are monastic refectories rather than secular halls. In our present state of knowledge, stone does seem to have been almost exclusively reserved for church buildings in Anglo-Saxon England.

Between Stanton Harcourt and Drayton (Oxfordshire) a cluster of unexcavated crop marks has been taken to indicate another group of large halls and their service buildings. They lie in a similar topographical location to those at Northampton, on a gentle slope looking towards a crossing point of the Thames near Abingdon. Here the largest hall, probably timber-built, was also about 25m long. Documentary sources say nothing helpful about Northampton or Drayton, but they do point to Tamworth (Staffordshire) as a settlement important to the Mercian royal dynasty in the late 8th and early 9th centuries, and we might have expected to find halls of this type there. Within a circuit of defences, which might have originated as an enclosure around a great hall, a group of timbers and other features were discovered in excavations in 1968, which hint at structures of this type.

The lord's hall was a long-lived architectural concept. Indeed, the large space in which the lord's entire community could be assembled proved useful into modern times, although after about 1600 it frequently became an ante-chamber to the house proper. By the later medieval period, the original form, with its open roof, centrally placed and open fireplace, and its 'high' and 'low' ends, had acquired great symbolic meaning. Here the entire community could be seen at a single glance, and yet individual members could also be clearly located socially relative to their companions. The careful, but largely intangible, divisions of space within the late Anglo-Saxon timber hall were glimpsed in excavations at Sulgrave (Northamptonshire), where a hall dating from about 1000 had opposed doors in the centre of the long walls, just like those of 500 years earlier. A detached building (also of timber) stood at either end, one of which was the kitchen. We can presume that that the kitchen was near the low end of the hall. The building near the opposite high end was presumably, the 'bower' of which we hear much in documentary sources. This was a more private chamber to which senior members of the household might retire. The most striking evidence for status in the Sulgrave hall, however, was the evidence for benches ranged along certain lengths of wall. Such benches would not be for honoured guests in the hall, who would have been seated at free-standing tables in the central spaces, nor would they be for servants who would stand, waiting to serve at the tables. The benches probably indicate an intermediate level of society in the hall: perhaps the lord's more humble tenants.

Sulgrave was probably typical of East Midlands halls around the turn of the first millennium. Similar buildings probably existed at all the more important manors, and this type of establishment has been excavated at Goltho (Lindsey), where it represents the manor of Bullington, eventually the headquarters of the Kyme barony.

At Goltho the halls were replaced about once every generation (Fig. 4.26), raising the intriguing possibility that the hall was a very personal symbol of lordship in the landscape. As was the case with the hall called *Heorot* in *Beowulf*, each Goltho hall may have symbolised not just the authority of the Kyme family in general, but that of an individual lord of the Kyme estate. The earliest hall was slightly bow-sided, in the Viking manner, and apparently stave-built, but it was also subdivided, with private spaces at one end and with a floor on two levels, one of which contained the hearth. In subsequent halls, the hearth was also asymmetrically located towards one end, indicating a gradation of internal space, and several of them had at least one aisle, which might also have functioned as a further marker of social distinctions. All the halls were accompanied by

Fig. 4.26 Eight successive generations of halls superimposed on each other over a period of less than 300 years, excavated by Guy Beresford at Goltho (Lindsey). Dates: A and B c.850–950; C and D 950–1000; E 1000–1080; F and G 1080–1150; H c.1150.

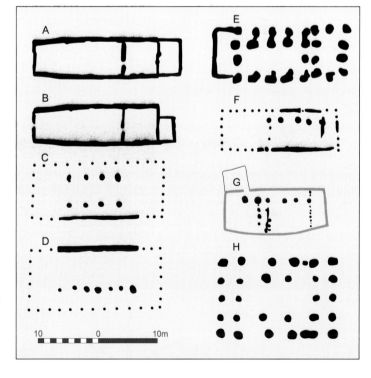

Fig. 4.27 Like all the English 'shire' castles, Oakham Castle (Rutland) was founded by William I, who raised a great motte within a large walled enclosure, adjacent to the principal church. *Although now isolated amongst its earthworks, the castle's late 12th-century aisled hall was originally joined to other buildings (see the blocked doors in the east wall) and surrounded by yet more.*

Fig. 4.28 Boothby Pagnell Manor House (Kesteven) is an icon of 12th-century domestic architecture, *yet only recently Edward Impey and Roland Harris showed that a much larger hall originally lay to the east (left).*

subsidiary buildings, thought to be either bowers, kitchens or agricultural buildings. The hall of the early 12th-century generation was enveloped by the bailey defences of a motte-and-bailey castle, but its form was little different from those it followed.

The Norman Conquest seems to have made little impact on the sociology of Goltho, as the post-Conquest hall reveals the same subtle subdivisions of internal space, including a single aisle, which had been a feature of the pre-Conquest halls. The final Goltho hall, however, probably of late 12th-century date, represented a new beginning. The castle structures had gone, and the hall now stood in the centre of a large moated platform. Yet its architecture was much more ambitious than anything here earlier. This timber hall was 19.5m by 12m, and apparently had a continuous aisle around all four sides with clerestory lighting. Oddly enough, there was less evidence for space allocation in this final hall than in any of its predecessors, but it did have opposed doors at the low end, with the central hearth shifted towards the high end.

Goltho's final timber hall would have resembled the contemporary stone hall at Oakham Castle (Rutland) (Fig. 4.27) and this design set the pattern for halls for public feasting, lordly judgment and displays throughout the remainder of the medieval period. Magnificent aisled halls of this type are known at the Bishop of Lincoln's palaces at Lincoln itself, at Buckden (Huntingdonshire) and Lyddington (Rutland), and they also existed at many of the more important castles and manors (Leicester Castle – built in timber, like Goltho – and Ashby-de-la-Zouche, Leicestershire – *see* Fig. 4.32). At his Lincoln palace, the bishop had two halls. The grand aisled building to the west, on the public side of the palace, was clearly for ceremony, and its architectural details represented a carefully considered essay in the display of status and power. The first-floor 'private' hall to the east, surrounded by comfortable chambers, was serviced by garderobes (latrines) and by the private chapel, and was much more representative of medieval lordly accommodation.

'Private' accommodation at Lincoln's Bishops' Palace was integrated with the bishops' personal hall, but we have seen that, at earlier dates, such accommodation was often provided in separate buildings, usually reached through a doorway in the high end of the hall. Such chamber blocks, containing suites of private lordly apartments, have sometimes been so well appointed that they have been mistaken for the principal buildings of the manor. The famous 12th-century stone-built hall at Boothby Pagnell (Kesteven) was originally just such a chamber block belonging to the manorial hall of the de Boby family, the foundations of which lie beneath the lawn further east (Fig. 4.28). Both of the other East Midlands stone chamber blocks of this type and date (at Hemingford Abbots, Huntingdonshire and the 'School of Pythagoras' in Cambridge) might also turn out to be the private chambers associated with halls that have now gone. Fine chamber blocks, or 'solars', were constructed alongside the lord's hall throughout late medieval times, taking the form, in cases like South Kyme (Kesteven), of bold stone towers attached to ground-floor halls. Here, and perhaps also at Halloughton (Nottinghamshire) and Longthorpe (near Peterborough) (Fig. 4.29), the hall has been joined in the landscape, as the architectural marker of lordship, by the tower: a feature visible from much further away. The gigantic four- and five-storey towers built by Ralph, Lord Cromwell at Tattershall (Lindsey) and South Wingfield (Derbyshire) (see Fig. 4.33) and by Lord Hastings at Ashby-de-la-Zouche (Leicestershire) (see Fig. 4.32) represent spectacular examples of the genre.

The Bishop of Lincoln also marked his lordship in the East Midlands landscape with a magnificent four-storeyed brick solar tower, located where it could be seen by the maximum number of travellers, on the Great North Road at Buckden (Fig. 4.30). Marking the estate centre in the landscape was an important function of the manorial hall, no matter how small the estate, and many East Midlands halls belonged to only minor lords, like the 12th-century example belonging to the de Furneus family, excavated at Raunds (see Fig. 7.13). These more typical manorial halls are represented by standing examples at Northborough (near Peterborough) and Shutlanger (Northamptonshire). At Stanton Harcourt (Oxfordshire), although the hall has gone, many of its associated buildings survive (Fig. 4.31). The survey of Lincolnshire lands of the barony of Bayeux undertaken in 1288 shows that the manor houses of Thoresby and Calcethorpe both had a hall and chamber; at Stewton there was a hall, a little chamber and a kitchen, while at each of the more valuable manors of Linwood and Welbourne there were halls, two chambers, kitchens and brewhouses. Linwood also had a bakehouse and a little chamber for the baker and his flour.

Linwood manor was also surrounded by a moat and, from the 12th century, these distinctive earthworks became very common in the East Midlands, as in

Fig. 4.29 Longthorpe Tower, Peterborough, was built between about 1300 and 1310 by local man Robert de Thorpe, Steward of Peterborough Abbey. *Robert may have thought it important to emphasise his status through such a demonstrative building because his family had risen to gentry status recently, from origins amongst the peasantry. Inside, flaunting further his sophistication, the principal chamber is decorated with wall-paintings with complex allegorical meanings.*

England as a whole. In 'village England' moats are found in the densest concentrations in and around the forest areas, where '-green' and '-end' place-names are common. They occur especially frequently in western Cambridgeshire, Huntingdonshire, central and eastern Bedfordshire and in the vale of Aylesbury.

Beggary manor seems a typical example of an East Midlands moated site although it only survives in part. The 'assart' settlement here (pp.71–2) would have contained a small hall for the manorial lord, from at least the 12th century, and other structures connected with the hall and farm also stood within the moat. By the late medieval period, Beggary manor-house was a timber-framed, apparently aisle-less, hall, with a cross range at one end, containing the more private apartments of the lord and his family. These moated buildings became the home of Richard Stocker (1579–1656) and his son Oliver (1612–67), who both called themselves 'gentleman'. The medieval hall at

ABOVE: *Fig. 4.30 Alongside the Great North Road (middle distance – west), the Bishop of Lincoln's palace at Buckden (Huntingdonshire) was rebuilt in the 1470s and 1480s using a prestigious new material – brick.* Within the boundary wall were a series of courtyards, the central of which contained a fine ground-floor hall, a chapel and a great chamber next to the fine solar tower, with its octagonal angle-turrets. To the north-east, earthworks indicate an elaborate garden layout, whilst the parish church, south of the tower, may also once have been within the site.

RIGHT: *Fig. 4.31 Stanton Harcourt Manor (Oxfordshire) contained similar components to Buckden (Fig. 4.30) but on a smaller scale, as befitted the local lords of the de Harcourt family.* Here the parish church lay east of the manor, which had two courtyards. The outer contained the gatehouse (within the scaffolded buildings along its northern side). The inner courtyard (marked by concentric planting) contained the hall, facing the gatehouse – linked to the surviving solar tower – and the magnificent detached kitchen, with its faceted conical roof.

Beggary was demolished, it is said, in the 1920s, but it apparently looked like houses still standing within comparable moated sites in the outlying parts of other nearby parishes, like Blackburn Hall, Thurleigh, which has an aisled hall and a 16th-century cross wing. Other examples of this simple plan occur widely across the East Midlands and can be accurately dated: that at Long Crendon (Buckinghamshire, with an aisled hall), for example, to 1205; at Fenlake Barns (Bedfordshire) to 1210–20; Sutton Courtney (old Berkshire) to 1370–1400; Sun House, Potton (Bedfordshire) to *c.* 1450; and The Gables, Little Carlton (Nottinghamshire) to *c.* 1580. This plan, ancient as it was, was not superseded in houses of this 'gentry' status until the late 17th century, when the 'double-pile' – the grouping of two rectangular ranges in parallel to form a single house of square plan – came into fashion. The earliest dated English example of this latter plan type may also be within our region, at The Priory, Brant Broughton (Kesteven), built for William Garnon ('gentleman'), which carries a date-stone of 1658.

Less conservatism was shown among house builders at higher levels of society. Whereas the gentry clung onto essentially medieval house types until after the Civil War, the aristocracy had become interested in new types of domestic building several generations earlier. Some later medieval houses belonging to the uppermost levels of society simply followed the traditional layout of many manorial halls. This was the case at Lord Burgh's ambitious, but conservative, house at Gainsborough when it was largely rebuilt between *c.* 1470 and 1500. Gainsborough Old Hall was originally set within a moat, and has a timber hall, but an extended solar block, with a tower, and an up-to-date lodgings range, all in brick. Timber was retained for the hall alone at this building, no doubt because this was the traditional material for such structures. Expensive, modern brick for the lodgings, however, would have advertised the generosity of Lord Burgh's hospitality. The Old Hall sat at the end of the main street of Gainsborough town, symbolising Lord Burgh's responsibility for, and engagement with, the life of his tenants. His superior status was marked out by the moat and by the form and size of his house, but he was locating himself clearly *within* his community, albeit at its apex.

Lord Hastings's castle at Ashby-de-la-Zouche was on a similar long-standing manorial site at the edge of a small town. Unlike at Gainsborough, the late 15th-century refurbishment, including the large solar tower, were part of a development of the 'private' side of the site, overlooking the extensive, secluded gardens. Although it is not certain that the impressive water garden south of the tower belongs to the same period, it seems clear that some sort of private garden in this area was intended, to provide vistas from the new solar tower (Fig. 4.32).

Lord Hastings's domestic buildings were about status, but he was less interested in locating his new buildings visibly within contemporary Ashby. He was more concerned to impress the (presumably quite limited) group of aristocratic guests entertained in his new garden. At South Wingfield (Derbyshire), the connection between the aristocracy and the remainder of the community was broken completely. The manor was acquired

Fig. 4.32 Ashby-de-la-Zouche Castle.
Lord Hastings's refurbishment in the 1470s involved new buildings (including the tower) on the south-facing, 'private' side of the castle and was focused on a substantial garden layout, which underlies the complex earthworks visible in this view from the south-west.

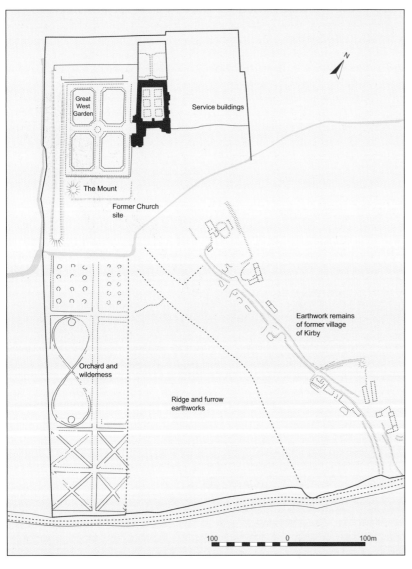

by Ralph, Lord Cromwell in 1439 or 1440, but he set about constructing his ideal home from scratch, providing us with a valuable example of the landscape aspirations of the contemporary aristocracy. The house is neither moated nor fortified, but more significant still, it is located a mile from the settlement to which the manor belonged, and even further from the parish church. Was the manor-house always isolated in this fashion? Or were tofts associated with the earlier manor-house relocated by Cromwell? Wingfield was certainly isolated within parkland by the 17th century (Fig. 4.33), but we might suspect that the park was actually created by Lord Cromwell to isolate his house from the surrounding community. Although subjected to considerable later reconstruction, Haddon Hall (also Derbyshire) has many similarities with Wingfield. It too was probably isolated from the associated village by its parkland from the mid-14th century.

Although considerably later in date, and dressed in Renaissance architectural details, Sir Christopher Hatton's house at Kirby Hall (Northamptonshire), begun about 1570, is similar to Haddon and Wingfield. It too had an outer and an inner court with an axially placed hall opposite the entrance. Its high-status private chambers were also behind the high end of the hall, and guests here were also housed in individual suites of lodgings around the inner court. The village of Kirby was certainly removed, in order that Sir Christopher's new gardens should be quiet, and so that the new house's setting would not be disrupted by his tenants' agricultural operations (Fig. 4.34). Although Kirby Hall's architecture imitated an ancient ideal, then, with the lord in his place among his community, in fact Sir Christopher had divorced himself in the landscape from the community in which he sat.

There are many examples of the Kirby mentality, where the presence, location and type of hall are the only visible reminder of the lord's position

in his community. Houses surrounded by hectares of newly created parkland, with agriculture pushed out of sight, became characteristic of the aristocracy during the late 16th century. In this region good examples were built in Derbyshire in the reigns of James I and Charles I at Hartington Hall (dated 1611), Renishaw Hall (c. 1625, for George Sitwell) and at Weston-upon-Trent (built c. 1633 for the Roper family, but apparently never completed). Holme Pierrepont, Staunton and Thrumpton halls survive in Nottinghamshire, while in Leicestershire spectacular examples are still to be seen at Quenby Hall (begun c. 1615 for George Ashby) and Shenton Hall (dated 1629). In Lincolnshire the restrained elegance of Doddington Hall, built in 1593–1600 for the diocesan recorder, Thomas Taylor – with its long vistas towards his former 'office' at Lincoln Cathedral – is of this type. Cambridgeshire examples include Madingley Hall (built c. 1547 and 1609 for the Hynde family) (Fig. 4.35) and Bourn Hall (dated 1607). Buckinghamshire includes Gayhurst (started 1597 by William Mulso), while in Oxfordshire, Broughton Castle and Rousham (c. 1635) remain, although Sir Henry Lee's house at Ditchley has gone.

Such houses are most frequently found in Northamptonshire, however; the county of 'Squires and Spires'. In addition to Kirby Hall itself, we can still visit Apethorpe (c. 1500–50), Boughton House (c. 1550), Canons Ashby (begun 1551) (see Fig. 3.31), Castle Ashby (begun 1574), Deene Park (substantially altered before 1585) and Rushton Hall (substantially altered in the 1590s). The original Holdenby Hall, a truly palatial building, was also a Northamptonshire house of this type (c. 1574–83) (see Fig. 4.38). It was built by the same Sir Christopher Hatton, Elizabeth's youthful Lord Chancellor, as Kirby Hall, but was demolished in the 1650s. Perhaps the finest of all, Burghley, was built here by Elizabeth's eponymous chief minister, Lord Burghley, on the Great North Road just outside Stamford between c. 1555 and 1587.

Why did so many members of the Tudor court find Northamptonshire a convenient location to build their new houses? John Norden called it 'the Herald's Garden' in 1610 because it contained so many armigerous families. In addition to Hatton and Burghley, Lord Compton (Castle Ashby) was a hunting companion of Henry VIII, Sir Edward Montague (Boughton) was an executor of Henry's will, Sir Walter Mildmay (Apethorpe) was a senior figure in Elizabeth's court, and Sir Edmund Brudenell entertained the queen at Deene in 1566. These men would have shared ideas on architecture and estate management, and the fact that they were all able to buy properties in Northamptonshire suggests that estates containing surplus land for conversion to parkland were to be had here. This may have been because such a large area of the county had been forest hitherto, and

ABOVE: *Fig. 4.35 Madingley Hall (Cambridgeshire) is typical of many grand country houses of the 16th century, built by prosperous gentry (in this case by the Hynde family, c.1547–96).* Today's landscaped grounds retain structure and planting from 'Capability' Brown's layout of 1756, when village houses were re-located by their landlords in the Cotton family (earthworks survive on the left – south-of this view) and roads were re-routed to permit satisfactory distant views of the house and attractive vistas from its windows.

OPPOSITE PAGE:

TOP: *Fig. 4.33 This early painting of Wingfield Manor (Derbyshire), made by Thomas Smith in the late 17th century, shows the house before it was abandoned.* It gives a good impression of the separation of the house in the landscape from the nearest settlement. Although Lord Cromwell was keen to show that he was the head of the community by using the architectural vocabulary of lordship, he did not want to be 'within' it and in the 1440s he placed his new house deep inside his hunting park.

BOTTOM: *Fig. 4.34 The setting of Kirby Hall (Northamptonshire).* The plan shows the earthworks of the evacuated village of Kirby and the layout of new gardens in the common fields.

Fig. 4.36 Close together physically, but far apart in concept, the Old Hall at Hardwick, part-way down the hill, is a confusing jumble of manorial ruins, originally located close to its home farm and its workers' houses. The New Hall, isolated on the crest of the hill above however, can be seen for miles across this part of Derbyshire and addresses the entire landscape. This visibility was Bess of Hardwick's main requirement in marking the birthplace of the dynasty she hoped to found.

the development of enclosed private hunting parks would have left large areas of former chase available for redevelopment. It also seems that, in the 16th century, Northamptonshire was thought to be sufficiently close to London for owners to 'commute' to court conveniently.

Not all aristocratic builders were members of the Elizabethan establishment, however. Some of the most innovative and advanced architecture of the age was built by more eccentric figures. Foremost among these must be Elizabeth Cavendish (Bess of Hardwick), Countess of Shrewsbury (*c.* 1520–1608). The story of this extraordinary woman's independent fortune, four husbands and formidable reputation as a plotter and schemer does not concern us here, but we cannot avoid noting her impact on the Derbyshire landscape and on English architectural history. We know little of the new house at Chatsworth, which she began in 1552, but Hardwick Hall is a very personal statement: this was where her (relatively lowly born) family came from (Fig. 4.36). Unlike the Old Hall (which Bess retained as a didactic feature in her new garden), Hardwick Hall was designed to be seen from the valley below, being set right on the skyline for maximum impact. With its huge glass windows flashing in the setting sun, and the openwork parapet with the letters 'ES' silhouetted against the sky, it appropriates the whole of the Doe Lea valley as its park. From the house itself, vertiginous views are offered from the same huge windows: the allegorical hunters decorating the long-gallery plasterwork on the upper floor seem to fly out through them into the hills beyond. Full use was also made of the roof as a walkway, with its own discrete chambers, where privileged guests could relax in privacy and enjoy the impression that the Cavendish estates were even larger than they were in reality.

Hardwick, standing so tall, was thought a great 'prodigy' by contemporaries and very clearly dominates and appropriates its landscape, yet it floats way above the communities on which the family's prosperity was based, and has no visual links with them. The same could be said of Wollaton House, 6km west of Nottingham. This is another 'prodigy', built (in 1580–8) by another social outsider, Sir Francis Willoughby, a coal-mine owner. Like Bess of Hardwick, he planted his new house in a highly visible location overlooking the landscape in which his money had been made. To ensure that his guests fully appreciated his dominance of the locality, Wollaton had a dining hall on the roof with huge glazed windows. Like that of Hardwick, the village of Sutton Passeys was cleared away to provide a large park around Wollaton. Both Hardwick and Wollaton were designed by Robert Smythson, who was also responsible for spectacular and novel houses at Worksop (Nottinghamshire) and Barlborough (Derbyshire). Houghton House, near Ampthill (Bedfordshire) was probably a similar type of building. Erected in about 1615 for Mary, Countess of Pembroke, it too sits on the hill crest and 'appropriates' its local landscape. As at Hardwick, Wollaton and several other prodigy houses, the hall at Houghton House is merely an ante-chamber to the main stairs and to other equally important rooms. It was suitable for brigading servants, but was not somewhere the mistress or master would want to dine in the midst of the community.

This aristocratic trend towards separating themselves from the communities over which they held lordship, looking 'over the heads' of the population into the landscape beyond, continued through the 18th century. In 1707 at Kimbolton Castle (Huntingdonshire), Sir John Vanbrugh and Nicholas Hawksmoor were asked by the 1st Duke of Manchester to turn a real manor-house, set at one end of the communal market place (as at Gainsborough), into a contemporary pastiche of a medieval house. Eventually (*c.* 1765), an imposing symmetrical gatehouse, in neoclassical style, was carefully designed to ensure that shoppers in the market could not see into the castle grounds. In fact the gatehouse and castle façades are so clearly symmetrically placed, but at the same time so out of kilter with the houses along the south side of High Street, that they still seem to threaten them with demolition (Fig. 4.37). Eighteenth-century inhabitants of the small town can have had little doubt about their lord's intentions regarding their homes and businesses.

Kimbolton High Street survived, but many similar communities were unable to resist the aristocratic drive for *lebensraum* between the Reformation and the Napoleonic Wars, and the list of settlements moved out of newly created parkland is a long one: from early examples like those at Holdenby, Kirby and Sutton Passeys, through Belton (Kesteven) in the 1680s, to later ones like Stowe (Buckinghamshire), in the first half of 18th century, Rousham (in the 1740s and 1750s) and Nuneham Courtney (Oxfordshire, 1760s). The aristocracy were able to put space between themselves and their compatriots both socially and physically. They were able to mould the landscape, along with its inhabitants, into any shape that pleased them, and they took full advantage.

Such changes in the balance of English society are sometimes seen as the product of the Reformation. The purchase of church lands following the Dissolution of the Monasteries (1536–40) had transferred great power over the landscape into secular hands. Because most church estates were already well run, the Dissolution itself resulted in few changes in farming practice or in the landscape created by it. There is little evidence for an increase in the rate or extent of enclosure, for example. However, the new landlords now had enlarged incomes to spend on their houses and, indeed, many of them had also acquired large building complexes – former churches and cloisters – as part of their new estates. There were over 100 monasteries in the old diocese of Lincoln and virtually all of them were converted into houses of some sort within a generation or two of the monks' departure. The new owners were not supposed to leave the former monastic church available for use, but such rules may not have been strictly followed. The canons' choir at Launde Abbey (Leicestershire), for example, became the domestic chapel of the new house. For the most part limitations on new owners were imposed only by their own

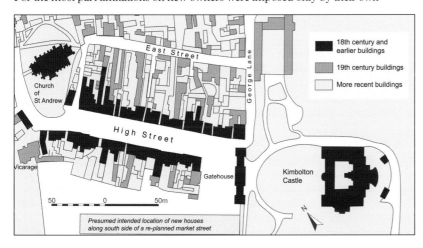

Fig. 4.37 Kimbolton (Huntingdonshire), showing the relationship of the medieval and later buildings on the High Street to the new buildings of the mansion erected by the Montague family in the 17th and 18th centuries.

ingenuity and purse. Frequently, a monastic cloister became the core of a new house, arranged around a three- or four-sided courtyard: there are examples at Hinchinbrooke Priory (Huntingdonshire); Woburn Abbey and Chicksands Priory (Bedfordshire); Thurgarton Priory and Welbeck Abbey (Nottinghamshire); Delapre Abbey (Northampton) and Stoneleigh Abbey (Warwickshire). An alternative was to build around a former infirmary, abbot's house or guesthouse (as at Wroxton Abbey, Oxfordshire; Barlings Abbey and Revesby Abbey, Lindsey; and Leicester Abbey).

At most of these houses traces of the monastery were not deliberately preserved: if the pre-existing buildings could not be easily re-used, they were demolished and the stone itself was re-used. However, in a number of interesting cases, the converters of monastic buildings took steps, for whatever reason, to preserve a memorial of the monastery. The most spectacular example of such careful conservation is at Newstead Priory, Nottinghamshire, where the Byron family carefully preserved the elaborate west façade of the monastic church alongside their grand new house, built around its cloister. It seems likely that a symbolic point was being made: by leaving this useless but dramatic remnant, the Byrons were making it clear, visually, that they were the secular successors of the medieval church's local power and prestige. Similar didactic motivations have been suggested for the conversion of the former abbot's house at Barlings Abbey (Lindsey) into something like a palace by the powerful Duke of Suffolk; the conversion of the remains of the canons' choir at Launde Abbey into the family chapel might be another example of similar impulses. This case is made particularly interesting because Launde was purchased by Thomas Cromwell himself, before his fall, and was intended as his own family's home. By the 18th century, of course, having a Gothick ruin in the landscape garden had become *de rigeur*. Monastic eye-catchers were created out of genuine monastic ruins at Barlings Abbey and Tupholme Priory (both Lindsey), but more frequently they now had to be built from scratch (as at Wimpole Hall, Cambridgeshire).

We have seen (pp.85–6) that, until the late medieval period, much hunting went on in the open chase rather than in enclosed spaces, but enclosed hunting within parks became increasingly common as the ceremony and theatre of hunting grew more elaborate. Some hunting parks were at a considerable distance from their owner's houses and, in such circumstances, the hunting party needed convenient accommodation on site; thus the hunting lodge developed. Unaltered examples of such buildings are now relatively rare. In some cases the family eventually relocated to the park, with the lodge becoming the core of a much larger house (as at Worksop Manor, Nottinghamshire or Goltho Hall, Lindsey). Elsewhere, the park became defunct and the lodge was demolished, in which case it may survive as a ruin (Tower-on-the-Moor, Lindsey), or as an earthwork, such as the moated site a mile south-west of Rockingham Castle (Northamptonshire). Each park would be surrounded by a 'pale' (a deer-proof stockade, usually distinguished from other linear ditches in the landscape because the ditch is on the inner side), with specialised gates ('leaps') to allow stock in and out, and with 'drives', 'lawns' and (in the later and more developed parks) 'stands'. These were specialised viewing platforms, usually erected at the ends of drives, from which the highly ritualised 'kill' could be watched by spectators at the end of the pursuit. At Beckley Park (Oxfordshire), a purpose-built hunting lodge was built in a former royal hunting park *c.* 1540 by Lord Williams to complement his houses a few miles away at Rycote and Thame Park.

Although parkland was also often established around new aristocratic houses on ancient sites, and settlements were sometimes moved to give the new house elbow-room, many parks were laid out over former arable fields, often those belonging to the more marginal settlements. As well as the remnants of the ridge-and-furrow of such fields, sometimes parkland around great houses also includes the highly informative earthworks of earlier, formal garden schemes. Such gardens have a long history. No spectacular garden remains of the Roman period, like those excavated at Fishbourne (Sussex), have yet been found in the East Midlands, but a small ornamental layout based around a central pond has been excavated at the Bancroft villa (Milton Keynes) and several old villa excavations might have encountered garden features without realising it (in 1859 at Apethorpe, Northamptonshire, for example). Even so, it is very likely that the 'palaces' at both Greetwell and Castor (p.137) stood above elaborate landscape gardens terraced into the hillsides on which they stood. In the medieval period, the possibility that gardens might have enhanced the setting of the palaces at Northampton, or the halls at Sulgrave or Goltho, has not yet been considered, but from at least the 13th century there is both documentary and archaeological evidence for such gardens. At Stow Park (Lindsey) for example, the setting of the Bishop of Lincoln's palace was enhanced with ornamental lakes and walks, while at the Bishop's Palace at Nettleham, just north of Lincoln, the layout of a later medieval garden can be reconstructed in greater detail. Something of the Bishops' garden at Buckden has also been recovered from surviving earthworks (*see* Fig. 4.30). Medieval gardens were probably far from rare; where moated sites occur in pairs – as, for example, at Linwood (Lindsey), Chalgrove (Oxfordshire) or Epperstone (Nottinghamshire) – one of the pair is likely to have been a moated garden. Sometimes such a moat forms one part of a more elaborate layout providing a spectacular water-garden setting for a late medieval country house, as at Papworth, Harlton and Caxton (all Cambridgeshire).

Earthwork remains of terraces, walks, canals and mounts enable us to appreciate formal gardening between the 16th and 19th centuries. Because of its relative density of aristocratic houses, the East Midlands probably contains several hundred such gardens. The earliest examples are relatively simple, like that at Collyweston (Northamptonshire), probably started in 1453 by the same Ralph, Lord Cromwell who built at Tattershall and South Wingfield. A number of important layouts survive from gardens of the 1540s associated with the conversion of former monasteries (the first house at Canons Ashby, Northamptonshire, of 1540–51 (*see* Fig. 3.31) and Brooke Priory, Rutland). From the great age of Elizabethan gardening come spectacular examples such as Lyvden New Bield (Northamptonshire, 1597), Kirby Hall (*see* Fig. 4.34), and Sir Christopher Hatton's other house at Holdenby (1579–87) (Fig. 4.38). At Holdenby the whole hillside was terraced to form a great stepped apron in front of the house: at the foot of the slope were several tiers of water gardens, isolating the former parish church which still occupies its own ecclesiastical terrace. The great house itself was viewed across the gardens from a huge mount in the south-west corner. We know from contemporary descriptions that gardens such as Lyvden and Holdenby would have been full of political and poetic meaning, such as those that pervaded the impressive earthworks of Sir Henry Lee's Quarrendon (Buckinghamshire). Sometimes, as at Sir Robert Cotton's great circular garden layout on Round Hill, Conington (Huntingdonshire), we can glimpse didactic points made by noted intellectuals. Cotton's garden was deliberately sited to show the visitor views of his fenland domain and to set his property within its local social and political landscape, literally and metaphorically. The garden was centred on an enigmatic ephemeral building, and we also know that Cotton's friend, the poet and

Fig. 4.38 Chris Taylor's plan of the surviving earthworks of the enormous landscaped garden at Holdenby House (Northamptonshire).

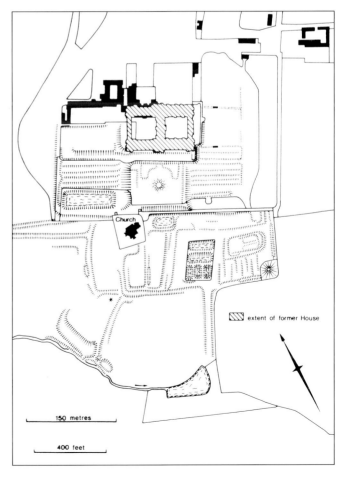

149

playwright Ben Jonson (who had visited Conington in 1603), was experimenting with outdoor drama involving such temporary structures.

Late 17th-century 'French' gardening styles are represented most fully in the complex of severely geometrical earthworks surrounding Boughton House (Northamptonshire), which was rebuilt in the 1680s once the first Duke of Montague had returned from his appointment as ambassador in Paris. The house and garden here were relegated to components within a busy landscape design, much influenced by the gardens of Louis XIV. The gardens laid out alongside Sir George Downing's house at Gamlingay (Cambridgeshire) in 1712 have both a greater scale and a greater simplicity, perhaps pointing towards more classicising tendencies. These are also seen in the magical surviving landscapes – replete with buildings, allegorical sculpture and political meaning – at Rousham Park (Oxfordshire). Here, the remodelled house of 1738–40 was accompanied by a fantasy landscape, by Charles Bridgeman and William Kent, who turned this secluded stretch of the Cherwell into a fragment of Elysium (Fig. 4.39). The grandest such garden in England, however, was created at Stowe (Buckinghamshire) by the Temple family where, starting in 1713, half a century's work went into removing the supposedly derelict village and creating, first, a formal rectilinear layout, and subsequently a smoother, more 'Elysian', landscape under Lancelot 'Capability' Brown. The Stowe landscape is dotted with buildings both predictable and

ABOVE: *Fig. 4.39 Rousham Park is a hidden gem. Initially laid out by Charles Bridgeman in the 1720s, the gardens were updated 1737–41 and then left more-or-less alone, leaving us today with a thrilling, miniature, landscape packed with classical allusion and symbolism. Visitors can still walk the prescribed route, which reveals vista after vista composed of carefully placed buildings, carefully chosen planting and, across the natural ha-ha of the Cherwell, the contrast between the Elysian fields and those of contemporary Oxfordshire.*

unexpected. In addition to looking stunning, most conveyed allegorical meanings, political statements (like the 'Temple of English Worthies'), or even contemporary jokes. Contemporary political messages were also concealed in the Temples of Romulus and Remus and of Pitt at Coleby Hall (Kesteven), whilst the Protestant succession may be celebrated in the immaculate pavilion (1709–10) designed by Thomas Archer to terminate the principal vista at Wrest Park (Bedfordshire). Brown himself was also busy elsewhere in the East Midlands. He swept away the formal gardens and created expansive new settings for many houses including Castle Ashby, Madingley Hall (*see* Fig. 4.35), Grimsthorpe (Kesteven) and Burghley. Brown's designs involved planting thousands of new trees, in clumps and shelter-belts, and by undertaking such planting the aristocracy were also re-connecting, if only symbolically, with their ancestors' role of maintaining the forests.

Specialised buildings, filling a variety of functions, had been a feature of gardens since Roman times, but in the 16th century they became a common feature in the East Midlands landscape. They tend to be highly visible, like Bess of Hardwick's Hunting Tower at Chatsworth, and they can be quite large, like that at Wothorpe (Northamptonshire), which was said to have been built for the second Lord Burghley as a place 'to retire to while his great house … was a-sweeping'. One of the most enigmatic is Sir Thomas Tresham's deeply symbolic Triangular Lodge at Rushton (Northamptonshire, built 1594–7), which juggles both with Trinitarian theology and St Augustine's symbolic uses of rabbits (the building was also a warrener's house) (Fig. 4.40). The theological allusions of Tresham's cruciform 'New Bield' at Lyveden (left unfinished at Sir Thomas's death in 1605) are easier to understand, perhaps. Given such preoccupations, it is not surprising that ordinary East Midlands parish churches also found themselves incorporated into the landscapes around great houses. At Stainfield (Lindsey), Gayhurst and Nuneham Courtney they were relocated, rebuilt and re-oriented to provide satisfactory terminations to vistas and to lend a symbolic weight to the house's context.

Around 1800, the same picturesque trend in English culture that had prompted Clare to write so movingly about the rural poor, had the ironic result that some parkland around great houses – from which the real poor had only recently been displaced – acquired collections of pretty cottages (sometimes copied from pattern books, like that by John Papworth of 1823), built of unsquared timbers, logs and thatch. At Aston Wold, Northamptonshire, an entire farmstead was built in this fashion. The lovely circular cottages on the park fringes at Langton and Scremby Halls (both Lindsey) are of this sort, and so is the small lodge at the west gate of Roxton House (Bedfordshire). This is probably also where the extraordinary Tea-Pot Hall (Lindsey) (Fig. 4.41) should find its eventual place in architectural history. This famous building, commemorated in the rhyme 'Tea Pot Hall, all roof, no wall', was a gigantic thatched 'tent' supported on beams set into the ground at complementary angles and resting against a ridgepole. For many years it was thought to be the only surviving example of the earliest type of English house. Unfortunately, it was burnt to the ground by revellers on VJ night 1945, so it cannot now be dated, but it was probably an unusual *cottage orné* on the edge of the Dymoke family's parkland around Scrivelsby Hall.

Although many great designers were involved, and although planting schemes changed greatly, the broad principles of 19th-century great houses and their settings drew greatly on the ideas of previous generations. In the East Midlands, this was perhaps clearest at the extraordinary Bayons Manor (Lindsey), where the Tennyson d'Eynecourt family built a complete imitation medieval manor in the 1840s, surrounded by an imitation deer park. The fantasy has now dissipated: the building was blown up in 1965 and the parkland devastated. At least Mentmore (Buckinghamshire; designed by Sir Joseph Paxton and built 1850–5) looks back to earlier architectural models from the English Midlands (mostly Wollaton). The

Fig. 4.41 'Tea-pot Hall', Scrivelsby (Lindsey), held a distinguished (if wholly undeserved) place in English architectural history from the 1890s until its destruction in 1945. Far from being representative of the earliest type of English house, as was once thought, it was probably an early 19th-century cottage orné on the Dymoke estate.

OPPOSITE PAGE:

BOTTOM: *Fig. 4.40 The famous 'Triangular' or 'Warrener's' Lodge, in a remote corner of the park at Rushton Hall (Northamptonshire), was a religious and political manifesto in stone for the Old Religion. It was designed and built in 1594–7 by Sir Thomas Tresham, who spent many years in prison for his Roman Catholic beliefs. In a typically intricate conceit, the building's design plays with the number three (standing not just for the Trinity but also for Tresham) as well as incorporating living symbols. According to St Augustine, rabbits (like those originally kept in the long mound visible behind the building) symbolised human souls needing to be kept safe in the 'burrow' of the Roman church.*

Fig. 4.42 The present outlandish house of 1834–6 at Wrest Park (Bedfordshire).

It was designed either by Philip 2nd Earl Grey himself (who considered himself an architect) or perhaps by an obscure Frenchman called Cléphane. The site is much older, however, and the foundations of earlier houses lie beneath the 19th-century geometrical beds on the south terrace, themselves the final phase in a magnificent, if complex, landscaped garden.

same cannot be said of the unusual house at Wrest Park, built within an earlier parkland for Earl Grey (the first president of the RIBA) (Fig. 4.42). No matter whose the design, it looks like an unsuccessful hotel at an unfashionable resort. Although more lovable than Wrest, Waddesdon Manor (Buckinghamshire) – built 1877–83 by a French designer called Destailleur – also intrudes into the East Midlands landscape. Both Mentmore and Waddesdon are examples of the same phenomenon represented earlier by Kirby Hall and Boughton House. They are the homes of individuals who found their social circle in an international world based in London. For such figures the East Midlands were within easy reach of the capital and estates were available for sale.

Milton Hall (Bedfordshire, built in 1856 by William Butterfield), on the other hand, is more successful in its setting, perhaps because it appropriated the layout and elevation of the hall and cross range so common in the area in the Middle Ages (though it is far from a replica). It was built, not for a cosmopolitan landlord, but for the architect's brother-in-law Benjamin Starey. Thoresby (Nottinghamshire, rebuilt 1865–75 by Anthony Salvin) also seems successful because it borrows details both from older local buildings, not least Chatsworth, and from more recent pastiches of such buildings (such as Harlaxton Hall, Kesteven). The Earls of Kingston, for whom it was rebuilt, had been part of this East Midlands community for 200 years and played little part in London life. This was less true of John Manners-Sutton, the local MP. His new house, Kelham Hall (Nottinghamshire), was built between 1859 and 1861 by George Gilbert Scott; although entertaining, it displays little acquaintance with the history of East Midlands architecture. It seems an uncoordinated assembly of Gothic details taken from textbooks and, with its clock tower and two-storey windows, it is hard to tell what its function might be: legislature, railway station or military academy.

FURTHER READING

General
Girouard 1978; Salzman 1967.

Villas
Hodder & Millett 1980; Mackreth 1984 (Castor); Percival 1976; Rivet 1964, 1969; Scott 1993; Simco 1984 (Bedfordshire); Stead 1976 (Winterton); Todd (ed.) 1978; Whitwell 1992 (Lincolnshire); Wild 1978 (Nene valley).

Anglo-Saxon palaces
Blair 1996b (Northampton); Williams *et al.* 1985 (Northampton).

Medieval great houses
Aberg 1978 (Moats); Bailey 1998; Blair 1993; Beresford 1975, 1987 (Goltho); Currie 1992 (Oxfordshire/Berkshire); Davison 1977 (Sulgrave); Grenville 1997; Impey & Harris 2002 (Boothby Pagnell etc); Munby 1993; Roberts & Wrathmell 2002; Thompson 1998 (Bishops' palaces); Wood 1965.

Later great houses and gardens
Airs 1995; Brown (ed.) 1991; Cooper 1999; Currie 1992 (Oxfordshire/Berkshire); Daniels & Watkins 1991 (*Cottages Ornés*); Elliott 1986; Everson 1991, 1998; Girouard 1983, 1985; Green 1976; Heward & Taylor 1996 (Northamptonshire); Howard 1987; Hussey 1967; Pevsner 1974; Taylor 1998; Turner 1985; Williamson 1995; Woodward 1982.

5

Patterns of Industry

INTRODUCTION

Agriculture is now, and always has been, the East Midlands' premier industry. Other regional industries (stone, coal, iron and pottery) have long pedigrees, but none has come to dominate more than discrete areas. Farming, on the other hand, unites the region. Whereas a Nottinghamshire coal miner might find little to discuss with a Witney blanket maker, farmers in both places would speak a common language: they faced similar problems and could share solutions. Because the landscape is also agriculture's factory floor, and because we are more familiar with our farming landscape than we are with coal mines, the entire East Midlands community shares an investment in agriculture quite unlike that in other industries. But since 1945 British agriculture has sought to emulate the rapacious economics of the coal mine. Farmers have considered agriculture as a purely industrial process, and in doing so they have risked ignoring its wider constituency in the community at large. Today the national and international subsidy regime has caught up and recognised the legitimate community interest in agriculture. We can now hope for more sympathetic styles of agricultural management.

There are major differences in lifestyle, after all, between raising crops and animals, and manufacturing commodities for sale, and we must ask whether the two activities generate different landscapes. In East Midlands' common-field settlements, most villagers would set out each day to manage their stock and arable, participating in an integrated agricultural economy. But a small group set out in a different direction, towards the community's managed woodlands; in the forest areas they lived amongst them. In both the limited woods around the fringes of common-field settlements and in the more extensive woods within the forest areas, woodland workers provided services for the common-field community, producing timber for fuel and construction and, in some cases, iron and ceramics as well. Like the agricultural workers, workers in woodlands would also have surpluses to sell to other communities at certain times of year. Indeed, they may have had products for sale more frequently than was the case in the annual agricultural cycle and they might, therefore, have become the community's specialists in sales and marketing. Although the connection has been made for generations, recent studies of Rockingham and Whittlewood forest industries have clearly shown that, before the industrial and agricultural revolutions of the 18th century, the important minority with business in the woodlands were responsible for most early industrial developments. The connection between industry and woodlands is simple: most industrial activities required fuel, which would be either wood or charcoal. Woodland workers not only supplied fuel when needed, but they made sure it was available in future seasons.

Like those who worked on the land, however, the lives of woodland workers were disrupted by the immense changes of the late 18th and 19th centuries. In particular the new methods of communication – first canals and then railways – meant that fuel and raw materials could be concentrated for large-scale industrial production at new locations. Most industrial processes moved out of rural communities altogether, taking their enlarged workforces with them. Many switched fuel source at the same time, from charcoal to mined or 'seacoal'; and, while the coalfields filled up with new coal-fired industries, the woodlands were gradually abandoned, or managed as cover for hunting. Men like John Clare (pp.91–2), who at the start of his short life might have expected both to plough the land and to manufacture lime, according to the season, would be forced to choose between earning a wage by ploughing or lime-burning full-time. Like Clare, many gave up the rigours of land labour only to find full-time industrial labouring was even more taxing.

This chapter will reflect these fundamental distinctions between agricultural and other industries. The landscape of agriculture itself is considered first and, as we have already considered the changing layout of fields and their crops in Chapter 3, we will look at the distinctive landscape contribution made by various agricultural building types. This part of the chapter will also consider the working of the land for other purposes: the digging of stone, coal and metal ore. None of these activities necessarily went on in the woodlands and all were initially community enterprises, undertaken as supplementary activities by people whose usual work was growing crops and raising livestock. Land workers would expect to realise money from winning such natural resources from their community's land, just as they would expect to sell their stock and crops at market. But not all resources gathered in this way would be used by the agricultural workers who had won them.

Manufacturing activities such as potting and metalworking, on the other hand, had always required specialised skills and were undertaken within a tight regulatory system, be it imperial or manorial. Along with similar industries which have also operated at one remove from the agricultural community, these activities are considered in the second part of the chapter.

Working the Land 1: Scratching the Surface

FARMING

Until quite recently, animals on East Midlands farms have not required many buildings at all, let alone distinctive ones. In the 18th century, cattle were still being over-wintered in open 'crew yards', as they had been in 13th-century Goltho, and probably also at Orton Hall Farm (Peterborough) a millennium before that. Similarly sheep required only a simple shed for winter lambing and milking. All livestock required winter fodder, typically hay, which until the relatively recent introduction of open-sided barns was stored in thatched ricks rather than buildings. On the other hand, the East Midlands contain a large and diverse collection of dovecotes – a very distinctive building type (Fig. 5.1). In this region they are frequently of stone, and often circular in plan, like the fine late-medieval example at Minster Lovell, Oxfordshire. Sometimes they have considerable architectural ambitions, like the great square brick block of about 1530, which was once part of the great court of Willington Manor (Bedfordshire), or the decorative 18th-century examples in the parks at Chastleton House and Wroxton Abbey (both Oxfordshire). Medieval sumptuary law dictated that pigeons could only be kept by the lord of the manor, so the dovecote itself became a decorative architectural symbol of lordship. And because it supplied fresh meat during the winter, it was a very practical emblem. However, as over-wintering livestock became easier and more common, the value of winter pigeon meat declined, until an Act of 1761–2 allowed any freeholder to keep the birds.

With its climate, topography and geology favouring arable agriculture, a less frivolous contribution to the East Midlands landscape has always been made by buildings associated with grain production. Even so, archaeology has identified very few specialised buildings associated with grain storage or processing before the Romano-British period. In the Bronze and Iron Ages large quantities of grain were certainly being grown, stored and processed, but these operations do not seem to have given rise to specialised building forms. Sickles of flint, bronze and iron are known, and there is evidence for the use of simple field kilns for drying the harvested grain. But evidently it was then threshed and winnowed outside, either in the field or on platforms with prepared clay floors, within settlements.

Roman Britain's economic success was partly based on improvements in what was, already, a successful agricultural economy and, between the 2nd and 4th centuries, we find the first archaeological evidence for specialised buildings dedicated to processing crops. These are mostly buildings for threshing and storing grain. We know of many large Romano-British barns and granaries through aerial photography and excavation. One of the most fully explored grain-producing farmsteads in Britain is at Orton Hall, where excavations have shown us a sequence of four large aisled barns, not all of which were used contemporaneously (Fig. 5.2). The largest of these barns was approximately 25m by 15m, not as big as the largest medieval examples (and only half the length of the largest barn excavated at Winterton villa, Lindsey – *see* Fig. 4.22), but still an impressive building; and at most periods there were at least two such barns working at Orton Hall farmstead. Presumably they would have been for storing different crops: barley and wheat, perhaps, or grains and peas. The sheer size of these examples demonstrates the productivity of the local Romano-British arable, whilst the number of other East Midlands barns identified shows that this productivity was not confined to the Peterborough area.

Indeed, the national distribution shows that most were in the territory of the Corieltauvi and the western Catuvellauni. Clearly, when Roman writers commented on Britannia's value as a bread-basket, it was the East Midlands they had in mind.

These great Romano-British barns highlight not just the productivity of the region's arable; they also make the point that the marketing of surpluses (p.46) necessitated storage before the crop was threshed. Before it could be stored the crop needed to be dry, and it is no coincidence that many simple Romano-British low-temperature 'corn-dryers' have also been discovered in the East Midlands, often at field margins. Barn floors would also be useful for threshing itself and for the storage of straw once the grain had been transferred to granaries or market.

ABOVE: ***Fig. 5.1 The dovecote (1685) at Rousham Park (Oxfordshire).*** *Both a status symbol and a practical necessity, it stands between the contemporary enclosed walled garden and the stable block. The doves originally came and went through the specially designed cowl in the roof's centre.*

BELOW: ***Fig. 5.2 Multi-phased Romano-British farmstead at Orton Hall Farm (Huntingdonshire).*** *Subsequent Anglo-Saxon buildings are superimposed (source: Mackreth 1996).*

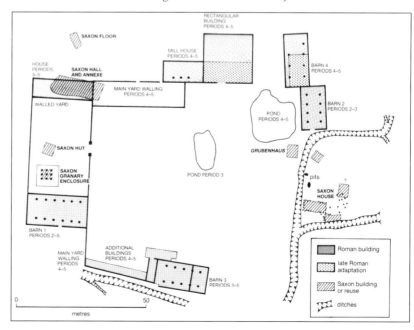

Although late-Roman and Anglo-Saxon farmers put large areas of former arable down to grazing, they still grew a relatively large hectarage of grain. However, few buildings from Anglo-Saxon excavations have been interpreted as barns; aisled structures of this date are usually presumed to be 'halls' (pp.137–8). Perhaps we need to reconsider such interpretations, but at present it seems that the Romano-British agricultural regimes which relied so heavily on their great aisled barns were replaced (perhaps during the late Romano-British period rather than the Anglo-Saxon) by regimes more reminiscent of the Iron Age, where grain surpluses were not so large, and grain was neither dried nor stored before threshing.

By the 10th century, however, grain was once again being dried and stored before threshing, in great barns descended from the Romano-British types. The East Midlands contains many examples, which divide into two distinct types. First, there are the flimsy vernacular buildings, rarely aisled, which sit behind dwellings in excavated tofts like those at Goltho or Barton Blount (Derbyshire). Most tofts have such structures, and they presumably represent the individual peasant family's store for crops, once dried (Fig. 5.3). No standing examples have been positively identified, but as dendrochronological dating proceeds, specimens may yet come to light. Such small, private produce stores would, nevertheless, have had the same function as the larger medieval barns, found on both ecclesiastical and lay estates.

Such barns are often called tithe barns, and the label is not always incorrect. Some were indeed intended primarily for storing produce due to the Church as tithe (a tax paid in kind). One of the largest and most famous of these structures in England was Boroughbury or Monk's Barn, west of the medieval abbey and town at Peterborough, within the monastic home farm courtyard. It was said to have been built between 1300 and 1350 and had two pairs of doors with threshing floors between each pair. This layout was widely adopted, as the through-draft between the doors blew away chaff when threshing or winnowing. Renouncing the medieval economy in favour of the steam age, Monk's Barn was demolished in 1888 to make way for railway extensions. The fine surviving aisled example at Great Coxwell (old Berkshire) (Fig. 5.4), which stored the surpluses from the local granges of Beaulieu Abbey (Hampshire), is somewhat earlier in date (early 13th-century) and more than 40m long by 15m wide. It was small, however, compared with that demolished in 1818 at Cholsey (old Berkshire), which was some 80m long. The much smaller barn at Colesden Grange (Bedfordshire), visible when looking south from Beggary, is also said to be of 13th-century date, and may have stored produce from the local lands of Caldwell Priory. Similar barns belonging to secular estates were also scattered across the region. The footings of a modest example of c.1200-50 were excavated at West Cotton (Northamptonshire), whilst those at

Fig. 5.3 Buildings and layout on a typical medieval toft, reconstructed from Guy Beresford's excavations at Goltho.

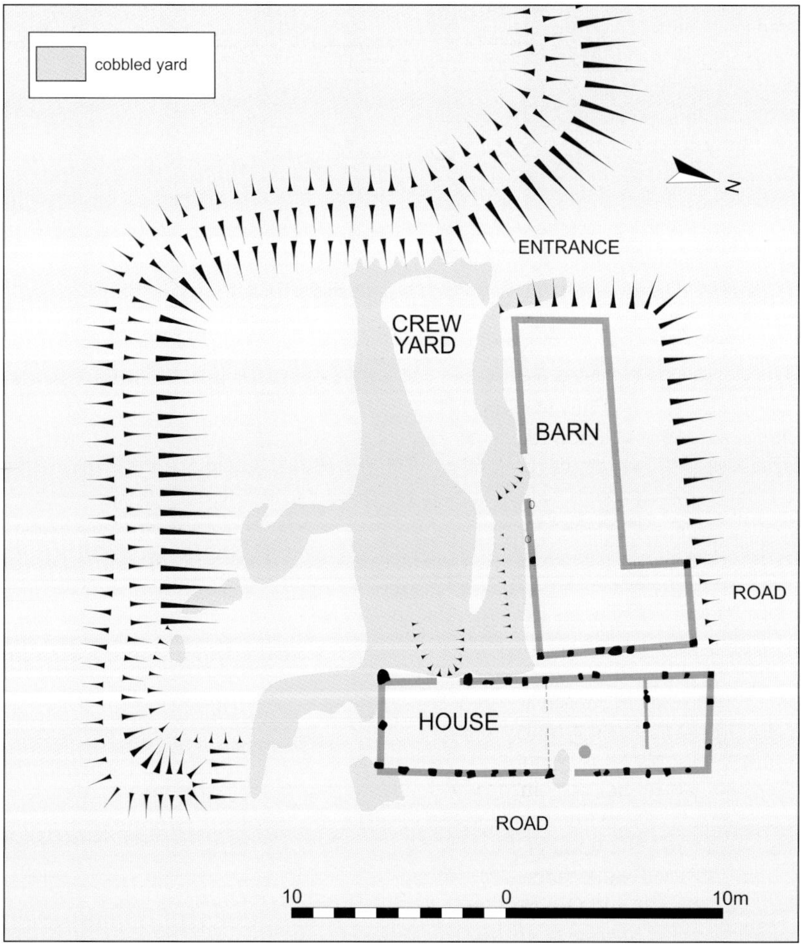

cobbled yard

ENTRANCE

CREW YARD

BARN

ROAD

HOUSE

ROAD

10   0   10m

Bray Manor, Harlestone (Northamptonshire), Bassingbourn Manor and Eversden (both Cambridgeshire) have threshing porches and probably date from the 15th century. During the 19th century, grain processing within barns became mechanised and power units were attached to older barns to drive threshing and winnowing machines. Sometimes these were permanent installations using wind or water power, but more frequently they were powered by mobile steam traction engines. Both the threshing machines themselves and the engines that drove them had an impact well beyond the farms where they worked; many were built in East Midlands towns such as Gainsborough, Lincoln, Grantham and Banbury (p.104).

Once threshed and winnowed, the grain needed dry storage, safe from pests, before it

TOP: *Fig. 5.4 The barn near Great Coxwell (old Berkshire). Though relatively small compared to some such monastic barns, it is a fine example of medieval building in Corallian limestone.*

ABOVE: *Fig. 5.5 A traditional box-framed granary on staddle stones. This example still stands north of a great barn (built by New College Oxford c.1400) at Manor Farm, Upper Heyford (Oxfordshire).*

could be ground, sold, or used for next season's seed. In the Iron Age grain was usually stored in pits dug into the ground, as at Gravelly Guy, for example. Experimental archaeology has shown that such pits actually prove to be effective storage vessels, provided they are sealed with a stout clay lid, which would have retained carbon dioxide, preserved the grain and killed pests. They would have been ideal for storing seed corn, which was not needed for a period following deposition, but less suitable for grain being used for food, which was probably kept in purpose-built granaries. Subsistence farmers have probably always kept their precious grain in pottery jars in the house for brief periods before use or sale, but larger operations require dedicated, specialised buildings. A particular pattern of four posts, arranged in a square, has been regularly interpreted as a type of Iron Age granary with a raised floor supported on the posts (for example at Pennylands, Milton Keynes, and at Gravelly Guy), although such a pattern might also represent a simple type of hay-rick cover.

Several excavated Romano-British structures have been proposed as likely granaries, including one at the Winterton villa, which had a raised timber floor to inhibit pests. Anglo-Saxon examples have also been identified, at Pennylands for example, while at Orton Hall an arrangement of padstones has been interpreted as a staddle-stone support for a box-framed granary of 6th- to 8th-century date. This was the form taken by most medieval and later granary buildings. Free-standing timber-framed boxes of this type, supported on staddle stones, are still to be seen on a few farms in Cambridgeshire, Bedfordshire and Oxfordshire (Fig. 5.5). Upstairs rooms within the farmyard could also be used as granaries, and in many 19th-century 'model farm' layouts, the granary is above the cartshed (for easy transport of grain to market) or above the stables or cowshed (for easy use of stored grain as animal food). During agricultural intensification after 1945, however, the granary was rendered obsolete by the grain silo. Sharing a name with facilities for concealing missiles, the distinctive, sinister, shapes and discordant colours of these structures were an appropriate symbol for the countryside in the era of Mutually Assured Destruction.

Such silos symbolised the re-equipping of East Midlands agriculture following 1945, but the impulse to re-engineer farmsteads to make them more efficient factories has a much longer pedigree. We know of 'model' husbandry units of medieval date in Yorkshire, but in the East Midlands such units are mostly products of 19th-century technology. Good farmers had always aimed to organise their buildings to ensure maximum efficiency in the handling of stock and materials, but in the late 18th and 19th centuries agricultural architects pioneered specialised buildings arranged in conveniently planned layouts, which maximised efficiency and minimised costs. Because they were often nearly self-sustaining, growing the food on the farm for the stock and using manure as a fertiliser, the mixed farms of the East Midlands were ideal subjects for such treatment, and many 'model' farms were built here by ambitious estate managers. Representative examples are the three farms built by the Dysert estate in Kesteven at Hanby Lodge (1883) (Fig. 5.6), Hanby Grange (1884) and The Pines, Great Ponton. Accountants had clearly already seized control of agricultural production and recommended cost-cutting through mechanisation and labour-saving. The attention to detail in such establishments is impressive: the purpose-built open-fronted cartsheds were always arranged to open to the north, for example, because direct sunlight would warp wooden wheels and axles.

In pre-history grain was ground by hand in various designs of quern (of which there are numerous East Midlands examples) but, although there is also some evidence for horse-driven mills in early periods, by the medieval period wind and water power were being harnessed to grind grain on a large scale. The earliest watermill (with horizontal mill-wheel) from which components have survived was excavated at Tamworth. It comes from the 9th century and may have belonged to a mill within the Mercian palace here (p 138). Even at this early date, the aristocracy had appropriated the right to grind corn on behalf of the community, and many East Midlands mills are listed in Domesday Book as valuable sources of income for their lordly owners. As most manorial lords insisted on corn being ground in the manor mill, there would usually have been at least one mill in each community, and by the 12th century many contained several, like that excavated at West Cotton (Northamptonshire). A watermill of 13th-century date, with vertically mounted wheel, was excavated at the Templar Preceptory at South Witham (Kesteven); with its mill pond, sluices and race, it differed only in scale from the many surviving large East Midlands watermills of much later date, like those at Osney (Oxford) or Ollerton (Nottinghamshire).

As medieval towns grew in size, their watermills were supplemented by wind power. The earliest documentary records of windmills date from the late 12th century; by the 16th century at least 11 windmills surrounded Lincoln and 13 were lined up along the northern edge of Nottingham's town fields. These mills were timber-framed structures, built around a central post whose base stood in a substantial horizontal timber frame, itself buried in a mound of earth to provide stability. Few such 'post-mills' now stand in the East Midlands, where the scale of the grain industry meant that most were replaced during the 19th century with

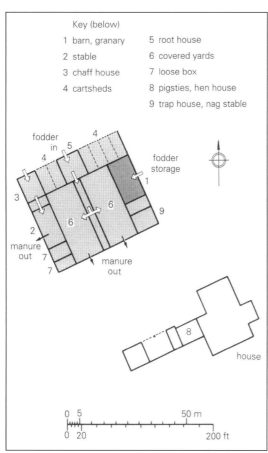

Fig. 5.6 Layout of the 'model' farm at Hanby Lodge (Kesteven), built in the early 1880s. *Such installations were not just efficient money-making machines for landlords, they were also potent symbols of the 'modernisation' of the countryside by exemplary landlords (source: Barnwell & Giles 1997).*

Key (below)

1 barn, granary
2 stable
3 chaff house
4 cartsheds
5 root house
6 covered yards
7 loose box
8 pigsties, hen house
9 trap house, nag stable

larger, more fully mechanised, and more structurally sound tower mills. Lincolnshire retains only a single post-mill (at Wrawby near Brigg) out of what must originally have been many hundreds, while among the handful of surviving examples in Cambridgeshire, that at Bourn is said to be the oldest standing in England, having been first mentioned in 1636. The post-mill on Brill's windy hilltop is said to date from the late 17th century (Fig. 5.7).

A century ago the distinctive shape of the tower mill, built of tarred brick and with a white domed or ogival cap, dominated the landscape of many East Midlands counties. They were always especially thick on the ground in Lincolnshire (where over 130 still stand today) but they also embellished skylines in Nottinghamshire, Cambridgeshire, Huntingdonshire and Bedfordshire. By 1900, however, grain could be crushed between high-speed rollers, typically driven by steam or electricity. Rolling mills were enormous multi-storey buildings, and their awkward square forms made an equally dramatic impact on the East Midlands skyline. Set alongside waterways or railways, typically on the edges of towns, they could prepare flour and animal feed in batches weighed in tons. There are good examples on the Ouse at Huntingdon (1863 – visible on Fig. 6.3), on the Nene at Wellingborough (1886) and on the Trent at Gainsborough (1936).

If grain was not ground for flour or used as seed for the next harvest, it would probably be malted for brewing. This process – whereby the grain is steeped in water, allowed partial germination, and then kilned to arrest that germination – has probably been undertaken since at least the Bronze Age. The simplest maltings, however, leave only a floor and a hearth for the excavator to find, so it is not surprising that so few early examples have been identified. A good example of Roman date was excavated among the agricultural buildings at the Bancroft villa (Milton Keynes), while at St Mary's Guildhall, Lincoln, an urban malting complex – in production between the 15th and 19th centuries – has been explored. Malt was often produced on larger farms (like that excavated at Irthlingborough, Northamptonshire) and standing maltings survive from the 18th and 19th centuries (for example at Burwell, Cambridgeshire – Fig. 5.8). The coming of the railways, however, destroyed the traditional trade in malt. No longer produced in small quantities on individual farms, its production was brought within the brewery industry (itself undergoing rapid mechanisation and

ABOVE: *Fig. 5.7 Brill post-mill (Buckinghamshire) on its windy eminence. (*See also *Fig. 5.36)*

BELOW: *Fig. 5.8 At Burwell a rural malting-house, of uncertain date, stands alongside Manor Farm, of which it once formed part.* It may have begun life within the estate of the medieval priory here, but the tiled kiln itself and, beyond, the long thatched building, containing granary (above) and couching floor (below), look 18th-century in date. Buildings of chalk blocks are rare in the East Midlands, being found only in the Lincolnshire Wolds and here, in eastern Cambridgeshire.

Fig. 5.9 Bass and Co.'s industrial malting complex on the railway outside Sleaford (Kesteven). It rises from amidst the barley that it was designed to process on such an unprecedented scale.

expansion). The huge new brewery combines centralised their malting, collecting the grain from whole regions into single maltings and taking malt to the brewery by railway. A few of these cathedrals of malting survive in the region, such as the stupendous complex built by Bass and Co. alongside the railway outside Sleaford between 1899 and 1905 (Fig. 5.9). Actually a group of eight distinct maltings each with six malting floors, the whole site was fully automated and powered by two large Robey steam engines, built in Lincoln. From here the malt was carried to Burton-upon-Trent each day by Bass's dedicated trains. In the sunshine, and from a distance, the many roofs of soft grey Welsh slate on their red-brick walls look like a model village set amid the golden barley by an Edwardian estate agent.

TEXTILE MANUFACTURING

East Midlands' agriculture, however, was never solely focused on grain. Pastoral farming was also significant, and for long periods between the 4th and 10th centuries, and between about 1350 and 1750, raising stock was probably more important to the local economy than arable. Animals were raised for food, of course (meat, milk, or both), but they were also important for wool and hides, and the processing of both has always been a major regional industry. Excavated sites of all periods suggest that spinning and weaving, tanning and leatherworking, were all undertaken within communities whose economy was largely devoted to working the land.

Prehistoric textile working is attested only by quantities of spindle-whorls, loom-weights and other equipment from late-Bronze Age and Iron Age sites. Dozens of such items were found at both Gravelly Guy and Dragonby, for example, representing textile manufacture on vertical looms, within dwellings. To judge from surviving loom-weights and spindle-whorls, little seems to have changed in textile manufacture during the Romano-British period, and although it is known that there were centres of more industrialised textile production (at Winchester and Silchester, for example), no evidence for 'factories' of this date has yet been forthcoming from the East Midlands.

Cloth making is said to be indicated by Anglo-Saxon place-names including the words 'thistle', 'teasel', 'woad' (for dyes) and 'bracken' (for mordant). Such associations are controversial, however, and archaeological evidence for regional cloth making between the 5th and 9th centuries is confined to yet more spindle-whorls and loom-weights. Long narrow buildings north of the 10th-century hall at Goltho were identified as weaving sheds on the strength of tools associated with weaving recovered from this part of the site. The spindle-whorls, however, came mostly from the 'bower' area, suggesting that spinning (unlike weaving) might have been associated with Goltho's private domestic chambers. Spinning may therefore have been a process undertaken, in private, by individuals of higher status, or at least in their presence. Very likely it was undertaken by women (as was preliminary 'combing' later in the medieval period), perhaps as a necessary accompaniment to polite conversation. Weaving at 10th-century Goltho, on the other hand, may have already become a more technical operation, presumably undertaken by individuals of lower status, perhaps already professional weavers, in a self-contained building. Even though it was within the lord's enclosure, Goltho's weaving shed might represent an early textile factory.

The basic distinction between spinning and weaving persisted until the 18th century, when both processes were mechanised. Spinning continued to be a responsibility of women. Perhaps it always indicated a certain social status; it was, at least, undertaken only by those whose manual work left them enough time. It was appropriate work for wives within an agricultural community. Hair or wool was just another product of the land, and could be given added value by being spun into a saleable yarn. Presumably savings on clothes could also be made if the spun yarn was woven within the community. In the 12th and 13th centuries some, if not most, weaving was undertaken in the towns (pp.72–4), but in the 14th century the industry changed fundamentally and self-employed weavers based in the countryside, close to the spinners, became the norm.

In late 14th-century Wyboston, not only did Thomas Stocker own a flock numbering perhaps several hundred sheep, but he was buying fleeces from sheep-farming neighbours up to 20km away (at Catworth, Huntingdonshire, for example). But Thomas was not just a wool producer; he also manufactured cloth, which he sold in Newark, Godmanchester, King's Lynn and, eventually, London. We can presume that he employed weavers to process yarn, spun by the wives of his shepherds in Wyboston and other Eaton hamlets. They might have worked in Thomas' own weaving-sheds, but it is more likely they had workshops within their own houses. He would also have had the cloth 'fulled' (washed and beaten to even out the fabric). The Ouse valley clays were a good source of 'fuller's earth' and water-powered fulling mills are documented in nearby Great Barford parish. He may also have had his cloth dyed with locally produced vegetable dyes or with more exotic imported materials. This might have involved taking the raw cloth to urban dyeworks like those documented in towns including Kettering, Brigstock and Wellingborough. The cloth would then be 'teased' with locally grown teasels (still abundant by the river in Wyboston), and 'sheared' to produce a finer finish. The cloth would then need storing whilst marketing was arranged. Not far away from Wyboston, at Fen Ditton Hall (Cambridgeshire), the upper storey has great open spaces which are thought to have been stores for fleeces and cloths belonging to a similar family wool and cloth business. On a smaller scale, two-storeyed warehouses attached to Docwra's Manor at Shepreth and Old Manor, Fowlmere (both Cambridgeshire) are very likely to have belonged to similar operations.

The long-woolled sheep breeds, Lincolns, Leicesters and Cotswolds, all originated in the East Midlands and by the late medieval period the highest prices were paid for Lindsey and Cotswold fleeces. In intermediate counties, such as Bedfordshire, wool of medium grade was produced, ideal for conversion into cloth. During the 16th and 17th centuries, however, the prodigious quantity of wool produced in Northamptonshire, Lincolnshire and Cambridgeshire was mostly shipped either to the South West or to East Anglia to be made into textiles. In 1662 Thomas Fuller observed 'that mid-England … having most of the wool, has least of the clothing therein'. Only lace continued to be made locally by womenfolk in their cottages in these eastern parts. Typically it was sold at the cottage door to passers-by; as recorded, for example, at Eaton Socon in 1596. By the late 16th century fine broadcloth 'kerseys' were being produced from south-western Northamptonshire south-westwards, and by the 17th century there were 60 blanket makers in Witney employing some 3,000 people, mostly carding and preparing the wool in surrounding villages. Subsequently both the wool-dressers and the weavers and finishers gravitated towards the town itself: the surviving Blanket Hall was built as their guildhall in 1721 and an industrial quarter grew up around West End and Newland (Fig. 5.10). In this way, Witney developed in a similar manner to the Gloucestershire and Somerset wool towns, with mechanised spinning machines and water-powered looms rather than the powered knitting frames, which came to dominate textile manufacture in Leicestershire and Nottinghamshire.

A frame for knitting woollen stockings mechanically is said to have been invented in 1589 by William Lee, curate of Calverton (Nottinghamshire); but it is also said that the frame remained unused in England because of Queen Elizabeth's concerns about unemployment. Under James I, however, such machines were established in London, making fine silks rather than woollen stockings. Such frames could obviously be used for woollen worsteds (smooth, closely woven cloths), and masters wanted to produce stockings nearer the source of raw materials: in the East Midlands. Two master framework-knitters recorded in Nottingham in 1641 may be the first sign that the industry had finally returned, and by 1700 at least 31 south Nottinghamshire villages had economies based on knitting. By 1750 there were 1,200 frame knitters in Nottingham itself.

Nottingham's 18th-century frame knitters worked mostly worsteds, but by 1799 eight lace manufacturers also operated in the town. Arkwright's Nottingham mill of 1768 (p.90) had produced lace mechanically, and eventually lace manufacture came to define the town in the 19th century. Ironically, the town had never produced hand-made lace. Nottingham owed its success to the improvements made possible by Heathcoat's 'bobbin net' machine (patented 1809), which adapted the frame-knitting machine to make cotton lace. The town grew alongside Victorian tastes for covering surfaces with lace cloths and veils and, by 1911, of 46,000 employed in lace-making nationally, 50 per cent worked in Nottingham itself and an further 25 per cent worked in surrounding centres such as Beeston, Long Eaton and Sandiacre. Strong reactions against Victorian design in the 1920s decimated the industry, however, and although money was made between 1939 and 1945 by knitting mosquito nets for jungle troops, by the 1960s only some 5,000 were employed. Even these low numbers have declined subsequently, as spun polymers have replaced cotton and computerisation has lead to fully automated factories.

Arkwright's real impact on East Midlands' textile production, however, was in the cotton and silk industries, produced by his mills in the Derwent valley (p.93). Arkwright and his contemporaries came to the East Midlands (before moving onto Lancashire and Yorkshire) because of the existing hosiery industry, which already made extensive use of silk and cotton ribbons and bows. Lombe's huge and innovative mill at Derby, established in 1717–18, spun silk from 1718. In 1771 Arkwright opened his new water-powered factory at Cromford (Derbyshire), producing cotton thread, and by 1788 there were 56 mills of this type operating in Nottinghamshire and Derbyshire alone. A fine, if architecturally pretentious, survivor from his generation, built in 1815, still looms over the little village of Cressbrook on the River Wye, where it replaced an earlier mill designed by Arkwright himself. Whole new communities were added to minor settlements where the water power was to be harnessed. The first of a series of large mills was built at the minor settlement of Belper (Derbyshire), for

Fig. 5.10 Originally water-powered, the New Mills at Witney (Oxfordshire) were established by Early Blanket Company along the Windrush in the late 18th century. Most of the surviving buildings (including the street-frontage and the engine house) were rebuilt following a fire in 1883, when they were converted to steam power. When the mills closed, surviving buildings were incorporated into a prestigious housing development.

example, by Jedediah Strutt in 1776, turning it overnight into a major centre of population.

By 1844, the towns and villages of the East Midlands contained some 44,000 knitting frames. The three materials which could be made on the frames – silk, cotton and worsted – were being spun largely in three different counties: Derbyshire produced mainly silk which was knitted into garments on frames, Nottinghamshire specialised in spinning cotton, which was knitted into lace, while in Leicestershire, wool was still spun into thread for knitting into garments. The main spinning towns (Mansfield, Sutton-in-Ashfield, Nottingham, Derby, Loughborough, Leicester and Hinkley) were all sited to take advantage of water power, and the great bulk of such mills still adds occasional vertical accents among the workers' housing (Fig. 5.11). Through the late 18th and early 19th centuries, frame knitters set up in the spinning towns (there were 1,000 frames in Leicester by 1750) or gravitated towards the surrounding villages, where they knitted garments in the local specialist material as piecework. In both towns and countryside, knitters' cottages can still be seen, with their distinctive enlarged windows (often on the top floor) designed to cast better light on the frame. Examples survive along Wollaton Road in Nottingham, at Calverton and Stapleford (Nottinghamshire) (Fig. 5.12), and Hinkley, Leicestershire.

Arkwright's water-powered frame had been adapted for worsted spinning in the 1780s, but it was only with the coming of the railways that steam-powered knitting frames were established in any numbers. The first was set up in Loughborough in 1839. With the change in fashion from breeches to long trousers in the second quarter of the 19th century, the hosiery industry reached a crisis and subsequently diversified into a bewildering variety of textile garments. From the 1850s new all-purpose textile factories produced anything that could be knitted on a frame. The whole basis of the industry had changed and, especially following

ABOVE: *Fig. 5.11 The large mill built by the Anglo-Scotian lace company in 1871.* *Its sub-gothic castellations dominate the skyline of the little town of Beeston (Nottinghamshire): an effective and enduring advertisement in the landscape.*

BELOW: *Fig. 5.12 Early 19th-century textile-workers' cottages in Nottingham Road, Stapleford (Nottinghamshire). They retain their characteristically large windows on the top floor for lighting knitting-frames.*

Fig. 5.13 Central Leicester looking north-east from St Martin's church.
This photograph was taken, perhaps, c.1867, whilst the new spire was under construction. Already, a number of chimneys indicate steam-powered mills.

improvements patented by Compton in 1864, frames were gathered together in steam-powered factories in Nottingham, Leicester, Loughborough and a number of small market towns on the railway network such as Fleckney, south of Leicester. By 1871, 74 Leicestershire mills were steam-powered. As the industry developed, more specialist finishing processes developed alongside the spinning and the knitting mills. These phases of expansion, after the arrival of the railways, swelled Nottingham and Leicester in the second half of the 19th century, and had contrasting impacts on both towns (pp.94–8) (Fig. 5.13).

The 20th century was a period of sustained decline in the textile manufacturing industries. Numbers employed dwindled through the 1920s and 1930s, but picked up again in the 1950s and 1960s, reaching 56,000 in Leicestershire by 1967, when textiles were the second largest employer in the county. Since 1970, however, the numbers employed have collapsed, although the industry has not. Small factories supplying niche markets still make a good living in Leicester.

TANNING, BOOTS AND SHOES

The hides of animals reared on East Midlands pastures have always been a valuable product. Skins were probably treated before animals were domesticated but, although tanning hide must have been an essential agricultural skill for millennia, we know little of how it was done at early periods. Even so, leatherworking awls and similar tools have been identified at Iron Age sites such as Gravelly Guy. Along with the retting of flax, tanning was an Oxford industry as early as AD 800, when it was apparently located in the Grandpont area. Given its noisome reputation, and indeed the need for lime and oak bark (or a similar source of tannin), it is perhaps surprising that there is not more evidence for tanning as a woodland industry. Yet in the 16th and 17th centuries, oak-bark was taken to urban markets like that in Northampton. Some tanning clearly did take place in the countryside, as the Assize of the Forest ordered in 1181 that thenceforth tanners and tawyers were to dwell within a borough, implying that they had not done so beforehand. In the 16th century, however, it was said 'in most villages of the realm there is some one dresser or worker of leather'. Even so, documentary evidence for medieval tanneries in the East Midlands comes mostly from the medieval shire towns, where they were often sited away from the centre: at St John's Street in Bedford, for example, and in southern Wigford, Lincoln. Here tanners used water from the Ouse and the Witham (even though the Wigford tanners were upstream of the city) and large quantities of lime. Both towns produced lime, but it was available in great quantities right along the Jurassic ridge (pp.173–4). Excavations are now revealing the industry in many small towns as well (for example at St Neots).

Leather was worked and sold by saddlers, shoemakers, glovers and lorrimers in most towns, but especially in Northampton, Oxford (which reported 144 in leatherworking trades in 1388) and Leicester (where there were around 30 master tanners alone at a similar date). All three towns had developed a reputation for their leatherwork by the late medieval period and had easy communications with London, where much of their output was sent. In Northampton large tanneries of the 16th and 17th centuries were excavated at The Green and St Peter's Street, perhaps indicating a tanners' quarter in the south-western part of the town, and providing archaeological evidence for the rise of the town's famous boot-and-shoe industry, the mainspring of Northamptonshire's economy for several centuries (pp.90 and 98–9).

By comparison, Leicester's footware industry was never as large or famous, but it developed from similar medieval origins and, as in Northampton, it was based on 'putting-out' manufacturing tasks to craftsmen working in domestic workshops on piece rates. In the long term, the Leicestershire industry's decision to focus on the mass-market now appears mistaken, but it was a successful strategy in the 19th century, when Thomas Crick developed ways of riveting the sole to the upper and mechanising part of the boot-making process. Crick's son John opened a factory, featuring a number of automated stages, in Highcross Street in 1851 and the industry then mushroomed in the town. There were 70 boot-and-shoe factories in Leicester by 1867 and more opened subsequently in surrounding villages. By 1891, the industry employed 30,000 workers in the county. Like the hosiery industry, however, boot-and-shoe making suffered greatly from increased competition from abroad in the 20th century and the numbers employed gradually declined. By 1967 only 16,500 were employed and by the 1990s that number had shrunk by more than half, although several Northamptonshire works (Barkers of Earls Barton, Sanders of Rushden and Loakes of Kettering) have found a niche making shoes for the top end of the market.

The leatherworking industry brought with it not only a distinctive landscape of terraces and factories (see Figs 3.40 and 3.52) but also a variety of ancillary industries, such as whip-making at Daventry, although packaging (typically in cardboard) and elastic webbing (used for the side panels in slip-on boots and shoes from the late 19th century) are probably more important. Both specialisations have developed into free-standing industries and in towns like Desborough (Northamptonshire), where the major shoemakers have closed, Rigid Containers' cardboard-box factory and the forbidding red-brick Co-op Corset Factory are still producing their very different types of packaging (Fig. 5.14).

Fig. 5.14 Both 'packaging' factories in modern Desborough (Northamptonshire) owe their origins to the boot-making industry. The former Co-op Corset Factory made elastic ribbon whilst Rigid Containers Ltd made cardboard shoe-boxes.

Working the Land 2: Digging Deeper

STONE QUARRYING

The East Midlands contains valuable stones. Granite from Charnwood, for example, has been highly prized since Neolithic times, when axes made of this material were carried across much of lowland Britain. This stone was also carted to Leicester by the Romans and used for building projects, alongside a local sandstone from Danehills, but it came to the fore during the 18th century when it was suddenly in great demand for 'setts' to pave both turnpikes and city streets. New quarries were opened and the stone was shipped to all parts of Britain and Europe via the Leicester Canal (opened in 1794), scarring the tranquil forest landscape. The railway boom intensified demand and the introduction of steam engines to drive crushers made a new product practical: 'granite chippings' for ballast on the railways themselves. Mountsorrel was the industry's centre, but surprisingly few buildings survive there today to reveal the industry's significance. Granite quarrying is still important, though the quarries are now more discrete, and in 1970 Leicestershire supplied the Department of Transport with more road-stone than any other county.

Charnwood produced a second important stone, at Swithland, which was exploited differently. Here, a fine greenish slate (geologically related to Mountsorrel granite) was exploited by the Romans as a roofing material, and quarrying is documented from the 13th century. Swithland slate was a versatile material and blocks could be worked into complex shapes, for water troughs, cheese presses, sinks, carved fireplaces and even clock faces. Today it is best known through the legacy of exquisite gravestones like those in the churchyard of St Mary de Castro, Leicester, carved between the late-17th and the mid-19th centuries, and found in many East Midlands churchyards. Far from benefiting from the railways, however, the Swithland slate industry was killed off by them. It could not withstand competition from the enormous Welsh slate mines and the last quarry closed in 1887.

Much coarser, but very attractive, the Jurassic limestone slates produced at Collyweston (Northamptonshire) also suffered from Welsh competition, but quarrymen here subsequently turned to producing stone for walling or cement. Here (and also at Stonesfield, Oxfordshire), blocks of Jurassic limestone were 'frosted' (ie brought out of the mine at dusk on clear winter nights and kept well watered, so that the frost would freeze the water in the stone, splitting them into thin slates), before being shaped and drilled. Frosting is only documented at Collyweston from the late 17th century, but finds of Roman and medieval frosted slates show that it was long understood (Fig. 5.15). Abbey Barn at Enstone (Oxfordshire), for example, was roofed in 1382 using Stonesfield slates made in this way. Collyweston and Stonesfield slates could only be produced from certain strata, which eventually had to be mined from adits (horizontal

Fig. 5.15 Having been soaked, 'logs' of newly mined Collyweston stone are laid out to be split by winter frosts at Harrod's Pit in the 1950s. Note the finished slates in the foreground.

OPPOSITE PAGE:

TOP: *Fig. 5.16 The long and controversial building campaign at Blenheim Palace (1705–25) employed several famous Jurassic building stones, identifiable by slight variations in colour and texture. Vanbrugh, the architect, specified Taynton stone from quarries 24km away, but this was supplanted by local Glympton stone in Kitchen Court (to the north – top), whilst Blisworth and Helmdon stone from Northamptonshire was also used.*

BOTTOM: *Fig. 5.17 The dramatic new museum building in Lincoln ('The Collection' opened 2005) employs Ancaster stone from quarries 32km away.*

passages) driven into the hillsides, increasing costs considerably. Stonesfield's last mine closed in 1909, and although re-used slates are still available from Collyweston, frosting has not been undertaken commercially there since 1969.

Neither slate nor granite is a good walling stone, although examples of its use do exist – like the church of St Mark's on Belgrave Gate, Leicester (1872), designed by the mainstream architect Ewan Christian. Unlike their counterparts in Cornwall, for example, East Midlands builders had access to a wide variety of much better building stones from other local hills. Indeed, two of the region's prime building stones, Jurassic and Magnesian limestone, have always been admired, and exported across the country.

Jurassic limestones from quarries around Lincoln, Ancaster, Clipsham, Stamford, Barnack, Ketton, Kings Cliffe, Weldon and Taynton have long been prized for their palette of light honey colours, excellent texture and robust weathering properties. Most occur in Roman London, sometimes in large quantities. Taynton stone, from quarries in the Windrush valley north-west of Burford, was used in some 11th-century London churches, is mentioned in Domesday Book and is still quarried today. It is seen best at Blenheim Palace, where Sir John Vanbrugh ordered it for the main buildings. Vanbrugh's dedicated enemy, Sarah, Duchess of Marlborough, countermanded his instructions, however, and obtained cheaper stone from Glympton, just north of Woodstock, for Kitchen Court. The Glympton stone failed within two centuries, whereas the Taynton has weathered well (Fig. 5.16). Barnack, Ancaster and Lincoln stones were also worked during the Roman period, and used for 9th- and 10th-century buildings; although Barnack 'ragstone' is said to have 'run out' during the 14th century, Ancaster continued to be transported around the Midlands (being used in Newark Castle, Wollaton Hall and Belvoir Castle, for example) and is still available. It has recently been used in the new Lincolnshire Museum (Fig. 5.17). Clipsham, another famous stone, was used for Edward III's rebuilding of Windsor Castle in the 1360s and in many East Midlands churches. It has become a popular stone in recent restoration projects at a number of English cathedrals (Canterbury, York, Norwich, Ripon and Salisbury) and also for projects at several Oxford colleges. Weldon stone, from quarries to the east of Corby, like others from this end of the Jurassic ridge, travelled widely by water and was taken to

Cambridge, London and Suffolk by this means in the 15th and 16th centuries. Weldon was used for Kirby Hall and several other Northamptonshire houses of the 16th century, and although Ketton stone was also used in the medieval period, it too was sought after for ashlar work at great houses (Audley End, Essex and Belton, Kesteven, for example) (*see* Fig. 5.25).

Praise for these famous oolitic limestones tends to obscure an important aspect of the stone industry along the Jurassic ridge. They were produced by quarries with permanently employed teams of specialist quarrymen, at least during the 18th and 19th centuries. Archaeological observation and ancient maps tell us, however, that every village on the limestone had its own quarry. At Ancaster (Kesteven), for example, Gregory's Quarry, just south of the village, has been supplying excellent building stone for about two centuries, and it is samples from this quarry that have found their way into geologists' reference collections. Yet Gregory's is a deep quarry, cutting back into the hillside, and typical of industrialised workings made possible only by mechanisation. Prior to mechanisation, quarrying around Ancaster extended not backwards into the hill face, but sideways along the exposures to east and west; earthwork remains extending to either side of Gregory's Quarry are still visible today. The spoil heaps, working platforms and trackways extend at least 10km along the ridge to the west and then south at least as far as Belton parish (Fig. 5.18), while to the east they extend at least another 7km as far as the Raucebys. Yet we still think (and write) of Ancaster stone as though it all came from Gregory's Quarry! Nor should we stop at Rauceby and Belton. Between Ancaster and Lincoln, just about every parish retains archaeological evidence for stone quarrying, and the same is probably also true of the parishes between Ancaster and Stamford and between Lincoln and Scunthorpe.

Most communities have always needed stone for building and many other purposes. When required, they have obtained the consent of the quarry owner, paid where necessary, and prized the stone away from the rock face themselves. Liberating rough blocks from an exposure is not a highly skilled operation and for communities along the Jurassic ridge, such quarrying would have been a skill learnt along with ploughing, fencing and the other tasks necessary to make a rural living. During the early modern period, house-building became more specialised, yet it is still likely that a large proportion of the honey-coloured cottages that make journeys through the limestone country so enjoyable today were actually built by their original owners, or at least by low-level specialists from within their own communities.

In central Oxfordshire, north Buckinghamshire and southern Bedfordshire, the Corralian beds produce a different type of Jurassic limestone. It is a dark, rubbly material, which is difficult to cut square, but as it forms both Cumnor Hill (to the west) and Headington Hill (to the east), it was used in Oxford from a very early date. Oxford's earliest standing stone structure, the city's 11th-century north gate

Fig. 5.18 Along the 'cliff' in Lincolnshire every parish had its quarry. Here, *looking north from Belton Park towards Honington, a continuous belt of trees has grown up along the line of rough earthworks left behind by generations of quarrying. The modern quarries at Ancaster lie 8km to the north-east.*

OPPOSITE PAGE:

TOP: *Fig. 5.19 Cottages in Rockingham (Northamptonshire).* They are largely built of iron-rich 'Northampton Sand' the colour of treacle, quarried from the cliff above the village.*

BOTTOM: *Fig. 5.20 The chapter house vault at Lincoln Cathedral:* a masterpiece of early 13th-century construction in the local Jurassic limestone (quarried no more than 100m to the east). But the webs between the ribs, originally intended to be plastered, are made of thin 'blue lias' slabs from the Trent valley, a few kilometres to the west.*

tower (subsequently St Michael's steeple), is built with it (*see* Fig. 6.5), and it is widely used in nearby villages. Quarries around Headington also produced a hard freestone, widely used in Oxford colleges in the 15th and 16th centuries, but weathering poorly. Even so, the quarries continued to be worked into the 20th century, and have left a legacy of incongruous deep holes full of old bicycles and blackberry bushes among the suburban housing.

Rich, dark tawny, red-brown building stones were quarried from the bottom of the Jurassic strata west of the ridge from Oxfordshire to the Humber. The red and brown stones, often called the 'Northampton Sands', are coloured by iron oxide and were, consequently, also quarried for iron-making (pp.176–7). Around Banbury many major buildings are of stone from quarries at Hornton (such as Broughton Castle and Wroxton Abbey, both in Oxfordshire), and many villages all along the ridge, such as Lyddington and Uppingham (both Rutland), contain many lovely buildings the colour of strong coffee. The most perfect display may be at Rockingham, just across the River Welland from Lyddington, where the road swings down the steep valley side to meet the uniform 17th- and 18th-century buildings of the relocated village, of stone as warm as gingerbread (Fig. 5.19). Older in geological date is 'blue Lias'. This is a smooth, slate-like stone, used for quite ambitious buildings where better stones are harder to come by. At Kineton (Warwickshire) it is used in bands in vernacular buildings to contrast with bands of dark brown ironstone, but in western Lincolnshire and eastern Nottinghamshire, complete cottages are built from it (for example, at Long Bennington, Kesteven), as are certain medieval churches (Marton and Upton, Lindsey, for example). At Lincoln itself it was used in evenly split slabs to form the 'webs' of 13th-century vaults in the cathedral. In the chapter house, its cool blue colour contrasts so well with the golden Lincoln limestone that, when the plaster was taken off in the 1960s, re-rendering was considered unnecessary (Fig. 5.20).

The East Midlands' Jurassic system provides the richest choice of fine building stone in England, but excellent magnesian limestone, of Permian age, is also quarried in the region. It outcrops in the ridge along the eastern side of the Pennines between Nottingham and the Yorkshire border – the same ridge on which Bolsover Castle and Hardwick Hall stand. This is a creamy white stone, with a more chalky texture than Jurassic limestone, and has also been much in demand since the Roman period, when it was used for many official buildings in York. At one time there were quarries in every parish on the Permian ridge, but since the 18th century famous 'deep' quarries have been worked for freestone by professional quarrymen around Mansfield Woodhouse and on Bolsover Moor. Worksop Abbey, Blyth Priory and Bolsover Castle (*see* Fig. 5.2) were all built from this material, along with most medieval churches in central and western Nottinghamshire. The villages of Nottinghamshire ought to shine with its glistening tones, as some Yorkshire villages do, but rebuilding in brick by the mining industry has dimmed them. The arrival of plentiful brick did not render the stone valueless, however, as it proved to be a good lining for

Fig. 5.21 The 'Little Castle' or 'Keep' at Bolsover (Derbyshire). This rich man's indulgence was built by Sir Charles Cavendish between 1612–21 in playful imitation of medieval examples (see also Fig. 2.11). According to the surviving buildings accounts (Knoop & Jones 1936), it was built of Permian limestone from three quarries; two within the parish and a third at Shuttlewood, 4km to the north-west.

Bessemer's new steel furnaces (introduced after 1856), and large quarries were opened at Steetley (Derbyshire) to supply this market.

Further south, the most famous quarries still working Permian stone are Gregory's at Mansfield (Nottinghamshire), which is famous for a stone known as 'Mansfield White', used at Southwell Minster and in the pompous neoclassical town hall at Newark (designed by York architect John Carr in 1773). To the east, sugary pink Triassic sandstones were greatly used in 17th- and 18th-century farm buildings between the Trent and Sherwood.

West of the Permian ridge, into Derbyshire, stones are less glamorous, but still very serviceable for building. Carboniferous limestone is harder, rougher and less attractively coloured than the Jurassic form, but it adds to the hard-bitten character of mountain villages like Castleton (Fig. 5.22) and dour fortified houses like Haddon Hall (both Derbyshire). Here the stone also makes an impact through field walls, which give the landscape as much character as the vernacular buildings. When rain-washed, the stone's dove grey colour is seen to good advantage, and it is a very pure source of calcium carbonate. A large modern mine, mostly below ground, at Middleton-by-Wirksworth exploits the stone's chemical purity and sells exclusively to the chemical industry.

All these East Midlands building stones have probably been in constant demand since methods were first devised to liberate them from the bedrock. Other East Midlands stones with special properties have also been sought out since earliest times. Gypsum has long been quarried along the Trent valley between Gotham and Newark. From the 17th century it has been made into a plaster and used over boards to make a robust floor covering, but now it has a variety of other uses. Today, Nottinghamshire and Derbyshire supply 40 per cent of Britain's output. Alabaster, a crystalline form of gypsum, has been quarried west of the gypsum deposits, especially between Ratcliffe-on-Soar and Burton-upon-Trent. In the medieval period it was quarried at Humberstone (Leicestershire), Chellaston

OPPOSITE PAGE:

TOP: *Fig. 5.22 The planned town of Castleton (Derbyshire), whose character derives from the dove-grey Carboniferous limestone of which it is built. Mam Tor rises behind.*

BOTTOM: *Fig. 5.23 Finished grindstones for the Sheffield cutlery industry, stacked near the gateway to Bole Hill Quarry near Grindleford (Derbyshire).*

(Derbyshire) and Tutbury (Staffordshire), where, as the locally available stone, it was used in the church. Unfortunately it is too soft for such external use, but this quality made it highly prized in the late medieval period for devotional sculptures as well as for monumental effigies. By the later 15th century, sculptors in Nottingham, Burton-upon-Trent and elsewhere were producing alabaster devotional panels, some sold in Nottingham's market place. After the Reformation these sculptors devoted themselves exclusively to monumental tombs for the aristocracy. This trade was only overtaken by imports of Italian and Greek marbles (and of continental sculptors themselves) after the Civil War; the Trent valley alabaster quarries' last commission is said to have been for the fascias at Keddlestone Hall (Derbyshire) in the 1760s. The workings at Chellaston (Derbyshire) left a moonscape of spoil heaps and working floors, which has now been mostly reclaimed.

Pennine Carboniferous sandstone – more commonly called millstone grit – is another specialist material, used for grinding-stones from the Roman period until the 20th century. It is difficult to work as a building stone, but because it is available in large uniform blocks, and no doubt also because it was sometimes available in an attractive red colour, the Romans used it for architectural columns in both Leicester and Lincoln, as well as in York and London. Whether early millstones were really slices of Roman columns remains a matter for speculation, but the fragments we have of early medieval millstones are certainly made from this same material.

We do not know where the Roman quarries were, but the millstone grit used at Chatsworth was quarried on Beeley Moor. Here, and at quarries around Hathersage (Derbyshire), millstones were a speciality. First documented in the 13th century, the output of millstones continued until a downturn in the 18th century, said to have coincided with the introduction of white bread. Derbyshire stones were not well suited for grinding such pure flours. Gardom's Edge Quarry, Baslow, used this stone to make edge-running grinding wheels for use on crushing circles in several industries, including the local processing of lead ore, but the failing millstone industry was given a new lease of life in the 19th century by the Sheffield cutlery industry, which needed large grindstones for polishing and sharpening. Unfortunately the grindstones produced at the quarries between Hathersage and Baslow were of poor quality, and the industry was already in steep decline before Edwardian factory legislation made such flawed and irregular grindstones illegal. Orders were left unfulfilled, and at the Bole Hill Quarry above Hathersage, the last consignment lies stacked for eternity in the dispatch bays by the entrance (Fig. 5.23).

LIME BURNING

As limestone occurs in many parts of the East Midlands, the region has also been a centre for lime burning. Lime has had three main functions: to make mortar for building, as an alkali in the tanning industry, and as a soil conditioner. Lime was already being spread on clay soils to reduce acidity in the 13th century and it became the principal soil preparation before the advent of chemical fertilisers in the 19th century. Traces of several Roman kilns have been found in the region, including excavated examples at Weekley and Wellingborough, Northamptonshire, Cardington, Bedfordshire, and Helpston, near Peterborough. These are all isolated kilns, perhaps constructed for single building projects. Barrow-on-Soar (Leicestershire), however, is said to have produced lime on an industrial scale in Roman times, burning the local Liassic stone, and it was certainly called upon for lime to build Kirby Muxloe Castle in 1480–3. Latterly, kilns here were fired by Derbyshire coal, shipped along the Soar Navigation, but Barrow lies across the river from Charnwood Forest, where charcoal has always been produced, and earlier charges were probably fired with this fuel. Being adjacent to large managed woodlands and also on a major river, Barrow was an ideal location for large-scale lime production for building projects across the East Midlands.

Although mortar would have been in great demand during the Roman period, Anglo-Saxon architecture had little call for it. Even so, the 9th-century mortar mixers used when constructing the second hall at the Northampton palace site (p.138) are among the few traces of the material in England at this early date. With the revival of stone building following the Norman Conquest, many building projects set up kilns on site for the duration – there was one at Bedford Castle, for example. Nevertheless, many building projects were not large enough to justify dedicated kilns, and so we find lime burning wherever limestone quarries, charcoal and communication routes (for transporting it to customers) coincided. They came together in 13th-century Lincoln, for example, where there is documentary evidence for lime kilns along the foot of the cliff just east of the walled city. These kilns were probably fired by charcoal made in the managed woodland south-west of the city; their customers would have been supplied by cart or barge and may have included contemporary building campaigns at the cathedral on the hilltop.

Simple lime kilns were common features in the medieval landscape and, with the emphasis on increasing agricultural efficiency in the 18th century, almost every farm in certain parts (such as Kesteven) had its own lime kiln for 'conditioning' the fields. It would have been simple 'flare kilns' or 'field kilns' of this type that John Clare tended at Pickworth (pp.91–3). Until recently, several were still visible amongst the earthworks of the abandoned village there (see Fig. 3.35).

In the late 18th century the industry expanded rapidly, with many larger scale kiln-banks being constructed to supply the booming construction industry. Such large facilities were sited, first, alongside the new canals (at Moira, Leicestershire, for example), and subsequently alongside the railways. A huge bank of 20 kilns was built in 1840 at Ambergate (Derbyshire) by George Stephenson, who foresaw that railways would provide an ideal means of transport for this bulky, but low value, product. Ambergate worked until 1965 but has now been demolished. Smaller kiln-banks still survive at Castle Bytham (Kesteven) and Millers Dale (Derbyshire), both located by railways.

The greatest regional investment in the lime industry, however, was made in the Derbyshire Peak between 1750 and 1950. Enormous workings were established on moorland at Grin Low and Dove Holes (above Buxton). At Dove Holes a weird landscape was created by dozens of circular flare and 'pot' kilns and their surrounding spoil heaps, while at Grin Low an even larger area of earthworks represents over 100 kilns (Fig. 5.24). These Derbyshire kilns were fired by Lancashire coal, which outcrops in the Goyt valley to the west; in fact their lime contributed mainly to the industrial development of the North West,

OPPOSITE PAGE:

TOP: *Fig. 5.24 Successive phases of lime-burning are revealed at Grin Low, Buxton (Derbyshire).* *The 17th- and 18th-century kilns (now represented only by earthworks) were lined up in rows along benches beneath the smaller quarry faces in the foreground, below the circular tower. The managed woodland towards Buxton would have provided fuel. This area became grazing land, divided regularly into fields at enclosure. Behind (north-west), although the huge kilns have gone, the great pit quarried vertically through the hill in the 19th century, and sustained by a branch railway, is now a dramatic caravan park.*

BOTTOM: *Fig. 5.25 Limestone has been quarried at Ketton (Rutland) since at least the Roman period and quarries extended for kilometres east and west along the exposures.* *Ketton stone is very even-grained, and this made it particularly suitable for the smooth ashlar finish sought in the 17th and 18th centuries. Fine clay, ideal for cement, is also found at Ketton, hence the Portland Company's buying-up small quarries in the 1920s and establishing the thriving cement works. Here the progress of stone on conveyors can be traced from the working faces through crushers and mixers to the kiln.*

until the railway from Buxton to Cromford was forced through the Wye valley gorge in 1860. Subsequently lime from here was used in the expansion of many East Midlands towns. The Derbyshire industry kept up with developments in kiln technology and in 1872 a 'hoffman' kiln with 'continuous firing' was built at Harpur Hill. It was closed in 1944 and has since been demolished.

Lime itself became a less important commodity in the late 19th and 20th centuries. Agriculture looked to imported or man-made materials for soil conditioning, while lime mortar's role in construction was supplanted by cement. Forms of cement, which is no more than lime mixed with clay and roasted, were known to the Romans, and a variety of recipes and production methods were patented in the late 18th and early 19th centuries. Chalk was more suitable than limestone for cement production, however, and the 20th-century industry became focused in the Thames estuary. Cement works were eventually established in most East Midlands counties, usually by companies based in Kent and Essex, but working local limestones where possible. A number (like those at Kirtlington, Oxfordshire and Pitstone, Buckinghamshire) have been closed and demolished in the last 20 years, but several large plants still dominate their local landscapes, such as the Earles Works in the Hope valley, Derbyshire (*see* Fig. 5.29), and the Portland Cement Company works (opened 1928) at Ketton, Rutland (Fig. 5.25).

COAL MINING

There are two coalfields within the East Midlands: one in south Derbyshire and north-eastern Leicestershire, and a much larger one extending south from Yorkshire into eastern Derbyshire and much of Nottinghamshire, north of the Trent (*see* Fig. 3.50). Here the coal seams slope down eastwards, so as one travels east from the outcrops on the Derbyshire–Nottinghamshire border, deeper shafts have been necessary to reach the coal. Although today we think of coal being produced from such deep shafts, for most of history it was simply not possible to excavate to such depths. Until the 19th century coal was either quarried from the faces of natural outcrops, where the coal seams reached the surface, or dug from shallow pits or shafts no more than 20m deep, known as bell pits. Examples of bell pits survive as earthworks at Strelley, Nottinghamshire, in Calke Abbey Park, Derbyshire and on Coleorton Moor, Leicestershire.

No clear evidence has yet been found for the use of coal during the Iron Age, although it would have been available from outcrops in certain Derbyshire and Leicestershire valleys. Coal from both the region's coalfields has been identified on Romano-British sites, but no mine of Roman date has yet to come to light either. It was evidently used as a fuel in northern England at that time, but it may have been regarded as a precious commodity with quasi-religious connotations; an indirect reference suggests that it was used to fuel a perpetual flame in a temple at Bath (Somerset).

Traces of East Midlands coal being exploited by the Anglo-Saxons are also absent, and there are no references to it in Domesday Book, which suggests that, if exploited at all, it was not a highly valued material. However, both East Midlands' coalfields have been worked since the 13th century, and recent discoveries during opencast reworking of north-eastern Leicestershire seams have revealed medieval galleries and shafts between 10m and 20m below ground. Coal mined at Cossall is mentioned in the late 13th century, at Selston a little later and at Wollaton in the 15th century. These places are a few kilometres north-west of Nottingham, and the town clearly played an important role in its marketing and transportation. By the 1530s output had reached 10,000 tons per annum and, although some was sold to fuel hearths in Nottingham, most was put onto river barges and sold into Lincolnshire and around the Humber estuary.

Having been powered in its initial stages by water, by the later 18th century the industrial revolution was turning to steam power, and steam was raised by coal. Once canals had linked them to the growing urban markets, East Midlands' coalfields expanded dramatically to meet demand. The Chesterfield Canal opened in 1777, with 65 locks connecting northern parts of the coalfield with the Trent, and was followed two years later by the Erewash Canal, which linked the river with the southern part of the coalfield. But output could not increase substantially without technological improvements, particularly in pumping and winding. Ironically, it was the steam engine that made such improvements possible, permitting cheap coal to be raised to fuel steam engines elsewhere. The earliest in the region may have been the Newcomen engine installed at Measham (Leicestershire) in 1720, and by 1777 seven atmospheric engines were at work in Derbyshire. Pumping and winding engines permitted the coalfields to expand eastwards. In Nottinghamshire, deep mining was now possible many kilometres from the outcrop and an industrial landscape developed slowly across previously agricultural land (p.106). The poorer soils of Sherwood Forest were particularly suitable for redevelopment. The land had not hitherto been very productive and coal was more profitable than trees. Many minor landowners (such as the Morewoods of Alfreton or the Drury Lowes of Denby) speculated by opening mines on their marginal land, and some acquired great wealth; but like the forest itself, a substantial number of new mines remained in aristocratic hands. As the winding and pumping engines became more powerful between 1850 and 1950, coal could be mined further and further east (see Fig. 3.50) until, between 1953 and 1958, large new mines were developed at Bevercotes, within a mile of the Great North Road, south of Retford, where the shafts were 900m deep (Fig. 5.26). The new mines of the Nottinghamshire Coalfield in the late 19th and 20th centuries were all much larger establishments than their predecessors and took full advantage of railway networks, developed to transport coal direct to customers. Since 1945 these have included a new generation of large power stations, established on the Trent (six in Nottinghamshire alone) to be close to the their fuel supply, and feeding the National Grid.

As in other coalfields, the new mines, with their railway networks, slagheaps and distinctive architecture, had a significant an impact on the East Midlands landscape. D H Lawrence saw the immense conical slagheaps as the most distinctive and representative feature of the Nottinghamshire Coalfield in which he grew up, but few now remain; most have been ruthlessly landscaped (see Fig. 3.58), with varying degrees of success. Many of the coalfield's distinctive buildings have also disappeared since the mine-closure programmes of the 1980s and 1990s. Markham, right beside the M1 near Bolsover, retained its 1891 winding gear, of the type once so typical of the region, until very recently. The site was dominated, however, by the outlandish shapes of raised tanks and conveyor belts belonging to the gigantic coal

Fig. 5.26 Bevercotes Mine (Nottinghamshire) typifies the recent history of this coalfield. Its very deep shafts were sunk (1953–8) in a rural setting (indeed in a wood), where there was no pre-existing village. But it was close to its main market, the new power-stations on the Trent (High Marnham – opened 1962 – is visible in the distance), with which Bevercotes was connected by both rail and road (via the A1M which passes north-west to south-east 1km to the east of the mine). Also characteristic was its closure in the 1990s.

*Fig. 5.27 **The unusual 'double' winding gear at Pleasley Colliery (Derbyshire) of 1898–1904** has been preserved now the mine has closed and will become a monument to the once-powerful local industry.*

preparation and washing facilities; these were built in the 1970s so that coal could be provided in large quantities, direct to the newly commissioned Central Electricity Generating Board's power stations on the Trent and in Yorkshire. The double-headed steam-powered winding gear of the same generation at nearby Pleasley has now been preserved (Fig. 5.27), as has the steam-powered winding gear of 1873 from Bestwood Colliery (Nottinghamshire). Here the wider landscape impact of the mine is recognisable. The whole settlement belonged to the mining company (which also ran four blast furnaces here until the 1920s), and miners and steelworkers were accommodated in a planned village of sombre red brick that flows down the hillside like an overturned pot of red paint on a green carpet. In the Leicestershire Coalfield, Snibston's winding gear has also been preserved within a heritage centre near Coalville, though it is domestic in scale compared with the big Nottinghamshire examples. Coalville was a company town as well, but it has a completely different landscape presence from Bestwood (*see* Fig. 3.51).

Although much more localised, coal processing to remove the impurities – to make coke – also had a profound effect on the wider landscape. Coke became important for the production of coal gas in Victoria's reign, and the coal of eastern Derbyshire and western Nottinghamshire was found to be particularly suitable for coking. By 1900 over 1,000 coking ovens are said to have been at work in the area between Dronfield and Chesterfield, filling the air with their distinctive, poisonous fumes. 'Beehive' ovens at Ramshaw and Summerley (Derbyshire) still survive, though the latter are somewhat later in date. Here also lies the enormous Coalite works north of Bolsover Castle, near Markham, which was the largest plant of its type in the world when it opened in 1937 (*see* Fig. 2.11). Coalite profited from the 1956 Clean Air Act and added further retorts at Bolsover to cater for increased demand.

IRON ORE MINING

The Iron Age metalworkers of Dragonby (p.43) would have smelted ore mined from the iron-rich limestone outcrops close to the settlement, and there is evidence for Roman ironstone quarrying at nearby Thealby. Ironstone quarrying must also have been widespread in the Anglo-Saxon period, but no dated evidence has yet emerged. In fact, the archaeological literature is largely devoid of references to the quarrying of ironstone for smelting. Nevertheless, quarrying must have occurred along the entire Jurassic ridge throughout the period between the Iron Age and the 18th century; perhaps its archaeological remains have been mistaken for quarrying for other purposes.

By the 19th century, however, quarrying for building stone can be distinguished from ironstone quarrying simply by the scale of extraction. Ironstone quarrying has made even greater scars in the east Derbyshire landscape than coal mining, and a

Fig. 5.28 View of open-cast ironstone working at Eaton (Leicestershire) c.1920. *This illustrates why the modern Northamptonshire and Leicestershire landscapes show relatively little sign of the massive extractions undertaken 1880–1980. The field on the left shows the original land surface before quarrying. The working face progressed across the landscape removing ironstone along a band some 15m wide, using a temporary light railway. Behind it, the field has been restored to use with topsoil saved to the right of the track. Now, however, the land surface is some 5m lower than it was.*

number of late 18th- and early 19th-century coal-mine owners (like the Bestwood Company) became better known as iron producers. For a period ore was available within the coalfield itself, but in relatively small quantities that were exhausted by 1900, after which Derbyshire ironmasters had to seek supplies elsewhere. As little was available locally, the furnaces of western Leicestershire used imported ore from the start, shipped in by canal and then railway. Ironmasters in both coalfields were always seeking alternative sources of ore, and in the 1870s the Wingerworth Company opened large-scale ironstone quarries around Stamford. At Scunthorpe in the 1880s, it was the Staveley Company's quarrying investment that inaugurated the phenomenal growth of that town (pp.108–9). Around Melton Mowbray extraction began in 1874 and by 1900 Leicestershire was the largest supplier of iron ore in England. In Rutland, the Cottesmore quarries opened in 1882 and spread north-east towards existing quarries around the Bythams (Kesteven) and south-east towards those around Stamford. In Northamptonshire, the cutting of main-line railways across the hill-and-dale landscape had stimulated a dynamic ironstone-quarrying industry (pp.109–10) and substantial complexes developed around Blisworth, Gayton, Duston and Desborough. With the introduction of mechanisation in the quarries in the late 19th century, particularly by Lloyds in Corby in the 1890s, production increased exponentially. The output of ironstone from the Jurassic ridge between 1870 and 1930 was prodigious and, as old photographs show (Fig. 5.28), ancient pasture was rapidly converted to devastated wasteland and back to pasture again. Once the ironstone had been removed, each field was backfilled with the spoil from the one next to it, so that, within 30 years, a whole geological zone had been inverted and displaced into the field beside it.

LEAD ORE MINING

Limited quantities of lead ore (galena) occur in western Charnwood, but in central Derbyshire there are substantial deposits, and here it has been mined even longer than iron. Late Bronze Age people used lead artefacts hereabouts, although we do not yet know whether it was smelted locally (perhaps at Ecton Hill in Staffordshire) or imported from elsewhere. Derbyshire lead was probably quarried and smelted during the Iron Age, but good evidence for its exploitation only arrives with the Romans. Roman sponsorship of mining and smelting is proved in a characteristically 'imperial' manner, through lead 'pigs' (ingots) stamped with taxation marks. Twenty-seven such pigs are known, from as far away as Sussex, but the earliest found (in 1777) had travelled no further than Cromford and dates from AD 117–38. The Romans may have come to the ore field in search of silver, of which lead was a by-product, but no Roman silver from Derbyshire has yet been identified.

Indeed, archaeological remains of the substantial Roman investment in the ore field are hard to find, although clear evidence of Roman (or pre-Roman) mining has been found underneath a wall of 2nd- or 3rd-century date at Royston Grange.

The Anglo-Saxons continued to work the ore field and by 835 it had become a valuable source of income for the church. A rental of that year records payment of a large sum (300 shillings) to Canterbury Cathedral by the Mercian abbey at Repton (Derbyshire) for exploiting mines in Wirksworth manor. Domesday Book records three lead 'works' at Wirksworth, out of seven mentioned in Derbyshire, all of which were probably smelt mills rather than mines. Later, smelt mills were considered to belong to the manors, like corn mills, and were sources of income for the manorial lords. As with their corn, miners were obliged to have their ore smelted in their own manorial mills, paying a fee to their lord for the privilege. Lead ore was therefore regarded simply as another manorial resource to be worked by the community, in the same way that farmland was worked. Until very recently, indeed, lead mining in Derbyshire was undertaken by miner-farmers, and was seen merely as another inherited farming skill.

Medieval mining was quite large in scale: the Tideswell mines were said to have produced 650 tons of ore in 1195 alone. Once located at the surface, the ore vein was followed vertically down into the earth, leaving distinctive linear spoil-heaps ('rakes') marching across the landscape. These features lend a rugged, striated, character to the moors north-west of Wirksworth and between Tideswell and Castleton (Fig. 5.29). But, although undertaken on a large scale, Derbyshire mining is actually characterised by its low intensity. The ore was either carried to the surface in baskets or wound on simple capstans, which were driven by horses or donkeys; their former presence is revealed today

Fig. 5.29 Looking eastwards along Dirtlow Rake, towards Hope (Derbyshire). It is easy to see, at the surface, the line of the lead ore vein beneath (left). The pits and other earthworks alongside it have been formed during 1,800 years of traditional mining. The enormous quarry on the right (south) supplies the Hope Cement Works beyond with limestone.

by distinctive circular earthworks. The galena was separated from the mother rock by a series of crushing, grinding and flotation processes. In Derbyshire, unlike other English ore fields, these were usually 'low-tech' operations, often animal-powered (like the surviving crushing circle at Odin Mine, Castleton) and sited as near the mine shaft as possible. They required water, however, which had to be stored and controlled, usually by small dams near the hilltops.

In the 16th century output increased and by the early 17th century most major veins had been exploited down to the water table. Drainage measures were required if the ore field was to continue in production, and a long campaign began in the 1630s to direct underground streams into artificial tunnels called soughs, draining eventually into the river valleys. Such measures avoided the need for pumping; by 1801 there was still only a single steam engine at work. The low level of investment in Derbyshire mining is sometimes forgotten because the most impressive standing remains belong to the handful of 'Cornish-style' engine houses (at Magpie Mine, near Shelton, for example, built in 1868). But these are atypical and the Derbyshire lead-mining landscape appears quite different from those in Shropshire or the South West, where larger-scale mines are more frequently encountered and each have several engine houses. This disparity in scale of investment, of course, is an indicator of differences in the mining economy. In the South West and Shropshire, investment was by large companies, often based outside the ore fields, and the miners were merely employees. Such operations were unusual in Derbyshire, although Millclose Mine (near Matlock) was one. It employed nearly 800 men in 1930, but ceased mining in 1939; now only a smelter remains.

In Derbyshire the ancient tradition of independent mining persisted, undertaken by local farmers, who mined on their own accounts and sold small quantities of ore to the smelter, just as they marketed their sheep and grain. The distinctive symbol of this mining economy was the 'coe' – a structure once scattered in great numbers across the ore field and almost unique to Derbyshire. It was a small shack, built of stone from the mine spoil, and located as close to the shaft top as was practical. It was a store for the individual miner-farmer's tools and clothes so that, when work on the land was slack, an afternoon could be spent winning ore. Unfortunately, coes are very vulnerable structures, but even 30 years ago there were still roofed examples to be seen on Bonsall Moor (Fig. 5.30).

Traditional mining suffered a downturn in the 1860s and slowly faded out of the landscape, although the largest mining companies survived until the 1920s. Ironically, the waste from two millennia of lead-working became highly sought after in the later 20th century. Until then, the fluorspar, barites and calcite, with which galena was combined in the vein, had been discarded. But now fluorspar was required as a flux in iron smelting and for plastics, barites was used as a paint additive and calcite had become a staple of the new chemical industries. Consequently, these minerals became as valuable as galena itself. Mining companies began to reprocess the ancient linear spoil tips, tearing long scars across the landscape and doing immense damage to the archaeological remains of the earlier industry. To local astonishment, new opencast mines for fluorspar at Eyam and Longstone Edge were opened to satisfy increasing demand. These workings, rather than the miner-farmer's coe, represent the Derbyshire mining industry today.

Fig. 5.30 A miner's 'coe' on Wirksworth Moor (Derbyshire). This is one of the last survivors of a once common building type in these parts.

Working the Woodlands

We have already suggested that, since at least the Iron Age, East Midland settlements seem to have divided into two broad types. Some settlement economies are dominated by farming the land and exploiting other resources of the landscape itself, such as stone; but other settlements, although growing food and raising stock, nevertheless have economies based on manufacturing. This second group of settlements, we can now see, needed an abundance of one resource in particular to break the rigid link with agriculture: managed woodland. The inhabitants of settlements with large areas of managed woodland could turn their hands to a variety of industries, generating useful products and materials for sale in regional markets. In particular, they could produce enough coppiced wood to fire iron furnaces and pottery kilns. Consequently, where large areas of managed woodland overlay clays suitable for pottery, or were near ironstone deposits suitable for smelting, communities were able to develop economies dominated by manufactured goods, rather than by agricultural produce.

Between at least the 6th century BC and the 17th century, there was enough managed woodland to produce fuel to meet industrial demand in the region. We have seen in Chapter 1 that such woodlands were most frequently found within forest landscapes, both around the East Midlands' borders (Sherwood, north-east Derbyshire, Needwood, Arden and Wychwood), and also within its boundaries (*see* Fig. 1.4). Charnwood, Rutland and much of Kesteven were dominated by large managed woodlands in 1086, and a smaller zone of managed woodlands ('Linwood') still runs along the southern boundary of Lindsey from Wragby to Tattershall. The three big forests of Northamptonshire (Rockingham, Salcey and Whittlewood) contained large areas of managed woodland. Further south, the poor soils of the Corallian and sandstone ridges from Faringdon (old Berkshire) to Sandy (Bedfordshire) also supported large managed woodlands. Its central part was formalised as the medieval forest of Bernwood. Harthay and Bromswold, which extended eastwards from Northamptonshire into Huntingdonshire, was another forest area that may once have contained much more managed woodland. If so, it disappeared relatively early, perhaps like that in eastern Leicestershire and eastern Lincolnshire, which may also have been well-wooded in the Anglo-Saxon period and which are linked by their '-wold' place-names.

CHARCOAL BURNING

Compared with the agricultural economy, huge quantities of coppiced wood were required to sustain industrial output. It has been estimated, for example, that 150kg of wood were required to fire a single pottery kiln. But for iron furnaces, wood was an inefficient fuel: it introduced chemical impurities and was unable to raise kiln temperatures sufficiently high. Charcoal, however, burns for longer with a more sustained high temperature and has fewer chemical impurities. Consequently charcoal-making became the basic industry of managed woodlands, on which other industries often depended. Charcoal burning was a seasonal activity (the wood is best cut in the winter and then kilned the following summer), allowing charcoal burners to follow other trades, often as managers of the woodland itself, felling trees, collecting underbrush, supplying timber and mending fences. Analyses of environmental data from Iron Age sites such as Gravelly Guy point to extensive managed woodland near the later prehistoric Thames valley, although whether charcoal was being made is unclear. There is also evidence of Iron Age coppicing of willow in the managed woodlands on the Bedfordshire sandstone from Ruxox. Plenty of evidence has been collected for charcoal use in the Romano-British period, although the sites of the 'stands', at which wood was kilned in carefully constructed piles under a covering of turf, can only be dated using radiocarbon. By the 13th century the English Crown was employing considerable numbers of charcoal burners in the royal forests (Wychwood, for example), presumably to provide fuel for other furnaces and kilns. Most of these furnaces probably produced iron, and charcoal and iron production in Rockingham Forest were closely integrated from the time of Domesday Book until the 18th century. In 1414 Henry V ordered small quantities of charcoal to be specially kilned in royal forests for milling into gunpowder in advance of the siege of Harfleur. Gunpowder mills became an increasingly important market for charcoal, and a number of 17th-century East Midlands works are reported (at Bedford, Stamford, Banbury and Oxford for example).

By the 18th century, however, charcoal had been replaced by coke in iron furnaces and the exhausted woodlands were vacated in favour of the coalfields.

Yet gunpowder (mostly for quarrying) remained a valuable market for industrial charcoal producers until after 1945. The traditional woodland stands had long been abandoned in favour, first, of brick kilns and finally of iron retorts, like the 'Blair kilns' at the Shirley Aldred Company's works at Worksop. Although it closed in 1970, the company kilned wood from Sherwood plantations right up to the end.

THE IRON SMELTING INDUSTRY

It is startling to think that, with the closure of the last Derbyshire furnaces in 1974 and those at Corby in 1980, only the Scunthorpe works remain to remind us that iron smelting has been part of the East Midlands scene for over two millennia (Fig. 5.31). Iron-making has been a routine activity in the region for almost as long as farming.

Iron Age furnaces would have been of the 'bloomery' type, producing only small quantities of iron, which needed much hammering to make it usable. Iron finds of the 3rd century BC from Ancaster (Kesteven), where ironstone outcrops in the hillside, may have been made in the immediate locality, but evidence for Iron Age smelting is extremely rare. Good evidence was found, however, for ironworking at Dragonby, which began in the 1st century AD and continued until the late Roman period. Metalworkers here may have combined both smelting and metalworking skills, as one small hearth seems to have been used for roasting ore. But, although iron ore was probably won locally, no other evidence of Roman smelting has yet emerged from north-west Lindsey. In Kesteven and Rutland, however, at least nine Roman iron furnace sites have been identified,

Fig. 5.31 Scunthorpe's skyline is dominated by the skeletal profile of the giant blast furnace array known as 'the four queens'. 'Mary' and 'Bess' to the right (north) here were first fired in 1939, and were joined by 'Anne' and 'Victoria' in 1954. With the demolition of similar structures at Middlesbrough in the 1990s, these are the last remaining smelters of this type in England.

and one has been excavated at Colsterworth. This was certainly fed by local ore, and we can guess that charcoal fuel was also produced near the site. Using evidence from the Weald, it has been calculated that it took more than 90kg of ore and 120kg of charcoal to produce 9kg of iron in furnaces of this type; such quantities must imply large managed woodlands in Kesteven and Rutland at this date, which are presumably those also recorded in 1086. 'Kesteven' is an intriguing place name in this respect because it incorporates a Celtic word meaning 'wood'. Similarly, the Iron Age and Romano-British smelting sites reported from Great Oakley, Harringworth, Laxton and Wakerley imply early managed woodlands within what subsequently became Rockingham Forest.

Smelting in the 6th and 7th centuries may be represented by 'tap-slags' (cooled molten impurities) and other debris from excavations at Shakenoak (Oxfordshire); more certain evidence from the 8th century has been found at Maxey, north of Peterborough. Contemporary smelting was reported at the Northampton 'palace' site (p.138), and has been presumed at Newton-le-Willows (Northamptonshire) where iron slag has been found alongside early pottery. Rockingham Forest has also produced extensive archaeological evidence for late Anglo-Saxon ironworking, while Domesday Book locates ironworkers at Gretton and Corby, as well as at Cranfield and Wilshamstead (Bedfordshire), Stow in Lindsey and Castle Bytham (Kesteven). These references probably represent iron smelters, not merely quarrymen or smiths. Smelting furnaces of somewhat later date have been excavated at Stanion and Little Weldon (Northamptonshire), both in Rockingham Forest.

Although close to the managed woodlands of Kesteven and Rutland, iron smelting in 11th-century Stamford may have been developed by a community of skilled workers in the town, capitalising on the new market there. Ore and charcoal would have been imported from the nearby sources. Thirteenth-century records report similar imports of large quantities of charcoal from Sherwood Forest into Nottingham, presumably to feed similar urban smelters. Along with imports of ore, this trade may have been controlled by those who sold iron artefacts in Nottingham's great markets. In Nottingham, the entire process (from the transport of raw materials to the sale of finished objects) may have been undertaken by individual smiths. Confirmation that urban metalworkers were indeed smelting their own iron comes from excavations at Godmanchester, where a 13th-century roadside blacksmith was using a smelting furnace in a back room.

Charcoal continued to fire iron smelters in the East Midlands through the 14th and 15th centuries, and it was not until after the Reformation that experiments using coal as a fuel began. The eventual success of such experiments was to have a great impact on the East Midlands landscape, relocating iron-making from the managed woodlands to the coalfields. The earliest and most important of these iron-making districts lay in the Erewash valley along the Nottinghamshire–Derbyshire border. Travelling up the River Erewash today, we find a distinctive combination of derelict sheds clad in corrugate, and brick walls enclosing nothing but weed-choked mounds, all separated from each other by blocks of red-brick terraced houses. The first furnace in the coalfield is said to have been erected here, at Codnor, by Sir John Zouche in 1582. However, it is not certain that coal was used for fuel at first, even though the Codnor furnace was bought in 1590 by Sir Francis Willoughby, a notable local coal-mine owner. This part of Derbyshire already contained large managed woodlands, and charcoal was certainly made locally; the late 16th- and 17th-century smelters here may have been fired with local charcoal, rather than local coal. The iron industry prospered, however, and by 1657 there were 19 furnaces in blast in Scarsdale Hundred.

Bar iron was shipped by waterway to London, Nottingham and Derby for working by local smiths, but by the mid-18th century Derbyshire iron had become too expensive to compete with Swedish imports and a mere 650 tons were produced at four furnaces in 1750. This poor performance may be evidence

OPPOSITE PAGE:

TOP: *Fig. 5.32 Abstract shapes of furnace stacks at Morley Park Ironworks stand incongruously amongst fields near Heage (Derbyshire). The earlier, to the right, was first fired using coke in 1780; its companion in 1825.*

MIDDLE: *Fig. 5.33 The original workers' village layout at Ironville (Derbyshire), established in the 1840s and 1850s along the Cromford Canal (bottom right), shows clearly in this modern view looking north-west. Completely surrounded by railway lines, the rectilinear village lay to the north-west (upper right). The lines of the nine original terraces, with evocative names like Foundry Row and Furnace Row, were retained when the houses themselves were replaced in the 1970s. Southwards, the characteristic curving streets of semi-detached houses were established over a coal-mine site and a brickworks in the 1920s and 1930s. The green field marking the site of the huge Codnor Park Iron Works (founded 1834), to which Ironville owed its origin, lies along the canal east of the railway (bottom centre).*

BOTTOM: *Fig. 5.34 Moira furnace, Ashby Woulds (Leicestershire), represented a major industrial investment in 1806. It was an attempt to capitalise on increasing output from the local coalfield by smelting local supplies of high-quality nodular iron ore, found in amongst the coal measures themselves. It was only fired until 1811, however, although the attached foundry survived until c.1844. Between the enormous furnace stack (foreground) and the Ashby Canal (beyond the tree) stands the contemporary 'bridgehouse' from which the ore was delivered into the top of the furnace. Blast was provided by a Boulton and Watt steam engine located in a separate building to the north (left).*

that the Derbyshire ironmasters were indeed still using charcoal as a fuel, as the cheaper iron with which they were competing was increasingly made with coke. Iron had been made using coke since Abraham Darby opened his furnaces in Coalbrookdale, Shropshire, in 1709; but it was not until 1780 that the Morley Park works, Ripley (Derbyshire), was opened using locally coked coal. It was followed by the nearby Butterley Iron Company in 1790 (who only started mining coal subsequently). The early blast furnace 'stacks' at both works still survive (Fig. 5.32), as does the symmetrical plan of Ironville village, built to house the workers at Codnor Park Smelter (Fig. 5.33).

The iron industry in the Leicestershire Coalfield developed along similar lines, but always on a smaller scale than in Derbyshire. Iron had been worked at Staunton Harrold, Whitwick and Hartshorne in the 17th century, probably using charcoal from the managed woodlands in Charnwood rather than local coal. As in Derbyshire, production fell away sharply in the early 18th century, to be reinvigorated in the 1780s by the introduction of furnaces using coal coked locally, at Measham, by Joseph Wilkes, who also sponsored other industries and backed the Ashby Canal to export regional manufactures. The most charming and spectacular remains of this period lie alongside this canal at Moira (Leicestershire). Here the monumental, multi-tier furnace stack opened in 1806 and closed less than 10 years later (Fig. 5.34). The extraordinary structure was then converted into a warren of individual cottages. The Moira furnace had been supplied by a new mine equipped with a Newcomen pumping engine house and model workers' housing, both of which survive, although the coke ovens have gone.

It required prodigious quantities of coke to fire these early furnaces – at least 5 tons per ton of pig iron produced. Even so, ironmasters continued to bring the ore to the coal, rather than vice versa. Relative quantities of coke and ore required to make iron were changing, however. In the late 19th century, purer ores and better furnace designs could produce more iron per ton of coke; the quantities of coke required continued to fall until by the 1970s it only took 0.75 tons of coke to produce a ton of iron.

As the quality of the ore remained similar throughout the late 19th and 20th centuries, economics pulled large-scale steel production away from the source of the coal and back into the ore field itself. A modern furnace had been fired in the ore field at Wellingborough (Northamptonshire) as early as 1853 and developed into a large works, and other mid-19th-century furnaces were established alongside the railways at Nevill Holt and Holwell (both Leicestershire) and Cransley (near Kettering). Scunthorpe also exploited the trend early and was already smelting c.1865, although Corby did not start smelting until 1907. Meanwhile the coalfield furnaces underwent a protracted decline, with 17 out of 35 furnaces in blast in Derbyshire closed between 1928 and 1931. Unlike Scunthorpe and Corby, the remaining Derbyshire furnaces failed to invest heavily in steel-making equipment and they became suppliers to a dwindling market for cast iron. The last Derbyshire iron smelter (at Stanton) was closed in 1974.

NON-FERROUS METAL SMELTING

Roman lead smelting used crucibles in open hearths worked by 'pedalled' bellows, and supposed sites of such hearths have been excavated near Duffield and at Scarsdale, east of Chesterfield. In addition to the three 11th-century smelters living at Wirksworth, Domesday Book also names smelters at Matlock, Ashbourn, Parwich and Darley; their entries suggest that their primary role might have been to recover not lead, but silver. We do not know what type of furnace was recorded by these entries, but subsequently 'bole' furnaces were widely used. These were kiln-like structures, set along a west-facing hill crest and relying on strong winds to heat the charges of wood and crushed ore to high enough temperatures to reduce the galena to slag and pure metal. They must have presented a dramatic sight to travellers on a windy night, lined up along the ridges on either side of the Derwent valley. Although their remains are hard to detect, 26 sites have been identified through earthwork survey and place-name study in recent years and a few, like those on Beeley and Totley Moors, have been excavated.

An important 16th-century innovation was the bole furnace's replacement with the 'ore hearth', which used 'whitecoal' (kiln-dried wood) rather than brushwood as fuel and was blown by bellows driven by waterwheels. Being no longer dependent on the wind, the ore hearths moved down-slope to sites such as Duffield (fired in 1550), where they could be nearer their fuel sources. Indeed, ore hearths (being mostly timber structures) are often difficult to locate except through the stone-built kilns in which their wood was dried. As with charcoal, whitecoal was best made from coppice poles, obtained from the managed woodland still present in the eastern Derbyshire valleys. By 1700 Wirksworth was described as 'the chief town of the Peak, and the greatest market for lead in England'. 'Near this town', it was said, 'are the furnaces where they melt down their lead ore with great fires' (Cox 1700, 433). In the 1730s further technical advances pushed the smelting furnaces back up the hillsides. The new 'cupola' furnaces (in which fuel was kept separate from ore, the ore being roasted in super-heated air rather than burnt) once again required strong draughts and, as they were fuelled by Derbyshire coal, they no longer needed to be near woodlands. Good examples survive at Stonedge near Chesterfield (established 1770), which is said to possess the oldest industrial chimney in the world (Fig. 5.35), and at Callow Field near Hathersage. Unlike the boles, however, the cupola furnaces were typically located just below the hill crests, on which a short chimney would be sited, linked to the furnace by a length of flue designed to enhance the draught and (eventually) to provide a condensation chamber for metal-rich flue gases. By 1811 there were 20 such cupolas in Derbyshire and some flues had reached several hundred metres in length. Some are still visible, looking like fossilised mole tunnels meandering through the heather moor.

CLAY INDUSTRIES: POTTERY

No pottery from the East Midlands (or indeed anywhere else in Britain) has been convincingly dated earlier than the middle of the 4th millennium BC, but one of the earliest wares is named 'Peterborough' from the region where it was first found. Such early pottery is grouped by style of decoration, however, not by its source of manufacture, and Peterborough ware is not specific to Peterborough. Furthermore, its decoration probably represents a symbolic language, with similar 'sayings' applied to many different types of pot, and studies of such pottery often show that they are made from clays dug close to the find site. With prehistoric pottery, then, it seems that the meanings of pottery designs travelled, rather than the vessels themselves.

With the much larger quantities of pottery from the Roman and medieval periods, we can study production and distribution patterns more meaningfully. Such studies show that much pottery manufacture before the coal-fired industry of the 18th century was another industry run by specialists often working in the more well-wooded regions. Urban pottery industries certainly existed, but rural potters were frequently members of distinctive communities, where woodland management was a more major part of the settlement economy than it was in common-field villages with their more intensive agricultural systems.

Excavations at Sidlings Copse, Oxfordshire explored the close relationship between Romano-British pottery production and managed woodland. Here it seems that the coppiced alder woodland slowly shrank in area, until by the 4th century it had been replaced by coppiced hazel and oak. As on many Romano-British sites an increase in willow pollen was also found, perhaps because willow was deliberately cultivated for fuel. Willow is fast growing and easily coppiced but it can also be pollarded (which enables a wood-pasture regime, with stock grazing the woodland floor). Chestnut may have been introduced by the Romans for the same purpose. The Romano-British pottery kilns at Sidlings Copse were just one of many production sites around Oxford, where the managed woodlands on the Corallian hills approached the Thames. After the 2nd century, this area became one of the largest manufacturing centres in Britain, producing many different wares, especially 'parchment ware' and a red-coated earthenware that mimicked Gaulish Samian ware. Oxfordshire pots were marketed across the north-western part of the British civilian zone, although few have been found north of the Fosse Way or north of the Welland.

The Romano-British managed woodlands in the area that subsequently became the forests of Salcey and Whittlewood also supported large potting communities, as did north-east Northamptonshire, in and around the woodlands that subsequently became Rockingham Forest and Bromswold. The important town of Durobrivae (pp.49–50) stood towards the eastern end of a scatter of at least 50 known kiln sites through these woodlands, typically located on the high clay-covered plateau land, above the settlements. Potting started hereabouts soon after the conquest, and what might be the earliest kiln in Britain (dating to the mid-1st century AD) has been excavated at Rushden (Northamptonshire). Most such kilns manufactured coarse wares, but fine wares were also produced. This was the centre of the 'colour-coated ware' industry, and it also produced an imitation Samian ware in the 2nd and 3rd centuries, as well as *mortaria* (bowls used for preparing food) for the army. No doubt the Nene was used for shipping finished pots, and it is thought that Durobrivae's commercial success was partly due to its role as a pottery market.

Romano-British kiln sites also concentrated around Hartshill, Mancetter and Chilvers Cotton (Warwickshire), at the northernmost tip of the extensive woodlands which would become the Forest of Arden and, eastwards, the woodlands of Charnwood. This industry was established by AD 100, and *mortaria* produced here were sold across Britannia; perhaps 30 per cent of this area's output was sold to the military in the Pennines and on Hadrian's Wall. North of

OPPOSITE PAGE:

Fig. 5.35 An elegant square chimney, originally providing up-draft for condensing flues at the lead smelter at Stone Edge (Matlock, Derbyshire), is the only substantial building remaining here. The poisoned landscape, however, colonised by willow-herb, clearly shows where smelting was undertaken between 1770 and the late 19th century.

Derby, managed woodlands along the Derwent valley probably produced distinctive pimply jars (known as 'Derbyshire ware') for the military base at Littlechester. The Derbyshire, Warwickshire and western Leicestershire kilns were located near coal exposures, but we only have evidence for the use of wood as fuel.

From the 2nd until the late 4th century, Lincolnshire was also an important centre of Romano-British pottery production, notable for its 'East Midlands burnished ware'. Lincoln itself was not located within any formally recognised area of managed woodland, but there was a substantial block of such countryside in the medieval period on the poorer sandy soils south-west of the city. It has been proposed that this was an area of managed woodland in the Iron Age and Romano-British periods, and the Romano-British pottery industry lies along its edge, at Swanpool. So-called 'Trent Valley ware' may also have been produced using these woodland resources – perhaps at kilns like that at Norton Disney (Kesteven).

Like other systems of intensive landscape management, large-scale pottery production in all these managed woodlands had come to an end by AD 500. Most early Anglo-Saxon pottery was grass-tempered, coil-built (rather than thrown on a wheel) and seems to have been fired, not in kilns, but in bonfires or 'clamps'. This technology was markedly different from the Romano-British industry and would not necessitate such an elaborate woodland management regime. In Northamptonshire and Lincolnshire, even better-made pots from 5th- and 6th-century cremation cemeteries are thought to have been manufactured by their respective communities within a few kilometres of their burial. In the 5th century, when empire-wide economic structures had been replaced by a multitude of self-reliant, but circumscribed, local economic regimes, intensive large-scale pottery production in the Anglo-Saxon woodlands seems less likely. This would be largely because distribution networks had broken down, because the woodlands themselves probably continued to be managed. According to this view, everyday pottery manufacture would have slipped from being a specialised activity, requiring full-time workers and high skill levels, to become just another low-level skill acquired as part of working the land. Most early Anglo-Saxon domestic vessels would now be fired in clamps, on individual farms, by the occupants, in the prehistoric manner. Although Anglo-Saxon cremation vessels are often made from the clay round each cemetery, however, they frequently display stylistic similarities with pots from many kilometres away. Consequently, rather than static production sites in the managed woodland, should we envisage bands of roving Anglo-Saxon potters moving from place to place, working each community's clay in turn, using each community's woodland resources?

Yet the East Midlands region does contain at least two candidates for genuine pottery 'industries' of the 5th and 6th centuries, apparently established in managed woodland and with long-distance trading connections, along Romano-British lines. Simple kilns of 5th- or 6th-century date at Cassington and Sutton Courtney (Oxfordshire), on the edge of Wychwood, have been put forward as evidence that Anglo-Saxon pottery manufacture continued in this fashion. More certainly, 'granite tempered' pots, probably made in woodlands on the eastern side of Charnwood, were used for both domestic and funerary purposes right across the East Midlands. This was not a rare or exotic pottery: at the contemporary settlement at Catholme (about 30km west), fully one third of the pottery was of this type. These exceptional sub-Roman 'industries' fade from sight during the 7th century, to be replaced by widely distributed 'Maxey-type wares'. Although it is not known where the 'Maxey-type ware' of the 7th and 8th centuries was actually made, its distribution, across the eastern parts of the East Midlands, but not in East Anglia, has suggested to some that it might have been produced in Northamptonshire woodlands. But it too is coil-built and clamp-fired, and it may represent a continuation of non-specialist Anglo-Saxon pottery-making traditions, even though a widespread distribution gives it the appearance of a genuine industry.

It seems unlikely that potters recolonised the East Midlands managed woodlands on any scale until after about 900, when a multitude of new woodland industries emerged at many locations contemporaneously. It is surely not coincidental that this occurs at precisely the same moment that the wider landscape was being reorganised into common fields and nucleated villages (*see* Chapter 3: A Landscape for Communities). This new generation of potters worked, not in the new common-field villages, but in more specialised settlements where the larger areas of managed woodland coincided with good quality clays. They used fast wheels and sophisticated kilns, like the Romans, and were clearly skilled specialists. Such potting communities were established around Wychwood, where they are reported in Domesday Book (at Bladon) and where the sites of more than 30 kilns of the 10th and 11th centuries have been identified. Production probably continued around Wychwood into the 18th century; although by then, the Bladon kilns were producing only poor-quality earthenwares for local use. The Crown Works at Leafield continued in production until about 1900.

By the 13th century a large industry had become established in Bernwood, across the Cherwell. There were potters at Boarstall (Buckinghamshire) between 1210 and 1220, and at least nine kilns have been tentatively identified among the earthworks of the deserted village there. Potters may have been confined to one zone of the settlement here, although there are also isolated kilns elsewhere in the landscape and the village fields are pockmarked with clay pits. At neighbouring Brill, where potters are first mentioned in 1255, the entire plateau of the dramatic hill on which the village sits has been gouged and moulded by clay-digging on an enormous scale (Fig. 5.36). Six kilns have been excavated here, dating between about 1300 and the mid-19th century. Later kilns hereabouts produced so-called 'Cistercian type wares', sometimes decorated with a white or yellow slip, and 'green wares', a type of pottery widely distributed in the Thames valley.

Fig. 5.36 Established on its dramatic hill is Brill (Buckinghamshire). *The common has been gouged and twisted by generations of clay diggers to feed the thriving local ceramics industry. Kilns were also established on the common, in amongst the diggings, where examples dating from the 13th to the 19th centuries have been excavated.*

The rather inferior, shelly 10th- and 11th-century pottery known as 'St Neots ware' might have been manufactured in the managed woodlands of the upper Nene and Ouse valleys. It too was a mass-produced ware, wheel-thrown, kiln-fired and widely traded, and it is of critical importance for our understanding of settlement development across the East Midlands, as it tends to be the earliest pottery found on the new common-field village sites. Currently, however, the only proposed production centre is in St Neots itself, where clamps or pits (rather than kilns) were discovered. Managed woodlands in Rockingham and Whittlewood forests were certainly producing pottery by the 13th century in considerable quantities, often in dedicated settlements, like those excavated at Lyveden (formerly Potters Lyveden). This was a highly specialised community with relatively little common-field agriculture and with properties more scattered across the countryside than is typical of Northamptonshire. But Lyveden was not an impoverished or marginal community, it was merely one whose economy was not wholly based on intensive agriculture. The specialists who lived here all worked the woodlands, though not all were potters; one of the tenements, for example, was occupied successively by a potter, an ironworker and a farmer. At Stanion, a few kilometres from Lyveden, potters formed part of another mixed industrial community, with ten 13th- and 14th-century pottery kilns in rectangular plots set out along a linear street. The 'potter-' prefix of the place-name Potterspury (in Whittlewood) first occurs in 1287 and production continued here through the 15th and 16th centuries, while kilns at neighbouring Paulersbury, Yardley Gobion and Yardley Hastings were also being worked throughout the same period. In Salcey Forest, at least 14 medieval kilns have been located amongst the earthworks of the deserted settlement of Olney Hyde; while in the area of extensive 12th- and 13th-century assarts in the managed woodlands on the Greensand ridge in Bedfordshire and Buckinghamshire, Great and Little Brickhill, Flitwick and Everton were also specialised industrial settlements producing both roofing and floor tiles and pottery between the 12th and 16th centuries.

One direct result of the dwindling of the Northamptonshire forests in the early modern period (pp.85–6) was that the Rockingham potteries did not last long into the 16th century. Yet green wares were produced in Whittlewood (at Paulersbury and Yardley Gobion) in the 16th and 17th centuries, along with slip-decorated Cistercian type wares, and the industry continued long enough to take advantage of increasing traffic on Watling Street during the 17th and 18th centuries. Wares of this date from here found their way to both London and the West Midlands.

In the managed woodlands of Arden and Charnwood the specialist pottery industry had been reinvigorated by the 12th century, with kilns at Nuneaton and Chilvers Cotton (once Potter Cotton). In addition to known kiln sites within the settlement, many clay pits in the parish are thought to have been located in the corners of the typical woodland closes, which were let for grazing when clay was not being dug. Between the 12th and 14th centuries, such kilns produced a hard reddish ware, but by the 15th century they were producing 'midland purple' and Cistercian type wares which were widely distributed around the East Midlands. At least 24 kilns of early modern date have been identified around Nuneaton, where bowls and pancheons (a type of large, flat dish) of midland purple ware continued to be manufactured until the mid-18th century.

Similar wares were also produced between the 16th and 18th centuries further north, east of Burton-upon-Trent, and several large potteries grew up around Ticknall, Swadlincote, Church Gresley and Melbourne, following the development of the coalfield in the late 18th century. But, although this area was on the western edge of Charnwood, there is little evidence for a pottery industry in these managed woodlands at much earlier dates. The Ticknall potters were set to using 'fireclay' raised from the new coal mines, rather than working clay dug in local fields, to making hard sanitary wares. There were 23 potteries here by 1840. None are still in production, although isolated buildings, like those of Green's Pottery, survive, hidden within the redeveloped centre of Church Gresley.

By the 18th century, of course, the Ticknall kilns were fired with local coal, rather than charcoal or coppice wood, but further north at both Burley Hill and in the village of Duffield (Derbyshire), excavations have revealed coal-fired pottery kilns of the 12th or 13th century. Although coal does not seem to have been widely used for firing local kilns in the medieval period, around 1700 the stoneware industry that developed at Crich (Derbyshire) exploited both clays and coal from the new mine workings. This fireclay was also used for sanitary ware manufacture – an industry which grew enormously with urban expansion and improvements in hygiene. Eventually it was made at several centres in the East Derbyshire Coalfield (Brampton, Ilkeston, Alfreton and Wirksworth). The famous Denby Pottery Company works was established in 1819, making similar products. Today a kiln at Smalley (near Ilkestone), where kitchenware was made until recently, and one at West Hallam (Fig. 5.37), are isolated survivors. The Hallam kiln is now the centrepiece of a gift shop, whilst at Green's in Church Gresley one can enjoy afternoon tea.

The pattern of medieval pottery production in rural Lincolnshire seems to have been somewhat different. Here little pottery was made in the countryside before about 1300, perhaps because the county was so completely devoted to intensive common-field agriculture. But with the collapse of the textile industry in Lincoln itself (p.79), and the restructuring of rural agriculture in the 14th century, the Lincolnshire villages of Bourne, Potterhanworth and Toynton All Saints devoted themselves to pottery manufacture. It is almost as though, rather than converting to sheep-farming they converted to industrial production. One suggestion is that potters followed the example of the textile workers and evacuated Lincoln to re-establish themselves in rural sites. All three villages contained many kilns (over 20 have been identified around Toynton, for example) and represent substantial commercial investments, perhaps by manorial lords, employing large communities of skilled specialists. These villages continued in production well into the early modern period. While they all used local clay, their fuel supplies have yet to be clearly identified. There is little evidence for abnormally large managed woodlands

Fig. 5.37 The upper part of the bottle kiln of the Peak Pottery Company at West Hallam (Derbyshire) dates only from the 1920s. *The site had been a brickworks previously, using clay dug immediately to the west, and the lower part of the surviving kiln might have been built originally to fire bricks or, perhaps, the brickworks made pottery as well. The Peak Pottery itself was established by John Derbyshire, c.1922 and closed in 1940.*

nearby, and we must presume that the villagers either imported wood or charcoal by the wagon load, or that they dug peat from adjacent fens. Indeed, there is some evidence that the Toynton kilns were fired in this way. The late medieval pottery industries at Potters Marston (Leicestershire) and Keighton (Nottinghamshire) may represent similar social and economic movements.

Pottery production in the major towns had been important since the 10th century. At the same time that potters were reoccupying East Midlands woodlands, others were setting up kilns inside the newly founded East Midlands towns, near their market places. The new 'professional' urban potters also used fast wheels and effective kilns and each developed a distinctive style and local markets. Kilns are known to have been established at this time in Torksey, Lincoln, Stamford, Nottingham (Halifax Square), Leicester (Southgate Street) and Northampton (Horsemarket). All produced broadly similar types of everyday pottery, which had limited distributions around the towns themselves. Indeed the foundation, or refoundation, of these towns seems to have been closely related to the establishment of these pottery industries, which all seem to belong to the earliest phases of urban development. Kilns in such new settlements may even have been the result of royal commercial policies, as several late Saxon kings enacted that trade should only take place in towns. The new urban kilns were all remote from their fuel supplies, if not their clay sources, but all were within a few kilometres of large managed woodlands and fuel to fire them would have been brought into town, perhaps by the rural poor who, by selling wood to the potters, would obtain coin to spend in the market. Clearly these early urban potters thought that the extra expenditure on their fuel was outweighed by the benefit of being next to markets at which their wares could be sold.

Lincoln kilns continued to produce 'Saxo-Norman wares' into the 13th century, when production fell right off, prompting some to propose the exodus to outlying villages such as Potterhanworth. Even so, potting continued on the city's outskirts, in Wigford, into the 16th century. Nottingham also continued to manufacture in the late medieval period, producing midland purple ware at kilns in Clinton Street and Parliament Street. Fuel for these kilns was brought from Sherwood and clay was probably dug in the town fields. Place-names like 'potterfield' and 'potterhill' around Northampton indicate clay digging and pottery production on the edge of the urban area here too in the late medieval period. Pottery may have been manufactured in Nottingham throughout the 16th century, and amongst potters recorded in the1630s and 1640s was at least one member of the Morley family. He probably made the so called 'Nottingham ware', with its distinctive manganese glaze. Between 1688 and 1693 James Morley began making earthenware and salt-glazed stoneware at kilns near the south end of Court Street. By the 1730s this brown stoneware had become famous, especially its beer mugs, and Charles Morley moved his kilns to Beck Barn Street. Although, like so many others, Nottingham ware was pushed out of the market before 1800 by competition from the Staffordshire industry, Morley's was a major regional factory and his stonewares found their way across the Midlands and North of England.

Like other early East Midlands towns, Stamford kilns of the 10th and 11th centuries produced a domestic ware of mediocre quality distributed only locally. But the town was also the source of 'Stamford ware', a much higher quality product, possibly made in imitation of northern French pottery by immigrant potters who came to England in the wake of the Viking armies. It was one of Europe's earliest glazed wares but it is not found in any greater quantities in the East Midlands than elsewhere. Instead it is found evenly distributed around the centres of contemporary international trade, as far away as Aberdeen, Dublin and Sweden. It is usually thought to be an indicator of high social status and would not have been found in most contemporary households. Because it was so technically advanced, the 'Stamford ware' industry has been credited with introducing improvements in English pottery manufacture from the 12th century onwards, but production apparently ceased during the 13th century, possibly in the face of competition from high-quality wares produced in Nottingham.

CLAY INDUSTRIES: BRICK

Until the coming of the canals and railways, brick manufacture was a localised activity (p.124). Where practical, major construction projects of the 17th and 18th centuries would have their own brick kilns, but for smaller projects bricks were available from specialist local manufacturers. Bricks made in 18th-century Lincoln, for example, travelled 15–25km into the surrounding countryside but, because of transport costs, the ability to compete with manufacturers nearer the building site was greatly reduced beyond such distances. Like iron smelting and potting, brick-making also required substantial managed woodlands, and wherever it was abundant, bricks were produced for local buildings. Along the Lindsey coast from Gainsborough to Barton-upon-Humber (Fig. 5.38), where bricks became an important building material in the 17th century, for example, fuel was provided by the managed woodlands on the sandy soils around Scunthorpe. In north Warwickshire, brick kilns around Nuneaton started work in the 15th century, using fuel from the Forest of Arden, and slowly came to dominate the local building market in the 16th and 17th centuries.

These Warwickshire and Lincolnshire bricks used clays that were often dug within metres of the kilns themselves, which were of the 'clamp' type. They were fired in the centre of a large, carefully constructed bonfire contained within a brick wall, like those excavated at Bow Brickhill (Buckinghamshire) and Atherstone (Warwickshire). This 'updraft' design culminated in the 'scotch kiln', a type which continued in use until the end of the 19th century or even later. They became increasingly sophisticated bonfires, contained within a roofed box, and with brick-built flues leading the flames through the bricks stacked inside for firing. Such kilns were simple and cheap to build and could be repaired and enlarged with bricks from subsequent firings. They stood at the centre of many 18th- and 19th-century brickworks in the region, along with their clay pits, drying and storage sheds. A typical group of buildings survives at Baumber (Lindsey); today they earn their living servicing an angling centre established in the former clay pit. Scotch kilns were never entirely replaced by the more efficient, but more complex, 'downdraft' 'beehive' kiln designs of which East Midlands examples survive at Great Linford (Buckinghamshire) and Coalville.

In the late 18th century, canals greatly reduced prices for transporting such commodities, and contracts were no longer awarded to the nearest brickworks, but to those which could guarantee the largest or most consistent output. Joseph Wilkes, an early entrepreneur in lime and iron around Measham, Leicestershire, also made bricks. He tried to overcome increasingly stiff competition by minimising his brick-tax bill. Ingeniously, he built a new brickworks in Bosworth Road in 1802, which would produce double-sized bricks and so (he calculated) pay half as much tax. Unfortunately in 1803 the Inland Revenue imposed a double tax on double-sized bricks. The result is that these double-size bricks (known as 'Wilkes' Gobs') are very rare and are best seen in the buildings that Wilkes himself built along the Ashby Canal at Measham to cater for the projected brick boom that never came (Fig. 5.39). It was, instead, the reinvigorated local collieries that capitalised on the booming brick market. Like most collieries, those of the East Midlands were raising more clay than coal, and some of it proved excellent for brick-making; consequently many collieries in both coalfields went into brick manufacture in the 19th century. Ibstock Colliery brickworks (Leicestershire), opened in the 1830s, was among the earliest, and remained an important producer – introducing one of the first 'Monnier' tunnel kilns to

Fig. 5.38 A long tradition of brick-making from the alluvial clays of the Humber foreshore, east and west of Barton-on-Humber (Lindsey), has left a grid of rectangular pools extending many miles along the water's edge (top). The clay is particularly suitable for tile-making. Tiles are dried in long, open-sided sheds before being fired in small 'scotch' kilns, typical of those found in 18th- and 19th-century brickworks across England. Both building types were still visible at the Barton Patent Works (bottom) in 1997.

England in 1934. Terracotta tiles were made from 1878 using the same clays at Hathern (Leicestershire) and were used to great effect on the façades of 'art-deco' public buildings, especially cinemas, in the 1920s and 1930s. At Watnall Colliery brickworks (Derbyshire) the four kiln chimneys of the ruined 'hoffman' kilns still stand sentinel beside the M1 as it sweeps out of the Erewash valley (Fig. 5.40).

Outside the coalfields, the history of the 19th-century brick industry is largely one of rapid engrossment, as large firms swallowed smaller ones, only to be gobbled up in their turn. By the century's end, only the larger local brickworks had survived. The consolidated Lincoln Brickworks did not finally disappear until 1969; the equivalent works in Loughborough (Tucker and Company), which had provided the bricks for both St Pancras Station and London's Heathrow Airport, closed recently; but Nottingham's consolidated brick company, with works at Arnold, is still producing. It was the railway links that gave these brickworks their commercial advantages. All such works were established along railway lines, and some found their way into more remote markets solely because of their rail links with the big cities. The large works at Arlesey (Bedfordshire), for example, was laid out alongside the St Pancras line in 1850 and distributed its distinctive cream-coloured bricks throughout the suburbs of north-east London.

By the early 20th century it was clear that the biggest cost reductions possible through large-scale working would occur along the deep Oxford clays, where huge mechanical 'shale-planers' could dig enormous clay pits quickly and safely. Clays of suitable thickness extended from Calvert (south of Buckingham) north-eastwards to the Nene, east of Peterborough. The deep clays also proved ideal for use in the latest 'Hoffman' kilns, which were designed to fire continuously. Although brickworks in these areas all began as independent makers, amalgamations of bewildering complexity resulted in their all being owned by the London Brick Company. The salmon-pink bricks ('Flettons') from these pits dominated the London market at the time of the greatest expansion of the city between 1870 and 1914. Brick-making is still an important industry around Peterborough, but the excitement of passing through the busy Fletton brickyards as one approached Peterborough railway station has now been lost. Both here and south-west of Bedford at Stewartby (p.112), an entirely new landscape was created by the shale-planers (Fig. 5.41). It is a disconcerting area today; with unnaturally square and impossibly blue lakes, nature reserves and scrubland, traversed by tree-lined roads on vertiginous causeways. But in the 1950s it was still a dusty, pink-tinged forest of chimneys, perhaps not inappropriate for the landscape that, in its rural past, once inspired Bunyan's 'Slough of Despond'.

ABOVE: *Fig. 5.39 Numbers 1 and 2 Navigation Road, near the former canal basin at Measham (Leicestershire).* *They were built in 1802–3 by Joseph Wilkes using his distinctive double-sized bricks known as 'Wilkes Gobs'.*

BELOW: *Fig. 5.40 This view from the north-west shows the last remains of large 'Hoffman' brick kilns at Oakwell or New Watnall colliery (Derbyshire).* *Bricks were made here from the start of deep mining in the 1870s and the brick pit enlarged as the colliery began to fail. It ceased work in 1966. The pithead itself lay in the scrub between the four chimneys and the M1 motorway, which approaches and leaves the site along the track-bed of the colliery's railway connection with the main line.*

Fig. 5.41 Bedfordshire's 'Slough of Despond'. *Today's clay-pits are now either water-filled, or back-filled with London's rubbish but, in 1982, the brick-kiln chimneys around the model village of Stewartby were still smoking. Although over 30 kilns can be seen in this view looking northwards towards Kempston Hardwick in the distance, only a handful now remain.*

FURTHER READING

General
Blair & Ramsey (eds) 1991; Brown 1989 (Nottinghamshire); Cossons 1993; Crossley (ed.) 1981; Fowkes 1984, 1986 (Derbyshire); Laws 1967 (Bedfordshire); Palmer & Neaverson 1992, 1998; Raistrick 1972; Starmer 1970 (Northamptonshire); Wright 1982 (Lincolnshire).

Farm and related buildings
Barnwell & Giles 1997 (model farms); Brunskill 1987; Fowler 1983a, b; Fussell 1966 (dairy); Harvey 1980; Hughes 1985 (barns); Lake 1989; OAU 1995 (dovecotes); Patrick 2004 (maltings); Rahtz 1981 (mills); Rigold 1971 (barns); Wade Martins 2002 (model farms); Wailes 1954 (windmills); Woodforde 1983.

Textiles
Cooper 1983 (Derwent Valley); Halls 1985 (Nottingham); Lloyd 1977; Mills 1982 (Leicestershire); Plummer 1934 (Witney); Rogers 1981 (Nottinghamshire); Walton 1991; Wells 1972.

Leather, boots and shoes
Allin 1981 (Leicester); Brown 1990 (Northampton); Cherry 1991; Granger 1965 (Leicester); Morrison with Bond 2004 (Northamptonshire); Mounfield 1964–5, 1966, 1967; Smith 1964 (elastics); Thomson 1982.

Stone
Arkell 1948 (Oxfordshire); Clifton-Taylor 1972; Earle 1971 (road-stone); Firman 1964 (Gypsum); Harrison & Adlam 1985 (Derbyshire); LUAU 1996a; Parsons (ed.) 1990, 1991; Purcell 1967 (Northamptonshire and Lincolnshire); Ramsay 1991 (alabaster); Sutherland 2003 (Northamptonshire); Tucker 1985 (millstones).

Lime burning
Boden 1963 (Derbyshire); Dix 1979; Francis 1977 (cement); LUAU 1996b.

Coal
Battye *et al.* 1991 (coke); Church 1986; Flinn 1984; Gould & Ayris 1995; Gould & Cranstone 1993; Hatcher 1993; Rawstron 1954 (electric power).

Lead
Blanchard 1981; Bramley 1991 (fluorspar); Cranstone 1993; Willies & Cranstone (eds) 1992; Young *et al.* (ed.) 1999.

Charcoal
Armstrong 1978; Foard 2001 (Rockingham).

Iron and steel
Armstrong 1981 (Scunthorpe); Beaver 1951 (Northamptonshire), 1982–3 (Rutland); Bellamy *et al.* 2000–1 (Northamptonshire) Condron 1997; Cranstone 1985 (Leicestershire); Crossley 1981; Riden 1990 (Butterley); Rimmington 1964–5 (Leicester); Schrufer-Kolb 1999; Tonks 1988 (Lincolnshire/Leicestershire/Northamptonshire); Tylecote 1962 (Lincolnshire); Warren 1961 (Derbyshire); Young (ed.) *et al.* 1999.

Clay industries and ceramics
Bond *et al.* 1980 (Oxfordshire); Cox 1979 (Bedfordshire); Foard 1991 (Northamptonshire); Fulford & Huddleston 1991; Hammond 1977 (brick kilns); McCarthy & Brooks 1988; Mellor 1994; Moorhouse 1981; Robinson 1999 (Lincolnshire); Simco 1998; Smith 1985; Spavold 1981 (Derbyshire); Swan 1984; Vince 1997 (Charnwood); Young 1977 (Oxfordshire).

6

A Defensive Pattern

In the East Midlands, defence was rarely an influential factor in the landscape before modern times. Furthermore, communities here have rarely united to consider defence regionally: typically they have either broken into smaller units for defensive purposes or coalesced with other English regions to make larger ones. Although individual locations of special importance were apparently defended, we have no reason to think that the Corieltauvi or the Catuvellauni attempted to defend their tribal boundaries. The region's incoherent Anglo-Saxon kingdoms and sub-kingdoms, similarly, have left us little evidence that regional defence was a high priority, so it seems best to consider the East Midlands' defences either as components of national strategy or as local initiatives.

NATIONAL AND LOCAL DEFENCES

In the overtly militaristic society of imperial Rome, community defences were an integral part of colonial government. The very existence of *coloniae* like that at Lindum (Lincoln), populated with former legionaries holding the rank of Roman citizen, resulted not just in the presence of a military reserve, but must have produced a settlement with the politics of the Chelsea Hospital combined with a regimental museum. Such a town would surely have taken a keen interest in building town walls, whether or not they were strictly necessary. Towns of *colonia* status required imperial permission to erect walls and, given the town's leadership, consent was expected. The stone walls at Lindum were begun early in the 2nd century, a few decades after the establishment of the *colonia*; and, no doubt to emphasise the community's military background, they were built on the line of the timber wall of the old legionary fortress, abandoned in the 1970s (*see* Fig. 3.9). The stone walls of the lower city at Lindum, which more than doubled the defended area, were not built until at least the end of the 2nd century. These cut across pre-existing settlement plots, yet the area enclosed was still not large and, furthermore, quite large areas of the interior were taken up with temples and other official buildings. One might ask whether this rectilinear layout too was not prompted by the desire to appear suitably military.

With its self-consciously military walls, Lindum provides a contrast with Ratae (Leicester) (*see* Fig. 3.10). Such regional capitals also had to gain imperial consent for defensive constructions and one might expect Ratae to have applied around the time of its foundation in the late 1st century. Although our knowledge of them is incomplete, however, it seems clear that no wall (of either stone or timber) was actually built here until the 3rd century. By this time, many much smaller Romano-British communities were also constructing defences: prompted, perhaps, by political instability and a genuine fear of attack, rather than a desire for aggrandisement. Ratae's walls enclosed nearly twice the area (6ha) of those at Lindum. Such great relative size also reinforces the impression that Ratae's defences were a genuine community effort. They clearly aimed to

include not just the finer buildings of the civic centre, but also poorer and less well-developed districts. Lindum's defences were also augmented (with turrets and a stronger wall) in the mid-3rd century and then completely rebuilt on an enormous scale, with a huge ditch, in the 4th century, once it had been promoted to the rank of provincial capital. But it must be significant that, even though great sums were spent, still no effort was made to enlarge the defended area. The wall continued to protect only the town's administrative core and its grand stone townhouses; traders' houses outside the various gates were still excluded. Despite its construction date, the final wall may thus also have related more to Lindum's political status than to community defence.

Fig. 6.1 Several fragments of the late 3rd-century defensive wall surrounding the Roman small town or fortress at Horncastle (Lindsey) still stand. This section of it is incorporated into property boundaries at Dog Kennel Yard.

Walls inevitably became an urban status symbol, if only because they were a tangible sign of imperial approval, and their imitation by the rulers of smaller towns in the later 3rd and 4th centuries may represent nothing more than an attempt to appropriate some of that *kudos*. In the East Midlands they were constructed at places such as Ancaster, Caistor and Horncastle (Lindsey) (Fig. 6.1), Margidunum (Nottinghamshire), Great Casterton (Rutland), Towcester (Northamptonshire) and Alcester and Dorchester (Oxfordshire) and Cambridge. All such walls were visible evidence that the community was prepared to defend itself and that aggressors would pay heavily for their aggression. Towers, such as those added to Lindum's wall, were similarly symbols of impregnability. They showed not only the community's resolution, but also that it had access to up-to-date military thinking and that even a professional siege might be unsuccessful. The main purpose of erecting both walls and towers, then, was to deter aggression, like the yellow and black colouring of the wasp. And, just as the wasp has many insect imitators with no powerful sting, so many towns with walls were, in fact, quite harmless.

Similar civic impulses and motivations were reprised during the medieval period, as East Midlands towns and cities once again looked to community defence. Putting aside Anglo-Saxon *burhs* and medieval castles for the moment, both of which require separate consideration, the towns of Lincoln, Newark, Nottingham, Leicester, Stamford, Northampton, Oxford and Cambridge were all walled in stone during the medieval period. Now the king, rather than the emperor, awarded the right to erect walls and gates; in 1174 he even exercised his right to remove the privilege, by ordering that Leicester's walls be razed as a punishment for rebelliousness. To emphasise the community's direct responsibility for providing defences, they were frequently paid for through 'murage', a local tax raised by town councils on goods passing through their markets. Having paid for the walls themselves, the citizens also held responsibility for manning them in times of strife. In mid-Tudor Stamford, John Leland reported 'there were seven principal towers or wards … to each of which were certain freeholders in the town allotted to make watch and ward in time of need' (Toulmin Smith 1964, V, 5).

The former Roman walled enclosures at Towcester, Great Casterton, Caistor, Ancaster and Horncastle were also still viable, and those at Towcester had been patched up to provide a strong point on Watling Street when Edward the Elder founded a *burh* here in 917. The continuing viability of such Roman defences probably also influenced the establishment of mints in Caistor and Horncastle by Æthelred the Unready, as neither were centres of large contemporary populations.

At a superior level to local community defence, 'the state' (whether Roman Empire or medieval kingdom) also sponsored defensive systems as part of national military campaigns. Within each of these, the East Midlands played a role. The system of forts established in the region by the conquering Roman armies after AD 43 did not remain long. Even so, large forts capable of supporting part, or all, of a whole legion have been identified at Longthorpe (west of Peterborough), Lincoln, Newton-upon-Trent (west of Lincoln) and Osmanthorpe (near Newark). The archaeology of such military installations is a popular topic of study, with new information coming forward each year. It is now generally thought that the Fosse Way, driving south-west to north-east across the East Midlands landscape, marks the approximate line of a pause in Roman assimilation of Britons into the Empire. Certainly the road remained an approximate boundary between the south-eastern zone of largely civilian settlement and the north-western one, where the military played a greater role. In addition to the legionary fortresses at either end – Lindum and Glevum (Gloucester) – there were additional military establishments along the road, at Ad Pontem, Margidunum (East Stoke and Castle Hills, both Nottinghamshire), and probably at Leicester. As with many early military installations in the East Midlands, however, we can say little about their character.

Yet many sites that flourished as civilian settlements in Britannia after the 1st century began life as military installations (pp.49–50). There are numerous examples in our region of towns that began in this way: Ancaster, Kirmington and Winteringham (Lindsey); Great Casterton (Rutland); Durobrivae (west of Peterborough); Godmanchester (Huntingdonshire) and Mancetter (Warwickshire). North-west of the Fosse Way, the military presence extended into the 4th century, and forts were more densely distributed: there were at least four in Derbyshire, for example (Strutts Park, Little Chester, Brough-on-Noe and Melandra Castle).

It is not until the 9th and 10th centuries that national systems of defensive strongholds were revived, with the establishment of *burhs*. It is not clear what the term *burh* implies; indeed it probably referred to a range of different contemporary establishments (p.66). *Burhs* were built, or rather instituted, by both sides in the long series of 9th- and 10th-century wars between the Wessex kings and the Vikings. Winter camps built by the Viking Great Army during their conquest of eastern Mercia were this war's earliest East Midlands fortifications. They were built at Nottingham in 867, Torksey (Lindsey) in 872, Repton (Derbyshire) in 873 (Fig. 6.2) and Cambridge in 874, but none of these sites is called a *burh* at this stage. The 'fortification' mentioned at Nottingham was presumably erected by the Vikings themselves (as there is no record of earlier fortifications there) and it might have been a ditched and banked enclosure with its back to the River Trent, of the type found at Repton, rather than the later enclosure around St Mary's church. Torksey is a natural island in the Trent and would have needed little additional defence, whilst at Cambridge the stone-walled enclosure of Roman Durolipons already had its back to the River Cam. Although these fortifications all served the same purpose (defending the Viking army and fleet while they over-wintered in hostile territory), there is no contemporary evidence that they were interconnected.

Fig. 6.2 The Viking fort at Repton (Derbyshire), apparently built in 873–4. It was revealed in excavations by Martin Biddle and Birthe Kjølbye-Biddle in the 1980s. Note the pre-existing Mercian royal church and mausoleum, incorporated into the defences, and also the Viking-age mausoleum, originally buried under a mound to the west.

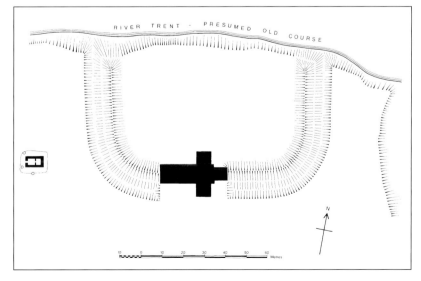

Fig. 6.3 Seen from the south-east, Huntingdon lies close to Roman Ermine Street north-west of its crossing of the Ouse. The modern bypass (re-using a former railway) clips the southern corner of the earthwork remains of the castle, in its roughly 'D shaped' enclosure against the river. The town, with its triangular market place, lies wholly to the north-west, and graphically illustrates the impact of modern service industries on a historic centre.

In less than a century, however, all except Repton had become sizeable urban settlements. The *Chronicle* had named Nottingham, Lincoln, Stamford, Derby and Leicester as fortifications and *burhs* by 942, and there were contemporary urban settlements at all these places. In the mid-10th-century Danelaw, then, it seems that the term *burh* implied both a fortification and an associated urban settlement. We have to guard against presuming, however, that settlements in such places were automatically located within the fortresses. We have seen that the Viking fortification at Nottingham may not have been identical with the *burh*, while according to the *Chronicle*, Huntingdon also began life as a fortress rather than an urban settlement. The Vikings established a fortress here, but in 921 they are said to have abandoned it in favour of one at Tempsford, whereupon Huntingdon was occupied by a division of Edward the Elder's forces. By 963, presumably thanks to Edward's efforts, it was described not as a fortress but as a 'market', so clearly, like Nottingham, the military installation had become a settlement. Edward is credited with the foundation of civilian settlements at a number of other former military sites acquired from the Vikings, and it is these, rather than the fortresses, that attract the contemporary description *burh*. There is no evidence that Edward's market at Huntingdon was ever fortified: the only serious fortification here, either in surviving documents or in the archaeological record, is the D-shaped enclosure against the river that subsequently became the castle (Fig. 6.3). Here, then, the urban settlement was apparently established outside the fortification and the Viking's initial fortress might be represented by the later castle.

At Lincoln the most viable fortification was the Roman upper city; yet, despite extensive excavation, we still have no evidence for dense 'urban' settlement within this enclosure before the 12th century. On the contrary, the evidence for the early urban settlement at Lincoln is downhill, by the river, and located both inside and outside the former Roman walls. Here, too, it may be that the early town was established outside the fortification (*see* Figs 3.8 and 6.4). Whether the contemporary term *burh* denoted the uphill enclosure or the downhill urban settlement, or both, remains uncertain. Similar divisions between fortifications and settlements may have occurred at Derby, Buckingham, Cambridge, Bedford and at Peterborough, where it seems that the defensive wall and ditch forming the large monastic enclosure was distinct from the market established by royal grant in 963 to the east. In all these cases it is hard to see the term *burh* as an Anglo-Saxon equivalent of the medieval walled town. It was more similar to the Roman fort with a trading community at its gate.

There were other types of *burh* locally, however. Settlements probably grew up within (rather than alongside) the fortifications at Leicester, Towcester and Tamworth, while at Oxford this was certainly the case. At Leicester and Towcester, fortification was provided by ancient Roman walls, but Oxford and Tamworth appear to have had newly constructed defences designed to contain an urban community. These enclosures seem to have been designed for community defence and, as if to confirm their strength, the gates into Oxford from north and south (the more important through-route at this period) were equipped with guardian churches both dedicated to St Michael (Fig. 6.5), the most military of angels.

All *burhs* were regional centres of power and administration, whether fortresses, settlements, or both. The *Chronicle* mentions in passing that lords and other ranks of society belonged to particular *burhs*. In 917 we hear that a host owing allegiance to Northampton came from as far north as the Welland, while in 918 we hear of 'all the lands belonging with' Oxford and of those 'who owed allegiance to' Bedford. These references reflect King Alfred's policy of organising civil defence around strong points and calling the *fyrd* (militia) together there in times of trouble. Oxford and Tamworth, the *burhs* where the settlement was apparently contained within the fortification, were on the fringes of the Danelaw closest to Wessex, and they may represent Alfred's concept of the *burh* more faithfully than those established in reconquered territory. This patterning may also suggest that the defended *burh* at Northampton (similarly close to the Danelaw boundary) contained, rather than excluded, the settlement. It was only after they had been re-integrated with southern England that civic functions became coincident with defence at those *burhs* with Viking military origins further north-east.

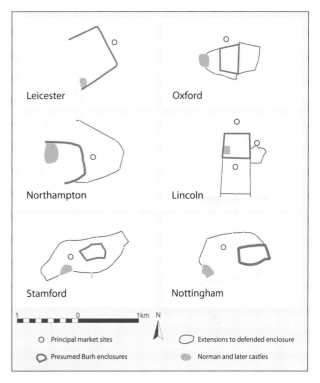

ABOVE: *Fig. 6.4 Six fortified East Midlands* **burhs,** *showing their locations relative to early markets and therefore, perhaps, to the early settlements at these places. Note that none of the markets identified here lie within the presumed* burh *enclosures.*

LEFT: *Fig. 6.5 Survey work on the tower of St Michael at the Northgate in Oxford in the 1980s* demonstrated that, although it was subsequently recruited as a conventional church bell-tower, it began life as a freestanding structure alongside the north gate of the late Anglo-Saxon burh.

199

THE PRIVATISATION OF DEFENCE

The Normans privatised fortification. From the time of the Conquest, the rapid development of military feudalism devolved responsibility for defence onto the individual lord. Like many other duties, the king devolved responsibility for security to his vassals, and they devolved security responsibilities to their vassals in turn, down the feudal pyramid. It was as though every subaltern in a modern army was given his or her own budget, and was expected to provide his or her platoon with its own fort. Such arrangements mirrored the centrality of personal obligations to social inferiors and superiors in feudal society more widely, and between the late 11th century and the 14th century, they resulted in the construction of that discrete group of defensive structures in the landscape that we call castles.

Sometimes lords were prepared to fulfil their feudal obligation to defend their own local community alongside their kin, and at both Bolsover and Castleton (Derbyshire) town defences were provided by the lord of the local castle. The lords who owned such towns and markets also wished, however, to defend their commercial investments and, although the town wall was a very public statement that the lord was living up to his feudal responsibilities, it was also useful for controlling movement of villagers and enforcing the collection of tolls. Many other villages were probably 'defended', to some extent: the remains of an earthwork circuit survive in part, for example, at Castle Bytham (Kesteven). At some East Midlands castles with two baileys – Thonock (Lindsey), Laxton (Nottinghamshire, Fig. 6.6) or Rockingham (Leicestershire) – the second bailey might have been intended initially to contain a settlement, although in all these cases settlements rapidly developed outside the castle.

There are more than 250 castles in the East Midlands, of which at least 60 per cent seem to owe their origins to 'motte and bailey' or another earthwork form,

Fig. 6.6 Laxton (Nottinghamshire) is famous for the survival of common-field farming into the present day, resulting in the partial retention of a landscape of strip fields around a central village, dominated by several competing farmsteads. *The castle, with its motte and two baileys (foreground), was probably built by the de Caux family in the 12th century. It stands to one side of the (evidently planned) village layout, but whether this implies that the village was laid out earlier, or later, remains uncertain.*

presumed to date from the 11th and 12th centuries. Although we have long assumed that these earthwork and timber structures were wholly defensive, the bailey is no more than the ditched enclosure that surrounded the lord's hall, like Goltho or Oakham (*see* Figs 4.26 and 4.27), and which persisted throughout the Middle Ages as the moated site (pp.141–2). Sometimes the bailey could possess substantial military potential, but more frequently it merely marks out the lord's hall and separates it from the remainder of the community. Similarly, the motte is often seen as an explicitly military structure: many mottes were indeed provided with specialised timber structures, equipping them as fighting platforms and as final refuges in sieges (as was also the case at Goltho). Yet the motte's origins lie, primarily, in the role of the great mound as an ancient symbol of lordship: it is thought to have been the lineal descendant of the mounds built at traditional meeting places (called 'moots'), from the top of which adjudications were pronounced. Only subsequently did it become a fighting platform. As enormous symbols in the landscape, mottes like that at Brinkhill (Warwickshire), Eaton Socon or Cainhoe (Bedfordshire), standing proudly above the East Midlands common-fields, were primarily intended to dominate the settlements and landscape for miles around, just as Iron Age hillforts and some Roman forts had done before them. Secondly, as mottes were structures dramatically superimposed on the existing landscape by the conquering Normans (Eaton Socon castle only one of many cases where the new castle displaced the people's houses), they also conveyed a symbolic message that the regime had changed (as did the Roman forts). Only thirdly did they provide a secure bolt-hole for their lords in armed disputes with their neighbours.

Patterns are evident in the distribution of these new symbols of power across the countryside. William the Conqueror was in haste to provide physical evidence for his 'regime-change' by building castles, including (significantly) new mottes, at all the East Midlands shire towns. Castles at Nottingham, Lincoln, Oxford, Huntingdon and Cambridge were all established between 1066 and 1071. Although we have no proper evidence for its date of foundation, a motte was also established within the *burh* at Buckingham which is said to have been Hereward the Wake's prison in 1070. The large motte and bailey castle established in the south-west corner of the presumed *burh* at Leicester is not mentioned until 1101, but it is likely to have been a member of this group founded immediately following the Conquest. At Bedford the motte and bailey castle seems particularly poorly documented, but it also existed by the late 11th century and, strategically, it belongs to this same group of sites. The Crown may have regarded Derbyshire as an administrative subdivision of Nottinghamshire and, although it had a *burh* (possibly located initially within the former Roman enclosure at Little Chester), this may explain why it never acquired a castle.

Subsequent groupings of castles in the landscape can also reflect the topography of later political battles, as well as military ones. A group of castles with distinctive rectangular plans around Cambridge may relate to King Stephen's attempt to restrain the Earl of Essex during the Anarchy, for example, while a group of deserted earthwork castles with prominent mottes around Leicester may reflect a peace treaty signed between 1148 and 1153. In both cases the distinctive new structures in the landscape reminded the local community whose forces were really in control of the body politic.

The Bishop of Lincoln's three contemporary castles at Newark, Sleaford and Banbury also form a stylistic group, being contained within rectangular earthwork enclosures, beside rivers that filled their moats. All three had high stone curtain walls, with major stone gatehouses, and the principal chambers were distributed around the curtains themselves, rather than being freestanding. Banbury may have had a central motte (though this is not certain) and perhaps also a detached great tower, of the type that became so characteristic of English castles in the 12th century and which is an early manifestation of the prominent

*Fig. 6.7 Just south of the Bishop of
Lincoln's mid-12th-century bridge,
which carried the diverted line of the
Great North Road for the next 800
years, Newark Castle's north curtain
wall is undoubtedly martial-looking,*
*but the architectural details are intended to
convey the visual message that this is also a
place of superior lordship and of hospitality to
travellers approaching from north. The solar
towers imply occupation by more than one
lordly entourage, whilst the large hall windows
imply that these different entourages are
brought together harmoniously here, under the
supervision of the castle's owner.*

'solar' as a symbol of status and lordship (p.141). Approaching across the water-meadows amongst which all three castles were set, they would have presented a more domestic appearance than the shire castles of a century earlier, but the symbolic message that this was a seat of lordship remained unmistakable. At Newark the bishop continued to embellish the façade facing the water-meadows, enhancing its domestic features, such as the windows of the main accommodation suites and the solar towers at either end (Fig. 6.7).

The water-filled ditches around such castles might be valuable in military emergencies, but they were also elements in spectacular garden designs – a very knowing enhancement of the castle's appearance in its landscape, aimed at capturing the admiration of visitors, as well as frightening off potential aggressors. This type of castle, set in the valley floor and surrounded with complex layouts of gardens, moats and ditches, was evidently highly desirable by the end of the 13th century and remained fashionable until the 16th century. Such castles were chivalric daydreams, entirely consistent with the world of symbolic poetry and Arthurian allusion sponsored and promoted amongst the aristocracy by Edward I. Symbolically, they still projected power in the landscape, but the language used had developed since the 11th century. The finest East Midlands example of this type of 'picturesque' castle may have been the retreat of the Earls of Lancaster and Lincoln at Bolingbroke (Lindsey), before it was slighted, but very similar in style was Somerton Castle (Kesteven), originally built by Anthony Bec, Edward's controversial Bishop of Durham in the 1280s. It was given to Edward II and then used as a royal residence by King John of France in 1359–60, while he was being held captive. Standing on the complex earthworks of outlying moats, and looking back at the surviving towers, one can appreciate that the fantastic multi-turreted castles seen in manuscripts like *Les Tres Riches Heures du Duc de Berry*, reflected in their surrounding gardens and lakes, once existed in England too.

Tattershall was also a castle of this type. It was converted into one by Ralph, Lord Cromwell between 1434 and 1456 (if it had not already been one previously) and when complete it must have looked just as spectacular as Bolingbroke and Somerton. Bourne and Folkingham castles (Kesteven) were probably also of this type and further examples at Barnwell and Titchmarsh (Northamptonshire) and Shirburn (Oxfordshire) survive in varying states of preservation. Kirby Muxloe (Leicestershire) was a late example of the genre, begun by Lord Hastings in 1481 (like Tattershall in fashionable brick) and left unfinished on his execution in 1483 (Fig. 6.8).

Such castles were intended to be admired and gazed down upon, and we might ask whether they are not more relevant to discussions of gardening than to defence. But military features had always been rapidly incorporated within the symbolic, chivalric, architectural language deployed to enhance lordly accommodation. It is, consequently, often hard to say where the 'castle' really ends and the 'house' begins, despite the fact that the two types of dwelling were given distinct legal identities in the Middle Ages through Royal grants of the right to 'crenellate'. Even so, the impact that the castle made in the landscape increasingly overrode any pretence of military potential and, by the 15th century, military architectural details were being used more like decorative veneers whilst moats were created more for decorative effect than to keep attackers at bay. The realistic-looking gun loops at Kirby Muxloe, for example, are without the necessary space behind them to mount cannon, whilst the moats could easily be drained by any attacking force.

Fig. 6.8 Lord Hastings's unfinished castle at Kirby Muxloe (Leicestershire) stands within a valley, overlooked by hills, and surrounded by water that is held back by undefended dams and earthworks. Its dramatic and beautiful appearance in the landscape was more important than its military potential, even though its architectural details were military in origin.

THE IMPACT OF THE CIVIL WAR

Although it could be argued that, through expanding particular royal castles or suppressing selected baronial ones, the English Crown did often pursue a co-ordinated national defence policy, it was not until the Civil War of 1642–50 that adversaries again built defensive lines and structures across the East Midlands. Even then, resources were short and many communities chose to remain neutral if they could. Although this part of England is sometimes said to have been natural recruiting country for the Parliamentary cause, many aristocratic houses held out for King Charles here, and the southern part of the region, particularly, was firmly Royalist, perhaps influenced by the proximity of the Royalist capital, set up at Oxford in 1643. In fact, the East Midlands was a 'front line'. The war began at Nottingham; the first battle was on Edgehill, north-west of Banbury; there were notable sieges at Newark, Leicester and Northampton; and Charles's most decisive defeat was at Naseby, Northamptonshire. The war ebbed and flowed across the region, making life miserable for the population in both town and country. Few East Midlands towns escaped military action, and key towns like Oxford and those on roads north, like Grantham and Newark, were permanently garrisoned throughout the war.

In the wider landscape, many castles and houses barricaded themselves in and mounted a few guns, if they had them. Church towers were used for sniping, but few places were provided with substantial new fortifications. Among the most substantial defensive circuits in England, however, were those around Oxford, Leicester and Newark. Around Newark, in particular, we can still visit the remains of earthwork bastions and forts, interconnected by siege lines built by

Fig. 6.9 Queen's Mount sconce, part of the earthwork siege defences of Newark, survives amongst the suburban housing at the southern end of the town. Its arrow-head bastions were the last word in artillery fortification when it was built in 1642–5.

Fig. 6.10 The proposed circular gun emplacement at Tout Hill, Sawtry (Huntingdonshire). It is typical of the simple earthwork fortifications thrown up in this war of rapid movement, in this case on land that had once been within the village common-fields. It was sited to command Ermine Street in both directions (north and south), perhaps using a single artillery-piece, which could be moved from side to side as necessary.

OPPOSITE PAGE:

BOTTOM: *Fig. 6.12 Bull Sands Fort was built in amongst the shipping lanes of the Humber estuary off Grimsby in 1915.* Like Haile Sands Fort, closer to shore, it was a self-sufficient fortress armed with searchlights and four 6-inch guns.

both attackers and defenders, and sense the scale and power of 17th-century siege warfare (Fig. 6.9). A large army was besieged in Newark, but the town's population continued to function and, to that extent, some of these siege-works could be seen as civil defence. This was equally the case at Oxford, where the remains are now less visible. At Nottingham, by contrast, the medieval wall had been demolished to ground level by 1625 and, apart from the new doors fitted to the Chapel Bar, the town's defence relied on three new earthwork forts built in meadows to the south and a bulwark to the north. Successive governors of Lincoln did even less, merely patching up the medieval castle walls in readiness for the siege of 1643, and in 1648 fortifying the Bishop's Palace.

In the countryside, new installations were sometimes sited along key roads, evidence of the importance of mobility during this war. A small earthwork redoubt, still surviving on the Great North Road just outside Sawtry (Huntingdonshire), is an excellent example. Here a small, circular raised gun platform, within a square ditched enclosure, could command the road in either direction with a single cannon (Fig. 6.10). Tout Hill, Sawtry, might have imitated a larger battery on the former motte of Huntingdon Castle (Fig. 6.3). Cambridge Castle, however, was more strongly fortified in 1643, with modern arrow-head bastions of earth and timber. Earthworks at Cornbury Park (Oxfordshire) and at South Kelsey (Lindsey) have also been identified as gun emplacements protecting the approaches to houses belonging to gentry.

The wars had a greater landscape impact, however, through the destruction of buildings, particularly once hostilities had ceased. Several great medieval buildings were 'slighted' by the victorious Parliament, worried that they might be used again in renewed hostilities. Newark Castle was demolished in 1645, once the siege was over, and Banbury Castle, Belvoir Castle (Rutland), Bolingbroke Castle, Cambridge Castle and Rockingham Castle went shortly afterwards. The tall solar towers of houses at South Wingfield (*see* Fig. 4.33) and Ashby-de-la-Zouche (*see* Fig. 4.32) were made uninhabitable by the removal of one wall in 1649, and Nottingham Castle was demolished with gunpowder in 1651. The Lincoln Bishop's Palace, besieged in 1648, was so badly damaged that the site was not reoccupied until the 18th century (*see* Fig. 2.7), and it remains ruinous. Some of Lincoln's churches were also destroyed for military reasons. The suburban churches of St Botolph, St Benedict, St Peter Eastgate and St Nicholas were all badly damaged (or even totally demolished) either as a precaution by defenders or by attackers during the assault. St Swithin's had been destroyed when the gunpowder magazine it contained exploded in 1644. Boarstall parish church (Buckinghamshire) is also said to have been destroyed by the royalist garrison of Boarstall House, to deny it to attackers, and they may have removed surrounding village buildings as well. Boarstall House itself was damaged and replaced later in the century. Nearby Hillesden House may have been treated in similar fashion, and in 1646 Faringdon House and Godstow House (both Oxfordshire) certainly were.

LATER DEFENCES AND THE LANDSCAPE

With the extraordinary exception of Weedon (Northamptonshire), the East Midlands played no very distinctive part in the preparations for war against, and invasion by, Napoleon. Stands of arms were distributed to magazines in all the county towns, and barracks were built along the west side of The Park in

Nottingham, but no defensive measures were taken along the Lincolnshire coast. It was thought too remote from invasion, either from Ireland or the continent. It was precisely this distance from likely invasion beaches that made Northamptonshire an ideal location for the central distribution of military stores and reserves. This was the function of the military barracks and stores complex at Weedon, which was begun in 1803 and joined to the Grand Junction Canal in 1804 (Fig. 6.11). A fortified site (with portcullises closing off the canals), it was not just intended to store reserves of gunpowder and many other vital military commodities; it also included a group of three yellow-brick pavilions to house the royal family in the event of any retreat from London. Until the coming of the railways, this important complex was the hub of national military logistics. Weedon can be seen as the canal-based equivalent of the large military supply bases around Bicester, which lie strung out across the Oxfordshire countryside, and along the former Great Central Railway, north-west of Aylesbury. Although none of these has the architectural pretensions of Weedon, taken as a whole they are much larger. Together they provide today's armed forces with a similar range of stores to those kept at Weedon, although some offer training in post-Napoleonic skills, such as train-driving.

ABOVE: *Fig. 6.11 The Weedon Depot (Northamptonshire) is one of England's most remarkable survivals from the Napoleonic Wars. Watling Street and the Grand Junction Canal pass the eastern (far) side of the site, whilst stores buildings line the wharfs inside the fortified canal gate (centre right). Gunpowder magazines stand within their own compound at the western (near) end of the complex; alternate buildings are dummies, filled with earth to absorb blast and prevent explosions in one store igniting the remainder.*

As elsewhere in England throughout the 19th century, all the East Midlands county towns were provided with militia barracks, but it was not until the 20th century that military technology, particularly the birth and rapid rise of military aviation, began to have a significant impact on the region's landscape. Both world wars resulted in fixed defences along the Lindsey coast, with large gun batteries built at Stallingborough, Killingholme and offshore at Haile Sand and Bull Sand forts (begun 1915), guarding the Humber estuary (Fig. 6.12). Even more

powerful was the massive railway gun, which trundled along the Humber foreshore between Grimsby and Cleethorpes. Between 1939 and 1945 a further 12 coastal gun batteries, of smaller calibre, were constructed in a line down the coast from Stallingborough to Boston. On the ground, evidence for secret 'stop' lines survives, composed of pill-boxes, trenches and natural features, prepared in advance of invasion. One of the longest extended from the Essex coast along the fen edge and then across the Jurassic ridge towards Newark.

Lincolnshire was more particularly associated with aviation. Ironically, the earliest military aerodromes in the county belonged to the Royal Naval Air Service (Skegness, which opened in 1914, and Killingholme), but in 1915 all RNAS pilot training was centralised at Cranwell. This major facility was also used by the early Royal Flying Corps. It included an airship station, although airship development shifted to Short's aerodrome at Cardington (Bedfordshire) in 1917, where the huge hangars, built for the R100 and R101, reached their present capacity in 1927. The RFC decided to centralise training in Lincolnshire in 1916, and aerodromes at Scampton (Fig. 6.13), South Carlton, Waddington and Spitalgate (east of Grantham) were all sited on the crest of the Lincoln Edge, facing west. It is said that this exposed position was necessary so that inexperienced pilots could take off into the prevailing wind over the cliff, and rise on the thermals usually to be found there. This substantial investment in training aviators meant that, when the newly founded RAF was looking for a prestigious site to rival Sandhurst and Dartmouth, Cranwell was chosen for the Royal Air Force College in 1918. The impressive, but wholly incongruous, formal buildings, rising uncannily above the barley-lands of Lincoln Heath, were designed in 1929.

Between 1939 and 1945 about 100 RAF stations were operational within Lincolnshire, and about half were home to front-line squadrons. As a typical bomber base swallowed up over 250ha of land, required nearly 6,000m of

Fig. 6.13 Of Lincolnshire's many airbases, RAF Scampton (Lindsey) is probably the most famous. First established as a fighter station in 1916, it was reopened in 1936 as a bomber base. Guy Gibson and the 'dambusters' flew from here in May 1943, B-29s flew from here during the Berlin Airlift and from 1958 to c.1970 it was one of nine V-bomber bases, before becoming the Central Flying School. The diversion of Roman Ermine Street around the eastern end of the extended runway is clearly visible (top right).

concrete runway and brought with it a population of 2,000, the impact of these bases on the landscape was enormous. It was much the largest single land-use change since Parliamentary enclosure and, although many bases have now reverted to other uses, they still make highly visible intrusions on the county's map. Large areas of land were also appropriated for decoys, whose lights, fires and other details were intended to mislead enemy air-crews into bombing fields instead of towns. Such a decoy was established at Branston Fen, imitating Lincoln, while Scunthorpe was mimicked on Risby Warren. Such decoys were not always successful: Lincoln was bombed in 1942, though damage was slight. Nottingham, Grimsby and Derby, however, suffered more serious bombing.

The scale of RAF investment in the north-eastern parts of the region between 1939 and 1945 meant that it became the location for many post-war defensive and offensive systems, a role which continues today. During the Cold War, 'Bloodhound' missile batteries were installed at Misson (Nottinghamshire), Dunholme, North Coates and Woodhall Spa (Lindsey) and Woolfox Lodge (Rutland), while Hemswell (Lindsey) and North Luffenham (Leicestershire) became home to Britain's first generation of ballistic missiles, the Thor series. All except three of Britain's airborne nuclear squadrons were also based in the East Midlands. Scampton (Fig. 6.13), Waddington and Coningsby (Lindsey), Wittering (west of Peterborough), Wyton (Cambridgeshire) and Gaydon (Warwickshire) were all 'V bomber' stations. Each made a local impact on its landscape because the security requirements surrounding the detached bomb stores were so extensive. Ancient Ermine Street, which had driven straight from Lincoln to the Humber for nearly two millennia, was also given a distinctive new curve, to avoid Scampton's extended runway. Even more important strategically, perhaps, was the establishment of RAE Bedford in the early 1950s on three wartime aerodromes (Little Staughton, Thurleigh and Twinwood). The facility included no fewer than five wind-tunnels and was the home of British research into supersonic aerial warfare.

At Stenigot the Lindsey Wolds' elevation (151m) was exploited in the late 1930s for four high masts in the 'Chain Home' RADAR system; the base here continued as a link in increasingly sophisticated NATO communications systems until it closed in 1996 (Fig. 6.14). Although

Fig. 6.14 RAF Stenigot, on the Lincolnshire Wolds. This view was taken in July 1996, before the demolition of the distinctive circular antennae of NATO's 'tropospheric scatter' communications system known as 'Ace High' (built in 1960). One mast of the earlier 'Chain Home' radar station (built 1939) remains a prominent landmark at the southern end of the site.

Fig. 6.15 From the moment of its construction in 1963, locals were intrigued by the enormous, but top-secret, aerial that dominated the southern Bedfordshire skyline on the hill north of Chicksands. It was one of the five antennae, world-wide, of the American FLaRe 9 secure global communications system. The array was nearly 400m across and the tallest masts were nearly 35m tall. It was dismantled in 1998.

Stenigot's parabolic reflectors were impressive, they were tiny compared with the astonishing FLaRe 9 aerial array above RAF Chicksands (Bedfordshire) (Fig. 6.15). This so-called 'steel stonehenge' or 'elephants' play-pen', was built in prefabricated parts in the USA and erected in 1963 on the crest of the sandstone ridge in southern Bedfordshire. It was sited here not so much because of the elevation (although it intercepted radio traffic arriving from any direction) but because this was poor land (mostly used for forestry) and could be spared for military use without controversy.

Changing defence requirements and the 'peace dividend' since 1989 have also left their mark in the East Midlands. The military have withdrawn from many long-established bases and NATO has refocused on different technologies. The Cruise missiles intended for the USAF base at RAF Molesworth (Huntingdonshire) were never installed, and the USAF Strategic Air Command base at Upper Heyford (Oxfordshire) has also closed, leaving unresolved questions over the site's use. Enormous TR-1 spy-planes no longer drift slowly and silently across the East Coast Main Line in the early morning on their approach to USAF Alconbury (Huntingdonshire), after keeping night-watch on the Soviet Union. Their huge hangars, specially widened to take their 32m wingspan, were set to be demolished, but they are so secure that they have become ideal depositories for sensitive commercial documents.

FURTHER READING

Roman
Buckley & Lucas 1987 (Leicester); Frere & St Joseph 1974 (Longthorpe); Jones 2003a, b (Lincoln); Todd 1968 (Great Casterton); Welfare & Swan 1995.

Medieval community defence
Barley 1969 (Nottingham), 1976; Biddle & Hill 1971; Blair 1994 (Oxford), 2000; Bond 1987; Buckley & Lucas 1987 (Leicester); Chapman 1998–9 (Northampton); Crawley & Freeman 2001 (Bedford); Dodd (ed.) 2003 (Oxford); Dyer 1972; Hall 2001; Mahany &

Roffe 1982 (Stamford); Marshall & Samuels 1997 (Newark); Stocker 2004 (Lincoln); Turner 1971; Vince 2003a, b, c (Lincoln).

Castles
The bibliographies in Coulson 2003 and Johnson 2002 offer a full picture of current thinking regarding castles and landscape. Renn 1973 is a useful analytical gazetteer. *See also*: Baker 1982 (Bedfordshire); Cantor 1978 (Leicestershire); Creighton 1999 (Rutland); Speight 1994 (Nottinghamshire).

Civil War
Butler 1949 (Nottingham); Courtney & Courtney 1992 (Leicester); Foard 1994 (Northampton); Harrington 2004; Royal Commission 1964 (Newark).

Early Modern and 20th century
Blake *et al.* 1984 (Lincolnshire); Cocroft & Thomas 2003; Coleman 1991 (Lincolnshire); Hancock 1978, 1985 (Lincolnshire); Lowry (ed.) 1995; Osborne 1997 (Lincolnshire).

7

Patterns of Community Belief

THE LANDSCAPE OF BELIEF

Since the 18th-century Enlightenment the western world has tended to divide religion and spirituality from the practical business of daily life. It has been only partially successful. We may think ours a secular society, but our lives are still hedged around with rituals both large and small. Today much western thought champions the secular society, in which religious activity is confined safely within the church walls or within the individual's own beliefs, but spirituality continually defies such constraints.

Even if the West really is a secular society in the 21st century, however, this was certainly not the case in the past. Until the 18th century, every activity in England was governed by religious codes, since every action was seen to have a religious connotation, to arise from a doctrinal requirement, or simply to require a particular auspicious procedure. For example, no matter how mundane, to be successful every medieval journey had to be accompanied by the correct prayers. Offerings had to made, in the appropriate order, to appropriate saints at appropriate chapels. Doing things in the 'right' way was essential, and this was as true for the everyday tasks of life as it was for great life events such as birth, marriage and death.

Different cultures have different ideas of appropriateness. Ideological frameworks have not remained constant and they have tended to borrow from each other. Thus the basic necessity of making an offering before or during a journey may have been expressed in a wide variety of ideologies through the last 8,000 years. In earlier mental worlds, dominated by powerful deities or by saints who had control over dangerous events, it was logical to believe that propitiating deities or honouring saints would offer protection from the perils of travel. Today we still say 'drive safely', or 'have a good trip'; many of us have talismans in the windscreen and some take more elaborate precautions. Exactly how such propitiations were conducted varied from age to age but, turning to the landscape, it is fascinating to see that such activities were frequently undertaken in the same place. It makes sense, then, to discuss the impact of 'beliefs' on the landscape by looking at different types of location: we will look in turn at locations associated with journeys, with water sources and then with gathering-places, before considering the development of Christianity at all of them.

Archaeology shows that propitiation rites connected with travel occur over long periods of time at river crossings. The Witham crossing at Lincoln has been the location for such rites of passage for millennia, though (as far as we know) it has only been marked by a building since the construction of St Thomas' Chapel on the new stone bridge in the late 12th century. St Thomas' was built, at community expense, to accommodate the correct prayers and gifts offered by those making the crossing. By the 12th century there were probably few fears of the bridge collapsing, but offerings were still made to mark the transition from one bank to another, and from one community to another, and to ensure that the enterprise necessitating the crossing would flourish. It was just 'what one did'.

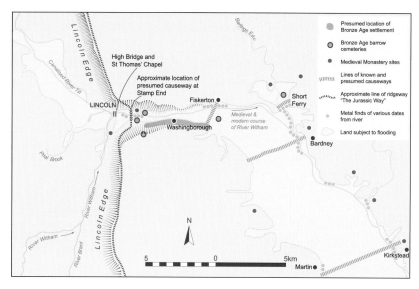

Fig. 7.1 River crossings in the middle Witham valley (Lincolnshire), showing the archaeological evidence for rituals marking crossings from the late Bronze Age to the medieval period.

Fig. 7.2 St Ives bridge (Huntingdonshire) retains its late-medieval chapel of St Leger. Bridge and chapel were built by Ramsey Abbey (1414-26) to provide easier access to their great market on the north bank (right). The chapel incorporates a room for a priest, who doubled as bridge-warden, and was retained to serve as a toll-house. Although relatively few were located over the river in this way, chapels were frequently associated with bridges in the medieval period.

Yet Lincoln's bridge-chapel was not the first place near this crossing point where such offerings had been made (Fig. 7.1). A few hundred metres away, a second causeway across the lowland had been the site of regular offerings since the Bronze Age. At this time, the appropriate rituals here also involved gifts, not to a saint, but to the water itself. Such rituals apparently recognised the river as some sort of personality; it was thought to represent a deity. During the Iron Age the River Thames was also seen as such a 'spirit', which was anthropomorphised as the god Thamesis in the Romano-British period, and the ancient sacred spring at Buxton (Derbyshire) was given the personality of a goddess named Arnemetia. At the early Lincoln crossing we know of at least 26 'gifts' to the river, dating from the late Bronze Age to the 11th century AD; all are of metal and many are valuable items of weaponry.

But this collection gives a misleading impression of the quantity and range of offerings actually made here. A more accurate picture was revealed in excavations at the crossing point near Fiskerton (Lindsey), a few kilometres downriver. Here not only were over 70 metalwork offerings discovered, but so also were the remains of many items of wood, pottery and even food. What was considered appropriate would depend on both the date and the journey's character. The most famous gifts made to the Witham are the many swords (of all dates from the late Bronze Age to the 14th century AD). In the medieval period these swords may have been placed in the river as part of the Christian funeral processions of local lords as they made the river crossing. But such journeys would have been infrequent; most would have been much more functional and much less elaborate, so less valuable offerings would have been appropriate – hence perhaps the many working tools, pots and food items found at Fiskerton. There were probably close connections between these rites of passage and the monastic houses that lined the Lindsey bank throughout that medieval period; thus all the causeways across the river, where such rites had been performed for at least 1,500 years, were eventually 'Christianised'. Slowly, gifts formerly made to the river itself were brought within the church.

Christian rituals at river crossings were not unusual in the East Midlands. Bridge chapels existed at Hethbeth Bridge across the Trent near Nottingham (built in the early 14th century by Nottingham's citizens), at West Bridge across

the Soar, Leicester (built 1365–6), on the Ouse at Bromham, Turvey, Bedford, Huntingdon and St Ives (Fig. 7.2) and on the Derwent at Derby. If there was no dedicated chapel, appropriate offerings could often be made in a hospital or monastery, deliberately founded near the abutment with responsibilities for maintaining the crossing, like St John's Hospital, Northampton, Duxford Hospital (Cambridgeshire), Bridge End Priory (Kesteven), and many others.

At Flag Fen east of Peterborough we also have evidence for the marking of river crossings at early dates. Here excavations have revealed a wooden island, apparently built as part of a route across the fen. The island was a massive undertaking in the late Bronze Age (built between 1000 and 700 BC); it consumed five times as much timber as one of Nelson's warships and is said to have been the largest structure ever built of wood in England (Fig. 7.3). However, although it was the location of many ceremonies and rituals, the island had no central idol; it seems to have celebrated the embayment in which it stands and the water within it. It may represent a period when an aristocratic priesthood claimed to offer protection against the inexorable rising water-levels which were, at this time, flooding more of the rich fen meadows each season. We should not lose sight of the fact, however, that it may have owed its origins to a much earlier route across the fen and that the later Bronze Age offerings made here may have derived from a long tradition of rituals made when crossing a drier valley. Whatever its precise significance, the Flag Fen platform was evidently a structure celebrating the power of the water, and the crossing over it. It is 2km or more from the great abbey of Peterborough (not founded until AD 655), but we have to ask whether there is a connection between the two structures. Was the abbey founded to stand guard for Christ over these same waters and their crossing? Should we see the abbey as the most recent structure reflecting community investment in this numinous area where a major route across the fen makes landfall? And, if Peterborough Abbey does stand within a continuous succession of rituals performed in this place, where were such devotions focused during the millennium from 400 BC to AD 600? Was it around Orton Meadows, to the south, where currency bars and Iron Age swords have been found in such numbers?

Perhaps it is not surprising that water has always attracted community interest and concern in the landscape; water is, after all, essential. In many Third World communities vital water resources are still governed by a framework of community ritual and belief, and this was also true in the East Midlands until the industrial era. Holy wells are frequently found in the East Midlands landscape and at least three villages take their names from such features (Holywell in Kesteven, Holywell in Huntingdonshire and Holwell, Oxfordshire). It has been estimated that there might be as many as 200 holy wells in Lincolnshire alone. Quite often the wells were not just 'holy' but under the patronage of particular saints, such as St Trunnian's Well, Barton-upon-Humber (Lindsey) or St Frideswide's Well, Binsey (Oxfordshire). Sometimes the symbolism of the spring emerging ('being born') from the ground has attracted official church interest and such sites may have been used for Christian baptism. One recent study of medieval church sites in Lincolnshire suggests that perhaps 20 per cent had been located alongside the community spring and, in many more cases, a local stream or brook close to the church was available for baptism.

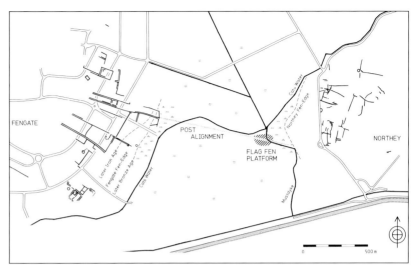

Fig. 7.3 Features of the complex prehistoric landscape around Flag Fen, east of Peterborough, recovered from aerial photography and excavation by Francis Pryor.

Although a close association clearly exists between church sites and water, however, secure archaeological evidence that East Midlands churches were founded specifically to Christianise pre-existing water cults is hard to find. Many such cults were connected with divination: foretelling the future. In many societies pools have been thought to represent gateways between this world and the domain of the gods. We still throw pennies into fountains and make a wish, much as the Romans threw lead plaques containing curses and prayers into the hot springs at Bath. In both cases the intention is to pass messages to other worlds. In this respect the regional distribution of churches dedicated to St Helen is interesting.

Fig. 7.4 St Mary's church, Thoresway (Lindsey), stands on a bluff adjacent to a powerful spring. *Although now brigaded into a mill pool, driving machinery, such a source of water right at the head of this remote valley in the dry Wolds would have seemed remarkable to earlier occupants and may have encouraged notions of divine intervention.*

They are particularly frequent in Lindsey (there are 25 of them, some near springs), and Helen has been connected less with the saintly mother of Constantine than with the Celtic Ellén, the guardian spirit of the gate to the underworld. A large temple complex by the pool in Lindum may be associated with Mercury, who also conveyed messages from humans to the gods. Does this indicate another watery gateway between this world and others? If so, should we think of Lincoln Cathedral as the successor to the temple of Mercury? Does it too stand guard in the landscape over a portal to the other world, only now in the name of Christ? At Thoresway, high on the dry Lincolnshire Wolds, surrounded by barrows, the church stands above a great pool fed by a powerful spring, which may have been named after the Norse god Thor (Fig. 7.4). At Uppsala (Sweden) victims were ritually drowned in another pool before Thor's principal shrine; did the tranquil, isolated pool at Thoresway ever witness such rituals? And does St Mary's church there now protect us from such memories? Echoes of such communication with the other world may also lie behind 'well-dressing', which is still sponsored by certain Derbyshire churches (at, for example, Barlow, Tissington, Tideswell and Wilne), whilst they might also be heard in the close association between the excavated church of St Paul-in-the-Bail in Lincoln and a large well shaft to the east, perhaps originally dug in the Iron Age.

It has always been important to lay claim to high ground as well as to water sources. Communities have often advertised their presence on hills and ridges, particularly if they overlook the 'home' territory. Throughout the Neolithic and early Bronze Ages (*c.* 4000–*c.* 1500 BC), the Thames valley was probably more notable for its ceremonial monuments than for its elaborate settlements or permanent agriculture. Such monuments were not always on the highest ground visible, but they were usually carefully sited. The earliest known are the so-called 'cursuses', 'causewayed enclosures' and the long barrows. The 25 East Midlands causewayed enclosures are all large, approximately circular enclosures, surrounded by interrupted ditches and banks, and typically located near the tops of rises. Aspect was clearly important: examples typically face across rivers with clear views along the valley. From them you could see and be seen. Recent palaeo-botanical studies suggest they were originally constructed in a well-wooded landscape, within which they would have formed large, obvious, clearings. They were all distributed in the central and southern parts of the region (none has yet been confirmed in Lincolnshire, Derbyshire and

Nottinghamshire), and they seem to have congregated along certain river reaches; nine sites have been identified within 32km of each other in the upper Thames valley and five cluster along the Welland north of Peterborough. Some were in pairs, facing each other across the river. The enclosure at Briar Hill faced that at Dallington across the Nene at Northampton; Etton enclosure may have faced a second across a branch of the Welland; while north of Abingdon, one enclosure faced a second at Radley across a branch of the Thames.

Excavations have failed to elucidate these enclosures fully. At Etton, construction itself was thought to have been a community activity, and part of the enclosures' meaning might have been that activity itself. The construction could have taken many years, and have been a ritualised community project, intended to reinforce group identity and to establish the community's specific location within the river-valley landscape. Certainly evidence for feasting was found at Etton and Abingdon, along with the ritualised burial of food – perhaps the remains of that feast – and this also hints at community gatherings. But it is also possible that the enclosures provided 'neutral' locations in the landscape where one community could meet another on friendly terms. In a world where distinctions were simply not drawn between secular and sacred events, however, all such activities would have been conducted within a religious framework. If a place was important in the lives of the community, it would also have had a religious aspect. This might have been reflected by a central division in the enclosure at Etton: feasting occurred on one side and rituals relating to the dead on the other.

The earliest enclosures may, in fact, have symbolised the community's world, with the rim of the bank, seen from inside, representing the horizon and providing a 'frame' for observations of the sky above. Millennia later, the layout of many medieval churches in a cross plan was also seen as encapsulating the beliefs of their builders. For churches, unlike prehistoric monuments, there are contemporary documents that explain how this symbolism was recognised and consciously promoted by both architects and patrons. Similar symbolic meanings have also been read into the circular plans of henge monuments – a problematic class of enclosure dating from the late 3rd and early 2nd millennia BC (Fig. 7.5). Their designers too were preoccupied with circular forms; a preoccupation mirrored in the architecture of contemporary burial monuments, the round barrows (pp.234–5). Like the causewayed enclosures, henges are typically sited to command good views, often also of river valleys. At Fengate a henge was one of a line of monuments (the others are barrows) along the edge of the contemporary fen, marking (as it were) the start of dry land and possibly acting both as boundary posts and meeting places between families and communities.

Although some stone circles in the modern landscape represent barrows, others played roles analogous to henges. But such circles are not common in most of the East Midlands, and this has sometimes led to the proposal that the region was occupied by a distinct lowland culture that simply did not build monuments in stone, even though it was so readily available. Of the 22 stone circles in Derbyshire, one of the finest, at Arbor Low, combined a stone

Fig. 7.5 Bull Ring at Dove Holes, near Chapel-en-le-Frith (Derbyshire). This fine earthwork henge is seen here from the north-east.

circle with an earthwork henge, demonstrating the close connections between these monument types. A henge and a stone circle also once stood together at the Devil's Quoits near Eynsham (Oxfordshire – a site excavated before the building of a wartime airfield). The smaller circles at Barbrook (on Big Moor) and Nine Ladies (on Stanton Moor), both in Derbyshire, also have surrounding earthworks, but are associated with landscapes dominated by burial monuments.

Although only about 30km north of Devil's Quoits, it is the isolation of the stone circle near Rollright (Oxfordshire) that is usually emphasised, but like Arbor Low, Bull Ring and many other enclosures, the Rollright Stones are most notable for their prominence in the local landscape (Fig. 7.6). The location has spectacular views to north, south and west. Furthermore, the circle itself is visible for some distance from the south while, from the north, the King Stone is also visible on the skyline for many miles. And why this hill in particular? Perhaps it is because the views north and south from this hill represent one of the great watersheds of England. Northwards the valleys unite to form the Stour, Avon and Severn, while to the south the valleys join in the Evenlode and Thames. It is still a numinous place on a blustery spring day and, indeed, continues to be the focus of folk rituals, now reinvented to satisfy modern preoccupations.

The wind also blows keenly at most Iron Age hillforts, like that on Hunsbury Hill across the Nene from modern Northampton. These monuments are traditionally interpreted, not as sites of community gatherings and celebrations, but as installations of defence and authority. Yet Hunsbury's notable hill, the top of which was ornamented with Iron Age

TOP: **Fig. 7.6 Folk-tales relating how an ancient army was petrified into the 'king's men' stone circle (Great Rollright, Oxfordshire)** *often revolve around their dramatic hilltop location, and the distant views that might be had from it. It is a spectacular eminence indeed, standing on the watershed between two great river systems; Thames and Severn.*

ABOVE: **Fig. 7.7 Borough Hill Daventry has been a meeting-place in the landscape for at least three millennia.** *Surrounded by earthwork banks and ditches since the Bronze Age (in the curving lines of trees), there is a smaller Iron Age enclosure at the north (far) end, also used for Romano-British cults. Community festivals (such as horse racing) were held here until 1801. The long-wave transmitter building (call sign 5XX), established here by the BBC in 1925, was an appropriate successor to such festivals for an age of mass communications. The thicket of masts that accompanied it, however, is now represented only by a lonely survivor earning its keep carrying relays for mobile phones. Yet this too represents a continuation of the hill's long-term use as a centre for communication.*

ramparts, was used for community gatherings in the Neolithic and early Bronze Age, at the Briar Hill enclosure on its northern slope. It is surely likely that the location was also thought auspicious by the local Iron Age community; especially so if iron was really smelted and worked there, as is suspected. Nevertheless the huge ditches and ramparts at Hunsbury are usually viewed as military structures. But is it possible to see these ramparts as symbolic defences as well as practical ones combining the demarcation of a special enclosure with military considerations?

At Borough Hill near Daventry (Fig. 7.7), there is clearer evidence for more-or-less continuous use of the hill as a special place in the landscape. This dramatic flat hilltop, from where it is said you can see clear across the East Midlands (from the Chilterns to the south-east to The Wrekin in Shropshire), may have been first ornamented in the Bronze Age, when it was considered a suitable location for significant barrow burials. In the Iron Age it acquired extensive ramparts, more complex than those at Hunsbury, and in the Roman period the hilltop enclosure was still thought a suitable place for making offerings. Did the Iron Age ramparts here really mark a 'military' phase sandwiched between two cultures who viewed the hilltop more as a religious site? Or would we be wiser not attempt to draw such distinctions between religious behaviour and other activities? It may be better to think of the hill an a major community meeting place, perhaps at times a place of defence, which inevitably attracted the support of the prevailing religious authorities. Thought of in this way, the ramparts might be seen as at least partly symbolic; a spiritual as well as a practical defence.

The hillfort at Beacon Hill, on a similarly dramatic hill in Charnwood Forest, was also once classed as an Iron Age defence, but Bronze Age votive finds from here may indicate that the ramparts here might also be viewed as symbolic. Military and religious explanations of such sites, then, need not be mutually exclusive; we need to think more subtly about the close connections between warfare and religion in the Iron Age. Many East Midlands hillforts clearly had Bronze Age predecessors within which votive objects have been found (like those at Mam Tor, Derbyshire (*see* Fig. 5.22), Burrough Hill, Leicestershire, and Chastleton and Lyneham, Oxfordshire). The fine symmetrical hillfort at Wandlebury, overlooking Cambridge, is also a good candidate for this sort of re-evaluation. Here, although the ramparts look very martial, the hill has been associated with the ancient gods since the very earliest written records (by Henry of Huntingdon in the 12th century).

Sometimes hillforts overlook, and must therefore be considered components of, much wider 'special' landscapes, known to have been the settings for rituals of many types. The impressive triple-ditched enclosure (often called a hillfort) at Honington, above the Ancaster gap in Kesteven, occupies one of the most numinous locations in Lincolnshire (Fig. 7.8). From here the views both west towards

Fig. 7.8 Landscape around Ancaster (Kesteven), showing features with ritual connotations from the Iron Age to the medieval period.

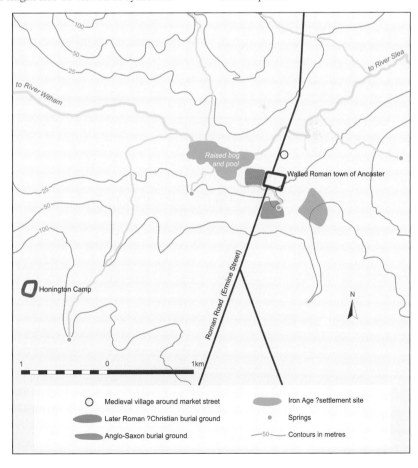

215

Nottingham and east towards Boston are breathtaking. It is easy to imagine that this place might have been singled out for gatherings by communities from both west and east. Although votive objects have been found here of both Iron Age and Romano-British date, the Camp is only one element in a larger landscape singled out for meaningful rituals over time. In the foreground of the stupendous view, in the valley below, lie the springs and bogs around Ancaster village. The valley has produced plentiful evidence for Romano-British cult practices. There was a major shrine here to the Romanised Celtic god Viridios, who we might presume could be reached through the pools and bogs. This is reminiscent of the topography at Lincoln, where the pool in the valley was also adjacent to Romano-British shrines and where the hilltop above was marked by the foundation of a church here by the missionary Paulinus in 627–8. At Ancaster early Anglo-Saxon investment in the site is represented by a cemetery overlooking the Roman enclosure, and (unusually) Roman cult sculptures might have been re-used here in pagan Anglo-Saxon rituals. There is no documentation for early churches at Ancaster equivalent to that from Lincoln, yet excavations revealed burials that may be of early Christian date, and it may be that pagan rituals here had been 'converted' to Christianity. Whatever the truth of this, in addition to the fine parish church (constructed, it is said, on the site of a Romano-British temple), by the 16th century Ancaster also possessed a mysterious hermitage and a holy well dedicated to St Mary. At Ancaster as at Lincoln, then, it seems that the distinctive topographical location, first marked by the enclosure on the hilltop at Honington Camp, subsequently attracted rituals belonging to successive ideologies, of which Christianity was only the latest.

As religion and political power were inextricable at earlier periods, Romano-British temples, like that at Ancaster, should be discussed alongside other expressions of political status. At Kings Hedges (Cambridgeshire), for example, the 3rd-century villa was preceded by a Romano-British temple, which may itself have had Iron Age origins, whilst the shrine at Woodeaton (Oxfordshire) was surrounded by a great market and fairground. In a society dominated by a wealthy imperial aristocracy, the rituals accompanying daily life were performed at shrines within villa complexes and at their other domestic locations. Most villas and farmsteads had such shrines, and they have been identified in excavations at the Stanwick villa (Northamptonshire). Such shrines will have influenced interior décor including the mosaics on the floor; the depiction of Ceres, the goddess of the harvest, in mosaic at the Winterton villa (Lindsey) would have been appropriate to the grain economy of the area.

Water sources and hills were not the only locations invested with both political and religious meaning. Alongside their economic importance, the woodlands of the Iron Age and Romano-British period were also accorded religious significance. It has been suggested that the extraordinary circular timber structure located within the 1st-century military establishment at The Lunt (Warwickshire) might have been a corral for the druid's sacred horses, mentioned by several classical writers. If true, there could be few clearer demonstrations of the inextricability of religion and political power than this. Such horses were associated with Iron Age tribal gathering-places in the woodlands known as 'groves', which were the centres of political decision-making. Such groves may have pre-dated Romano-British settlements at Vernemetum ('the great grove') near Willoughby-on-the-Wolds (Nottinghamshire) and Mancetter (Warwickshire). The major Romano-British temple complexes at Brigstock (Northamptonshire), Thistleton (Rutland) and Frilford (old Berkshire) also have their origins in the late Iron Age and were located in well-wooded areas. Such Iron Age sites were not exclusively reserved for ritual practices, but they may still have been referred to as 'groves' by classical writers. The large temple complex at Collyweston (Northamptonshire) was also in an area that was well-wooded subsequently, but it seems to have been established after the Roman conquest. All of these temple complexes covered large areas of land and incorporated specialised cult buildings (sometimes circular or octagonal) as well as more mundane ones. At Frilford there may even have been an amphitheatre, a discovery which re-emphasises the inextricable links between political and social gatherings and religious celebrations, and connects this site directly with the causewayed enclosures.

At Ancaster, the Anglo-Saxons invested in the Romano-British cult centre (Fig. 7.8), and some continuity of cult has been suggested, but we do not know how common this might have been. Most pagan Anglo-Saxon cult sites are known from place-names. Fourteen place-names incorporating the Old English words *weoh* and *hearg* have been identified within the East Midlands; both approximate to our word 'sanctuary' or 'shrine'. Of these, Harrowdonehill ('the shrine on the hill', in Woodeaton parish, Oxfordshire) was on the site of a Romano-Celtic temple, while Great Harrowden (Northamptonshire) is also near a Romano-British site on a distinctive high spur projecting into the Ise valley. Many such sites are associated with hilltops. Harrowden (Bedfordshire) stands on the same pronounced low ridge as Elstow, where an important Benedictine nunnery was founded in about 1075. Earlier Anglo-Saxon burials have been found on this ridge, along with contemporary pottery, all of which may suggest that the nunnery's broader location had an inherited significance.

An unlocated place in Northamptonshire called Weedon (also meaning 'shrine on the hill') is associated with a 7th-century monastery founded by St Werbergh, and the story of her chasing geese from the meadows hereabouts may retain an echo of the release of captured birds used in pagan ornithomancy (divination of the future from the behaviour of birds). Although St Werbergh's monastery is often associated with modern Weedon Bec or Weedon Lois, neither village is 'on the hill', and a more likely site for it might be the dramatic adjacent hill where St Michael's, Stowe-Nine-Churches now stands (Fig. 7.9). The 'nine churches' at Stowe have been taken as evidence that this was a 'minster' site, referring to eight other churches in the surrounding countryside that were once dependent on Stowe. Nevertheless the place-name could imply that there were nine churches at Stowe itself, within Werbergh's putative monastery. Such early monasteries commonly had such 'families' of numerous small chapels rather than a single large church, as is thought to have been the case at Crowland and Bardney (Lindsey).

Evidence for the church taking over sites of earlier religious devotions, however, has to be treated cautiously. Because parochial churches were provided for so many small communities in the 10th and 11th centuries, many East Midlands church sites post-date the introduction of Anglo-Saxon Christianity by several hundred years. Furthermore, churches are certainly not found on every site of known prehistoric, Romano-British or Anglo-Saxon religious significance. At Breedon-on-the-Hill (Leicestershire), however, the Iron Age enclosure

Fig. 7.9 St Michael's Stow-Nine-Churches (Northamptonshire) is dramatically sited on a hilltop, and contains both Anglo-Saxon fabric and pre-Viking stone sculpture. Richard Morris has suggested that it was the heart of the monastery founded 'at Weedon' by St Werbergh in the late 7th century.

Fig. 7.10 Breedon-on-the-Hill (Leicestershire) demonstrates contrasting attitudes to a distinctive natural feature through time. *The isolated limestone hill, rising abruptly from the Trent plain, has been a focal point and community meeting place for a hundred generations. However, today the Iron Age ramparts and the Anglo-Saxon monastic site, both tokens of this community respect, have now been mostly destroyed. Once steam-driven excavating equipment made it possible, the community seems to have respected the hill only for the commercial value of its stone.*

ornamenting one of the most dramatic hills in the region was adopted by the early church as a monastic centre 'to bring baptism to the area around' (Fig. 7.10). The hilltop was probably used continuously from the 4th century BC through to the 4th century AD, and surviving sculpture testifies to its continuing importance to the religious life of the locality in the 8th and 9th centuries. The enclosure's religious significance may have been indistinguishable, however, from its role as a gathering-place for community celebrations, including (to judge from the range of pottery discovered here) trading with distant groups. Aylesbury church was established in a similar, though less dramatic, topographical location. Here too an early church was established on a prominent hill within an Iron Age enclosure, and here too there have been Middle Saxon finds. Such churches are not numerous in the East Midlands, but they include Burgh-on-Bain (Lindsey), Binsey (Oxfordshire) and perhaps St Peter and St Giles in Cambridge, if the recently proposed hillfort there is confirmed.

The early church may have been attracted to pre-existing enclosures of all dates, however. At Lincoln the Roman stone-walled enclosure on the hilltop was selected for Paulinus' early church, while the walls of Roman Leicester provided an enclosure for St Nicholas's church, if we presume that this church was founded in the 7th century. At a number of other locations, natural enclosures surrounded by water were selected by the early church: at Bardney and Crowland, monasteries were founded on near-islands which had long been a focus for ritual gatherings.

Why was the early church prompted to invest in such a variety of ancient sites? The connecting thread, once again, may be not so much the earlier rituals performed at such places but their role as traditional gathering-places for local communities. As religion and daily life were inextricable, such community gatherings (for trade, politics or entertainment) would also have had religious aspects, so we may be framing the question poorly by asking whether such locations were pre-existing religious sites. At some locations of integrated community gatherings and religious rituals, the early church evidently invested heavily without placing a church at the topographical centre. Dorchester (Oxfordshire) has perhaps the most impressive of all sequences of ritual monuments in the East Midlands (Fig. 7.11), starting with a cursus (of *c.* 3000 BC) and including a henge and many mortuary structures dating from the 3rd and 2nd millennia BC. In the late Bronze Age votive offerings were made into the river hereabouts, and in the Iron Age (if not before) Wittenham hillfort had been constructed overlooking the tongue of land between the rivers Thame and Thames. By the Roman conquest this tongue was occupied by a settlement contained within earthwork dykes (*see* Fig. 3.5). The nature of community rituals here during the Romano-British period has been little discussed, but there is an enclosed graveyard of this date nearby, and by the 5th century, if not before, there was intensive burial by Anglo-Saxon peoples. As it was such a long-term focus for local communities, it is not at all surprising that Dorchester should have been adopted by St Birinus as the headquarters for his conversion project in the upper Thames valley early in the 7th century.

Although the ideologies celebrated at Dorchester in gatherings, rites and rituals changed continuously over 5,000 years, the communities of this part of the Thames valley seem to have

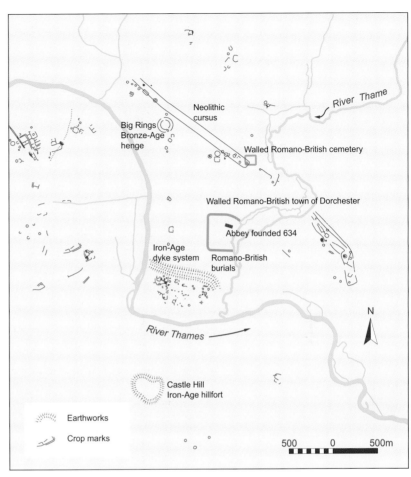

Fig. 7.11 Landscape around Dorchester-on-Thames (Oxfordshire), *showing locations of sites with ritual connotations from the Neolithic to the Anglo-Saxon periods (various sources). The church of the Augustinian abbey was founded by St Birinus in the north-eastern corner of the former Roman walled enclosure, which extended down to the River Thames (source: Cook & Rowley (eds) 1985).*

returned here for celebrations again and again. Each celebration would have been held within a framework of religious beliefs and, occasionally, changes in those beliefs resulted in new monument types in the landscape. Consequently, when he arrived, Birinus had many earlier enclosures to choose from, but he seems to have chosen the walled Roman enclosure for the site of his new church. Although it might have served as a quarry, the Roman enclosure may not have been the most actively used part of the landscape in the 7th century (that would have been, presumably, the contemporary burial grounds to the north and east), but the Roman walls would have been the most impressive monument architecturally. Birinus, anyway, wanted to associate his new Christianity with the prestige of Rome, and the repair and re-adoption of the Roman enclosure in preference to the more recent pagan Saxon burial grounds would make good propaganda.

The selection of site for the great church at Dorchester therefore reminds us that incoming Christianity did not feel the need to plant its churches right on top of the most recent activity. It may have been more important to dominate this 'special' landscape. Thus it may be legitimate to view Eynsham Abbey, founded about 1005 about 2km from the Bronze Age Devil's Quoits and a group of later ritual monuments now known only as crop marks, as the inheritor of that gathering-place. The 7th-century monastic site at Peakirk (north of Peterborough) might have been related to community gatherings in the landscape, represented at much earlier dates by prehistoric monuments at Etton and Northborough, less than a mile away. Whilst at nearby Crowland, an early 8th-century account tells how St Guthlac swept out pagan 'devils' from a probable Bronze Age chambered tomb, itself perhaps associated with a Romano-British temple, before founding his monastery within its former sanctuary. But none of these examples should be taken as evidence for direct continuity of worship. Placing an early church near a 3,000-year-old earthwork cannot, of itself, indicate any religious continuity; the earthwork may even have been invisible when the church was founded. It is more likely that such coincidences of location reflect a continuity of uses of these areas of landscape by successive local communities. These were long-term gathering-places in the landscape and, as all gatherings took place within a religious framework, these locations were occasionally marked by distinctive ritual monuments. It was the gatherings themselves towards which the new Christian church was drawn, not necessarily the remains of the earlier monuments.

Throughout the 8th and 9th centuries, the church developed through a network of missionary centres or minsters, of which there were dozens in the East Midlands. These too were often located in places with pre-existing landscape significance to their local communities. Oundle, Brixworth (Northamptonshire) and Bedford are documented as early monasteries and all three churches stand proudly above important river crossings. As well as Weedon, early saints' lives mention churches at Kings Sutton and Brackley (Northamptonshire) and Stowe (Buckinghamshire), while the place-name Wistow (Leicestershire) indicates a cult of St Wystan. Buckminster and Misterton (Leicestershire) are also known to have been minsters from their place-names while at Wing (Buckinghamshire) and at Great Paxton (10km north of Wyboston), minster status can be deduced from the surviving architecture. Given its close control of the outlying 'hamlets', and the fact that it retained its own secular jurisdiction through its Soke, it is likely that St Mary's Eaton Socon owes its origin to a minster church of this period.

One of the most extensively and imaginatively explored minster churches is Bampton (Oxfordshire), where the churches of St Beornwald's community focus on the remains of a Bronze Age barrow and a Romano-British settlement, both of which, we can presume, had a place in community lore and already attracted gatherings before the saint and his team arrived. Many Nottinghamshire and Derbyshire minsters were located in similarly numinous locations. At Southwell (Nottinghamshire) a group of important springs had been the focus of Romano-British rituals, and the large contemporary building known here was probably a temple. Although most commentators now discount the late medieval tradition that St Paulinus conducted baptisms here in the 7th century, nevertheless the wells were clearly appropriated by the Anglo-Saxon church.

During the late Anglo-Saxon period, church organisation in the East Midlands underwent a parallel revolution to that occurring on the land – the introduction of the parish system. The relationship between the two revolutions is not yet well understood, but the installation of common-field agriculture in the 10th and 11th centuries, and the nucleated communities that went with it, must have had a profound impact on church organisation. Prior to the establishment of the common fields, when smaller settlements had been more scattered across the landscape, most communities had no local church building. Such scattered communities had their own regional gathering-places, like Southwell or Bampton, often at some distance, and these had long been appropriated by the church. The scattered community would have taken their children for baptism and their dead for burial in such places. But for the most part these dispersed communities would have seen only the occasional priest and would have drawn heavily on traditional beliefs, albeit overlaid by Christian forms.

We have already seen in Chapter 3: 'A Landscape for Communities' that the concept of 'village community' was fundamental to the coalescing of these scattered communities into large nucleated villages surrounded by new common fields in the 10th and 11th centuries. The village 'idea' was founded on a community working together within a stable social (feudal) hierarchy, and if that hierarchy was to be complete, it needed to include the church. The church responded by reorganising itself into an approximately parallel hierarchy to that of the laity, with a priest as a spiritual 'lord' of his church, at the centre of each village, mirroring the lay lord of the manor. Ideally the village would be a single parish and would be coterminous with the lands of the secular manor, although in the East Midlands such tidiness was only rarely achieved. In the same way that various village lords would be grouped under great noblemen, who exercised authority on behalf of government, so village priests would be grouped together into dioceses under bishops. Across parts of the East Midlands (Oxfordshire and Derbyshire, for example), the creation of parishes involved little more than subdivision of former minster territories, with new churches in each new village. Elsewhere, though (Lincolnshire, for example), reorganisation seems to have been more radical. In the East Midlands this dramatic revolution in church organisation is poorly documented. The boundary described in a charter of 969 at Aspley Guise (Bedfordshire) is followed by the boundary of the modern parish, indicating that parishes had been created here by the mid-10th century, and a similar date has been deduced from documentary sources for the foundation of Badby parish (Northamptonshire). Fortunately these dates accord with archaeological studies: for example, in mid-Kesteven, where a study of stone sculpture from the first generation of parochial graveyards suggests that they were founded within 25 years of the year 1000.

In the new common-field landscape, churches needed to be conveniently located within each village and, consequently, the creation of parishes might sometimes involve the construction of new churches on sites without previous associations with community gatherings and rituals (Fig. 7.12). Even so, many new parochial foundations sought out distinctive locations within the new villages, such as springs. Although one might expect many new parochial churches to have been founded within or near the lord's new manorial enclosure, this proved to have been the case in only some 40 per cent of examples in a Lincolnshire study. Nearly as many new churches were founded on the village's public open space; that is to say, on their local gathering-place.

Churches founded during the 'village moment' have been encountered in numerous excavations, and much the best East Midlands example is that discovered within the enclosure of Furnells' Manor, Raunds (Northamptonshire). Here, a church with a nave only some 5m long, and a chancel half that, was built in the 10th century out of local stone, near the centre of a rectangular graveyard (Fig. 7.13). It was not entirely clear whether the graveyard or church was built first, but they were approximately contemporary. Immediately to the south-east, the lord of the manor and his family were buried in a plot marked by simply-carved stone monuments. Similar monuments are frequently

Fig. 7.12 St John's church, Strixton (Northamptonshire). We can't confirm that it was founded at the same date as the nucleated village that surrounded it and alongside its manorial site to the east (now represented by the rectilinear earthworks of its post-medieval garden). Similar physical relationships are, however, typical of many East Midlands villages, where the establishment of a parochial church was one aspect of the re-organisation of the landscape that included the nucleation of villages and the consolidation of manors in the 10th or 11th centuries. Strixton was fully occupied when mapped in 1588, but abandoned and enclosed in 1619.

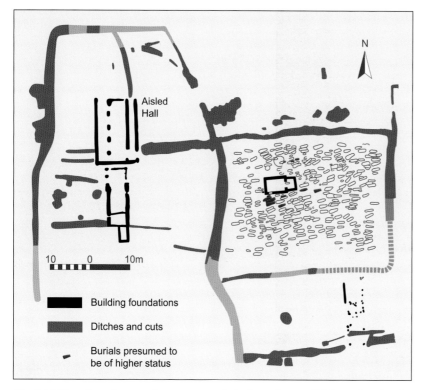

Aisled
Hall

10   0   10m

Building foundations

Ditches and cuts

Burials presumed to
be of higher status

N

*Fig. 7.13 Church and manor house
complex of the 10th and 11th centuries
in the Furnells area of Raunds
(Northamptonshire), as revealed
in excavations by Andy Boddington.*

OPPOSITE PAGE:

TOP: *Fig. 7.14 In Northamptonshire, the
'county of spires and squires', the
steeple of St Mary's Raunds is not
unusual and can be seen throughout
the parish. These days, however, the
'squires' make their biggest landscape impact,
not through their houses, but through their
horses' paddocks.*

BOTTOM: *Fig. 7.15 The large church of St
Mary, Eaton Socon, was the parochial
church of medieval Wyboston. Like
many of its more wealthy parishioners, Robert
Stocker, a junior wool-man in the family firm,
left £1 towards the construction of its new
western bell-tower in his will of 1484.*

found in Lincolnshire, Derbyshire, Nottinghamshire and Cambridgeshire, and studies of their distributions have concluded that many late 10th- and 11th-century lordly families established similar family burial plots in new churchyards across most of our region.

Simple nave-and-chancel plans, similar to that at Raunds, underlie many parish churches in the region, but there are virtually no unaltered examples of such buildings still standing. Even though it is a 19th-century re-creation, however, we can get close to experiencing the intimacy and simplicity of such buildings at Haugh, remote in the Lindsey Wolds. Many Lindsey churches are now small, intimate spaces with just a nave and a chancel, but most (like Croxby) have reached this form having once been much larger. Here, where many small parishes were severely affected by agricultural crisis and depopulation in the 14th century (p.76), churches have frequently been shorn of their aisles and sometimes of their chancels as well. Many churches hereabouts (like Haugh) have also been patched up or rebuilt in the 18th or 19th century, reflecting the return of arable cultivation following the agricultural revolution and the concomitant rise in rural population numbers.

Further south and west, churches (and parishes) tend to be larger and altogether grander, and big stone churches seem to stand closer together on the East Midland limestone than elsewhere in England. So many proud buildings are a consequence of the combined effects of settlement nucleation into villages and the economic success of common-field agriculture. The bringing together of scattered settlements into nucleated villages had the effect of focusing community effort on the fabric of the church itself, as well as on the fields around. It also drove adjacent communities into competitive building campaigns, and we know from the handful of surviving commissioning documents that competition with neighbours was a prime motivation in the construction of towers and spires. Given these strong parochial loyalties, the community would also feel it important that the parish church tower or spire could be seen (and the bells heard) at its centre when its members were out working in the furthest fields. In this way the parish church stood guard over the common-field landscape.

Only a handful of medieval stone spires were built in Lindsey; here towers more frequently imitated Lincoln Cathedral by erecting lead spires on their stocky stone towers. But in Kesteven spires frequently punctuate the skyline, as they do in Northamptonshire and Leicestershire (Fig. 7.14). It is sometimes said that the number of spires in these counties is due to the quality of local building stones, but this can only be partly true. Good building stone is found throughout the region (*see* Chapter 5), and anyway, by the 14th century, East Midlands stone was being shipped all round England. The patchy distribution of spires must be due, in part, to variable success in raising funds for such projects. While the repair of the chancel was the responsibility of the rector (who was not necessarily a priest, although frequently a monastic house held this position), the nave and the tower were the responsibility of the community. In a successful common-field economy, many small donations might fund a tower; but after the 14th-century agricultural crisis, major gifts were increasingly obtained from a few wealthy donors. Such individuals left heraldry carved into the stonework to record their gifts (as at Boothby Pagnell, Kesteven) and also their names (as at Great Carlton, Lindsey), but more frequently donors remain anonymous. We only know that Robert Stocker (*c.* 1440–84), one of the London wool merchants originally from Wyboston, gave £1 towards the construction of the massive west tower at Eaton Socon church, because his will survives (Fig. 7.15).

The church building was a reflection of the common-field village community in every respect and, while the community was engaged in communal arable farming, additions to the fabric also tended to be communal. New altars were established in new aisles, rather than in distinct chapels, for example. But as social divisions between landowners and tenants became more evident in the 14th and 15th centuries, and as the economically successful wished to distinguish themselves from their fellow villagers, many more 'private' additions were made to fabrics. In particular, the wealthy established chantries, which often took the form of enclosed chapels, screened off from the laity. By 1390 Eaton Socon parish church had a staff of 10 (excluding the absentee rector) servicing at least two chantries and the parish guild of Corpus Christi. About this time the nave was reconstructed, no doubt with donations coming from both the prosperous small town of Eaton, and also from the outlying hamlets, which still had no ecclesiastical provision of their own. Parishioners who lived here still walked up to 8km across the common fields to bring their children to baptism and their dead to burial, or merely to attend church on Sundays.

The inhabitants of the largest hamlet, Wyboston, were at last relieved from the weekly trek to Eaton church in 1476 when the two London wool-merchant brothers, Sir William and John Stocker joined with their cousin Henry (still resident in Wyboston) to

found a chantry chapel here. The new resident chantry priest was to pray for the brothers' souls, those of their family and the king. The little free-standing chapel of St Mary at Wyboston, which probably looked like the building at Brentingby (Leicestershire – Fig. 7.16), lasted less than a century. It was dissolved in 1546 and demolished shortly afterwards. It was just one of hundreds of similar chapels scattered across the landscape by the 16th century (there were more than 200 in Lincolnshire alone), many of which have long gone. The exquisitely carved 12th-century chapel at Steetley (Derbyshire), however, is not typical of this class of building. Most would have been simple rectangular boxes, sometimes with a distinct chancel like that excavated at Burnham (Lindsey), but often without even that elaboration, as at Brandon (Kesteven).

Fig. 7.16 The simple rectangular parochial chapel of St Mary, Brentingby (Leicestershire), was similar to the building provided by the Stocker family at Wyboston in 1476. *This building actually dates from the 14th century, although rebuilt in 1660. The belfry is 19th-century in date and the building was ideal for conversion into a desirable house in 1977–8.*

THE TOWNSCAPE OF BELIEF AND THE LANDSCAPE OF DISSENT

With the newly introduced Roman town came the diverse belief systems of the Empire, and interactions between Roman religion and indigenous beliefs were clearly just as complex as later encounters between Christianity and paganism. Just like saints of the 7th-century church, officials of incoming Roman cults attempted to associate their new gods with indigenous ones. Consequently, what was probably a pre-Roman cult centre near the strong spring called Roaring Meg just north of Lindum (Lincoln) was rededicated by the Romans to Mars Rigonemetos (Mars, 'king of the grove'). Although a kilometre distant, this cult was clearly within Lindum's urban sphere, and Lindum has produced far more evidence for Roman religion than any other East Midlands town. The large temple complex associated with the cult of Mercury has already been mentioned and evidence both for other temples and cults has been found in the town. Devotions to Mars (the god of war) are recorded, and would have been appreciated in a town containing so many army veterans. Similarly, two altars to the *Numina Augustorum* and a third inscription, found a few kilometres away but thought to come from Lindum, unites Mars and the imperial cult. Cults of Apollo and the *Matres* (mother goddesses) were also celebrated, along with the near-eastern god Atys and (perhaps) a cult of Mithras. These will all have been public cults; more private devotions to a smith-god and the *dea nutrix* are attested in smaller artefacts. In addition to evidence from sculptures and inscriptions – rare classes of find anyway – several excavated structures are thought to represent temple buildings.

Compared with evidence from elsewhere in the East Midlands (or indeed elsewhere in Britannia), evidence for Romano-British religion from Lindum is plentiful. In quantity it compares only with places like Bath, which were primarily cult centres. By comparison there is very little similar material from Ratae Corieltauvorum (Leicester) although the grand niches in the bath-house *palaestra* might have housed statues of gods and goddesses, such as Fortuna. There may also have been a cult of Mercury at Ratae, though the evidence is disputed; and although the building excavated beneath the Holiday Inn was probably a temple, whether it was dedicated to Mithras is still hotly debated.

Is the relatively large body of evidence for Romano-British religion in Lindum merely the product of more extensive excavations? Or should we be drawing the conclusion instead that Romano-British cults were particularly active in Lindum? We have already seen that the Witham pools and crossing point were the foci for prehistoric rituals and, according to Bede, Lincoln was also the first place in the East Midlands to have attracted the missionary Paulinus in 627–8. Was Lindum, then, primarily a Romano-British religious centre gathering-place, as it seems to have been both before and afterwards? Remembering that, in the past, the secular and sacred were not as sharply divided as they are today, we might argue, instead, that Lindum was not especially cult-oriented, merely relatively large. Yet is it much smaller in area than Ratae, which has produced far less evidence for ritual. If it was not Lindum's size that resulted in its apparently being a focus for Roman cults, could this be due to its association with imperial government? After all, three cult inscriptions mention the *Numina Augustorum*, the cult of the Emperor and the Empire.

Although the evidence from Roman Dorchester is much thinner, it too may have been primarily a cult focus. It has produced two dedicatory inscriptions: one is to Jupiter, but the other is to the same *Numina Augustorum* so well represented in Lindum. Dorchester, of course, has a much longer (and better attested) pre-history as a community gathering-place than Lindum (p.219) and, like Lincoln, it also became a 7th-century church centre. Does their long-term role as regional gathering-places account for their having shared the honour of seating the East Midlands diocese for most of the period between the 7th to the 19th centuries?

Romano-British urban religion was also strong at Durovigutum (Godmanchester, Huntingdonshire). This town was also established at a long-term gathering-place, where cursuses and other types of ritual monument were erected in the Neolithic and Bronze Ages. Excavations here have shown that the Romano-British town was dominated by a large *mansio* and its economy may have been dependent, at least in part, on travellers and visitors to the town's shrines. One temple, adjacent to the *mansio*, was dedicated to an otherwise unknown god, Abandinus, while a second, larger temple lay nearby. The prefix *Ab-* probably suggests that Abandinus was a river god, like Thamesis and Arnemetia, presumably relating to the River Ouse which was crossed near here. It is likely that such a cult would have pre-dated the Roman invasion.

Evidence for Romano-British Christianity in East Midlands towns is rare, but by the 4th century this was primarily a religion of the sophisticated urban elite (who often, nevertheless, lived in villas outside the towns – pp.135–7) who defined themselves in distinction to *pagani* ('pagan'), a word recently translated as 'backwoodsmen'. The most clear-cut evidence for urban Christianity is the astounding 'Water Newton Treasure', found in 1975 within the town of Durobrivae. Although the purpose of certain objects remains mysterious, this hoard of one gold and 27 silver objects represents the accoutrements of an early 4th-century Christian priest or patron. We cannot be certain that the church in which the equipment was used was at Durobrivae, but we have seen that the town was of considerable importance, and so might expect an early Christian presence here. It has been supposed that, along with a lead baptismal tank from Ashton (8km south-west) and a tag from excavations at Orton Longueville, the treasure represents a well-established aristocratic Christian community associated with the group of late villas around the town.

Archaeological evidence for Romano-British Christianity at Lindum is less clear-cut, although a bishop was based here in AD 314. Here one interpretation of the excavations at St Paul-in-the-Bail insists that a Romano-British church was constructed in the forum's central courtyard during the 4th century. The evidence for this view seems quite persuasive, and the alternative view (that the apsidal church discovered here was built by St Paulinus in 627–8) is based on documents rather than archaeology. Christianity was certainly present in Ratae (as a single brick from the forum there carries a Chi-Rho), but more than this cannot be said. Silver spoons found at Great Horwood (Buckinghamshire) and lead baptismal tanks with Chi-Rho monograms at Bishop Norton and Walesby (both Lindsey) and East Stoke (Nottinghamshire) might represent this same elusive urban elite, when 'at home' at their country villas.

Although archaeologists once mounted a rather desperate search for continuity between late Romano-British urban Christianity and the re-imported Roman church of the 7th century, in the East Midlands, no evidence has been forthcoming. Durobrivae does not seem to have been adopted by the 7th-century church at all; the early monastery associated with St Kyneburga 2km away, in the ruins of the former Roman complex at Castor (*see* Fig. 4.23) overlooking the town, might be considered its Christian successor. Lincoln's St Paul-in-the-Bail excavations offer more hope than most others, but even here (presuming the apsidal church in the forum courtyard is indeed late Roman) it is still not clear that the burials subsequently made around it were Christian. At one time many churches in medieval East Midlands towns were thought to have been established around early Christian mausolea in late Roman suburban cemeteries. Today, hopes of establishing such direct links with Romano-British Christianity have faded, and continuity is no longer sought quite so anxiously.

Instead, we celebrate the towns of the late 9th and 10th centuries as new foundations (pp.65–7). When re-founded they were fully equipped with the newly invented parochial churches also being established in the countryside. Most East Midlands towns already had at least one major church before their 're-foundation': Nottingham had St Mary; Stamford, St Peter; Leicester, St Nicholas and possibly St Margaret; Derby, St Alkmund; Oxford, St Frideswide; and Northampton, St Peter (Fig. 7.17). These churches were already at least a century old when true urbanism re-emerged; they were minsters and were an integral part of rural provision. In contrast to towns like Worcester, however, none of them seem to have exercised much influence over the new parochial foundations.

Sometimes the new East Midlands towns contained prodigious numbers of parish churches: by the end of the 12th century Lincoln probably had 47, Oxford had 20, Stamford 14, Leicester nine, Northampton nine and Nottingham three. The total numbers of parish churches are less a sign of a town's relative size than an indicator of the relative date at which it achieved its maximum growth. The earlier the town's expansion in the 10th and 11th centuries, the more likely it is to have large numbers of parochial churches. Towns whose maximum expansion came later, in the 12th century as at Oakham for example, tend to have fewer and larger parish churches. This rule can be explained by charting the

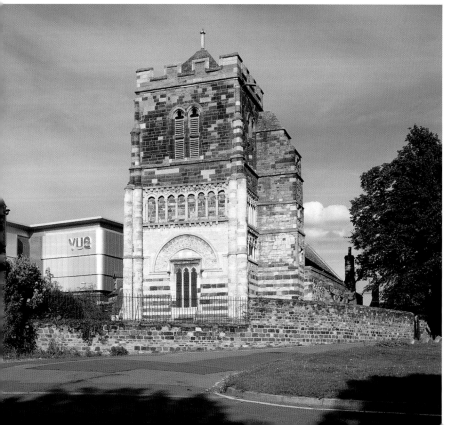

Fig. 7.17 St Peter's church in central Northampton probably pre-dates the establishment of a recognisable town here. *It was probably part of the 8th-century 'palace' complex revealed by excavations just to the east (behind the tree – see Fig. 4.25). St Peter's is one of the finest Romanesque structures in the Midlands and combines the local Northampton sandstone with finely carved architectural details in limestone of the Blisworth group, the nearest exposures of which are less than 5km away.*

growth of episcopal power through the 10th and 11th centuries. In the 10th century, bishops were unable to limit foundations of parochial churches, and consequently they were founded by every landlord, or group of laymen, with the means to do so. As bishops grew in confidence and authority through the 11th century, they were able to restrict foundations; and following the Norman Conquest, the foundation of new parish churches became a more elaborate and expensive procedure. In towns, new foundations became very much rarer. The numbers of medieval churches in East Midlands towns are therefore probably reliable indicators of the relative dates at which each town rose to economic maturity. Accordingly, Lincoln would be the earliest town to have reached economic prosperity, and this corresponds well with archaeological evidence suggesting a large town already flourishing by the mid-10th century. Oxford, Stamford, Leicester and Northampton would, by this measure, be attaining similar prosperity around the end of the 10th century, while Nottingham would be a relative latecomer, perhaps not rising to a peak of commercial prosperity until the mid-11th century.

Usually we have little idea who founded such churches. Domesday Book for Lincoln, however, records two of the last parochial church foundations, made between 1066 and 1086. The local lord Colsuein owned a block of land on the eastern fringe of the expanding town, which he developed during these two decades as commercial housing for new town dwellers, and on which he founded two churches (probably St Peter-ad-Fontem and St Clement-in-Butwerk) for his new tenants. But the city had reached its maximum expansion and these two churches remained marginal; they disappeared, along with their communities, in the late 13th-century recession. Many Lincoln churches must have been founded in this way, by landlords seeking to provide spiritual care for their tenants, and to make money in the process from church dues. Sts Peter and Clement were both sited on ordinary rectangular plots extending back from the street, like any secular burgage plot, and such plots may be typical of churches founded in this manner. About 20 of the 47 medieval churches in Lincoln sat in plots of this type, and many (though not all) may have been similar 'estate' churches. About 15 of the remainder were founded on street corners and these too might represent estate foundations. At least two, St Mary-le-Wigford and St Mark, are likely to represent foundations of a quite different type. From their archaeological remains it has been suggested that both were founded by communities of free townspeople coming together to found a church for their own benefit. Although no documents reporting this type of foundation survive for any town churches in the East Midlands, they are known from documentary sources in London and York.

Some churches in Lincoln's upper city (All Saints-in-the-Bail, and perhaps St Clement) may have been founded by lords, not so much for their tenantry but as 'chapels' for their own townhouses. At least 10 of Lincoln's other churches were established within public open space or market places, highlighting, once again, the inextricable connections between religion and daily life. In such cases, it is hard to say whether the presence of the church attracted the market (perhaps held within its churchyard) or whether the market came first and the church capitalised on the new gathering-place. It is likely, however, that a church was thought an essential item of market infrastructure (like the public wells with which many were also provided), not only legitimising commerce generally, but providing a practical service: mediating in disputes, for example, and witnessing oaths.

Churches in other East Midlands towns fall into similar categories. St Mary Magdalene and St Giles, Oxford (Fig. 7.18), are clearly churches founded on a market place, as are All Saints, St Mary and St George, Stamford (*see* Fig. 3.24). As befits a town with such a famous medieval market, many of Northampton's churches may have been established in market places; All Saints clearly was, but St Giles, St Thomas and St Edmund may have been as well (*see* Fig. 3.25). Market churches are less easy to spot at Leicester, although St Leonard and St Sepulchre

Fig. 7.18 St Giles' is one of two churches established adjacent to Oxford's great northern market, in this case in the early 12th century. Like many urban churches, St Giles' parishioners have capitalised on their valuable commercial site by letting plots along their churchyard frontage to traders. The buildings west of the church tower were certainly established by the 17th century, and may have originated during medieval expansion of the urban area.

look like clear candidates and St Martin (the modern Anglican cathedral) might be another (*see* Fig. 3.23). In Nottingham, St Peter's and St Nicholas' (*see* Fig. 3.22) are said to have been founded by the king to service the new great market (the French Borough); and St Werbergh in Derby may also have been founded within a market place (*see* Fig. 3.32). Presumably such churches are the urban equivalent of the 10th- and 11th-century rural examples we have noted founded on public open spaces.

Urban parish churches waxed and waned with their communities; like the towns themselves, they suffered from depopulation after the 13th century and were all greatly affected by the Reformation. From the 12th to the 18th century, they reflected back the gentle urban decline going on around and, as they disappeared, they left islands of open space in the townscape. At Lincoln the number of parishes was reduced from around 40 to 13 by Act of Parliament in 1547, but even these churches were not all viable; by the late 18th century, only 11 still had roofs. Not all East Midlands towns lost churches at this rate, but all except Nottingham contain lost church sites.

From the 17th century, the Anglican church, heir to the medieval church, also lost many souls to the growing Dissenting movements. Elizabethan puritans, like Richard and Christian Stocker of Wyboston (who died in 1614 and 1622, respectively), had remained Anglicans throughout their lives, but breakaway groups were becoming increasingly numerous and respectable. After the Act of Uniformity (1662) many Dissenting groups constructed their own places of worship. In Lincoln in 1701 the visitor could see the medieval Anglican parish church of St Benedict serving a handful of parishioners and still crumbling (despite being patched up after Civil War damage), alongside the trim and busy new Baptist chapel at Brayford Head, which served a Dissenting community that had been growing for a century and served a wide rural area. Leaders of industrial development in Nottingham were mostly Nonconformists, often Unitarians, from the chapel in High Pavement (founded in 1690). Members of this congregation occupied the mayoral chair for 66 years between 1700 and 1800. Methodism, established by John Wesley (1703–91) of Epworth (Lindsey), also became strong in Nottingham, and was particularly popular amongst the workers living north-east of English Borough who worked in the potteries, glassworks and textile mills owned by the Unitarians. Nottingham's first Methodist chapel, The Octagon, was built in Milton Street in 1764, and for a time social status was closely aligned with the chapel attended. In this respect Nottingham contrasted with Leicester, where (it was said) the Tory council refused to suppress riots in 1787 because they were aimed primarily at the firm of Coltman and Whitstone, Nonconformists who had recently introduced water-powered knitting frames. Even so it was the Unitarian Thomas Corah who introduced the first steam-powered mill into Leicester in 1865.

Various branches of Protestant Dissent made an enduring mark on East Midlands townscapes, from St Ives' peaceful, pocket-sized, Quaker meeting house (of 1691 and 1725) to its giant Congregational Free Church (built 1863–4), whose spire dominates the town. Early Dissenting chapels were often tucked away from the main streets, like that of the Quakers at Ampthill (of 1726), and were often built on the rear parts of burgage plots owned by sympathisers: examples include Keach's Chapel, built in 1695 at Winston (Buckinghamshire) and the Quaker meeting house (1696–7) at Saltergate, Chesterfield (Derbyshire). Such discretion arose partly from a desire for self-preservation. In the late 17th century few legal sanctions were applied to those who attacked Nonconformist meeting houses. Later Dissenters became more confident, and it is often Nonconformist buildings, rather than Anglican churches, that dominate East Midlands city centres. Look northwards along Trumpington Street, Cambridge, for example, and see the medieval church of Little St Mary's dwarfed by the bulk of the Emmanuel Church of 1872–5 (Fig. 7.19). This monster is in aggressive Gothic dress, but urban chapels were often incongruously neoclassical in design, like the Weslyan's huge Roman temple (built in 1863), which rises high above the humble skyline of Market Rasen (Lindsey).

Ironically, perhaps, the demolition of so many urban chapels since 1945 has meant that many of the most interesting are now found in the countryside. The Baptist chapel of 1701 at Monksthorpe (Lindsey) still has its outside baptistery, and looks magical (if cold) in the early morning mist, while the simplicity of the little meeting house at Brant Broughton (Kesteven) perfectly expresses the Friends' ideals of respect and simplicity (Fig. 7.20). Likewise, Congregationalists did not always deploy architecture like a bludgeon. At Roxton (south of Wyboston), in the 1820s the barn they used as a meeting house was converted by squire Metcalfe into a delightful chapel in the same rustic style as the *cottages ornés* elsewhere on the estate (p.151) (Fig. 7.21). Whether whimsical, brutal or tasteful, all this architectural ostentation seemed blasphemous to some working-

ABOVE: *Fig. 7.19 The small medieval parish church of Little St Mary, Cambridge (left),* is completely out-faced on Trumpington Street by the swaggering gothic of the Emmanuel Congregational Church, by the architect Cubitt.

BELOW: *Fig. 7.20 Looking north towards the 'stand' in the serene interior of the Quaker meeting house at Brant Broughton (Kesteven),* converted from a barn that stood well back from the street in 1702.

TOP: *Fig. 7.21 Since 1808, Congregationalists at Roxton (Bedfordshire) had used a barn as their meeting house.* The barn (centrally placed here) was subsequently enlarged with wings to north and south to include a vestry and a schoolroom. This was probably done in 1825, when the whole chapel was dressed in picturesque thatch and rustic external woodwork to match other similar buildings on the edge of the ornamental park.

ABOVE: *Fig. 7.22 The Primitive Methodist ('Ranter') chapel at Little Hale (Kesteven),* built by members of the connection themselves in 1837, is characteristically unpretentious, yet careful inspection reveals that even this small structure has been extended, by one third c.1887.

class Dissenters, and groups of Primitive Methodists (or Ranters) started breaking away shortly after Wesley's death. In Lincolnshire and the Trent valley, the Ranters were a large and influential force in society, gaining support among both rural and urban poor, especially those dispossessed by Parliamentary enclosures and impoverished by the depression following the Napoleonic Wars. Until their members became more comfortable, their buildings were assertively simple, completely without architectural decoration: for example at Claypole (Kesteven) and Little Hale (Fig. 7.22). Where they survive today (mostly in rural contexts) many have been readily converted into outbuildings.

The Anglican church responded to the Dissenters' challenge only slowly. There was relatively little new Anglican church building in the East Midlands following the Reformation. In Huntingdonshire some church towers, formerly thought to be late medieval, are now considered to have been built (in a medieval style) in the 16th and 17th centuries. For the most part, however, new churches only came about either through the energy of certain landlords (like Dr Richard Busby, headmaster of Westminster

School, who replaced St Mary Magdalene, Willen, Buckinghamshire, in 1678–82), or because of some disaster such as Northampton's 1675 fire, which prompted the reconstruction of All Saints. By the 19th century, however, even though many potential parishioners were now attending Dissenting chapels, Anglican pew-space was very scarce.

In 1818 the established church finally reacted with the Church Building Act, which provided for new churches, especially in the burgeoning towns. St George's, Rutland Street, Leicester is a good example of the type of suburban church built by the Act's Commissioners during the next generation throughout the region. Built in 1823–7, it was always intended to have a small tower and spire (marking it out above the roofs of the new terraced houses). St George's originally had the typical shallow recess in place of a chancel, which was replaced in 1879 by Blomfield to accommodate the more lavish style of Victorian liturgy. The church now ministers to Leicester's Serbian Orthodox community.

Prior to the development of official toleration, Roman Catholic buildings were very unassuming, like, for example, the discrete combined chapel and farmhouse of 1793 at Osgodby, Lindsey. After 'emancipation' in 1829 however, the newly established Roman Catholic hierarchy set out to make an impact on the East Midlands townscape with increasing confidence. Most dramatic is the enormous Roman Catholic cathedral, paid for by opera star Yolande Duvernay, at Cambridge (built 1885–90), which stands to one side of the university town but completely dominates the new working-class and industrial suburbs to the east and south. Furthermore, arriving by train, this is the first grand building encountered (Fig. 7.23). Most other Roman Catholic churches of the period also make substantial contributions to the skyline, although at Derby (where the hierarchy employed A W N Pugin with financial support from the Earl of Shrewsbury) the projected spire was never built. All are examples of the Gothic Revival, the only architectural style likely to appeal to 19th-century Roman Catholics. That style had also been championed by a revived Anglican church, especially following the foundation of the Cambridge Camden Society in 1839 and the Tractarian controversy of the 1840s. As between medieval village churches, the architectural result was unrestrained Gothic competition in the towns. The Lincoln skyline was provided with three large Gothic spires between 1876 and 1893: to the west, the large Congregational chapel; in the centre, the new Anglican church of St Swithin (with the grandest and most expensive spire, actually the gift of the Nonconformist Shuttleworth family); and to the east the blunt cone of St Hugh's Roman Catholic church (Fig. 7.24).

Other religions have also made an impact on the townscapes of the East Midlands. Before the Expulsion of 1291, Jewish synagogues served several communities in our medieval towns, and all these had cemeteries outside their gates. The Nottingham synagogue was on the corner of Castlegate and Listergate in the 13th

Fig. 7.23 The Roman Catholic Cathedral, Cambridge. Excluded from the University for so long, when it finally came to Cambridge the new cathedral (1885–90 – architects Dunn and Hansom) addressed itself to the newly built suburbs south-east of the city centre, towards the railway. The Anglican church of St Paul (built of brick in 1841 – architect Ambrose Poynter – far right) could scarcely compete.

LEFT: *Fig. 7.24 Lincoln Cathedral stands above competing 19th-century church spires of the commercial city.* On the far left the Congregational spire of 1874–6 was carefully sited to dominate the foreground in views of the cathedral from the new railway. Towards the right (east) the spires of Anglican St Swithin's (1884–7) and Roman Catholic St Hugh's (1893) both aim to impress travellers arriving on the road from Canwick.

BELOW: *Fig. 7.25 Two faces of Islam in contemporary Oxford:* the Madinah Mosque (left) in Stanley Road was an innovative conversion of a suburban villa in the mid-1990s, whilst the new Central Mosque (right) in Manzil Way (completed 2002) takes a more traditional form and makes a distinctive statement in the townscape.

century, while in Lincoln it was also centrally located, somewhere near the Jew's House, but not necessarily on the site of the present Jew's Court. Although its most famous ancient monument is called Jewry Wall, little evidence has been produced for Jews in medieval Leicester; but Northampton had one of the largest Jewries in England, with a synagogue in Silver Street. Oxford's medieval synagogue lies beneath the north-west tower of Tom Quad at Christ Church but, in a wonderfully English way, its modern equivalent stands across the road from the city's best Lebanese restaurant. Today Oxford, Leicester and Nottingham also have a number of mosques (three in Oxford and more than 15 in Leicester). Some of these have been carefully built in traditional styles, adding yet another layer to the palimpsest of East Midlands urbanism, but many are conversions of older buildings. The mosque in Stanley Road, Oxford, must rank as one of the most audacious conversions of a terraced house anywhere (Fig. 7.25). Gudwaras in Leicester and Nottingham, used by the Sikh community, now add their banner poles to the skyline (Fig. 7.26), although the many Buddhist buildings now found in the East Midlands tend not to be so distinctive externally. How these newcomers respond to the landscape of English belief is not much considered. Typically they occupy convenient buildings and sites for the communities to which they belong. Although Oxford's Stanley Road mosque is very much a piece with its community's surrounding fabric of terraces and villas, the new Central Mosque makes more of a didactic statement in the townscape. All, however, continue the tradition of close association between religious buildings and community gathering-places.

Fig. 7.26 Although it has now moved to nearby Forestfield, the Nottingham Sikh community (Siri Guru Singh Subha) made appropriate use of this former vicarage site opposite the Old Dye Works in New Basford. To what extent did the previous use of the site influence its establishment?

A FINAL JOURNEY

Our exploration of landscapes of belief in the East Midlands is almost complete; it remains only to review landscape as a place where our own remains have been laid to rest. The earliest explicit East Midlands memorials to the dead are the Neolithic long barrows and their kindred monuments, which survive in clusters as earthworks around the heads of dry valleys in the Lindsey Wolds, but which are now also known from crop marks and excavations across the area in many other locations. In particular they occur alongside groups of so-called 'cursuses' and other monuments along all the major river valleys. An example has recently been excavated at Eynesbury, just down-river from Wyboston. Some of these structures evidently contained not burials as such, but mementoes of the dead. They were bone-houses, storing remains of individuals, who were initially disposed of elsewhere; these are not so much monuments to death and burial, but to the continuing vitality of the dead and the role the ancestors played in contemporary lives. Bones were probably removed from such barrows to play occasional dramatic roles in community celebrations. In date they are also approximately contemporary with the causewayed enclosures, which also represent community gatherings (pp.212–13), and we might hypothesise beliefs based on interactions between communities of ancestors with communities of the living.

Such bone-houses with their related monument types, are quite different in character from the later round barrows. Unlike long barrows, round barrows marked the primary burial sites of individuals, who were accompanied on their individual journeys into the afterlife by gifts tailored for them, individually. These people were commemorated as individuals, not as communal ancestors, and the role they played amongst the living did not require them to be physically present in contemporary ceremonies. Instead they stood apart from the living in their barrows and exercised influence on the living through their imagination. The power of the dead over the living was probably just as strong, perhaps stronger, but it was not so tangible. The shift towards individual burial, which occurred during the 3rd millennium BC, marks a fundamental change in humanity's relationship with the gods. It represents the physical separation between the living and the dead, between humanity and its deities, which was to last until the present day.

In the landscape, the change from long barrow to round barrow burial was equally profound. Round barrows were woven into the layout of the agricultural landscape at Fengate. The landscape here could not be farmed without being aware of the ancestors' presence. Barrows were deliberately sited so that they would be regularly passed by, no doubt with appropriate rituals being performed. Many of those known from other East Midlands river floodplains were probably similarly integrated with grazing. Individual ancestors, represented by the barrow mounds, were deliberately placed in the contemporary farmer's foreground. On the one hand the barrow was a marker of the farmer's right to the land. It had been his ancestors' land and now it was his. But, on the other, these ancestors probably had to be propitiated, in the appropriate way, during ploughing or sowing, else the agricultural enterprise would fail.

Thousands of round barrows are known from the East Midlands, and so few have been systematically excavated that drawing typological conclusions is not helpful. Outside Derbyshire only a relatively small number survive as earthworks. The line of large mounds along the skyline at Bully Hills near Tathwell (Lindsey) still make an impact on travellers; and another still stands, prominently crowned by scrub, on the brow of the hill rising beyond

Fig. 7.27 Round Hill barrow north of Roxton (Bedfordshire) overlooks *the settlements of Chawston and Wyboston to the north (right)* (see also *Fig. 3.1*).

Chawston, in Roxton parish (Figs 3.1 and 7.27). It has not been excavated in modern times and is only one of a group of such burial mounds known from crop marks in the area. It is angled towards the community occupying the terrace land where Wyboston would eventually develop, and it may have played a role, not just in subdividing the Bronze Age landscape, but also in connecting the local Bronze Age agricultural community with their cosmos.

Many of these ancestors continued to play a role in the lives of successive cultures. Some Bronze Age barrows subsequently attracted burials of the Romano-British and the Anglo-Saxons, such as those at Harrold (Bedfordshire), where Bronze Age barrows became the focus of Anglo-Saxon cemeteries. Even though these later peoples cannot have known the original ancestor commemorated, they clearly understood that such mounds contained deceased spirits who could help their own dead in some way, and who therefore played some part in their own lives. Such appropriation of the indigenous ancestors' power is, after all, a sure way of laying claim to a new territory.

Before considering the landscape of Anglo-Saxon burials, we should note, in passing, the lack of evidence for Iron Age burial. The old adage that we only know about the Bronze Age dead and the Iron Age living is not so true now as it once was but, even so, remarkably few East Midlands Iron Age burials have been discovered. We have already seen that rivers were a focus for the 'burial' of objects during the Iron Age and it may be that most of the Iron Age population found their permanent resting-place here also, perhaps following cremation. Only once Mediterranean influence is felt in northern Europe, during the final century BC, do a few high-status Iron Age burials occur. The 'Belgic' style burials at Stanfordbury (Bedfordshire) or the 'sword burial' at Sutton Courtney (Oxfordshire) are East Midlands examples. The impressive pair of barrows by the gentle Claydon Brook at Thornborough (Buckinghamshire) belonged to warriors from similar Belgic backgrounds (Fig. 7.28). Given the burials' wealth and the scale of the barrows, these must represent important Catuvellaunian chiefs, and their location quite close to the presumed northern border of Catuvellaunian territory may also be significant. It may have been intended that potential aggressors would see land on the far side of the river defended by the spirits of these warlike ancestors and wonder whether their own ancestors were quite as powerful. As at other periods, then, late Iron Age monument building could reflect competition among the living as well as among the dead.

Although Romano-British burial behaviour may seem superficially similar to ours, it too was governed by fears about the power of the dead and by anxiety that

Fig. 7.28 Two giant late Iron-Age barrows stand by an ancient river crossing at Thornborough (Buckinghamshire). They still challenge onlookers to contemplate the impressive power of the ancestors of the people who live on the far bank and ask: 'how do your ancestors compare?'

they should be propitiated. Some Romano-British burials imitate their Iron Age forebears and are made in great barrows. But why the wealthy occupant of the large 2nd-century barrow, easily visible from Ermine Street at Riseholme (Lindsey), chose this form of burial among the many available remains uncertain. Was he or she aping Belgic customs perhaps, or associating with even older insular traditions? Many small, presumably family-owned, Romano-British graveyards also lie scattered across the region, like that excavated at Blue Bridge (Milton Keynes) which was probably based around the mausoleum of the owner of the Bancroft villa, but the majority of burials were made in large, carefully tended cemeteries, often located outside the new towns. The impact of these huge Romano-British cemeteries on the landscapes around each settlement must have been enormous. They were typically sited on approach roads and so, as the traveller arrived or departed, he or she would be reminded of the eternal verities by a mixture of small mounds, monuments, mortuary temples and inscriptions. The greatest landscape impact may have been made not so much by the monuments as by the planting of trees. Roman superstition and ritual associated certain types of trees with the dead: the laurel, juniper, cedar and cypress. Most such plants are not indigenous and so, having travelled through an agricultural landscape whose vegetation we would recognise today, the Romano-British traveller would first encounter any town through exotic imported trees scattered through its graveyards.

The Anglo-Saxons of the 5th century were both aware of, and respectful towards, the ancestors of previous insular cultures, hence their re-use of earlier barrows. Sometimes such respect might result in their siting of large cemeteries adjacent to the ruins of Roman towns, as may have been the case at Duston (Northamptonshire) and Thurmaston, which overlooked the ruins of Ratae. Indeed the Thurmaston cemetery might have been a regional or 'tribal' gathering-place for the Anglo-Saxons, as Ratae had been for the Romans. Although a much less significant precursor, it may be that the burial ground of this period on the hill north-west of Eaton Socon was deliberately sited to overlook the villa site north of St Mary's church. It has never been excavated, but it is quite likely that the villa itself will also have had Anglo-Saxon burials dug into its ruins. Almost all ruins of Roman towns and villas were used for Anglo-Saxon burials: 9 out of 10 recorded Anglo-Saxon burial grounds in Bedfordshire lie close to known Romano-British settlements and it seems likely that such burials were thought to interact in some way with the spirits of the ruin's occupants. Presumably they were intended to interact or negotiate with Roman ancestors as they were with the barrow builders of earlier cultures. Indeed the Anglo-Saxons may not have known the difference between a Bronze Age barrow and a Romano-British earthwork. Were the Anglo-Saxon dead to negotiate title to the new land with the ancestors of conquered or displaced peoples, no matter how long deceased?

Such burials were not, however, the numerically most significant method of disposal of the Anglo-Saxon dead. More typical were the large burial grounds in the countryside containing hundreds of inhumations, cremations, or both. Many such burial grounds in Lindsey (Elsham Wold, Fonaby near Caistor, Cleatham, South Elkington, West Keal, Castledykes at Barton-upon-Humber) do not seem to have had any comprehensible Romano-British background. All of them are sited, however, in magnificent locations, on the tops of hills and scarps commanding large views – often towards the west, facing the setting sun. Are these topographical similarities coincidental, or was a clear sight of the western horizon important in the burial rites used at such places? Alternatively it may have been important for the smoke from burial pyres to be seen across a specific territory.

Although they stood at a distance, such major Anglo-Saxon cemeteries seem to have been associated with large estates of the 7th to 9th centuries. In Lindsey, for example, the presumed Middle Saxon estate based at Caistor was overlooked by the cemeteries of Nettleton and Fonaby; at Bolingbroke the estate centre was overlooked by West Keal cemetery; and Kirton-in-Lindsey was overlooked by that at Cleatham.

In Kesteven neither estates nor cemeteries are quite so numerous, but the enormous cemetery on the westward-facing slopes of Loveden Hill north of Grantham was sufficiently important to become the wapentake meeting place. Here, too, the ancestors' domain was host to contemporary politics: the dead oversaw decision-making by the living. All these Anglo-Saxon cemetery sites lie away from the settlements they served, but the ancestors had their own dedicated locale in the landscape and it was used by the living for particular purposes such as law-giving.

Between the latest regional burial grounds of the 7th century and the parochial burial grounds of the 10th century, there was a transition. The inhabitants of each locality ceased to dispose of the dead within their traditional burial ground and started to make burials in cemeteries associated with the local minster church. In fact, there may have been more than one shift of site, as there is an intermediate group of Saxon burial grounds that contain exclusively 7th-century burials. Some of these contain extremely rich burials – among the richest ever made in England – and at least five such burials lay under large East Midlands barrows: at Caenby (Lindsey), Asthall (Oxfordshire), Wollaston (Northamptonshire), and Benty Grange and Cow Low, Derbyshire. All stand at the highest point for miles around and dominate views along adjacent river valleys, some are located quite close to known minster church sites (Asthall barrow is on the hill above Minster Lovell, for example whilst Caenby stood across a large gathering-place from the enigmatic church of Spital-in-the-Street). Some contemporary burials – for example, Grave 8 from the cemetery excavated at Standlake, Oxfordshire or the burial from Desborough, Northamptonshire – contain overtly Christian objects, and it seems clear that there was a period in the 7th century when Christian and pagan burial rites were combined.

Once the community burial ground was firmly united with the parochial church site in the 10th century, however, the cemetery merely contributed to the impact made by the church itself on the landscape. As East Midlands churches were now typically within settlements, this linking of settlement and burial must have appeared revolutionary to contemporaries. Not since the Neolithic period had the remains of the dead been invited into the settlement to share it with the living. Perhaps it was trepidation about this which ensured that most Christian burial grounds were equipped with a wall to divide the dead from the living, and that the act of passing through the gate of the churchyard was often deliberately marked during the funeral service (Fig. 7.29).

As they believed that such attentions to the human body contradicted the primacy of the immortal soul, Protestants laid much less stress on elaborate ceremonies accompanying the body's disposal. Some Protestant sects, like the Quakers and Baptists, deliberately put little effort into demarcating burial grounds at all. By the 18th century the aristocracy were also incorporating their family burials within their domestic landscapes. For a period in the 18th and 19th centuries the wealthiest built mausolea intended to contain dynastic burials, set carefully within the landscape gardens laid out around their new houses. The mausoleum's presence was viewed as integral to the Whig political manifesto: promoting the solidity and permanence of the aristocratic regime, like the planting of seedling oaks and other slow-growing trees. Like these trees, the mausoleum was also an expression of absolute confidence in the future. A distinguished East Midlands example

Fig. 7.29 Great St Mary's cemetery, central Cambridge. Although modern crematoria tend to be sited on the fringes of towns, the living and the dead still share the same landscape here, though separated from each other by a stout fence.

survives at Markham Clinton, Nottinghamshire (built in 1831–2), but the elaborate early 18th-century rotunda and its moated ziggurat at Boughton Park (Northamptonshire) have gone. Much the finest of these mausolea surviving, and also one of the furthest from its associated house (Brocklesby Hall, Lindsey), is that built by the Pelhams in the late 1780s to commemorate Sophia Aufrere, who died tragically young (Fig. 7.30). In Nollekens's marble statue, she stands poignantly, like some neoclassical Hermione, in the ghostly light that seeps through the stained-glass dome above. The building's main floor is raised above a complex crypt in which family burials were to be made. The Brocklesby mausoleum employs both the careful parkland planting around it, and all the architectural and sculptural symbolism of the classical world, to evoke the Elysian Fields. Here the ancestors were once again taken out of the community and set high on a neighbouring hill, very visible to the living, but playing only a managed role in daily life.

Fig. 7.30 A recreation of Elysium. The Yarborough family's magnificent mausoleum (foreground), above Great Limber (Lindsey), was one focus in an enormous landscape garden planted with informal belts of trees and clumps, forming a linear parkland uphill from Brocklesby Hall (in the middle distance). It was created in the final quarter of the 18th century.

OPPOSITE PAGE:

Fig. 7.31 A final journey. The modern city of Leicester from the large Welford Road cemetery of 1849 and later. This landscape also recalls, however, the Roman city of Ratae, which would also have been approached through such a graveyard, with generically similar monuments (tablets, pillars and obelisks) and would have been planted with a range of similar trees, also endowed with symbolic meanings.

Similar thinking lay behind the establishment of the great urban necropolises of the early 19th century. A need for extra burial space outside the churchyards had become urgent following urban population growth, and the form that many new cemeteries took in the landscape was strongly influenced by contemporary studies of antiquity. Like the aristocracy, the wider population also wished to adjust their relationship with their ancestors, and (as had been the case in Roman Britain) the most impressive of these new 'cities of the dead' were established at the edges of contemporary settlement, alongside the roads leading into town. The new cemetery opened in 1842 off Huntingdon Road, Cambridge, was a grand example. Planned by the doyen of contemporary cemetery design, J C Loudon, who had been involved in the model example at Kensal Green in London, it had a strictly geometrical plan and was planted with imported Taurian pines, yews and cedars. Nottingham, which scarcely had enough room for the living (p.95), nevertheless acquired a large cemetery on Alfreton Road in 1837, in what were then still the common fields. It acquired a second cemetery, with even more elaborate planting, on Mansfield Road in 1856. Lincoln's new civic cemetery was established, following a public outcry, in the same year and was situated on a gentle slope overlooking the town. It too was planted with imported trees and typically it was open to all denominations. In this respect too, the Victorian necropolis deliberately imitated Britannia's Romano-British urban cemeteries, which had also contained a great variety of burial rites. The landscaping and planting of these new urban cemeteries was imitated by many burial grounds around country churches. Some of the finest and most unexpected trees in the East Midlands landscape were planted at this time in an effort to associate parochial burial grounds with the Elysian Fields. There are spreading cedars at Edenham (Kesteven), stubby yews at Saxby (Leicestershire) and tall pines at Manby (Lindsey). Reappearance of similar cedars, cypresses, laurels and yews meant that, when approaching modern Leicester along the Welford Road, past the new city cemetery (opened in 1849 – Fig. 7.31), the traveller would catch a glimpse of the approach to Ratae 1,500 years earlier, and perhaps draw inspiration from this inheritance.

FURTHER READING

Landscapes of pre-Christian belief

Bamford 1985 (Briar Hill); Barnatt 1989 (stone circles), 1990 (henges); Blair 1988a (Binsey); Bradley 1981 (hillforts),1993, 1998a, b, 2000; Bradley & Chambers 1988 (Dorchester); Ellis 2004 (Eynesbury); Everson 1993a (Thoresway); Field & Parker Pearson 2003 (Fiskerton); Harding & Lee 1987 (henges); Jackson 1993–4 (Hunsbury Hill), 1996–7 (Borough Hill); Jones, M 2003b (Lincoln); Jones & Stocker 2003 (Lincoln); Lambrick 1988 (Rollrights); Mallim 2000 (Ouse valley); Oswald *et al.* 2001 (causewayed enclosures); Pryor 1998b (Etton), 2001 (Flag Fen); Rodwell (ed.) 1980; Stocker & Everson 2003 (causeways); Todd 1981(Ancaster); Wait 1985 (hillforts); Whittle *et al.* 1992 (Dorchester).

Landscapes of Christian belief

Ambler 2000 (Lincolnshire); Blair 1985, 1987, 1988b, 1992 (Bampton), 1994 (Oxfordshire), 1996a, b (Northampton), 1996c (Thames valley); Blair & Pyrah (eds) 1996; Blair & Sharpe (eds) 1992; Boddington 1996 (Raunds); Brandwood 1987 (Leicestershire); Bryant 1994, 2003 (Barton-on-Humber); CBA 1985 (Nonconformists); Cook & Rowley 1985 (Dorchester); Coppack 1986 (Burnham); Dornier 1977 (Breedon-on-the-Hill); Gem 1988, 1993; Gilchrist & Morris 1996 (post-Reformation); Hadley 2000 (Nottinghamshire/Derbyshire/Lincolnshire); Keevill 2003 (Dorchester); Liddle & Hughes 1979 (Brentingby); Morris 1989; Owen 1981 (Lincolnshire); Richmond 1986 (Northamptonshire); Rodwell 1981, 1984; Stell 1986, 2002 (nonconformists); Stocker 1993 (Crowland, Bardney); Stocker & Everson 2001.

Townscapes of Christian belief

Brandwood 1984 (Leicester); Green 1977 (Godmanchester); Mahany & Roffe 1982 (Stamford); Morris 1983, 1989; Sheils 1977; Thomas 1981; Vince 2003a, b, c (Lincoln); Whiffen 1947–8.

Burial landscapes

Barnatt & Collis (eds) 1996 (Derbyshire barrows); Bassett (ed.) 1992; Bradley 1987; Chambers 1987 (Dorchester); Colvin 1992 (Mausolea); Curl 1993 (Loudon etc.); Evans & Simpson 1991 (Skendleby); Everson 1993b (Caenby); Everson & Stocker 1999 (Lincolnshire); Hadley 2001; Leahy 1993 (Lindsey); Lewis 1992 (Thornborough); Lucy 2000; McAvoy 2000 (Godmanchester); Parker Pearson 1999; Pearce 1999; Whitwell 1992 (Riseholme); Williams 1983 (Thurmaston).

Bibliography

Aberg, A (ed.), 1978, *Medieval Moated Sites*. CBA Research Report 17. London: CBA.

Addyman, P V, 1965, 'Saxon Settlements and Norman Castle at Eaton Socon, Bedfordshire', *Proceedings of the Cambridge Antiquarian Society* **58**, 38–73.

Addyman, P V, 1972, 'The Anglo-Saxon House: a new review', *Anglo-Saxon England* **1**, 273–307.

Airs, M, 1995, *The Tudor and Jacobean Great House, A Building History*. Stroud: Alan Sutton.

Alcock, N W, 1969, 'Timber Framed buildings in North Bedfordshire', *Bedfordshire Archaeological Journal* **4**, 43–68.

Alcock, N W, 1981, *Cruck Construction: An Introduction and Catalogue*. CBA Research Report 42. London: CBA.

Alcock, N W and Woodward, P J, 1976, 'Cruck-Frame Buildings in Bedfordshire', *Bedfordshire Archaeological Journal* **11**, 51–68.

Aldcroft, D H and Freeman, M J, 1983, *Transport in the Industrial Revolution*. Manchester: MUP.

Allen, T G and Robinson, M A, 1993, *The Prehistoric Landscape and Iron Age Enclosed Settlement at Mingies Ditch*. Oxford: OUCA.

Allin, C E, 1981, *The Medieval Leather Industry in Leicester*. Leicester: Leicestershire Museums Service.

Allison, K J, Beresford, M W, Hurst, J G, *et al.*, 1965 and 1966, *The Deserted Medieval Villages of Oxfordshire, and Northamptonshire*. Leicester, University of Leicester Department of English Local History, Occasional Papers 17 and 18. Leicester: Leicester University Press.

Ambler, R W, 2000, *Churches, Chapels and Parish Communities of Lincolnshire 1660–1900*. History of Lincolnshire 9. Lincoln: History of Lincolnshire Committee.

Andrews, C B (ed.), 1934, *The Torrington Diaries. Containing the tours through England and Wales of the Hon. John Byng …*, 4 vols. London: Eyre and Spottiswood.

Arkell, W J, 1948, *Oxford Stone*. London: Faber.

Armstrong, L, 1978, *Woodcolliers and Charcoal Burning*. Horsham: Coach Publishing.

Armstrong, M E, 1981, *An Industrial Island: A History of Scunthorpe*. Scunthorpe: Scunthorpe Museum and Art Gallery.

Astill, G and Grant, A (eds), 1988, *The Countryside of Medieval England*. Oxford: Blackwells.

Aston, M, Austin, D and Dyer, C (eds), 1989, *The Rural Settlements of Medieval England: Studies Presented to Maurice Beresford and John Hurst*. Oxford: Blackwells.

Aston, M and Bond, J, 1976, *The Landscape of Towns*. London: Dent.

Bailey, J, 1998, 'The development of carpentry in Bedfordshire, 1200–1550', in Stenning (ed.), 55–67.

Bailey, J, 1998 (ed.), *Science in Archaeology*. London: English Heritage.

Bailey, J, 2001, 'The development of the medieval buildings adjoining the Abbey at Elstow', *Bedfordshire Archaeology* **24**, 57–75.

Baker, A H R and Butlin, R A, 1973, *Studies of Fields Systems in the British Isles*. Cambridge: CUP.

Baker, D, 1982, 'Mottes, moats and ringworks in Bedfordshire: Beauchamp Wadmore revisited', *Chateau Gaillard* **9–10**, 35–54.

Baker, D, 1983, *Coalville: The first seventy-five years*. Leicester: Leicestershire Libraries.

Baker, D, Baker, E, Hassall, J and Simco, A, 1979, *Excavations in Bedford 1967–1977*, (Bedfordshire Archaeological Journal 13). Bedford: Bedfordshire Archaeological Society.

Baker, P, Forcey, C, Jundi, S and Witcher, R (eds), 1999, *TRAC98*. Oxford: Oxbow.

Bamford, H, 1985, *Briar Hill. Excavations 1974–1978*. Northampton: Northampton Development Corporation.

Barclay, A, Bradley, R, Hey, G and Lambrick, G, 1996, 'The Earlier Prehistory of the Oxford Region in the light of recent research', *Oxoniensia* **61**, 1–20.

Barley, M W, 1949, 'Newark in the sixteenth century', *Transactions of the Thoroton Society* **53**, 15–25.

Barley, M W, 1952, *Lincolnshire and the Fens*. London: Batsford.

Barley, M W, 1961, *The English Farmhouse and Cottage*. London: Routledge & Kegan Paul.

Barley, M W, 1969, 'Nottingham', in Lobel (ed.), unpaginated.

Barley, M W, 1976, 'Town defences in England and Wales after 1066', in Barley (ed.), 57–71.

Barley, M W (ed.), 1976, *Plans and Topography of Medieval Towns in England and Wales*. CBA Research Report 14. London: CBA.

Barnatt, J, 1987, 'Bronze Age settlement on the gritstone East Moors of the Peak District of Derbyshire and South Yorkshire', *Proceedings of the Prehistoric Society* **53**, 393–418.

Barnatt, J, 1989, *Stone Circles of Britain: Taxonomic and Distributional Analyses and a Catalogue of Sites in England Scotland and Wales*. BAR (BS) 215. Oxford: BAR.

Barnatt, J, 1990, *The Henges, Stone Circles and Ringcairns of the Peak District*. Sheffield Archaeological Monographs 1. Sheffield: Sheffield University Press.

Barnatt, J and Collis, J (eds), 1996, *Barrows in the Peak District: Recent Research*. Sheffield: John Collis Publications.

Barnatt, J and Smith, K, 1997, *The Peak District. Landscapes through time*. London: Batsford.

Barnwell, P S and Giles, C, 1997, *English Farmsteads, 1750–1914*. Swindon: RCHME.

Barrett, J and Bradley, R, 1980, 'The Later Bronze Age in the Thames Valley', in Barrett and Bradley (eds).

Barrett, J and Bradley, R (eds), 1980, *Settlement and Society in the British Later Bronze Age*. BAR (BS) 83. Oxford: BAR.

Bassett, S (ed.), 1992, *Death in Towns: Urban responses to the dying and the dead, 100–1600*. Leicester: Leicester University Press.

Battye, K, Doncaster, R, Mitchell, I and Newing, D, 1991, 'Summerley Coke Ovens, Derbyshire', *Industrial Archaeology Review* **13/2**, 152–161.

Beastall, T W, 1978, *The Agricultural Revolution in Lincolnshire*. History of Lincolnshire 8. Lincoln: History of Lincolnshire Committee.

Beaver, S H, 1951, 'The Development of the Northamptonshire Iron Industry', in Stamp and Woolridge (eds), 33–58.

Beaver, S H, 1982–3, 'Ironstone in Rutland 1882–1982', *Rutland Record* **3**, 110–17.

Beckett, J, 1988, *The East Midlands from AD 1000*. London: Longman.

Beckwith, I S, 1988, *The Book of Gainsborough*. Buckingham: Baracuda.

Bellamy, B, Jackson, D and Johnston, G, 2000–1, 'Early iron smelting in the Rockingham forest area: a survey of the evidence', *Northamptonshire Archaeology* **29**, 103–28.

Bennett, S and Bennett, N (eds), 1993, *An Historical Atlas of Lincolnshire*. Hull: University of Hull Press.

Benson, D and Miles, D, *et al.*, 1974, *The Upper Thames Valley. An Archaeological Survey of the River Gravels*. Oxford: Oxfordshire Archaeological Unit.

Beresford, G, 1975, *The Medieval Clay-land Village: Excavations at Goltho and Barton Blount*. London: Society for Medieval Archaeology.

Beresford, G, 1987, *Goltho: the development of an early medieval manor c.850–1150*. London: English Heritage.

Beresford, M W, 1967, *New Towns of the Middle Ages*. London: Lutterworth Press.

Beresford, M W, 1983, *The Lost Villages of England*. Stroud: Alan Sutton.

Beresford, M W and Hurst, J G (eds), 1971, *Deserted Medieval Villages*. London: Lutterworth Press.

Bewley, R H (ed.), 1998, *Lincolnshire's Archaeology from the Air*. Occasional papers in Lincolnshire History and Archaeology 11. Lincoln: SLHA.

Biddle, M and Hill, D, 1971, 'Late Saxon planned towns', *Antiquaries Journal* 51, 70–85.

Biddle, M and Kjølbye-Biddle, B, 2001, 'Repton and the "great heathen army" 873–4', in Graham-Campbell *et al.* (eds), 45–96.

Bigmore, P, 1979, *The Bedfordshire and Huntingdonshire Landscape*. London: Hodder & Stoughton.

Birch, C, 1994, *The Book of Aylesbury*. Place of pub. not stated: Baron Birch Ltd.

Blair, J, 1985, 'Secular Minsters in Domesday Book', in Sawyer (ed.), 104–42.

Blair, J, 1987, 'Local churches in Domesday Book and before', in Holt (ed.), 265–278.

Blair, J, 1988a, 'Thornbury, Binsey: A Probable Defensive Enclosure associated with Saint Frideswide', *Oxoniensia* **53**, 1–20.

Blair, J, 1988b, 'Minster churches in the landscape', in Hooke (ed.), 35–58.

Blair, J (ed.), 1988, *Minsters and Parish Churches. The Local Church in Transition 950–1200*. Oxford: OUCA.

Blair, J, 1992, *The Bampton Project, Interim Report 1992*. Oxford: The Bampton Project.

Blair, J, 1993, 'Hall and Chamber: English domestic planning 1000–1250', in Merion Jones and Jones (eds), 1–21.

Blair, J, 1994, *Anglo-Saxon Oxfordshire*. Stroud: Oxfordshire Books.

Blair, J, 1996a, 'Churches in the early English landscape: social and cultural contexts', in Blair and Pyrah (eds), 6–18.

Blair, J, 1996b, 'Palaces or Minsters? Northampton and Cheddar reconsidered', *Anglo-Saxon Studies* **13**, 97–121.

Blair, J, 1996c, 'The minsters of the Thames', in Blair and Golding (eds), 5–28.

Blair, J, 2000, 'Small towns 600–1270', in Palliser (ed.), 245–70.

Blair, J and Golding, B (eds), 1996, *The cloister and the world: essays in medieval history in honour of Barbara Harvey*. Oxford: OUP.

Blair, J and Pyrah, C (eds), 1996, *Church Archaeology. Research directions for the future*. CBA Research Report 104. York: CBA.

Blair, J and Ramsey, N (eds), 1991, *English Medieval Industries. Craftsmen, Techniques, Products*. London and Rio Grande: Hambledon.

Blair, J and Sharpe, R (eds), 1992, *Pastoral Care before the Parish*. Leicester: Leicester University Press.

Blake, R N E, Hodgson, M and Taylor, W J, 1984, *The Airfields of Lincolnshire since 1912*. Leicester: Midland Counties Publications.

Blanchard, I S W, 1981, 'Lead Mining and Smelting in Medieval England and Wales', in Crossley (ed.), 72–84.

Boddington, A, 1996, *Raunds Furnells. The Anglo-Saxon Church and Churchyard*. London: English Heritage.

Boden, P K, 1963, 'The limestone industry of North Derbyshire', *Geographical Journal* 129/1.

Bond, C J, 1985, 'Medieval Oxfordshire Villages and their Topography', in Hooke (ed.), 101–24.

Bond, C J, 1987, 'Anglo-Saxon and Medieval Defences', in Schofield and Leech (eds), 92–115.

Bond, J, Gosling, S and Rhodes, J, 1980, *The Clay Industries of Oxfordshire. Oxfordshire Brickmakers*. Woodstock: Oxfordshire Museums Service.

Bourne, J (ed.), 1996, *Anglo-Saxon Landscapes in the East Midlands*. Leicester: Leicester University.

Bourne, J C, 1839, *Drawings of the London and Birmingham Railway. With an historical and descriptive account by John Britton*. London: J C Bourne.

Boutwood, Y, 1998, 'Prehistoric Linear Boundaries in Lincolnshire and its Fringes', in Bewley (ed.), 29–46.

Bowman, P, 1996, 'Contrasting Pays: Anglo-Saxon Settlement in Langton Hundred', in Bourne (ed.), 121–146.

Bradley, R, 1981, 'From ritual to romance: ceremonial enclosures and hill-forts', in Guilbert (ed.), 20–7.

Bradley, R, 1987, 'Time Regained: the creation of continuity', *Journal of the British Archaeological Association* **140**, 1–17.

Bradley, R, 1993, *Altering the Earth. The Origins of Monuments in Britain and Continental Europe. The Rhind Lectures 1991–2*. Edinburgh: Society of Antiquaries of Scotland.

Bradley, R, 1998a, *The Passage of Arms. An archaeological analysis of prehistoric hoards and votive deposits*. 2nd edn. Oxford: Oxbow.

Bradley, R, 1998b, *The Significance of Monuments. On the shaping of human experience in Neolithic and Bronze Age Europe*. London: Routledge.

Bradley, R, 2000, *An Archaeology of Natural Places*. London: Routledge.

Bradley, R and Chambers, R, 1988, 'A new study of the cursus complex at Dorchester on Thames', *Oxford Journal of Archaeology* **7/3**, 271–89.

Bramley, J V, 1991, 'Fluorspar mining in Derbyshire', *Bulletin of the Peak District Mines Historical Society* **11/3**, 153–8.

Brandwood, G K, 1984, *The Anglican Churches of Leicester*. Leicester: Leicestershire Museums Service.

Brandwood, G K, 1987, 'Anglican churches before the restorers: a study for Leicester and Rutland', *Archaeological Journal* **144**, 383–408.

Branigan, K, 1985, *The Catuvellauni*. Stroud: Alan Sutton.

Brazier, S, Hammond, R, and Waterman, S A, 1985, *A New Geography of Nottingham*. Nottingham: Trent Polytechnic.

Briggs, G, Cook, J and Rowley, T (eds), 1986, *The Archaeology of the Oxford Region*. Oxford: OUDES.

Broad, J and Hoyle, R (eds), 1997, *Bernwood: the Life and Afterlife of a Forest*. Preston: University of Central Lancashire.

Brown, A E (ed.), 1970, *The Growth of Leicester*. Leicester: Leicester University Press.

Brown, A E (ed.), 1991, *Garden Archaeology*. CBA Research Report 78. London: CBA.

Brown, A E and Foard, G, 1998, 'The Saxon Landscape: a regional perspective', in Everson and Williamson (eds), 67–94.

Brown, A E and Taylor, C, 1989, 'The origins of dispersed settlement: some results from fieldwork in Bedfordshire', *Landscape History* **11**, 61–81.

Brown, A E and Taylor, C, 1991, *Moated Sites in Northern Bedfordshire*. Vaughan Paper 35. Leicester: Leicester University Press.

Brown, C, 1990, *Northampton 1835–1985: Shoe Town, New Town*. Chichester: Philimore.

Brown, D, 1974, 'Problems of Continuity' in Rowley (ed.), 16–19.

Brown, I, 1989, *Nottinghamshire's Industrial Heritage*. Nottingham: Nottinghamshire County Council.

Brunskill, R W, 1987, *Traditional Farm Buildings of Britain*. 2nd edn. London: Gollancz.

Brunskill, R W, 1990, *Brick Building in Britain*. London: Gollancz.

Brunskill, R W, 1992, *Traditional Buildings of Britain: An Introduction to Vernacular Architecture*. London: Gollancz.

Brunskill, R W, 1994, *Timber Buildings of Britain*. 2nd edn. London: Gollancz.

Bryant, G F, 1994, *The Early History of Barton-upon-Humber*. 2nd edn. Barton: WEA.

Bryant, G F, 2003, *The Later History of Barton-on-Humber: Part One. The Church in Late Medieval Barton-on-Humber*. Barton: WEA.

Buckley, R and Lucas, J, 1987, *Leicester Town Defences*. Leicester: Leicestershire Museums Service.

Burnham, B C and Wacher, J, 1990, *The 'Small Towns' of Roman Britain*. London: Batsford.

Butler, L A S and Morris, R K (eds), 1986, *The Anglo-Saxon Church: Papers on history, architecture and archaeology in honour of H M Taylor*. CBA Research Report 60. London: CBA.

Butler, R M, 1949, 'The Civil War defences of Nottingham', *Transactions of the Thoroton Society* **53**, 26–33.

Campbell, B M S and Overton, M, 1991, *Land, Labour and Livestock. Historical Studies in European Productivity*. Manchester: MUP.

Cantor, L, 1970–1, 'The Medieval Parks of Leicestershire I', *Transactions of Leicestershire Archaeological and Historical Society* **46**, 9–24.

Cantor, L, 1976–7, 'The Medieval Parks of Leicestershire II', *Transactions of Leicestershire Archaeological and Historical Society* **52**, 73–6.

Cantor, L, 1978, 'The medieval castles of Leicestershire', *Transactions of Leicestershire Archaeological and Historical Society* **53**, 30–41.

Cantor, L, 1980, 'The Medieval Hunting grounds of Rutland', *Rutland Record* **1**, 13–18

Cantor, L (ed.), 1982, *The English Medieval Landscape*. London and Canberra: Croom Helm.

Cantor, L, 1982, 'Forests, Chases, Parks and Warrens', in Cantor (ed.), 56–85.

Cantor, L, 1983, *The Medieval Parks of England. A Gazetteer*. Loughborough: University of Loughborough, Department of Education.

Carver, M O H (ed.), 2003, *The Cross Goes North, Processes of Conversion in Northern Europe AD 300–1300*. Woodbridge: Boydell.

CBA, 1985, *Hallelujah! Recording chapels and meeting houses*. London: CBA.

Chadwick, G, 1966, *The Park and the Town*. London: Architectural Press.

Chambers, J D, 1957, *The Vale of Trent 1670–1800: A regional study of economic change*. Economic History Review Supplement. London: London University Press.

Chambers, J D, 1966, *Nottinghamshire in the Eighteenth Century*. 2nd edn. London: Cass.

Chambers, J D and Mingay, G E, 1966, *The Agricultural Revolution 1750–1880*. London: Batsford.

Chambers, R A, 1987, 'The late- and sub-Roman cemetery at Queenford Farm Dorchester-on-Thames Oxon.', *Oxoniensia* **52**, 35–70.

Chapman, A, 1998–9, 'Excavation of the town defences at Green Street Northampton 1995–6', *Northamptonshire Archaeology* **28**, 25–60.

Cherry, J, 1991, 'Leather', in Blair and Ramsey (eds), 295–318.

Church, R A, 1966, *Economic and Social Change in a Midland Town: Victorian Nottingham*. London: Cass.

Church, R A, 1986, *The History of the British Coal Industry Volume 3, 1830–1913*. Oxford: OUP.

Clark, P, 1984, *The Transformation of English Provincial Towns 1600–1800*. London: Hutchinson.

Clarke, H and Ambrosiani, B, 1995, *Towns in the Viking Age*. 2nd edn. Leicester: Leicester University Press.

Clifton-Taylor, A, 1972, *The Pattern of English Building*. London: Faber.

Cocroft, W D and Thomas, R J C, 2003, *Cold War. Building for Nuclear Confrontation 1946–1989*. London: English Heritage.

Cole, G and Roper, J, 1801, *The British Atlas*. London.

Coleman, E C, 1991, *The Royal Navy in Lincolnshire*. Boston: Richard Kaye.

Colvin, H, 1992, *Architecture and the After-life*. New Haven: Yale University Press.

Condron, F, 1997, 'Iron production in Leicestershire, Rutland and Northamptonshire in antiquity', *Transactions of Leicestershire Archaeological and Historical Society* **71**, 1–19.

Cook, J and Rowley, T (eds), 1985, *Dorchester through the Ages*. Oxford: OUDES.

Cooper, A, 1971, 'Victorian Newark', *Transactions of the Thoroton Society* **75**, 103–14.

Cooper, B, 1983, *Transformation of a Valley: The Derbyshire Derwent*. London: Heinemann.

Cooper, N, 1999, *Houses of the Gentry 1480–1680*. New Haven: Yale University Press.

Coppack, G, 1986, 'St. Lawrence Church, Burnham, South Humberside. The Excavation of a Parochial Chapel', *Lincolnshire History and Archaeology* **21**, 39–60.

Cossons, Sir N, 1993, *The BP Book of Industrial Archaeology*. 3rd edn. Newton Abbot: David & Charles.

Coulson, C, 2003, *Castles in Medieval Society*. Oxford: OUP.

Court, W H R, 1938, *The rise of the Midland Industries 1600–1838*. Oxford: OUP.

Courtney, P, 1998, 'Saxon and Medieval Leicester: The Making of an Urban Landscape', *Transactions of Leicestershire Archaeological and Historical Society* **72**, 110–45.

Courtney, P and Courtney, Y, 1992, 'A Siege examined: the Civil War archaeology of Leicester', *Post Medieval Archaeology* **26**, 47–90.

Cousins, R, 2000, *Lincolnshire Buildings in the Mud and Stud Tradition*. Heckington: Heritage Lincolnshire.

Cox, A, 1979, *Survey of Bedfordshire Brickmaking: A History and Gazetteer*. Bedford: Bedfordshire County Council /RCHME.

Cox, T, 1700, *Topographical, Ecclesiastical and Natural History of Derbyshire*. London: Nutt.

Cranstone, D, 1985, 'The Iron Industry of the Ashby Coalfield', *Leicestershire Industrial History Society Bulletin* **8**, 23–31.

Cranstone, D, 1993, *Monuments Protection Programme: Minor Metals and Vein Minerals. Step 1 Report*. London: English Heritage.

Crawley, A and Freeman, I, 2001, 'Bedford – An Alfredian Burgh?', *Bedfordshire Archaeology* **24**, 40–6.

Creighton, O H, 1999, 'Early castles in the medieval landscape of Rutland', *Transactions of Leicestershire Archaeological and Historical Society* **73**, 19–33.

Croft, R and Mynard, D, 1993, *The Changing Landscape of Milton Keynes*. Aylesbury: Buckinghamshire Archaeological Society.

Crossley, D W, 1981, 'Medieval Iron Smelting', in Crossley (ed.), 29–41.

Crossley, D W (ed.), 1981, *Medieval Industry*. CBA Research Report 40. London: CBA.

Cunliffe, B, 1991, *Iron Age Communities in Britain*. 3rd edn. London: Routledge.

Cunliffe, B and Miles, D (eds), 1984, *Aspects of the Iron Age in Central Southern Britain*. Oxford: OUCA.

Curl, J S, 1993, *A Celebration of Death*. 2nd edn. London: Batsford.

Currie, C J, 1992, 'Larger Medieval Houses in the Vale of the White Horse', *Oxoniensia* **57**, 81–244.

Daniels, G and Watkins, C, 1991, 'Picturesque Landscapes and Estate Management', *Rural History* **2/2**, 141–70.

Darby, H C (ed.), 1973, *A New Historical Geography of England before 1660*. Cambridge: CUP.

Darby, H C, 1977, *Domesday England*. Cambridge: CUP.

Dark, K, 1994, *Civitas to Kingdom*. Leicester: Leicester University Press.

Dark, P, 2000, *The Environment of Britain in the First Millennium AD*. London: Duckworth.

Davison, B K, 1977, 'Excavations at Sulgrave, Northamptonshire, 1960–76', *Archaeological Journal* **134**, 105–14.

Dawson, M (ed.), 2000, *Prehistoric, Romano-British and Post-Roman Landscapes of the Great Ouse Valley*. CBA Research Report 119. York: CBA.

De Beer, E S (ed.), 1959, *The Diary of John Evelyn*. Oxford: OUP.

Dearlove, P, 2000, 'Fen Drayton, Cambridgeshire: An Estate of the Land Settlement Association', in Thirsk (ed.), 323–35.

Defoe, D, 1724–6, *Tour thro' England and Wales*. London: Dent. (1962 'Everyman' reprint – 2 vols.)

Dix, B, 1979, 'Roman Lime-Burning', *Britannia* **10**, 261–2.

Dix, B, 1981, 'The Romano-British Farmstead at Odell and its setting: some reflections on the Roman landscape of the south-east Midlands', *Landscape History* **3**, 17–26.

Dixon, P, 1982, 'How Saxon is the Saxon House?', in Drury (ed.), 275–87.

Dixon, P, 2002, 'The reconstruction of the buildings', in Losco-Bradley and Kinsley (eds), 89–99.

Dodd, A (ed.), 2003, *Oxford before the University*. Oxford: Oxford Archaeology.

Dodgshon, R, 1981, *The Origins of British Field Systems: An Interpretation*. London: Academic Press.

Dornier, A, 1977, 'The Anglo-Saxon monastery at Breedon-on-the-Hill, Leicestershire', in Dornier (ed.), 155–68.

Dornier, A (ed.), 1977, *Mercian Studies*. Leicester: Leicester University Press.

Douglas, D C (ed), 1981, *English Historical Documents, Volume 2 1042–1189*. 2nd edn. London: Eyre Methuen.

Drury, P, (ed.), 1982, *Structural Reconstruction*. BAR (BS) 110. Oxford: BAR.

Dunn, C, 1977, *The Book of Huntingdon*. Chesham: Barracuda.

Dyer, C, 1986, 'English peasant buildings in the later Middle Ages', *Medieval Archaeology* **30**, 19–45.

Dyer, C, 1989a, *Standards of Living in the Later Middle Ages*. Cambridge: CUP.

Dyer, C, 1989b, '"The Retreat from Marginal Land": the Growth and decline of Medieval Rural Settlements', in Aston *et al.* (eds), 45–58.

Dyer, C, 1994, *Everyday Life in Medieval England*. London: Hambledon.

Dyer, C, 1996, 'Rural settlements in medieval Warwickshire', *Transactions of Birmingham and Warwickshire Archaeological Society* **100**, 117–32.

Dyer, J, 1972, 'Earthworks of the Danelaw Frontier', in Fowler (ed.), 222–36.

Earle, J B F, 1971, *A Century of Road Materials. The history of the Roadstone Division of Tarmac Ltd*. Oxford: Blackwell.

Edwards, K C (ed.), 1966, *Nottingham and its region*. Nottingham: Nottingham University Press.

Elliott, B, 1986, *Victorian Gardens*. London: Batsford.

Ellis, C J, 2004, *A Prehistoric Ritual Complex at Eynesbury, Cambridgeshire. Excavation of a Multi-period site in the Great Ouse Valley 2000–2001*. Salisbury: Wessex Archaeology.

Emery, F, 1974, *The Oxfordshire Landscape*. London: Hodder & Stoughton.

Evans, J G and Simpson, D D A, 1991, 'Giants' Hills 2 Long Barrow, Skendleby, Lincolnshire', *Archaeologia* **109**, 1–45.

Everitt, A, 1974, 'The Banburys of England', *Urban History Yearbook 1974*, 28–39.

Everson, P, 1991, 'Field Survey and garden earthworks', in Brown (ed.), 6–19.

Everson, P, 1993a, 'Reviews', *Lincolnshire History and Archaeology* **28**, 75–6.

Everson, P, 1993b, 'Pre Viking Settlement in Lindsey', in Vince (ed.), 91–100.

Everson, P, 1998, '"Delightfully Surrounded with woods and ponds": Field Evidence for Medieval Gardens in England', in Pattison (ed.), 32–8.

Everson, P and Stocker, D, 1999, *The Corpus of Anglo-Saxon Stone Sculpture, Volume 5. Lincolnshire*. Oxford: British Academy/OUP.

Everson, P, Taylor, C and Dunn C, 1991, *Change and Continuity. Rural Settlement in North-west Lincolnshire*. London: HMSO.

Everson, P and Williamson, T (eds), 1998, *The Archaeology of Landscape*. Manchester: MUP.

Fasnacht, R, 1954, *A history of the City of Oxford*. Oxford: Blackwell.

Faul, M (ed.), 1984, *Studies in Late Anglo-Saxon Settlement*. Oxford: OUDES.

Faulkner, P A, 1966, 'Medieval undercrofts and town houses', *Archaeological Journal* **123**, 120–35.

Field, N, 1984, 'A mud cottage from Withern with Stain', in Field and White (eds), 92–5.

Field, N and Parker Pearson, M, 2003, *Fiskerton. An Iron Age Timber Causeway with Iron Age and Roman Votive Offerings: the 1981 Excavations*. Oxford: Oxbow.

Field, N and White, A, 1984, *A Prospect of Lincolnshire, collected articles … in honour of Ethel H Rudkin*. Lincoln: The Editors.

Firman, R, 1964, 'Gypsum in Nottinghamshire', *Bulletin of the Peak District Mines History Society* **2/4**, 189–203.

Flinn, M W, 1984, *The history of the British Coal Industry, Volume 2, 1700–1830*. Oxford: OUP.

Foard, G, 1978, 'Systematic fieldwalking and the investigation of Saxon Settlement in Northamptonshire', *World Archaeology* **9**, 357–74.

Foard, G, 1991, 'The medieval pottery industry of Rockingham Forest, Northamptonshire', *Medieval Ceramics* **15**, 13–20.

Foard, G, 1994, 'The Civil War defences of Northampton', *Northamptonshire Past and Present* **9**, 4–44.

Foard, G, 1995, 'The early topography of Northampton and its suburbs', *Northamptonshire Archaeology* **26**, 109–122.

Foard, G, 2001, 'Medieval Woodland, Agriculture and Industry in Rockingham Forest, Northamptonshire', *Medieval Archaeology* **45**, 41–96.

Foss, P, 1996, 'Market Bosworth and its region – clues to its early status and connection', in Bourne (ed.), 83–106.

Foster, P, 1994, 'The Brigstock Survey: an intensive field survey on upland boulder clay in Northamptonshire', in Parker Pearson and Schadla-Hall (eds).

Fowkes, D V, 1984 &1986, *Derbyshire Industrial Archaeology: A gazetteer of sites. Volumes I and II: Borough of High Peak*, and *Borough of Erewash*. Derby: Derbyshire Archaeological Society.

Fowler, P J, 1983a, *The Farming of Prehistoric Britain*. Cambridge: CUP.

Fowler, P J, 1983b, *Farms in England: Prehistoric to Present*. London: HMSO.

Fowler, P J (ed.), 1972, *Archaeology and the Landscape. Essays for L.V. Grinsell*. London: David Baker.

Fox, H S A, 1989, 'The People of the Wolds', in Aston *et al.* (eds), 77–104.

Fox, H S A, 1992, *Origins of the Midland Village*. Leicester: Leicester University Press.

Fox, H S A, 2000, 'The Wolds before *c.*1500', in Thirsk (ed.), 50–61.

Francis, A J, 1977, *The Cement Industry, 1796–1914: A History*. Newton Abbot: David & Charles.

Freeman, J (ed.), 1952, *History of the Worthies of England …* London: Allen & Unwin.

French C, Macklin M G and Passmore D G, 1992, 'Archaeology and paelochannels in the Lower Welland and Nene valleys', in Needham and Macklin (eds), 166–76.

French, C and Wait, G A, 1988, *An Archaeological Survey of the Cambridgeshire River Gravels*. Cambridge: Cambridgeshire County Council.

Frere, S S, 1987, *Britannia*. 3rd edn. London: Guild Publishing.

Frere, S S and St Joseph, J K, 1974, 'The Roman fortress at Longthorpe', *Britannia* **5**, 1–129.

Fulford, M and Huddleston, K, 1991, *The Current State of Romano-British Pottery Studies*. London: English Heritage.

Fussell, G E, 1966, *The English Dairy Farmer, 1500–1900*. London: Cass.

Garton, D, 1987, 'Dunston's Clump and the brickwork plan field systems at Babworth, Nottinghamshire', *Transactions of the Thoroton Society* **91**, 16–73.

Gelling, M, 1984, *Place Names in the Landscape*. London: Dent.

Gem, R D H, 1988, 'The English parish church in the eleventh and early twelfth centuries: a Great Rebuilding?', in Blair (ed.), 21–30.

Gem, R D H, 1993, 'Architecture of the Anglo-Saxon Church, 735–870: from Archbishop Ecgberht to Archbishop Ceolnoth', *Journal of the British Archaeological Association* **148**, 29–54.

Gilchrist, R and Morris, R, 1996, 'Continuity, reaction and revival: church archaeology in England *c.*1600–1880', in Blair and Pyrah (eds), 112–126.

Gillett, E, 1986, *The History of Grimsby*. 2nd edn. Hull: Hull University Press.

Girouard, M, 1978, *Life in the English Country House: A Social and Architectural History*. New Haven: Yale University Press.

Girouard, M, 1983, *Robert Smythson and the Elizabethan Country House*. 2nd edn. New Haven: Yale University Press.

Girouard, M, 1985, *The Victorian Country House*. 2nd edn. New Haven: Yale University Press.

Glasscock, R A, 1973, 'England circa 1334', in Darby (ed.), 177–85.

Godber, J, 1984, *History of Bedfordshire 1066–1888*. Bedford: Bedfordshire County Council.

Goodburn, D, 1992, 'Woods and woodland: carpenters and carpentry', in Milne (ed.), 106–30.

Gould, S and Ayris, I, 1995, *Colliery Landscapes. An aerial survey of the deep-mined coal industry in England*. London: English Heritage.

Gould, S and Cranstone, D, 1993, *Monuments Protection Programme: The Coal Industry. Step 1 Report*. London: English Heritage.

Graham-Campbell, J, Hall, R, Jesch, J and Parsons, D N (eds), 2001, *Vikings and the Danelaw. Papers from the …13th Viking Congress, Nottingham and York, 21–30 August 1997*. Oxford: Oxbow.

Granger, A, 1965, 'History of the Boot and Shoe Industry in Leicester', *British Boot and Shoe Institution Journal*, March, 1–23.

Gray, H L, 1915, *English Field Systems*. Cambridge Mass.: Harvard University Press.

Green, D, 1976, *Blenheim Palace*. Woodstock: Blenheim Estate Office.

Green, H J M, 1977, *Godmanchester*. Cambridge: Oleander Press.

Greenall, R L, 1975, 'The rise of industrial Kettering', *Northamptonshire Past and Present* 5/3.

Greenwood, J, 1987, *The Industrial Archaeology and Industrial History of the English Midlands: A Bibliography*. Cranfield: Kewdale.

Grenville, J, 1997, *Medieval Housing*. London and Washington: Leicester University Press.

Grimes, W F, 1961, *Settlements at Draughton, Northants., Colsterworth, Lincs. and Heathrow, Middlesex*, Institute of Archaeology, Occasional Paper 11. London: London University.

Guilbert, G (ed.), 1981, *Hill-Fort Studies. Essays for A.H.A. Hogg*. Leicester: Leicester University Press.

Hadfield, C, 1970, *The Canals of the East Midlands*. Newton Abbot: David & Charles.

Hadley, D, 2000, *The Northern Danelaw. Its Social Structure, c.800–1100*. Leicester: Leicester University Press.

Hadley, D, 2001, *Death in Medieval England. An Archaeology*. Stroud: Tempus.

Hall, D, 1989, 'Field Systems and township structure', in Aston *et al.* (eds), 191–206.

Hall, D, 1995, *The Open Fields of Northamptonshire*. Northamptonshire Record Society 38. Northampton: NRS.

Hall, D, 1997, 'Enclosure in Northamptonshire', *Northamptonshire Past and Present* **8**, 350–67.

Hall, D, 2001, *Turning the Plough. Midlands Open Fields: Landscape Character and Proposals for Management*. Northampton: English Heritage/Northamptonshire County Council.

Hall, R A, 2001, 'Anglo-Scandinavian urban developments in the East Midlands', in Graham-Cambell *et al.* (eds), 143–55.

Hallam, H E (ed.), 1988, *The Agrarian History of England and Wales. Volume II: 1042–1350*. Cambridge: CUP.

Halls, Z, 1985, *Machine Made Lace in Nottingham*. Nottingham: Nottingham City Council.

Hamerow, H, 2002, *Early Medieval Settlements*. Oxford: OUP.

Hammond, M, 1977, 'Brick Kilns an Illustrated Survey', *Industrial Archaeology Review* **1/2**, 171–92.

Hancock, T N, 1978, 1985, *Bomber County: A History of the RAF in Lincolnshire*. Lincoln: Lincolnshire County Council. 2 vols.

Harding, A F and Lee, G E, 1987, *Henge Monuments and related sites of Great Britain*. BAR (BS) 175. Oxford: BAR.

Harrington, P, 2004, *English Civil War Archaeology*. London: Batsford.

Harrison, D J and Adlam, K A McL, 1985, *Limestones of the Peak*. London: HMSO.

Hartley, R F, 1983, *The Medieval Earthworks of Rutland*. Leicester: Leicestershire Museums Service.

Hartley, R F, 1984, *The Medieval Earthworks of North-West Leicestershire*. Leicester: Leicestershire Museums Service.

Hartley, R F, 1987, *The Medieval Earthworks of North-East Leicestershire*. Leicester: Leicestershire Museums Service.

Hartley, R F, 1990, *The Medieval Earthworks of Central Leicestershire*. Leicester: Leicestershire Museums Service.

Harvey, N, 1980, *The Industrial Archaeology of Farming in England and Wales*. London: Batsford.

Harvey, P D A, 1969, 'Banbury', in Lobel (ed.) unpaginated.

Harvey, P D A, 1989, 'Initiative and authority in settlement change', in Aston *et al.* (eds), 31–44.

Hatcher, J, 1977, *Plague, Population and the English Economy 1348–1530*. London: Macmillan.

Hatcher, J, 1993, *The History of the British Coal Industry, I. Before 1700: Towards the Age of Coal*. Oxford: OUP.

Hatley, V A, 1966, *Snobopolis: Northampton in 1869*. Northampton: Northampton Historical Series.

Heal, F and O'Day, R (eds), 1977, *Church and Society in England: Henry VIII to James I*. London: Methuen.

Heath, J E and Christian, R, 1985, *Yesterday's Town: Derby*. Buckingham: Barracuda.

Heward, J and Taylor, T, 1996, *The Country Houses of Northamptonshire*. London: HMSO.

Hill, D, 1981, *An Atlas of Anglo-Saxon England*. Oxford: Blackwell.

Hill, Sir F, 1948, *Medieval Lincoln*. Cambridge: CUP.

Hill, Sir F, 1956, *Tudor and Stuart Lincoln*. Cambridge: CUP.

Hill, Sir F, 1966, *Georgian Lincoln*. Cambridge: CUP.

Hill, Sir F, 1973, *Victorian Lincoln*. Cambridge: CUP.

Hinchcliffe, T, 1992, *North Oxford*. New Haven: Yale University Press.

Hingley, R and Miles, D, 1984, 'Aspects of the Iron Age Settlement in the Upper Thames Valley', in Cunliffe and Miles (eds), 52–71.

Hodder, I R and Millett, M, 1980, 'Romano-British Villas and Towns: a systematic analysis', *World Archaeology* **12/1**, 69–76.

Hodges, R, 1982, *Dark Age Economics. The Origins of Towns and Trade AD 600–1000*. London: Duckworth.

Hodgett, G A, 1975, *Tudor Lincolnshire*. History of Lincolnshire 6. Lincoln: History of Lincolnshire Committee.

Holderness, B A, 1972, 'The agricultural activities of the Massingberds of South Ormsby, Lincolnshire, 1638–1750', *Midland History* **1/3**, 15–25.

Holmes, C, 1980, *Seventeenth Century Lincolnshire*. History of Lincolnshire 7. Lincoln: History of Lincolnshire Committee.

Holt, J C (ed.), 1987, *Domesday Studies*. Woodbridge: Boydell.

Holt, R and Rosser, G (eds), 1990, *The Medieval Town. A Reader in English Urban History 1200–1540*. London: Longmans.

Honeybone, M, 1980, *The Book of Grantham*. Buckingham: Barracuda.

Hooke, D, 1985, *The Anglo-Saxon Landscape. The Kingdom of the Hwicce*. Manchester: MUP.

Hooke, D (ed.), 1985, *Medieval Villages*. Oxford: OUCA.

Hooke, D (ed.), 1988, *Anglo-Saxon Settlements*. Oxford: Blackwell.

Hooke, D, 1998, *The Landscape of Anglo-Saxon England*. Leicester: Leicester University Press.

Hooke, D (ed.), 2000, *Landscape. The Richest Historical Record*. Society for Landscape Studies Supplementary Series 1.

Hoskins, W G, 1946, 'The deserted villages of Leicestershire', *Transactions of the Leicestershire Archaeological and Historical Society* **22**, 241–64.

Hoskins, W G, 1949, *Midland England*. London: Batsford.

Hoskins, W G, 1955, *Making of the English Landscape*. London: Hodder & Stoughton.

Hoskins, W G, 1957a, *The Leicestershire Landscape*. London: Hodder & Stoughton.

Howard, F E, 1987, The *Early Tudor Country House. Architecture and Politics 1490–1550*. London: George Philip.

Hughes, G, 1985, *Barns of Rural Britain*. London: Herbert.

Hurst, J G, 1988, 'Rural building in England', in Thirsk (ed.), 854–930.

Hussey, C, 1967, *English Gardens and Landscapes 1700–1750*. London: Country Life.

Impey, E and Harris, R, 2002, 'Boothby Pagnell Revisited', in Merion Jones *et al.* (eds), 245–69.

Innocent, C F, 1916, *The Development of English Building Construction*. Cambridge: CUP.

Jackson, C (ed.), 1870, *The Diary of Abraham de la Pryme. The Yorkshire Antiquary*. Publications of The Surtees Society 54. Durham: Surtees Society.

Jackson, D A, 1993–4, 'Iron Age and Anglo-Saxon settlement and activity around Hunsbury Hill-fort, Northampton', *Northamptonshire Archaeology* **25**, 35–46.

Jackson, D A, 1996–7, 'Further evaluation at Borough Hill, Daventry, Northants', *Northamptonshire Archaeology* **27**, 143–64.

Jackson D A and Foard, G, 1993–4, 'Anglo-Saxon Occupation at Yardley Hastings, Northants', *Northamptonshire Archaeology* **25** 93–8.

Jervoise, E, 1932, *The Ancient Bridges of Mid and Eastern England*. London: Architectural Press.

Johnson, M, 1993, *Housing Culture. Traditional architecture in an English landscape*. London: UCL Press.

Johnson, M, 2002, *Behind the Castle Gate. From Medieval to Renaissance*. London: Routledge.

Jones, G D B and Mattingley, D, 2002, *An Atlas of Roman Britain*. Oxford: Oxbow.

Jones. M J, 2003a & b, 'The Roman Military Era' and 'The Colonia Era', in Stocker (ed.), 36–137.

Jones, M J and Stocker, D A, 2003, 'Settlement in the Lincoln area in the Prehistoric Era. The archaeological account', in Stocker (ed.), 19–33.

Jones, R B, 1954, *The Pattern of Farming in the East Midlands*. Nottingham: University of Nottingham Press.

Jones, R H, 1980, *Medieval Houses at Flaxengate, Lincoln*. Archaeology of Lincoln 11/1. London: CBA.

Jones, S, Major, K, Varley, J and Johnson, C, 1984, 1987, 1990, 1996, *Survey of Ancient Houses in Lincoln Volumes 1–IV*. Lincoln: Lincoln Civic Trust.

Keevill, G D, 2003, 'Archaeological Investigations in 2001 at the Abbey Church of St Peter and St Paul, Dorchester-on-Thames, Oxfordshire', *Oxoniensia* **68**, 313–62.

Keighley, C, 2000, *Discovering Wychwood*. Charlbury: Wychwood.

Kellett, J R, 1969, *The impact of railways on Victorian cities*. London: Routledge & Kegan Paul.

Kinvig, R H, Smith, J G and Wise, M J, 1950, *Birmingham and its Regional Settling*. Birmingham: British Association for the Advancement of Science.

Kirley, T and Oosthuigen, S (eds), 2000, *An Atlas of Cambridgeshire and Huntingdonshire History*. Cambridge: APU.

Knoop, D and Jones, G P, 1936, 'The Bolsover Castle Buildings Account, 1613', *Ars Quatuor Coronatorum* **49/1**, 1–56.

Lake, J, 1989, *Historic Farm Buildings, An Introduction and Guide*. London: Blandford.

Lambrick, G, 1988, *The Rollright Stones, Megaliths, Monuments and Settlement in the Prehistoric Landscape*. London: English Heritage.

Lambrick, G and Allen, T, 2004, *Gravelly Guy. Excavations at Stanton Harcourt*. Oxford: Oxford Archaeology.

Lane, T, 1995, *The Archaeology and Developing Landscape of Ropsley and Humby, Lincolnshire*. Heckington: Heritage Lincolnshire.

Laughton, J and Dyer, C, 1999, 'Small towns in the east and west midlands in the later middle ages: a comparison', *Midland History* **24**, 24–52.

Laws, P, 1967, *Industrial Archaeology in Bedfordshire*. Bedford: Bedfordshire County Council.

Leadham, I S, 1897, *The County of Nottingham and the Domesday of Enclosures 1517–18*. London: Longmans Green.

Leahy, K, 1993, 'The Anglo-Saxon Settlement of Lindsey', in Vince (ed.), 29–44.

Lelux, R, 1984, *A Regional history of the Railways of Great Britain. Volume 9, The East Midlands*. 2nd edn. Newton Abbot: David & Charles.

Lewis, C, Mitchell-Fox, P and Dyer, C, 1997, *Village, Hamlet and Field. Changing Medieval Settlements in Central England*. Manchester: MUP.

Lewis, S, 1992, *Buried Around Buckingham*. Buckingham: Buckingham Museum.

Liddle, P and Hughes, S R, 1979, 'St Mary's Chapel Brentingby – Excavations and Observations', *Transactions of the Leicestershire Archaeological and Historical Society* **54**, 1–13.

Limbury, S and Evans, J G (eds), 1978, *The Effect of Man on the Landscape: The Lowland Zone*. CBA Research Report 21. London: CBA.

Lindley, P (ed.), 2004, *The Early History of Lincoln Castle*. Society for Lincolnshire History and Archaeology Occasional Paper 12. Lincoln: SLHA.

Linton, D L (ed.), 1956, *Sheffield and its Region*. Sheffield: British Association for the Advancement of Science.

Lipscomb, G, 1847, *The History and Antiquities of the County of Buckingham*. London: J & W Robins. 4 vols.

Lloyd, T H, 1977, *The English Wool Trade in the Middle Ages*. Cambridge: CUP.

Lobel, M D, 1975, *Historic Towns Atlas Volume 2*. London: Scholar.

Lobel, M D (ed.), 1969, *Historic Towns Atlas Volume 1*. London and Oxford: Lovell, Johns-Cook, Hammonds and Kell.

Losco-Bradley, S and Kinsley, G (eds), 2002, *Catholme. An Anglo-Saxon Settlement on the Trent Gravels in Staffordshire*. Nottingham: Nottingham University Archaeology Department.

Lowry, B (ed.), 1995, *20th century defences in Britain. An Introductory Guide*. York: CBA.

LUAU, 1996a, *Monuments Protection Programme: The Quarrying Industry. Step 1 Report*. London: English Heritage.

LUAU, 1996b, *Monuments Protection Programme: The Lime, Cement and Plaster Industries. Step 1 Report*. London: English Heritage.

Lucy, S, 2000, *The Anglo-Saxon Way of Death*. Stroud: Sutton.

Mackreth, D, 1984, 'Castor', *Durobrivae* **9**, 22–5.

Mackreth, D 1996, *Orton Hall Farm: a Roman and early Anglo-Saxon farmstead*. East Anglian Archaeology 76. Manchester: Nene Valley Archaeological Trust.

Mahany, C and Roffe, D, 1982, 'Stamford: the development of an Anglo-Scandinavian borough', *Anglo-Norman Studies* **5**, 197–219.

Mallim, T, 2000, 'The ritual landscape of the Neolithic and Bronze Age along the middle and lower Ouse Valley', in Dawson (ed.), 57–88.

Margary, I D, 1967, *Roman Roads in Britain*. 2nd edn. London: John Baker.

Markham, Sir F, 1973–5, *History of Milton Keynes and District*. 2 vols. Luton: White Crescent.

Marshall, A and Marshall, G, 1993, 'Differentiation, change and continuity in Anglo-Saxon buildings', *Archaeological Journal* **150**, 366–402.

Marshall, P and Samuels, J, 1997, *Guardian of the Trent. The Story of Newark Castle*. Newark: Newark Castle Trust.

Martin, A F and Steel, R W (eds), 1954, *The Oxford Region. A Scientific and Historical Survey*. Oxford: OUP.

May, J, 1976, *Prehistoric Lincolnshire*. History of Lincolnshire volume 1. Lincoln: History of Lincolnshire Committee.

May, J, 1996, *Dragonby. Report on Excavations at an Iron Age and Romano-British Settlement in North Lincolnshire*. 2 vols. Oxford: Oxbow.

McAvoy, F, 2000, 'The development of a Neolithic monument complex at Godmanchester, Cambridgeshire', in Dawson (ed.), 51–6.

McCarthy, M and Brooks C, 1988, *Medieval Pottery in Britain AD 900–1600*. Leicester: Leicester University Press.

Mellor, M, 1994, *Medieval Ceramic Studies in England: A Review*. London: English Heritage.

Merion Jones, G and Jones, M (eds), 1993, *Manorial and Domestic Buildings in England and Northern France*. Society of Antiquaries Occasional Paper 15. London: Society of Antiquaries.

Merion Jones, G, Impey, E and Jones, M (eds), 2002, *The Seigneurial residence in Western Europe AD c.800–1600*. BAR (IS) 1088. Oxford: BAR.

Miles, D, 1986, *Archaeology at Barton Court Farm, Abingdon, Oxon*. CBA Research Report 50. London: CBA.

Miles, D, 1997, 'Conflict and Complexity: The Later Prehistory of the Oxford Region', *Oxoniensia* **62**, 1–19.

Miller, E (ed.), 1991, *The Agrarian History of England and Wales. Volume 3, 1348–1500*. Cambridge: CUP.

Millett, M, 1990, *The Romanisation of Britain*. Cambridge: CUP.

Mills, D R, 1982, 'Rural industries and social structure: framework Knitters in Leicestershire, 1670–1850', *Textile History* **13/2**, 183–204.

Mills, D R (ed.), 1989, *Twentieth Century Lincolnshire*. History of Lincolnshire 12. Lincoln: History of Lincolnshire Committee.

Milne, G (ed.), 1992, *Timber Buildings techniques in London c.900–1400*. London and Middlesex Archaeological Society Special Paper 15. London: LAMAS.

Milner, T, 1847, *Visitor's Guide to the Show of The Royal Agricultural Society: and Handbook to Northampton*. Northampton: Abel & Sons.

Moorhouse, S A, 1981, 'The Medieval Pottery Industry and its Markets', in Crossley (ed.), 96–126.

Morris, C (ed.), 1949, *The Journeys of Celia Fiennes*. London: Cresset Press.

Morris, R, 1983, *The Church in British Archaeology*. CBA Research Report 47. London: CBA.

Morris, R, 1989, *Churches in the Landscape*. London: Dent.

Morrison, K with Bond, A, 2004, *Built to Last? The buildings of the Northamptonshire Boot and Shoe Industry*. London: English Heritage.

Mounfield, P R, 1964–5, 'The footwear industry of the East Midlands, I', *East Midlands Geographer* **3**, 293–306.

Mounfield, P R, 1966, 'The footwear industry of the East Midlands IV, Leicestershire to 1911', *East Midlands Geographer* **4/1**, 8–23.

Mounfield, P R, 1967, 'The footwear industry of the East Midlands V, the modern phase: Northamptonshire and Leicestershire since 1911', *East Midlands Geographer* **4/2**, 154–75.

Munby, J, 1993, 'Manorial building in timber in central and southern England, 1200–1550', in Merion Jones and Jones (eds), 49–64.

Needham, S and Macklin, M G (eds), 1992, *Alluvial Archaeology in Britain*. Oxford: Oxbow.

OAU, 1995, *Dovecotes. Monuments Protection Programme, Step 1 Report*. London: English Heritage.

Olney, R J, 1979, *Rural Society and County Government in Nineteenth Century Lincolnshire*. History of Lincolnshire 10. Lincoln: History of Lincolnshire Committee.

Orwin, C S and Orwin, C S, 1967, *The Open Fields*. 3rd edn. Oxford: OUP.

Osborne, M, 1997, *20th Century Defences in Britain. Lincolnshire*. London: Brassey's.

Oswald, A, Dyer, C and Barber, M, 2001, *The Creation of Monuments Neolithic Causewayed Enclosures in the British Isles*. London: English Heritage.

Ottaway, P, 1992, *Archaeology in British Towns: From the emperor Claudius to the Black Death*. London: Routledge.

Owen, C, 1978, *The Development of Industry in Burton-on-Trent*. Chichester: Philimore.

Owen, D, 1981, *Church and Society in Medieval Lincolnshire*. History of Lincolnshire 5. Lincoln: History of Lincolnshire Committee.

Page, M and Jones, R, 2001, 'Medieval Settlements and Landscapes in the Whittlewood area. Interim Report', *Medieval Settlement Research Group Annual Report* **16**, 15–25.

Palliser, D, 1976, *The Staffordshire Landscape*. London: Hodder & Stoughton.

Palliser, D (ed.), 2000, *The Cambridge Urban History of Britain, Volume 1*. Cambridge: CUP.

Palmer, M and Neaverson, P, 1992, *Industrial Landscapes of the East Midlands*. Chichester: Philimore.

Palmer, M and Neaverson, P, 1998, *Industrial Archaeology. Principles and Practice*. London: Routledge.

Pantin, W A, 1947, 'The development of domestic architecture in Oxford', *Antiquaries Journal* **27**, 120–50.

Pantin, W A, 1962–3, 'Medieval English Town-house Plans', *Medieval Archaeology* **6–7**, 202–39.

Parker Pearson, M, 1999, *The Archaeology of Death and Burial*. Stroud: Sutton.

Parker Pearson, M and Schadla-Hall, R T (eds), 1994, *Looking at the Land: Archaeological landscapes in Eastern England*. Leicester: Leicestershire Museums Service.

Parry, S, 1994, 'Raunds Area Survey', in Parker Pearson and Schadla Hall (eds), 36–42.

Parsons, D (ed.), 1990, *Stone. Quarrying and Building in England AD 43–1525*. Chichester: Philimore.

Parsons, D, 1991, 'Stone', in Blair and Ramsay (eds), 1–28.

Patrick, A, 2004, *Strategy for the Historic Industrial Environment Report No.1. Maltings in England*. London: English Heritage.

Pattison, P (ed.), 1998, *There by Design. Field Archaeology in Parks and Gardens*. Swindon: RCHME.

Pawley, S, 1996, *The Book of Sleaford*. Place of pub. not stated: Baron Birch Ltd.

Pearce, J, 1999, 'The dispersed dead: preliminary observations on burial and settlement space in rural Roman Britain', in Baker *et al.* (eds), 151–162.

Percival, J, 1976, *The Roman Villa: an historical introduction*. London: Batsford.

Perring, D, 1981, *Early Medieval Occupation at Flaxengate Lincoln*. Archaeology of Lincoln 9/1. London: CBA.

Pettit, P A, 1968, *The Royal Forests of Northamptonshire: A Study of their Economy 1558–1714*. Northamptonshire Record Society 23. Northampton: NRS.

Pevsner, Sir N (ed.), 1974, *The Picturesque Garden and its influence outside the British Isles*. Dumbarton Oaks: Harvard University Press.

Pickering, J and Hartley, R F, 1985, *Past Worlds in a Landscape*. Leicester: Leicestershire Museums Service.

Phythian-Adams, C, 1977, 'Rutland Reconsidered', in Dornier (ed.), 63–84.

Phythian-Adams, C, 2000, 'Frontier Valleys', in Thirsk (ed.), 236–262.

Platts, G, 1985, *Land and People in Medieval Lincolnshire*. History of Lincolnshire 4. Lincoln: History of Lincolnshire Committee.

Plummer, A, 1934, *The Witney Blanket Industry*. London: Routledge.

Potts, W, 1958, *History of Banbury*. Banbury: Banbury Guardian.

Pryor, F, 1998a, *Farmers in Prehistoric Britain*. Stroud: Tempus.

Pryor, F, 1998b, *Etton: Excavations at a Neolithic causewayed enclosure near Maxey Cambridgeshire 1982–87*. London: English Heritage.

Pryor, F, 2001, *The Flag Fen Basin. Archaeology and environment of a Fenland Landscape*. London: English Heritage.

Pryor, F, 2002, *Seahenge: a quest for life and death in Bronze Age Britain*. London: Collins.

Purcell, D, 1967, *Cambridge Stone*. London: Faber.

Pye, N (ed.), 1972, *Leicester and its Region*. Leicester: Leicester University Press.

Quiney, A, 1990, *The Traditional Buildings of England*. London: Thames and Hudson.

Rackham, J (ed.), 1994, *Environment and Economy in Anglo-Saxon England*. CBA Research Report 89. London: CBA.

Rackham, O, 1986, *The History of the Countryside*. London: Dent.

Rahtz, P A, 1981, 'Medieval Milling', in Crossley (ed.), 16–28.

Raistrick, A, 1972, *Industrial Archaeology: an historical survey*. London: Eyre Methuen.

Ramsay, N, 1991, 'Alabaster', in Blair and Ramsay (eds), 29–40.

Rawstron, E W, 1954, 'Power Production and the River Trent', *East Midlands Geographer* 1/2, 23–30.

Reed, M, 1979, *The Buckinghamshire Landscape*. London: Hodder & Stoughton.

Reed, M, 1993, *History of Buckinghamshire*. Chichester: Philimore.

Renn, D, 1973, *Norman Castles in Britain*. 2nd edn. London: John Baker.

Richmond, H, 1986, 'Outlines of church development in Northamptonshire', in Butler and Morris (eds), 176–87.

Riden, P, 1990, *The Butterley Company 1790–1830*. Derby: Derbyshire Record Society.

Rigold, S E, 1971, 'The distribution of aisled timber barns', *Vernacular Architecture* 2, 20–21.

Rimmington, G T, 1964–5, 'Leicester foundries 1845–1914', *Transactions of Leicestershire Archaeological and Historical Society* **40**.

Rivet, A L F, 1964, *Town and Country in Roman Britain*. 2nd edn. London: Hutchinson.

Rivet, A L F, 1969 (ed.), *The Roman Villa in Britain*. London: Routledge & Kegan Paul.

Roberts, B K, 1976–7, 'The historical geography of moated homesteads: the forest of Arden, Warwickshire', *Transactions of Birmingham and Warks. Archaeological Society* **88**, 61–70.

Roberts, B K, 1977, *Rural Settlement in Britain*. Folkestone: Dawson & Son.

Roberts, B K, 1987, *The Making of the English Village*. London: Longmans.

Roberts, B K and Wrathmell, S, 2000a, *Atlas of Rural Settlement in England*. London: English Heritage.

Roberts, B K and Wrathmell, S, 2000b, 'Peoples of wood and plain: an exploration of national and local regional contrasts', in Hooke (ed.), 85–96.

Roberts, B K and Wrathmell, S, 2002, *Region and Place*. London: English Heritage.

Roberts, D, 1974, 'The persistence of archaic framing techniques in Kesteven, Lincolnshire', *Vernacular Architecture* 5, 18–20.

Robinson, D N, 1999, *Lincolnshire Bricks. History and Gazetteer*. Heckington: Heritage Lincolnshire.

Robinson, M, 1992, 'Environment, archaeology and alluvium on the river gravels of the south Midlands', in Needham and Macklin (eds), 197–208.

Rodwell, K (ed.), 1975, *Historic Towns in Oxfordshire*. Oxford: Oxfordshire Archaeological Unit.

Rodwell, W (ed.), 1980, *Temples, churches and religion: recent research in Roman Britain …*, BAR (BS) 77. Oxford: BAR.

Rodwell, W, 1981, *The Archaeology of the English Church*. London: Batsford.

Rodwell, W, 1984, 'Churches in the Landscape: aspects of design and construction', in Faul (ed.), 1–24.

Rogers, A, 1965, *The Making of Stamford*. Leicester: Leicester University Press.

Rogers, A, 1981, 'Rural industries and social structure: framework knitters in Nottinghamshire, 1670–1840', *Textile History* **12**, 7–36.

Rogers, A, 2001, *The Book of Stamford*. Stamford: Spiegl Press.

Rowley, T (ed.), 1981, *The Origins of the Open-Field Agriculture*. London: Croom Helm.

Royal Commission on Historical Monuments, England, 1964, *Newark on Trent: the civil war siegeworks*. London: HMSO.

Russell, E and Russell, R C, 1982, *Landscapes changes in South Humberside*. Hull: Humberside C.C.

Russell, E and Russell, R C, 1983, *Making New Landscapes in Lincolnshire*. Lincoln: Lincs. C.C.

Russell, E and Russell, R C, 1985, *Old and New Landscapes – Horncastle Area*. Lincoln: Lincs. C.C.

Russell, E and Russell, R C, 1987, *Parliamentary Enclosure …* Lincoln: Lincs. C.C.

Salway, P, 1981, *Roman Britain.* Oxford: OUP.

Salway, P, 1999, 'Roman Oxfordshire (The Tom Hassall lecture for 1997)', *Oxoniensia* **64**, 1–22.

Salzman, L F, 1967, *Building in England down to 1540.* Oxford: OUP.

Sawyer, P, 1981, 'Fairs and Markets in Early Medieval England', in Skyum-Neilsen and Lund (eds), 153–168

Sawyer, P (ed.), 1985, *Domesday Book A Reassessment.* London: Edward Arnold.

Sawyer, P, 1998, *Anglo-Saxon Lincolnshire.* History of Lincolnshire 3. Lincoln: History of Lincolnshire Committee.

Scaife, R G, 2000, 'The prehistoric vegetation and environment of the River Ouse valley', in Dawson (ed.), 17–26.

Schofield, J, 1994, *Medieval London Houses.* New Haven: Yale University Press.

Schofield, J and Leech, R (eds), 1987, *Urban Archaeology in Britain.* CBA Research Report 61. London: CBA.

Schofield, J and Vince, A, 1994, *Medieval Towns.* Leicester: Leicester University Press.

Schrufer-Kolb, 1999, 'Roman Iron production in the East Midlands, England', in Young *et al.* (eds), 227–33.

Scopes, Sir F, 1965, *The development of Corby Works.* Northampton: NRS.

Scott, E, 1993, *A Gazetteer of Roman Villas in Britain.* Leicester Archaeology Monograph 1. Leicester: Leicester University Archaeological Research Centre.

Seebohm, F, 1915, *The English Village Community.* London: Longmans Green.

Seeley, I H, 1974, *Planned Expansion of Country Towns.* London: Godwin.

Selwood, L, 1984, 'Tribal boundaries viewed from the perspective of numismatic evidence', in Cunliffe and Miles (eds), 191–204.

Sheils, W J, 1977, 'Religion in provincial towns: innovation and tradition', in Heal and O'Day (eds), 156–76.

Short, B, 2000, 'Forests and Wood-Pasture in Lowland England', in Thirsk (ed.), 122–149.

Simco, A, 1984, *Survey of Bedfordshire. The Roman Period.* Bedford: RCHME/Bedfordshire County Council.

Simco, A, 1998, *Monuments Protection Programme: The Clay Industries. Step 1 Report.* London: English Heritage.

Simco, A and McKeague, P, 1997, The *Bridges of Bedfordshire.* Bedford: Bedfordshire County Council/ Bedfordshire Archaeological Council/RCHME.

Simmons, I G, 2001, *An Environmental History of Great Britain.* Edinburgh: Edinburgh University Press.

Simmons, J, 1974, *Leicester Past and Present.* 2 vols. London: Methuen.

Skyum-Neilsen, N and Lund, N (eds), 1981, *Danish Medieval History: New Currents.* Copenhagen: Museum Tusculaneum Press.

Smith, D M, 1964, 'The Location of elastic web manufacturing in England and Wales', *East Midlands Geographer* **3**, 326–37.

Smith, J T, 1965, 'Timber-framed building in England: its development and regional differences', *Archaeological Journal* **122**, 133–58.

Smith, J T, 1970, 'The evolution of the English peasant house to the 17th century: the evidence of the buildings', *Journal of the British Archaeological Association* 3rd ser. **33**, 122–47.

Smith, T P, 1985, *The Medieval Brickmaking Industry in Britain, 1400–1450.* BAR (BS) 138. Oxford: BAR.

Snow, P, 1991, *Oxford Observed,* London: John Murray.

Spavold, J, 1981, 'The sanitary pottery industries of south Derbyshire, 1840–1914', *Industrial Archaeology Review* **5/2**, 143–54.

Speight, S, 1994, 'Early Medieval Castle Sites in Nottinghamshire', *Transactions of the Thoroton Society* **98**, 58–70.

Squires, A E and Humphrey, W L, 1987, *The Medieval Parks of Charnwood Forest.* Wymondham: Sycamore Press.

Stafford, P, 1985, *The East Midlands in the Early Middle Ages.* Leicester: Leicester University Press.

Stamp, L D and Woolridge, A (eds), 1951, *London Essays in Geography.* Cambridge: CUP.

Stamper, P, 1988, 'Woods and Parks', in Astill and Grant (eds), 128–48.

Starmer, G (ed.), 1970, *Industrial Archaeology: Northamptonshire.* Northampton: Northampton Museum and Art Gallery.

Stead, I M, 1976, *Excavations at Winterton Roman Villa and other Roman sites in North Lincolnshire.* London: HMSO.

Steane, J, 1974, *The Northamptonshire Landscape.* London: Hodder & Stoughton.

Steane, J and Bryant, G F, 1975, 'Excavations at the deserted medieval settlement of Lyveden', *Journal of the Northampton Museums and Art Gallery* **12**.

Steers, J A (ed.), 1965, *The Cambridge Region.* Cambridge: CUP.

Stell, C, 1986, *An Inventory of Nonconformist Chapels and Meeting-houses in Central England.* London: HMSO.

Stell, C, 2002, *An Inventory of Nonconformist Chapels and Meeting-houses in Eastern England.* London: English Heritage.

Stenning, D, 1985, 'Timber-framed shops 1300–1600: comparative plans', *Vernacular Architecture* **16**, 35–9.

Stenning, D (ed.), 1998, *Regional Variation in Timber-framed building in England and Wales down to 1550.* Chelmsford: Essex County Council.

Stocker, D, 1993, 'The Early Church in Lincolnshire. A Study of the Sites and their Significance', in Vince (ed.), 101–22.

Stocker, D, 2004, 'The two early castles of Lincoln', in Lindley (ed.), 9–22.

Stocker, D (ed.), 2003, *The City by the Pool.* Oxford: Oxbow.

Stocker, D and Everson, P, 2001, 'Five Towns Funerals: decoding diversity in Danelaw stone sculpture', in Graham-Campbell *et al.* (eds), 223–43.

Stocker, D and Everson, P, 2003, 'The Straight and Narrow Way. Fenland causeways and the Conversion of the Landscape in the Witham Valley, Lincolnshire', in Carver (ed.), 271–88.

Sutherland, D S, 2003, *Northamptonshire Stone.* Wimborne: Dovecote Press.

Swan, V G, 1984, *The Pottery kilns of Roman Britain.* London: HMSO.

Taylor, C, 1973, *The Cambridgeshire Landscape.* London: Hodder & Stoughton.

Taylor, C, 1975, *Fields in the English landscape.* London: Dent.

Taylor, C, 1977, 'Polyfocal settlement and the English village', *Medieval Archaeology* **21**, 189–93.

Taylor, C, 1979, *Roads and Tracks of Britain.* London: Dent.

Taylor, C, 1983, *Village and Farmstead: A History of Rural Settlement in England.* London: George Philip.

Taylor, C, 1995, 'Dispersed settlements in nucleated areas', *Landscape History* **17**, 27–34.

Taylor, C, 1998, *Parks and Gardens of Britain.* Edinburgh: Edinburgh University Press.

Tebbs, H F, 1979, *Peterborough – A History.* Cambridge: Oleander Press.

Tebbutt, C F, 1957, 'A Belgic and Romano-British Farm at Wyboston, Bedfordshire', *Proceedings of the Cambridge Antiquarian Society* **50**, 75–84.

Tebbutt, C F, 1978, *St Neots. The History of a Huntingdonshire Town.* Chichester: Philimore.

Thirsk, J, 1957, *English Peasant Farming. The Agrarian History of Lincolnshire from Tudor to Recent Times.* London: Methuen.

Thirsk, J, 1973, 'Field systems of the East Midlands', in Baker and Butlin (eds), 232–80.

Thirsk, J, 1987, *England's Agricultural Regions and Agrarian History 1500–1750*. London and Basingstoke: Macmillan.

Thirsk, J (ed.), 1988, *Agrarian History of England and Wales. Volume 2: 1042–1350*. Cambridge: CUP.

Thirsk, J (ed.), 2000, *The English Rural Landscape*. Oxford: OUP.

Thomas, C, 1981, *Christianity in Roman Britain to AD 500*. London: Batsford.

Thompson, F M L (ed.), 1982, *The Rise of Suburbia*. Leicester: Leicester University Press.

Thompson, M, 1998, *Medieval Bishop's Houses in England and Wales*. Aldershot: Ashgate.

Thomson, R S, 1982, 'Tanning, Man's First Manufacturing Process?', *Transactions of the Newcomen Society* **52–3**, 139–56.

Tiller, K, 1985, 'Charterville and the Chartist Land Company', *Oxoniensia* **50**, 251–66.

Tipper, J, 2004, *The Grubenhaus in Anglo-Saxon England*. Yedingham: LRC/English Heritage.

Todd, M, 1968, *The Roman Fort at Great Casterton, Rutland*. Nottingham: University of Nottingham.

Todd, M, 1981, *The Roman Town at Ancaster, Lincolnshire*. Nottingham and Exeter: Universities of Nottingham and Exeter.

Todd, M, 1991, *The Coritani*. 2nd edn. Stroud: Alan Sutton.

Todd, M (ed.), 1978, *Studies in the Romano-British Villa*. Leicester: Leicester University Press.

Tonks, E, 1988, *The Ironstone Quarries of the Midlands: Part 1, Introduction*. Cheltenham: Runpast Publishing.

Toulmin Smith, L (ed.), 1964, *The Itinerary of John Leland …*. Carbondale Illinois: Southern Illinois University Press.

Trollope, E, 1857–8, 'The captivity of John, King of France, at Somerton Castle, Lincolnshire', *Associated Architectural Societies Reports and Papers* **4**, 49–68.

Tucker, D G, 1985, 'Millstone making in the Peak District of Derbyshire: the quarries and the technology', *Industrial Archaeology Review* **8**, 42–58.

Turner, H L, 1971, *Town Defences in England and Wales. An architectural and documentary study AD 900–1500*. London: John Baker.

Turner, R, 1985, *Capability Brown and the Eighteenth Century English Landscape*. London: Weidenfeld and Nicholson.

Tylecote, R F, 1962, *Metallurgy in Archaeology*. London: Edward Arnold.

Unwin, T, 1983, 'Townships and early fields in north Nottinghamshire', *Journal of Historical Geography* **9**, 341–6.

Van der Veen, M and O'Connor, T, 1998, 'The expansion of agricultural production in Late Iron Age and Roman Britain', in Bailey (ed.), 127–44.

Vince, A (ed.), 1993, *Pre-Viking Lindsey*. Lincoln Archaeological Studies 1. Lincoln: CLAU.

Vince, A, 1997, 'The Characterization and Interpretation of Early to Middle Saxon Granitic Tempered pottery in England', *Medieval Archaeology* **41**, 214–20.

Vince, A, 2003a, b & c, 'Lincoln in the Early Medieval Era, between the 5th and 9th centuries', 'The new town: Lincoln in the High Medieval Era (c.850–c.1350)' and 'Lincoln in the Early Modern Era (c.1350–c.1750)', in Stocker (ed.), 141–337.

Vyner, B (ed.), 1994, *Building on the Past*. London: Royal Archaeological Institute.

Wacher, J, 1995, *The Towns of Roman Britain*. 2nd edn. London: Batsford.

Wade Martins, S, 2002, *The English Model Farm. Building the Agricultural Ideal 1700–1914*. Macclesfield: Windgather.

Wailes, R, 1954, *The English Windmill*. London: Routledge and Kegan Paul.

Wait, G, 1985, *Ritual and Religion in the Iron Age*. BAR (BS) 149. Oxford: BAR.

Walton, J K, 1983, *The English Seaside resort: a social history 1750–1914*. Leicester: Leicester University Press.

Walton, P, 1991, 'Textiles', in Blair and Ramsey (eds), 319–54.

Warren, K, 1961, 'The Derbyshire iron industry', *East Midlands Geographer* **2**, 17–33.

Watkins, A, 1993, 'The Woodland Economy of the Forest of Arden in the later Middle Ages', *Midland History* **18**, 19–36.

Wedlock, G H, 1954, 'Loughborough: an outline urban survey', *East Midlands Geographer* **1**, 12–19.

Welfare, H and Swan, V, 1995, *Roman Camps in England*. London: HMSO.

Wells, F A, 1972, *The British Hosiery and Knitwear Industry: its History and Organisation*. Newton Abbot: David & Charles.

Whiffen, M, 1947–8, *Stuart and Georgian Churches. The Architecture of the Church of England outside London 1603–1837*. London: Batsford.

Whittle, A, Atkinson, R J C, Chambers, C and Thomas, N, 1992, 'Excavations … at Dorchester-on-Thames, Oxfordshire 1947–52 and 1981', *Proceedings of the Prehistoric Society* **58**, 143–202.

Whitwell, J B, 1992, *Roman Lincolnshire*, History of Lincolnshire 2. 2nd edn. Lincoln: History of Lincolnshire Committee.

Wild, J P, 1974, 'Settlement in the Lower Nene Valley', *Archaeological Journal* **131**, 140–70.

Wild, J P, 1978, 'Villas in the Lower Nene Valley', in Todd (ed.), 59–69.

Williams, J H, 1984, 'A Review of Some Aspects of Late Saxon Urban Origins and Development', in Faul (ed.), 25–34.

Williams, J H, Shaw, M and Denham, V, 1985, *Middle Saxon Palaces at Northampton*. Northampton: Northampton Development Corporation.

Williams, P W, 1983, *An Anglo-Saxon Cemetery at Thurmaston, Leicestershire*. Leicester: Leicestershire Museums Service.

Williamson, T, 1995, *Polite Landscapes*. London: Alan Sutton.

Williamson, T, 2002, *The Transformation of Rural England: Farming and the Landscape 1700–1800*. Exeter: Exeter University Press.

Williamson, T, 2003, *Shaping Medieval Landscapes*. Macclesfield: Windgather.

Willies, L and Cranstone, D (eds), 1992, *Boles and Smeltmills*. Matlock: Historical Metallurgy Society.

Withington, L (ed.), 1876, *Elizabethan England by William Harrison, with an introduction by F J Furnivall*. London: Walter Scott.

Wood, M E, 1965, *The English Medieval House*. London: Dent.

Woodforde, J, 1983, *Farm Buildings in England and Wales*. London: Routledge & Kegan Paul.

Woodward, F, 1982, *Oxfordshire Parks*. Woodstock: Oxfordshire Museums Service.

Wrathmell, S, 1994, 'Rural settlements in medieval England: perspectives and perceptions', in Vyner (ed.), 187–94.

Wright, N R, 1982, *Lincolnshire Towns and Industry 1700–1914*. History of Lincolnshire 11. Lincoln: History of Lincolnshire Committee.

Young, C J, 1977, *The Roman Pottery Industry of the Oxford Region*. BAR (BS) 43. Oxford: BAR.

Young, C R, 1979, *The Royal Forests of Medieval England*. Leicester: Leicester University Press.

Young, S M M, *et al.* (eds), 1999, *Metals in Antiquity*. BAR (IS) 792. Oxford: BAR.

Index

Picture Credits

Images on the following pages © Crown copyright.NMR or © English Heritage: 11 (NMR 23943/11); 13 (AA050215); 17 (NMR 23215/16); 21 (NMR 17844/16); 22t (NMR 24032/19); 24t (NMR 23412/05); 24b (K990959); 27left (NMR 23899/08); 27right (NMR 24080/08); 33 (NMR 24032/21); 34 (NMR 23286/20); 39 (NMR 4518/36); 43 (NMR 15551/30); 56 (NMR 4222/18); 68 (NMR 24035/12); 71 (NMR 23903/23); 75 (NMR 23762/06); 78 (NMR 17389/23); 83 (NMR 24105/09); 86 (NMR 23414/05); 92 (NMR 23947/13); 99 (NMR 23031/03); 104t (RAF 30023 SFFO 0229); 104bl (NMR 20296/23); 105 (NMR 23284/02); 109 (20294/005); 110t (RAF 30032 SFFO 0006); 113t (RAF 542 37 F21 0071); 113b (NMR 20256/23); 114 (24047/035); 124t (AA049181); 132 (AA048533); 134 (J930069); 140t (BB013525); 141 (J850527); 142t (NMR 23215/24); 142b (NMR 23576/09); 143 (NMR 17464/15); 146 (NMR 12814/12); 150b (K930707); 152 (NMR 23622/21); 167t (NMR 21770/02); 168 (NMR 20258/13); 170 (J000063); 172t (NMR 20083/25); 172b (NMR 24082/033); 175 (NMR 20257/12); 178 (NMR 20213/007); 181 (20320/008); 183m (NMR 20496/23); 183b (AA046465); 187 (23948/002); 192t (20295/025); 192b (NMR 17000/18); 193b (NMR 20496/13); 198 (NMR 24032/01); 200 (NMR 17876/12); 203 (NMR 21871/09); 204t (NMR 20257/14); 205t (NMR 23900/03); 206 (NMR 12854/12); 207 (NMR 12852/34); 208 (BB94 12090); 210b (BB93 09467); 212 (20293/018); 213 (NMR 20283/19); 214b (NMR 21477/11); 218 (NMR 17824/14); 221 (NMR 23762/18); 231 (NMR 24035/67); 233 (AA050636); 238 (NMR 20260/05).

English Heritage ground photography was taken by Alun Bull, Derek Kendall and Peter Williams. Additional English Heritage photography by Steve Cole, Patricia Payne and Bob Skingle.

Additional photographs: Alamy: © Detail Nottingham: 89, © Mike Disney: 28, © fotolincs: 205b, © Travelshots.com: 171t; © Dr N W Alcock: 121; © John Bailey: 133t; © Martin Biddle and Birthe Kjolbye-Biddle: 197; Reproduced by permission of the British Geological Survey. © NERC. All rights reserved. IPR/62-03C: 15; British Steel: 177; Ashley Cooper: 102; Courtesy of Cambridge Antiquarian Society: 59; Courtesy of the National Coal Mining Museum for England: 106; Philip Dixon: 116, 118; Edifice: Gillian Darley: 157b; Purcell 1967, fig 29a. © Faber & Faber: 166; Field, F J 1984 'A Mud Cottage from Withern with Stain' in N Field and A White (eds) *A Prospect of Lincolnshire*. Lincoln pp.92–95: 119; Heritage Trust of Lincolnshire: 232t; Tony Holmes: 179; Leicester Museums, Arts and Records Service: 49l, 164; © Lincolnshire County Council. The Collection: 138; The National Trust: Andrew Butler: 157t; Northampton Central Library: Visitor's Guide to the Show of The Royal Agricultural Society: and Handbook to Northampton, by Thomas Milner. Published by Abel and Sons, 1847: 90; Nottingham East Midlands Airport: 9; Ordnance Survey: 107; Oxford Archaeological Unit: 40, Danyon Rey: 125; Francis Pryor: 211; Sabin Galleries: 144; Simmons Aerofilms: 44; David Stocker: 22, 81, 88, 124b, 127, 129, 151, 160, 196, 223b, 232b; Unit for Landscape Modelling, University of Cambridge: 194, 204b; Dr Kate Tiller: 130; © Woodmansterne Publications Ltd: 169b; © Dr P J Woodward: 120.

Aerial survey acknowledgements

New English Heritage aerial photographs were taken by Damian Grady, Peter Horne, David Macleod and Jane Stone. The Aerial Reconnaissance team would like to thank the following people for their help: a special note of thanks must go to the skills and patience of the pilots Chris Penistone, Mark Julian, Chris Penistone, Mick Webb, Marten White and David Williams; the aircraft owners Anthony Crawshaw and David Sanders; the NMR cataloguing team Rose Ogle, Katy Groves, Catherine Runciman, Cinzia Bacilieri, Philip Daniels, Geoff Hall; Jon Proudman for all the publication scanning; Sarah Prince for laser copying thousands of aerial photographs to send to the authors; and Kate Bould for post reconnaissance administrative support in York.